WEB**DESIGN**:

START HERE!

First published in the United Kingdom in 2003 by
ILEX
The Old Candlemakers
West Street
Lewes
East Sussex BN7 2NZ
www.ilex-press.com.

This book was conceived by
ILEX
Cambridge
England

Publisher: Alastair Campbell
Executive Publisher: Sophie Collins
Creative Director: Peter Bridgewater
Editorial Director: Steve Luck
Design Manager: Tony Seddon
Editor: Chris Middleton
Designer: Andrew Milne
Development Art Director: Graham Davis
Technical Art Editor: Nicholas Rowland

British Library Cataloguing-in-Publication Data
A catalogue record for this book is available from the British Library

ISBN 1-904705-03-0

Printed and bound in China

For more information on this title please visit:
www.webdesign.web-linked.com

WEB**DESIGN**

START HERE!

ALL THAT YOU NEED TO CREATE YOUR
OWN FANTASTIC WEBSITES

NICK NETTLETON

ILEX

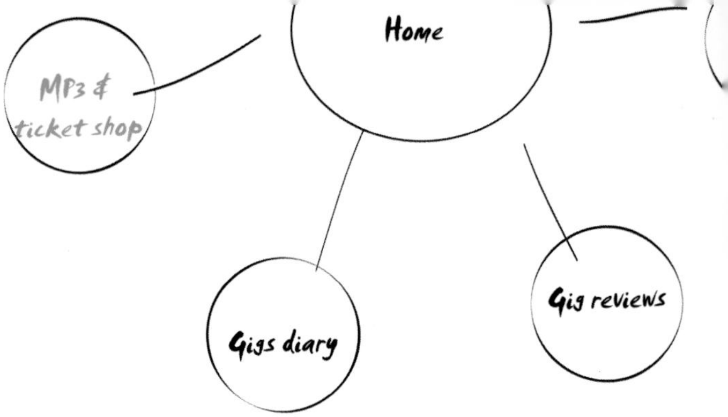
Home
MP3 & ticket shop
Gigs diary
Gig reviews

CONTENTS

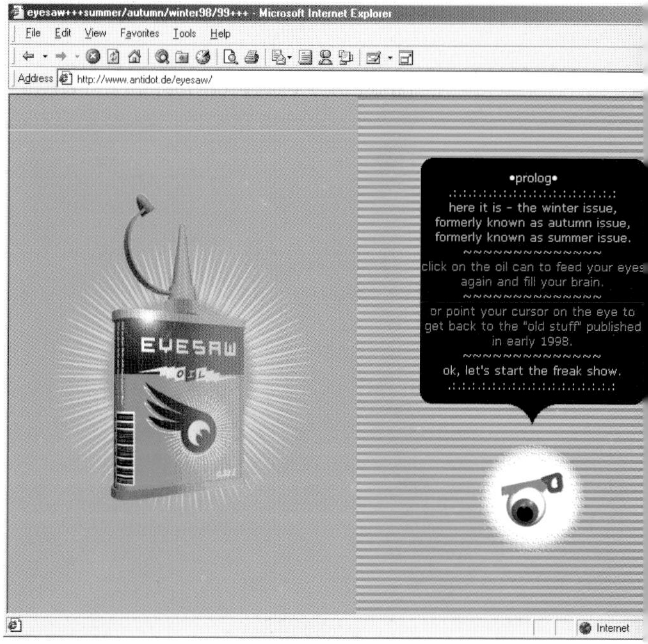

eyesaw+++summer/autumn/winter98/99+++ - Microsoft Internet Explorer
File Edit View Favorites Tools Help
Address http://www.antidot.de/eyesaw/
•prolog•
here it is - the winter issue, formerly known as autumn issue, formerly known as summer issue.
click on the oil can to feed your eyes again and fill your brain.
or point your cursor on the eye to get back to the "old stuff" published in early 1998.
ok, let's start the freak show.
EYESAW
Internet

Introduction

***Web Design: Start Here!* is the indispensable guide to developing all the skills you need to design and build innovative websites that work, and which people will want to visit again and again. And it's not just a step-by-step guide – within these pages you'll find inspirational ideas that you'll want to run with until you develop the confidence to take your own ideas to the world...**

Websites are everywhere. From fan sites on the latest bands, bulletin boards for people to share knowledge, and personal weblogs (blogs) that say, '*Hi, this is me, this is what I do*', to huge corporate portals, news services, research facilities and even online radio and video sites.

The Internet explosion has changed the way people interact forever: you can now find and communicate with like-minded people thousands of miles away with just a couple of clicks of a mouse (or the tap of a key on your Web-enabled phone). You can publish your work to a global audience, download software, share music, video and pictures, set up store online, or have goods delivered to your door. The Cyberspace Age has also proved that a fan site, like *aintitcoolnews*, can become a global player with the ear of multinational corporations.

But alongside all of this has been an explosion of bad design, sites that take minutes to load over a dial-up connection, broken links, clashing colours, browser problems, faulty fonts and fuzzy graphics. Even some big-budget websites went under because, while they were pouring millions of marketing dollars into finding their customers, they forgot to build an interface that worked. This book is designed to put a stop to all that, and show you how to go from beginner to expert in the space of some easy-to-follow projects.

Web Expert: Design puts all the information at your fingertips, from an in-depth explanation of the building blocks of a website right through to image editing, typography and animation. Whether you're on a PC or a Mac, just follow the projects step by step and you'll learn about HTML, creating links, acquiring, editing and optimizing images for the Web, and how to brainstorm and create a design scheme that works. We'll show you how to design a navigation, preview your work in all the major browsers and upload your site to the Internet for the world to see.

Right now you're probably wondering what equipment you'll need to turn your ideas into action. We'll tell you about that too, whether you want to know about hardware, such as digital cameras and flatbed scanners, or find out about the latest website building, graphics and image-editing packages. But don't panic: we'll also show you how to get around not having all of the equipment we talk about, and how to work within the restrictions of a tight budget.

You'll get off to a flying start: by the end of project one, you'll have created your first simple webpage, and by the end of the book you'll know how to build a complex website, work with fonts, turn an average photo into an innovative Web graphic, and use all the market-leading software.

Like the other titles in the growing *Start Here!* series, *Web Design: Start Here!* is not just a book; it's also a website, an online resource that includes all of the projects in this book for you to explore with whatever software package you've chosen, and whichever of the two main computing platforms you've opted for.

As long as you've got the ambition, the ideas and the confidence, we'll help you turn them into your own personal space on the World Wide Web.

www.webdesign.web-linked.com

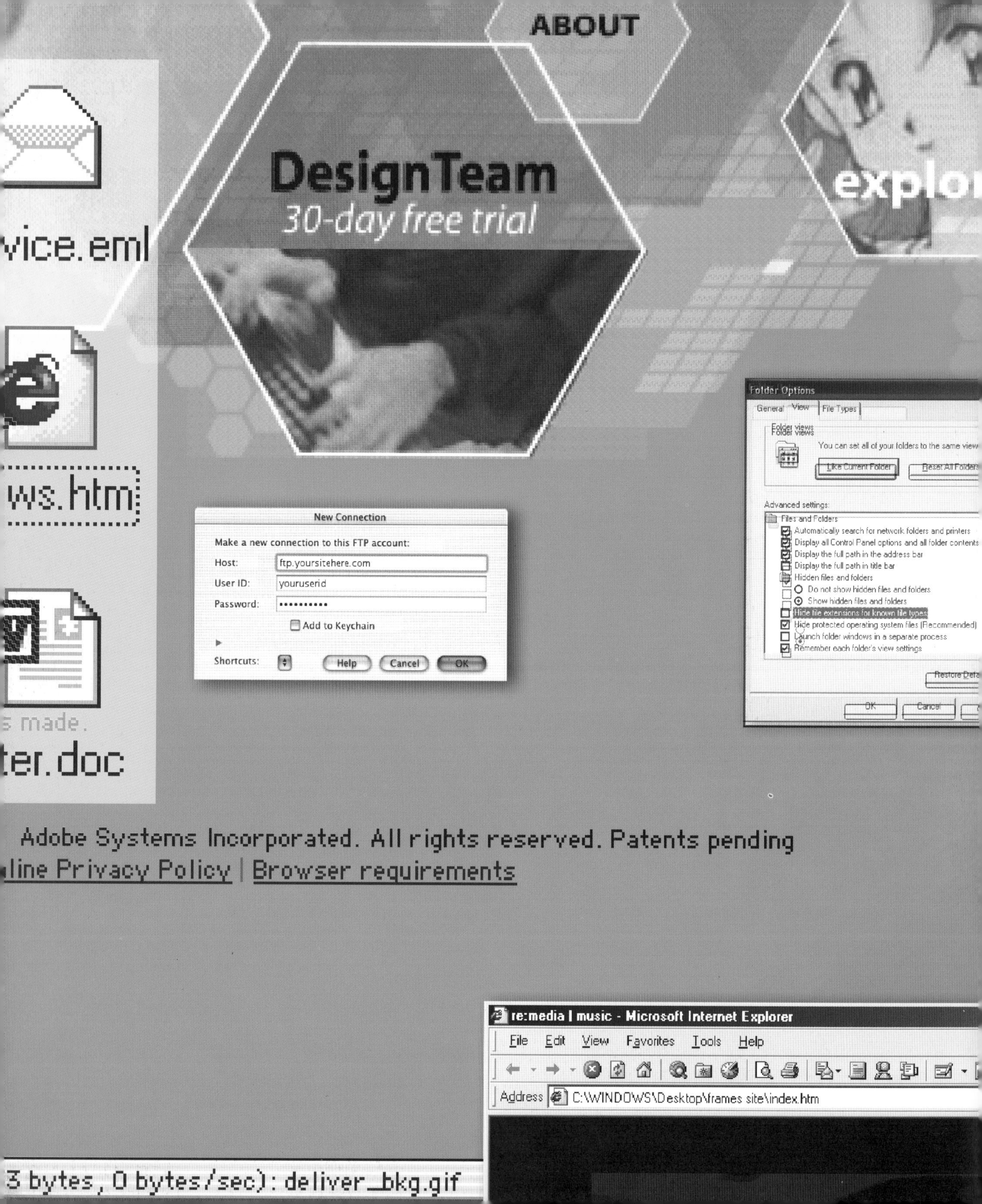
ABOUT
DesignTeam
30-day free trial
explor
vice.eml
ws.htm
s made.
ter.doc
New Connection
Make a new connection to this FTP account:
Host: ftp.yoursitehere.com
User ID: youruserid
Password:
Add to Keychain
Shortcuts:
Help
Cancel
OK
Folder Options
General
View
File Types
Folder views
You can set all of your folders to the same view
Like Current Folder
Reset All Folders
Advanced settings:
Files and Folders
Automatically search for network folders and printers
Display all Control Panel options and all folder contents
Display the full path in the address bar
Display the full path in title bar
Hidden files and folders
Do not show hidden files and folders
Show hidden files and folders
Hide file extensions for known file types
Hide protected operating system files (Recommended)
Launch folder windows in a separate process
Remember each folder's view settings
OK
Cancel
Adobe Systems Incorporated. All rights reserved. Patents pending
line Privacy Policy | Browser requirements
re:media | music - Microsoft Internet Explorer
File Edit View Favorites Tools Help
Address C:\WINDOWS\Desktop\frames site\index.htm
3 bytes, 0 bytes/sec): deliver_bkg.gif

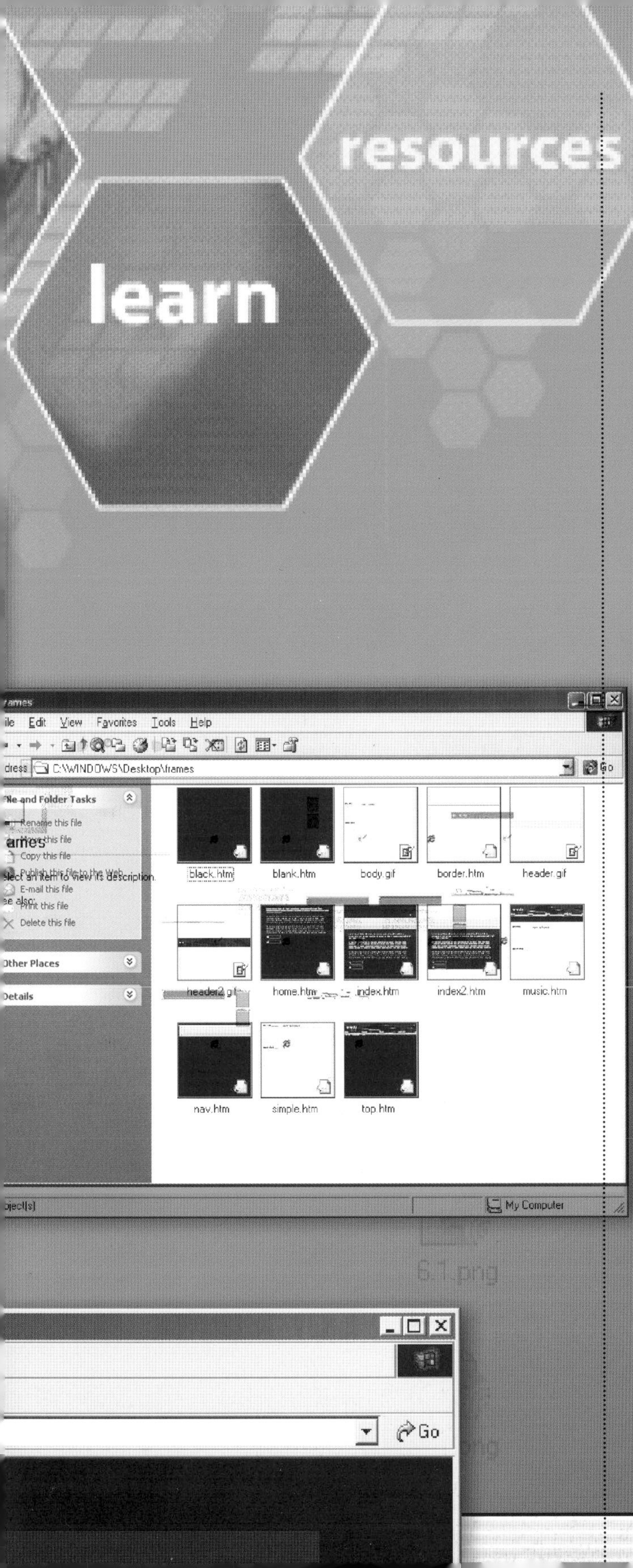

CHAPTER 1

Getting Started

Creating websites can be baffling for the beginner, because there seems to be so much to sort out first. You may be wondering what equipment you need, how you can get a Web address – or simply want someone to explain how a website is made. Don't worry – all will be explained...

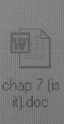

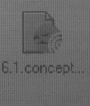

WHAT IS A WEBPAGE?

In essence, a webpage is a document that resides on a remote computer site. That site could be anywhere in the world, yet you can still view the page from your computer when you 'browse' the Internet. A website is made up of any number of these pages linked together.

Creating a webpage is incredibly easy. It's not that different from producing a newsletter in Microsoft Word, or sending an e-mail with pictures in it. In fact, if you have your e-mail program's Preferences set to send messages in HTML format (if you're using Outlook Express or Netscape 6, this will probably have been done automatically), then you're already creating a mini webpage every time you tap in a new message and send it!

HTML – HyperText Markup Language – is the code that underpins webpages. It's simple too but, in truth, you don't need to know anything about it to be a great Web designer. In this day and age there are many software applications out there that take care of all the HTML for you; you just need to concentrate on the design and content. The software tools that do this are called WYSIWYGs, which stands for 'What You See Is What You Get'. This simply means that you can see how your webpage looks as you create it – and there is also a bunch of user-friendly tools to enable you to amend text and graphics to an almost infinite degree.

1

1 *A webpage is usually made in HTML, although you don't need to understand it to create a webpage. Think of HTML as a file format, like a Microsoft Word document (which has the filename ending .doc), or an e-mail saved to your desktop (which may have the ending .eml, depending on your e-mail software). A simple HTML file, or webpage, has the ending .htm or .html – it usually doesn't matter which.*

2 *If you're using Windows and you can't see any endings like this on your files, your* Folder Options *are probably set to hide them. It's useful to be able to see file endings in Web design, so open a folder – any folder – and click* Folder Options *in your* Tools *menu. Choose the* View Tab *and uncheck the box marked 'Hide file extensions for known types'.*

2

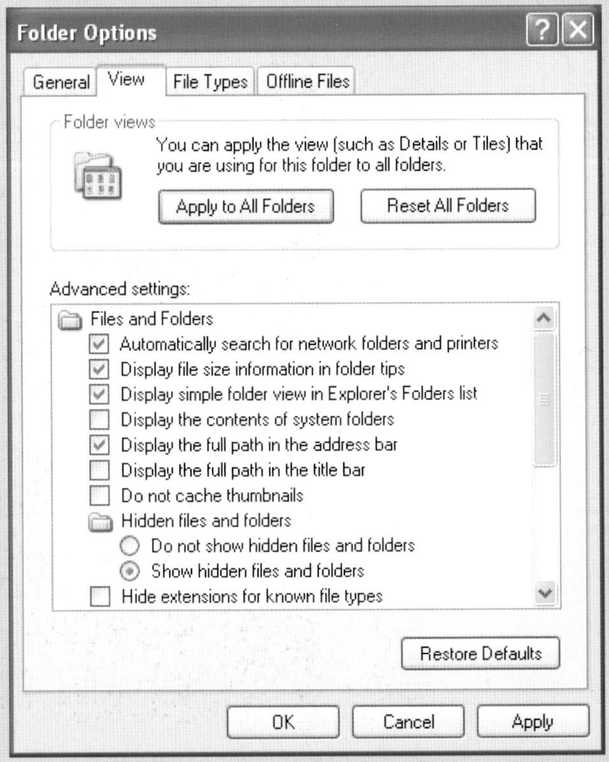

3

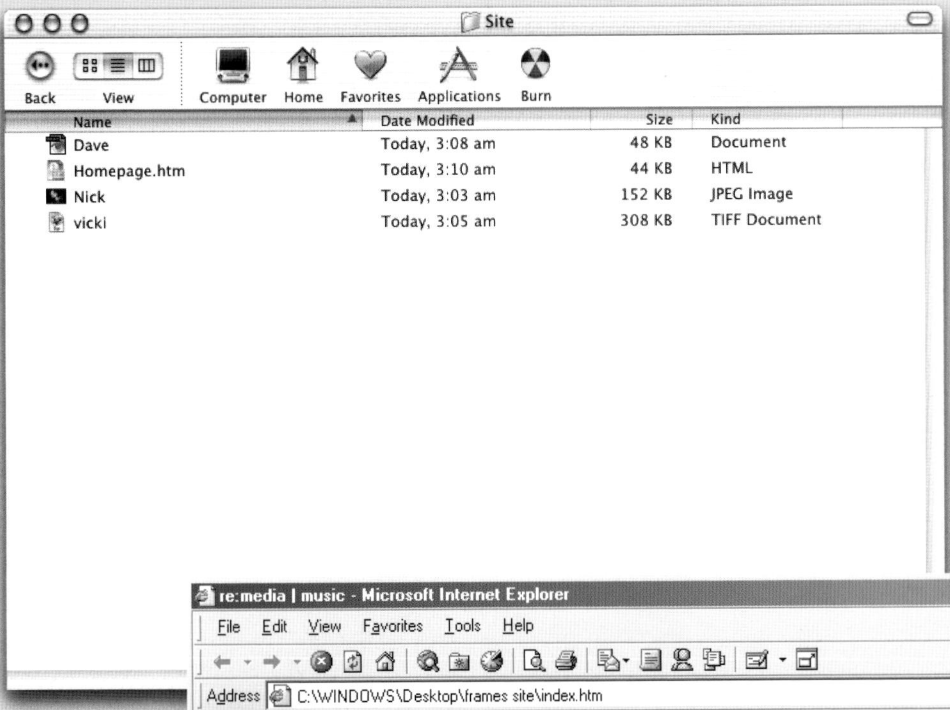
Site
Back
View
Computer
Home
Favorites
Applications
Burn
Name
Date Modified
Size
Kind
Dave
Today, 3:08 am
48 KB
Document
Homepage.htm
Today, 3:10 am
44 KB
HTML
Nick
Today, 3:03 am
152 KB
JPEG Image
vicki
Today, 3:05 am
308 KB
TIFF Document

3 If you're on a Mac, though, you might never have seen a file extension, since Mac OS doesn't traditionally use them to identify file types. However, you will need to use them when you're creating webpages. This is very simple – the most important thing to remember is to put .htm on the end of your webpage file names. (But don't use a dot elsewhere when you're naming your files!)

4 If you doubleclick an HTML file to open it, it should automatically open in your default Web browser. This will give you an indication of how the file will look on the Internet.

index.htm

4

re:media | music - Microsoft Internet Explorer
File
Edit
View
Favorites
Tools
Help
Address
C:\WINDOWS\Desktop\frames site\index.htm
Go
re:media
home
books
music
video/dvd
music
Lorem ipsum dolor sit amet, consetetur sadipscing elitr, sed diam nonumy eirmod tempor invidunt ut labore et dolore magna aliquyam erat, sed diam voluptua.
At vero eos et accusam et justo duo dolores et ea rebum. Stet clita kasd gubergren, no sea takimata sanctus est Lorem ipsum dolor sit amet. Lorem ipsum dolor sit amet, consetetur sadipscing elitr, sed diam nonumy eirmod tempor invidunt ut labore et dolore magna aliquyam erat, sed diam voluptua.
At vero eos et accusam et justo duo dolores et ea rebum. Stet clita kasd gubergren, no sea takimata sanctus est Lorem ipsum dolor sit amet. Lorem ipsum dolor sit amet, consetetur sadipscing elitr, sed diam nonumy eirmod tempor invidunt ut labore et dolore magna aliquyam erat, sed diam voluptua.
My Computer

WEB BROWSERS

A Web browser is what you use to view the Internet, and the two most common are Internet Explorer and Netscape Navigator (or Communicator). A browser is the software you will use to view the webpages at a particular Internet address (or URL), and the browser should also open automatically whenever you doubleclick a webpage, or HTML file, on your desktop.

Everyone needs a Web browser and, whether you have a Mac or a PC, chances are it will have come pre-installed with either Microsoft's Internet Explorer, which is known as IE for short, or Netscape's Navigator, which tends to be known as Netscape or NS. But if you're designing a website, you really need to have both, so that when you're creating your pages you can constantly check how they'll look to your viewers and make sure everything's working the way you want it to in both browsers.

1 *Internet Explorer and Netscape are currently still the most popular Web browsers, and, if you want to design a website, you should have both. You can download the latest versions of these for free at www.microsoft.com and www.netscape.com, although if you're not on a fast Internet connection you might prefer to ask for a CD. You can often get the latest versions on magazine cover CDs, too.*

2 *Installing and running IE and Netscape on your computer at the same time should be no problem, although you'll need to choose which you want to use as your day-to-day ('default') browser. This is so you don't end up with half your Bookmarks/Favorites in one place, and the other half somewhere else.*

1

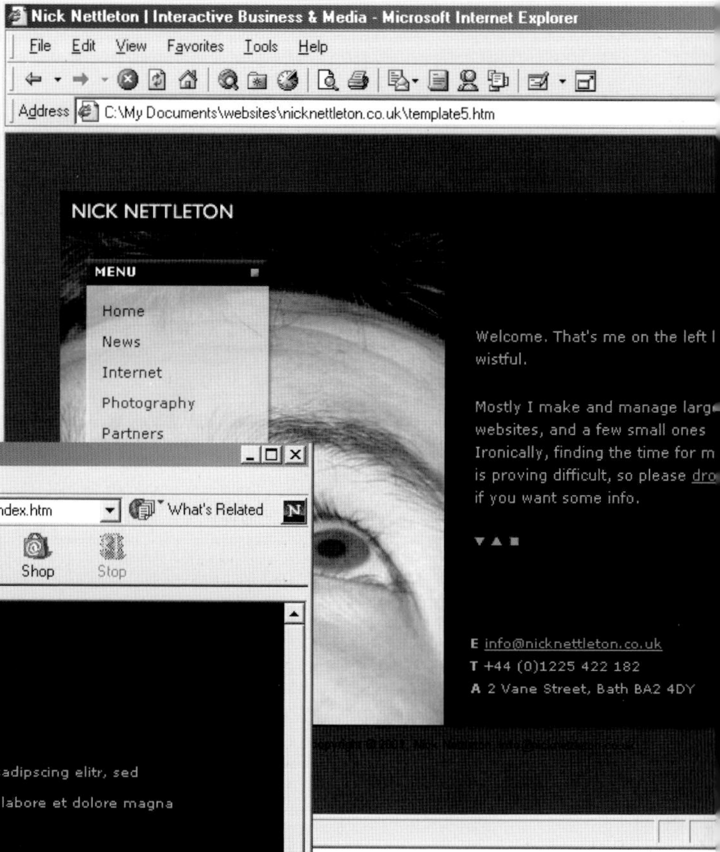

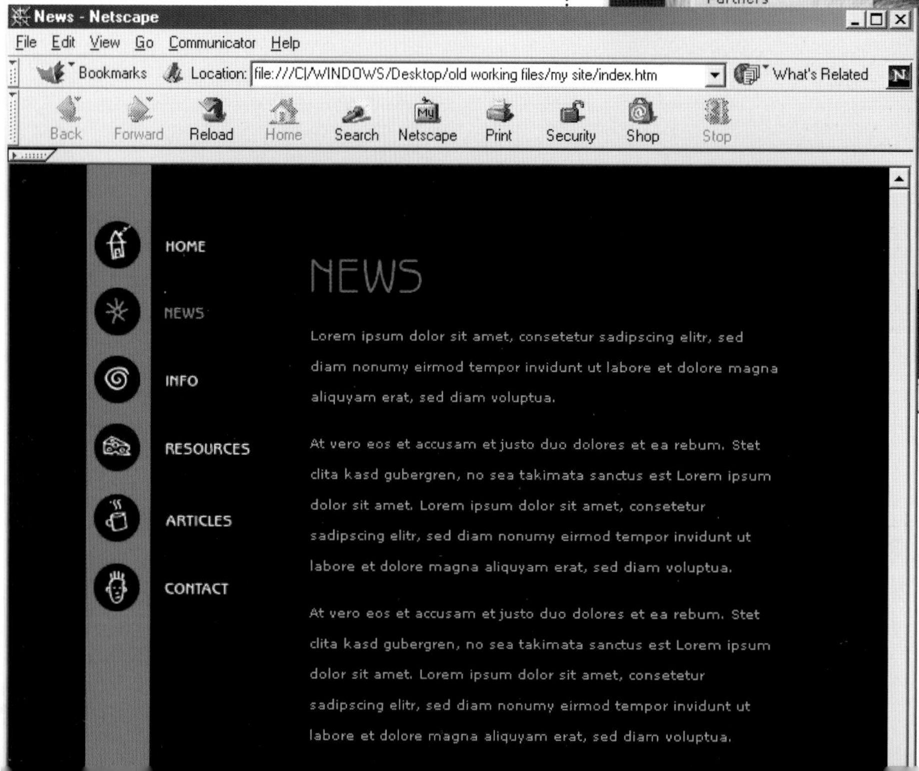

2
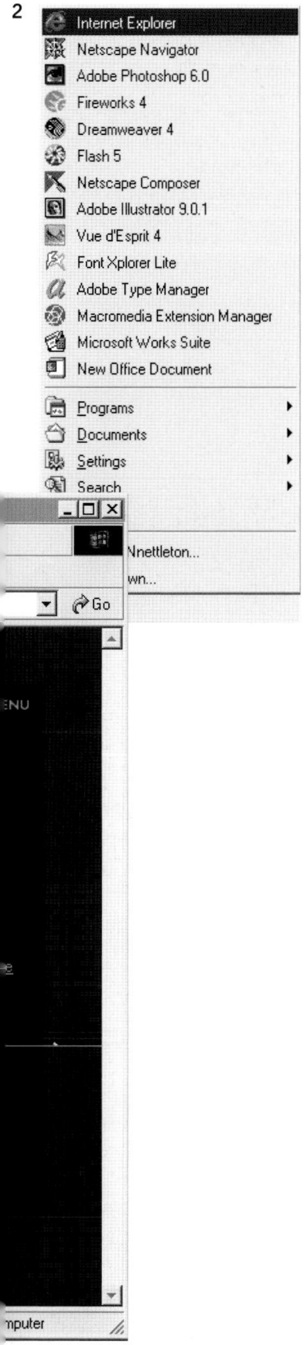

3 *But IE and Netscape are by no means the only options. There are a number of other browsers gaining popularity fast, which you might want to consider. For example, both Opera (**www.opera.com**) and Mozilla (**www.mozilla.org**) are packed with features, and are fast, free and have legions of hardcore fans. Many claim they are more secure than the big two established rivals. Usually you'll find that a webpage which works in IE and Netscape works well in other browsers too.*

By and large Netscape and IE work in the same way, but there are times when they don't and the results can be devastating. A great many new designers have had a terrible shock after working on a site using one browser as a guide, and then checking it in another browser only once the site is done. It's a galling experience, after all that work, so get into the habit of regularly checking with both.

You should make sure you're not using outdated versions of the Web browsers either; they tend to be updated and improved every six months or so. It takes a few months for the general public to catch on, so work towards creating a site that works best in the most popular browsers of the time.

3
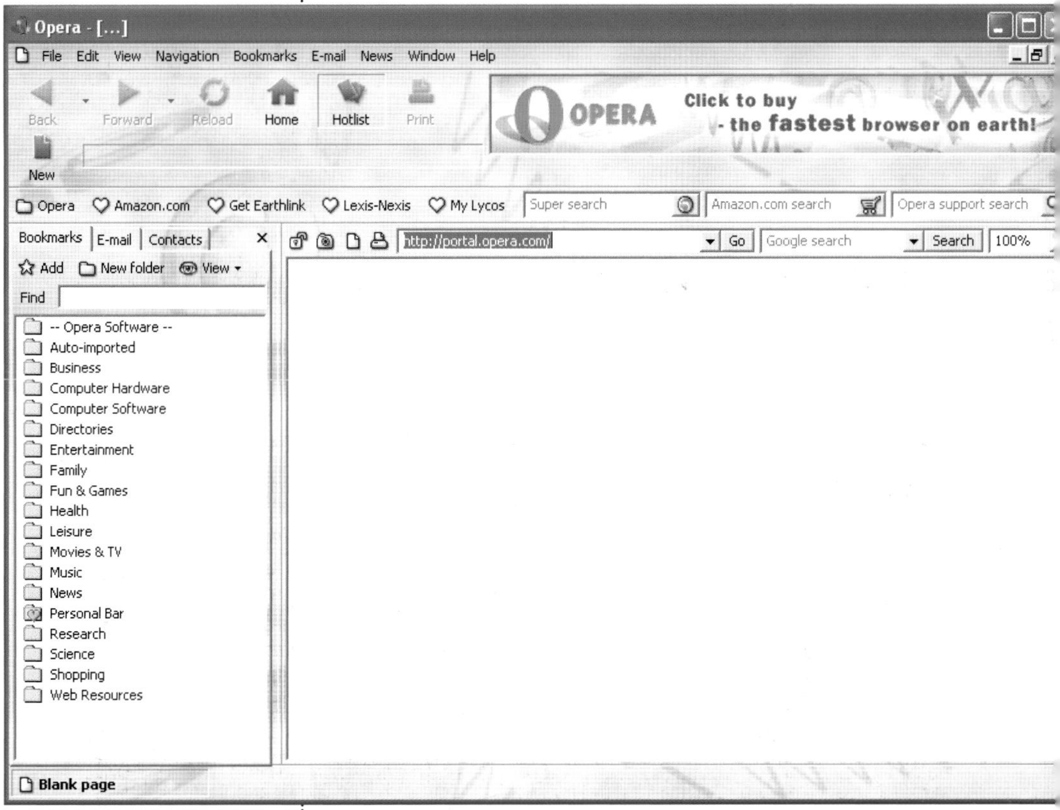

HOW A WEBPAGE IS MADE

So how do you create a webpage? Let's go back to the example of writing e-mails for a moment, since this has more in common with Web design than you might think. Imagine that in a few days it is your birthday. You didn't think about it much before today, but you woke up this morning thinking that you want to have a big day out. The only thing is, it's too late to mail invites and there are too many people to telephone. An e-mail invite is the perfect solution. You can make something pretty cool in Outlook Express or Netscape; throw in a picture or two, colour up the text and make it different sizes, and perhaps centre-align the whole thing.

Well, that's just what a webpage is: words + formatting + pictures + layout. And if you are playing around with colours and font sizes within your e-mails, you have to be using HTML, although you are probably not aware of it. Your software will have written all the code for you, in the background while you worked.

1

1 *You can take e-mail design to the limit – there's a project coming up in the next chapter to help you do this...*

2 *A webpage is made up of several elements – text with formatting, images, links and layout – all held together with HTML. To bring all these items together, you need software for creating the HTML. You can use Microsoft Word's* Save As HTML *option, and many other standard tools have similar functions, but most people choose to use dedicated Web design software to get a better result.*

2

E-mail design

Practise and experiment with your design skills by sending your friends unusual and exciting e-mails with pictures, colours and so on...

3

3 Text is the key element in most websites, especially those that are geared to giving people information, providing a service or selling a product. You can type text directly into your Web design application, but it's often better to write it in a word processing program first and then copy and paste it in as you do the design.

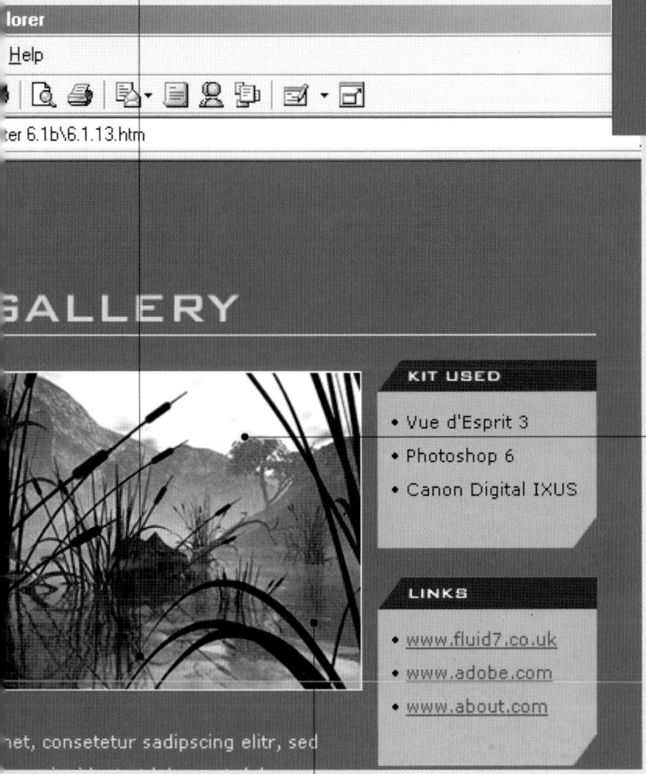

4

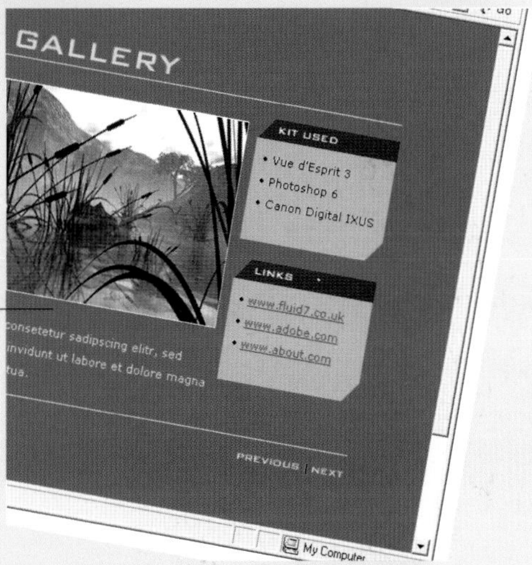

4 Images, which can be either graphics or photographs, are the key to making your webpages attractive and interesting, as well as providing a distinct visual identity. You need a separate bit of software to create these before adding them to your webpage – most graphics tools today have the features you need.

5 All the formatting – such as bolding, font sizes, alignment and so on – are done in the Web design application. This works just like a Word processor, so it is relatively straightforward to use – although bear in mind the font issues described on page 38.

5

WHICH WEB DESIGN SOFTWARE?

To build a website, you need to create HTML pages. You could still do this by learning HTML code and writing it directly into Notepad, SimpleText or something similar, but to be honest it's not much fun and you'd have to spend ages learning the language. Fortunately there are plenty of applications available today in which you can design your site visually, in just the way you would a newsletter in Microsoft Word. The best thing about them is that they write all the HTML for you.

Web design software ranges from the most basic, entry-level packages such as FrontPage Express (free with Windows 98) and Netscape Composer (free with the Netscape suite), to more professional applications such as Dreamweaver and Adobe GoLive.

It's worth starting off by using the free packages, but after a month or so you'll probably find their features just don't match up to your creative ideas, and they can be awkward to use too. Choosing a more appropriate application can be baffling at first – there are hundreds out there – but to be honest they all have similar underlying features and differ only in how easy they are to use (usually in relation to their price). Use the recommendations opposite as a guide.

Free software

You can get free software and trial versions of most Web design applications on the cover CDs of magazines like .net and Computer Arts or over the Internet – try ***www.cnet.download.com*** or ***www.zdnet.com***. Sometimes you can even get older versions of expensive software for free.

1

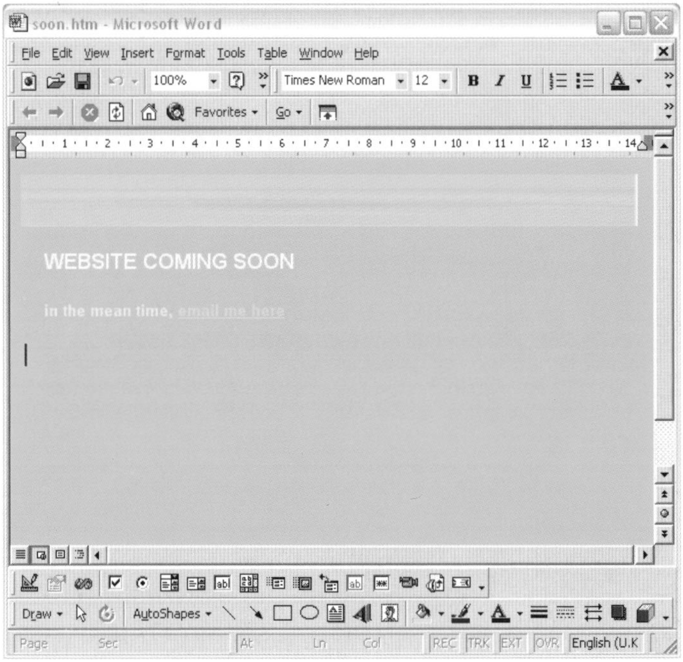

2

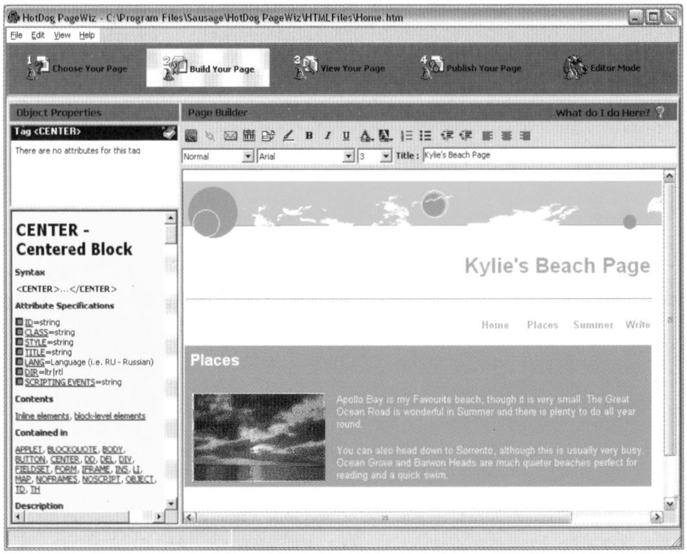

1 *If you have Microsoft Word, you can use this for designing basic webpages: select* Save As Web Page *before you begin, and then you can use the slightly modified interface to design your pages.*

2 *Aimed at the novice user, HotDog PageWiz is a simple, low-cost package that combines WYSIWYG and text-based authoring with some useful templates, so you can get a site up and running quickly.* **www.sausage.com**.

3

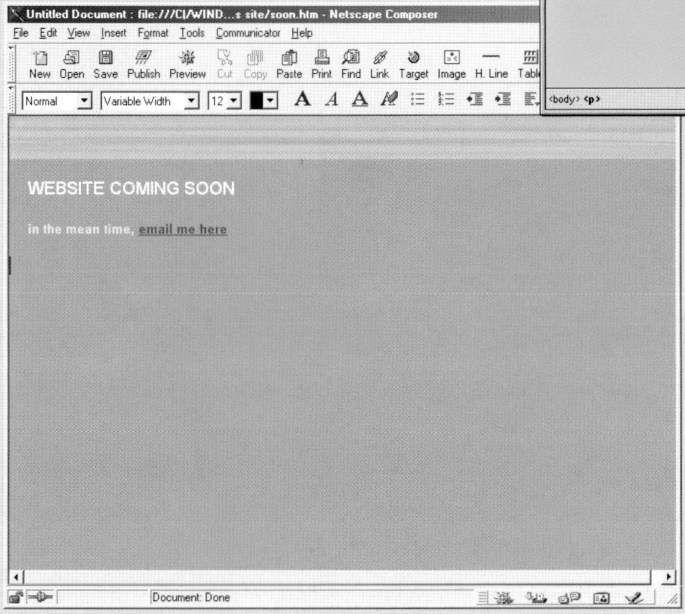

3 *Netscape Composer is a free add-on to the Netscape package for creating webpages – get the latest version at* **www.netscape.com**. *The features are very basic, which can make it frustrating for creative minds, but it's not a bad place to begin for free.*

4

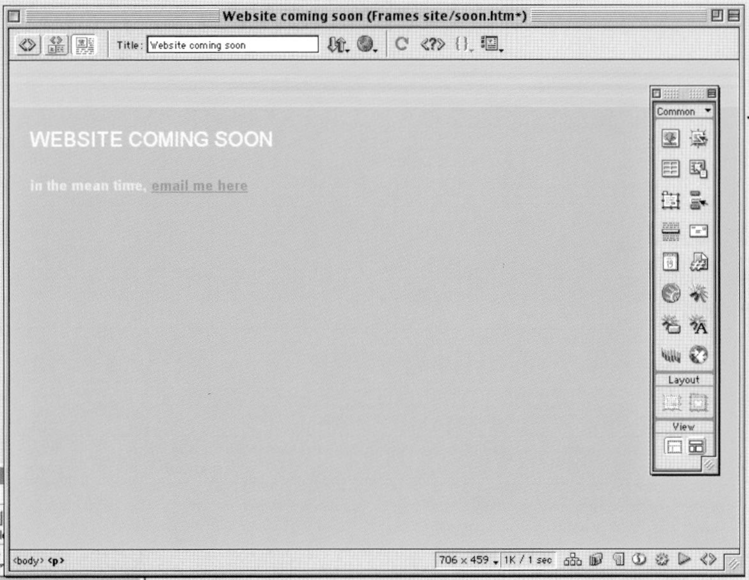

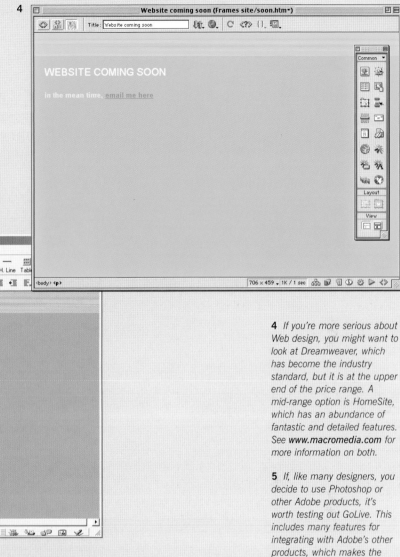

4 *If you're more serious about Web design, you might want to look at Dreamweaver, which has become the industry standard, but it is at the upper end of the price range. A mid-range option is HomeSite, which has an abundance of fantastic and detailed features. See* **www.macromedia.com** *for more information on both.*

5 *If, like many designers, you decide to use Photoshop or other Adobe products, it's worth testing out GoLive. This includes many features for integrating with Adobe's other products, which makes the whole Web design process much easier.*

5

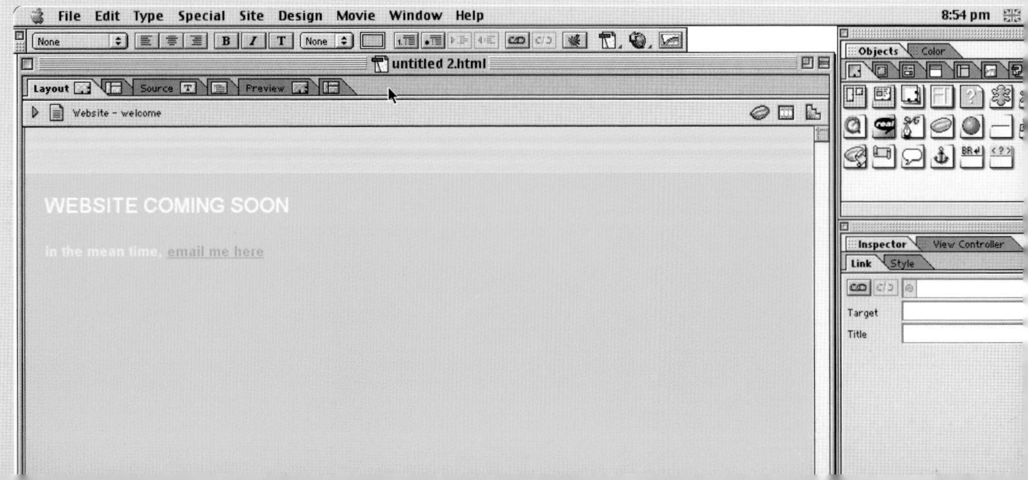

WHICH GRAPHICS SOFTWARE?

To create a website, you need more than just Web 'authoring' software such as FrontPage, HomeSite or Dreamweaver. Like your e-mail or word-processing program, these can add size, colour, positioning, links and so on to the things in your webpage – but they can't create or modify pictures. To do this you need a dedicated graphics application, and for Web design you need it to have Web-related features – so Microsoft Paint won't do! Most graphics applications today do have these features, but it's important to doublecheck before buying.

In Web design, graphics software is used to create headings with type; to prepare, resize and crop photos and to add icons and drawings to your design. You also need optimization, or compression, tools, which will be explained in more detail in chapter three (see page 82 onwards).

You don't need to spend a fortune to get hold of graphics software: head to our website, which is at ***www.webdesign.web-linked.com***, or check out magazine CDs, and you'll be able to find something for free. But you'll get infinitely better results if you can get your hands on some commercial software, and fully functional trial versions of most of these applications are available for you to try out. Normally, you can use them for 30 days – plenty of time to get up to speed and build your first website!

1 *Photoshop is the leading graphics application in the world – for professionals and amateurs alike. Few would deny that it is also the most powerful, with superb creative tools and features that put you in control of every aspect of your images. But that kind of functionality doesn't come cheap. It can also seem overwhelming at first, and it's likely that you won't use the full range of tools, so you might want to save money and take a look at* ***www.adobe.com*** *for more information before taking the plunge.*

2 *Photoshop Elements: this is a 'lite' version of Photoshop but it still includes all the most popular features for beginners, including special Web design tools, plus filters and effects. Its toolset is more than ample for you to complete all the projects in this book, and it's affordable. See* ***www.adobe.com*** *for further information.*

1

2

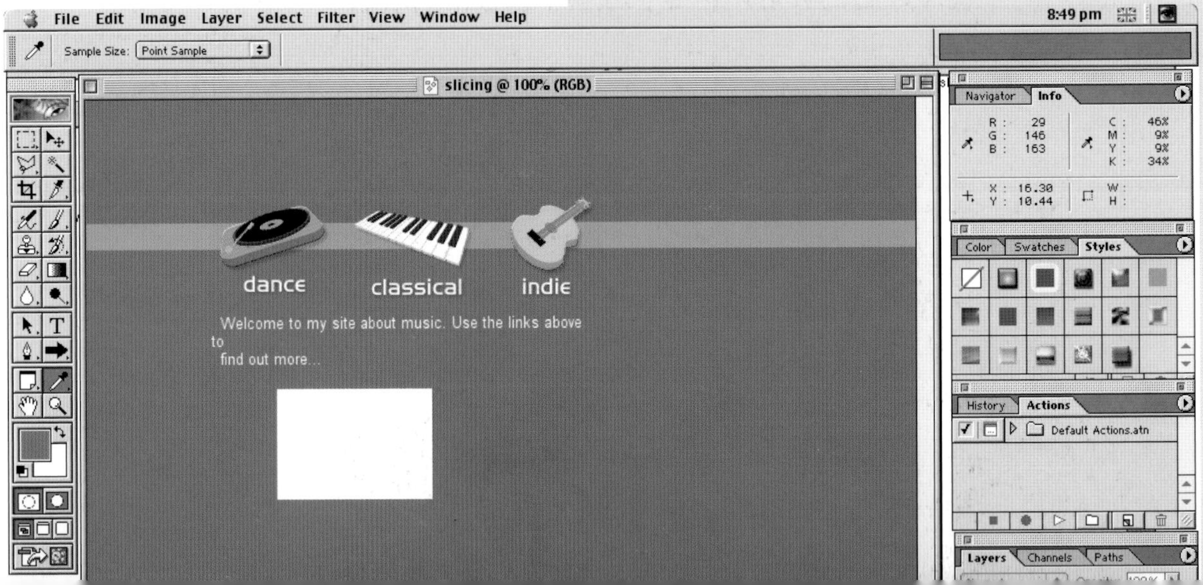

3 *At a similar price to Photoshop Elements, one of the most popular graphics applications for beginners is Paint Shop Pro. This has many of the features of a professional graphics application, is fairly easy to learn, and has a good range of features for automatically doing more complex tasks – but you may find it hard to achieve exactly what you want. See* **www.jasc.com** *for more information.*

3

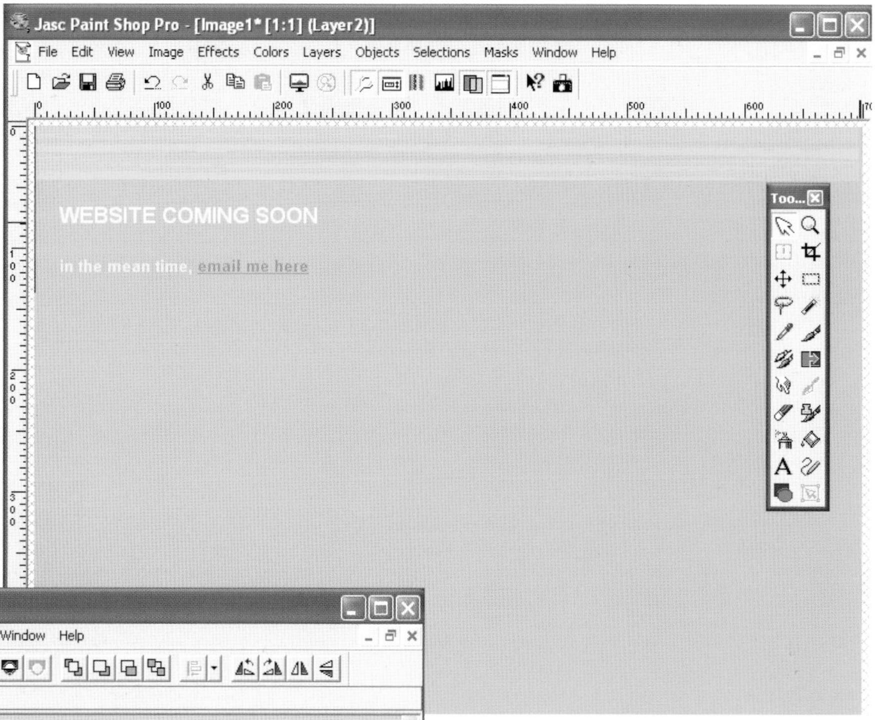

4

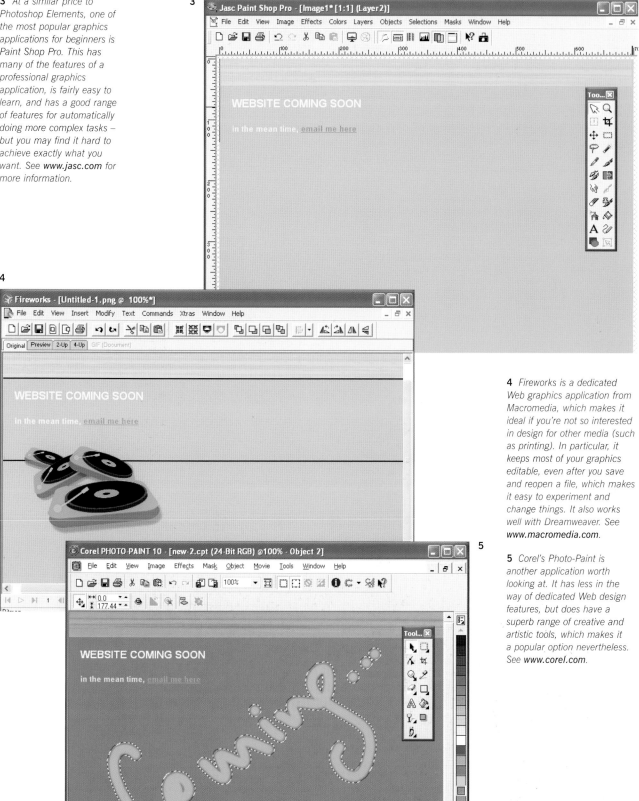

4 *Fireworks is a dedicated Web graphics application from Macromedia, which makes it ideal if you're not so interested in design for other media (such as printing). In particular, it keeps most of your graphics editable, even after you save and reopen a file, which makes it easy to experiment and change things. It also works well with Dreamweaver. See* **www.macromedia.com**.

5

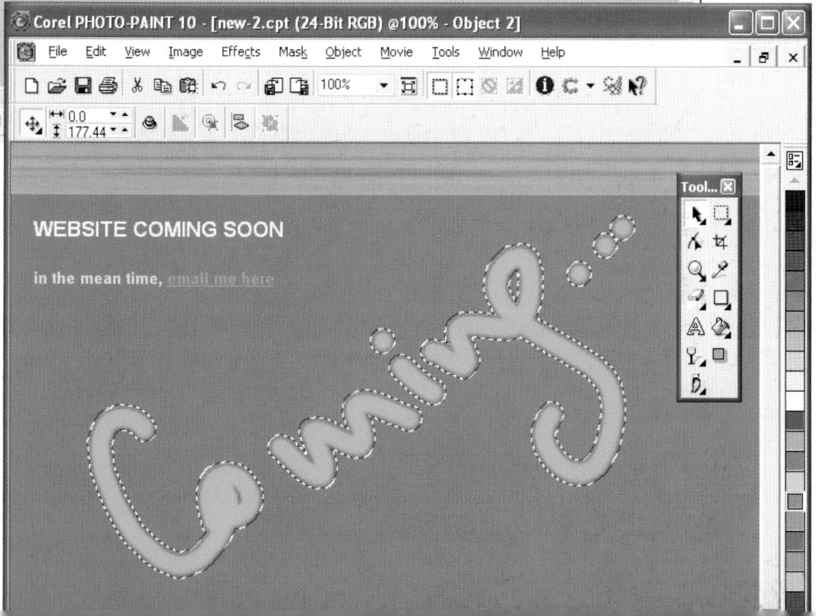

5 *Corel's Photo-Paint is another application worth looking at. It has less in the way of dedicated Web design features, but does have a superb range of creative and artistic tools, which makes it a popular option nevertheless. See* **www.corel.com**.

ORGANISING YOUR SITE

Of course, there's a lot more to a website than just a nice-looking page that works a bit like an e-mail. For a start, a website means a whole bunch of pages with links between them, not just one page on its own. Obviously these pages also have to actually be on the Web, and have a distinct Web address to go with them so that people can choose to take a look. So how do you get them from your computer and onto the Web?

Let's start with the pages. Each webpage has its own HTML file, and if there are images in there, then you'll have a file for each of those too. This is because images aren't included in HTML, but are saved as graphics format files, usually GIF or JPEG (see page 86).

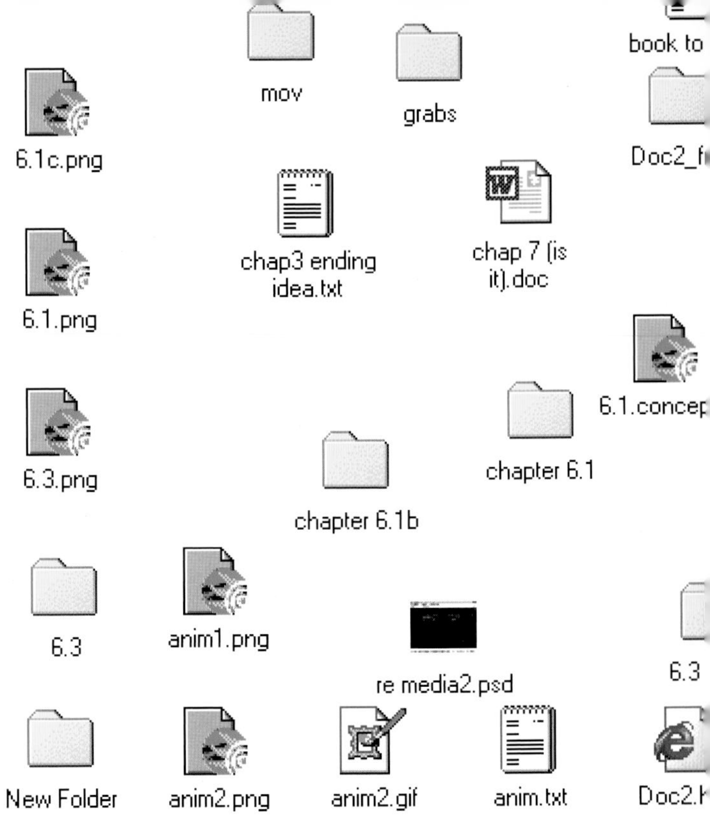

1

2

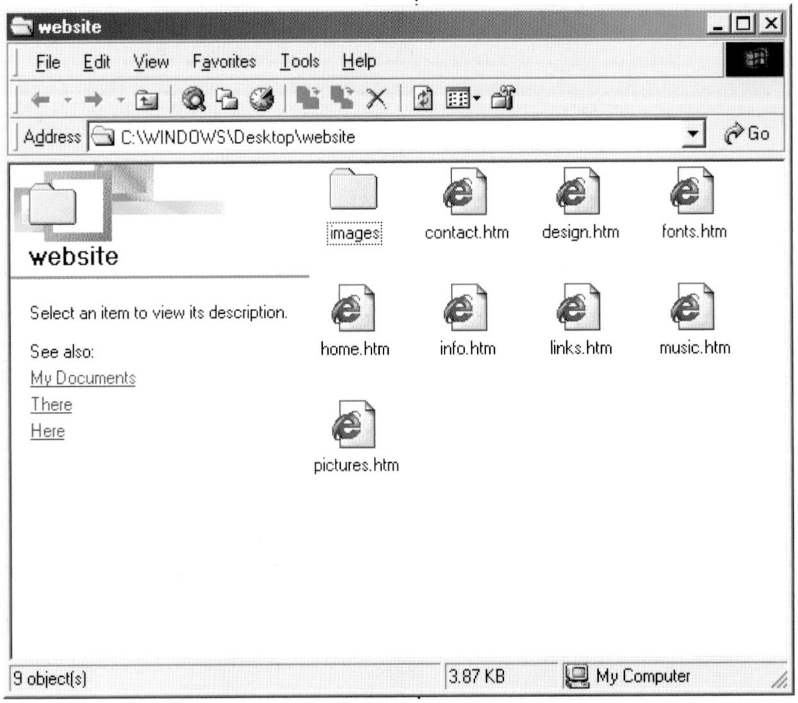

1 *While you're building your website, you'll soon find that you end up with loads of different files, and in different formats too. You will have HTML files, graphics files, text files, probably odd notes you've written to yourself, and loads of experiments as well.*

2 *It's a good idea to sort all your files into folders and to label them well. Most important, though, is to make sure that all the files for a particular website are in a single folder of their own. This is essential for making your links work properly. Otherwise, when you put your site on the Internet, there's a good chance you'll find that nothing works.*

3 *Don't be tempted to start throwing things away! Whatever you do, keep everything you do, unless it really is a complete disaster. You never know when you might want to go back to it and try again. Lots of designers keep a single folder called 'experiments' or 'help me', just in case.*

4 *Always try to keep copies of your work in their original, editable formats – 'software-native' formats, as they are called. Some examples are a Photoshop PSD file, Paint Shop Pro PSP file, Fireworks PNG, etc. GIFs, JPEGs, BMPs and similar common formats 'flatten' a design, which means you can change it only by adding something on top of the finished image, or by going back to the software-native version, changing it, then re-saving it as a JPEG or GIF etc. HTML is itself, however, a fully editable format.*

3

4

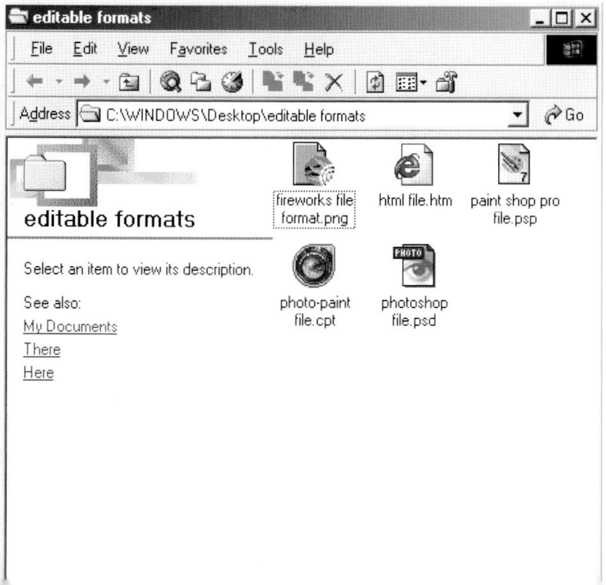

When you open a webpage, your browser first loads in the HTML, then has a look through to see what instructions it contains for images, and finally individually loads each of the graphics files into the right place on the page. So if you've got a five-page site (let's keep things simple for now!), then you will have five HTML pages and maybe four or five graphics files for each page, which makes at least 20 files in all.

Once you've designed your pages, you can use your Web design software to set up the links between them, so that visitors to your site can get around. It's very easy, and every Web design application includes simple tools for adding links.

HOW A SITE GETS ON THE INTERNET

Once you've got a website designed on your computer, and everything's working just fine from there, you need to post it onto the Web, complete with a www. address so that people can visit it. This process is also called uploading.

In order to do this, you need an ISP (Internet Service Provider), to give you some Web space and fix you up with a domain name – your own Web address. Soon you could be a dot com! In many cases, the ISP you use to connect to the Internet will be able to offer you Web space and an address for a small fee, although sometimes it's free. This space is, quite literally, a certain number of megabytes (spare disk space) on one of their computers. 20–50MB (the abbreviation for megabytes) is fairly standard, although you're unlikely to need much more than 10MB unless you want to use hundreds of images, or post some sound and video files.

Your ISP, or 'host', will create a folder on their computer that is specifically yours and add entries to databases on computers around the world, so that whenever someone taps in your website address, they automatically get forwarded to the files in your folder on their computer – or 'server' as it is known. All you have to do is get your files onto the server…

1

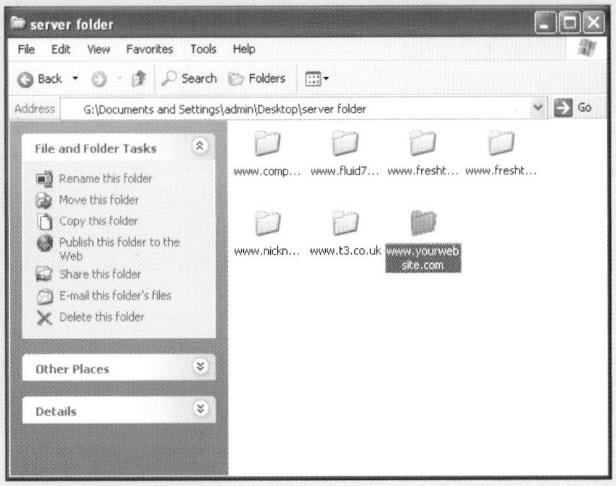

1 *To get your site on the Web, you first need a Web address and some Web space, which you can usually get from your existing ISP. Web space is a folder on a computer that's permanently connected to the Internet, and set up with special software for sending HTML pages to other computers. This is called a Web server.*

2

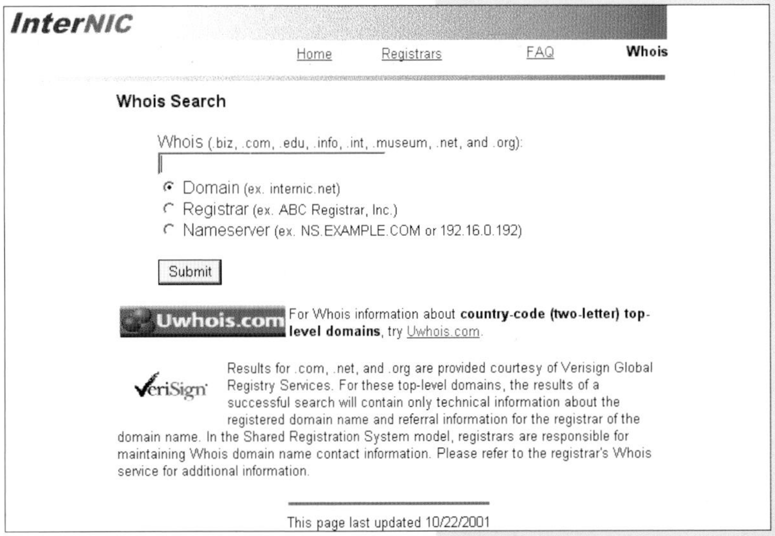

2 *To get a domain name, such as (and this is by way of example only) 'www.thisismywebsite.com', you need to register it. The authority through which you need to do this will depend on the ending of the domain name. For instance, .com addresses are managed by InterNIC. Your hosting company should take care of this for you, but you can check to see whether your ideal domain name is available at* ***www.internic.org/whois****. It may take you some time to find an available address to register!*

3

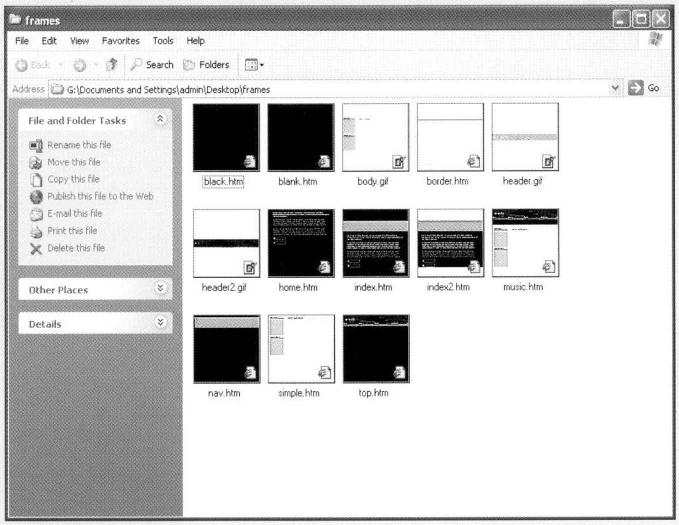

4

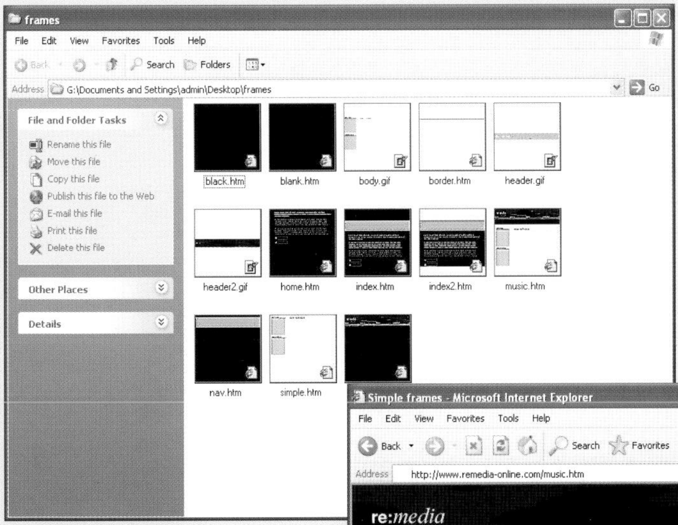

5

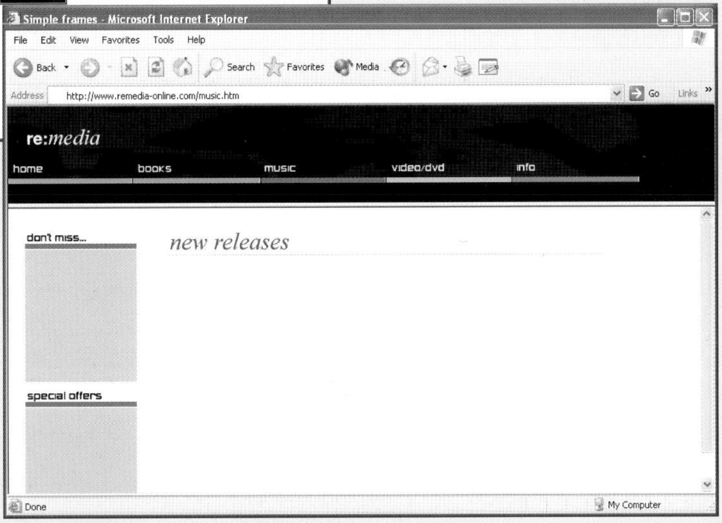

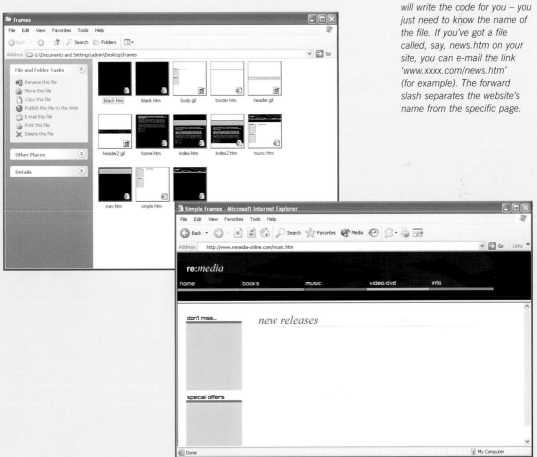

3 *When someone types in your Web address (or 'URL') from anywhere in the world, they will be directed to your Web space, and one of the files there will open automatically in their browser. Usually this page is called index.htm (or index.html), because in the early days of the Web the first page of a site was an index of the site's contents. So you should almost always give your homepage this name.*

4|5 *A link is a bit of HTML that says, 'When someone clicks here, get this file from the server.' Most Web software will write the code for you – you just need to know the name of the file. If you've got a file called, say, news.htm on your site, you can e-mail the link 'www.xxxx.com/news.htm' (for example). The forward slash separates the website's name from the specific page.*

1
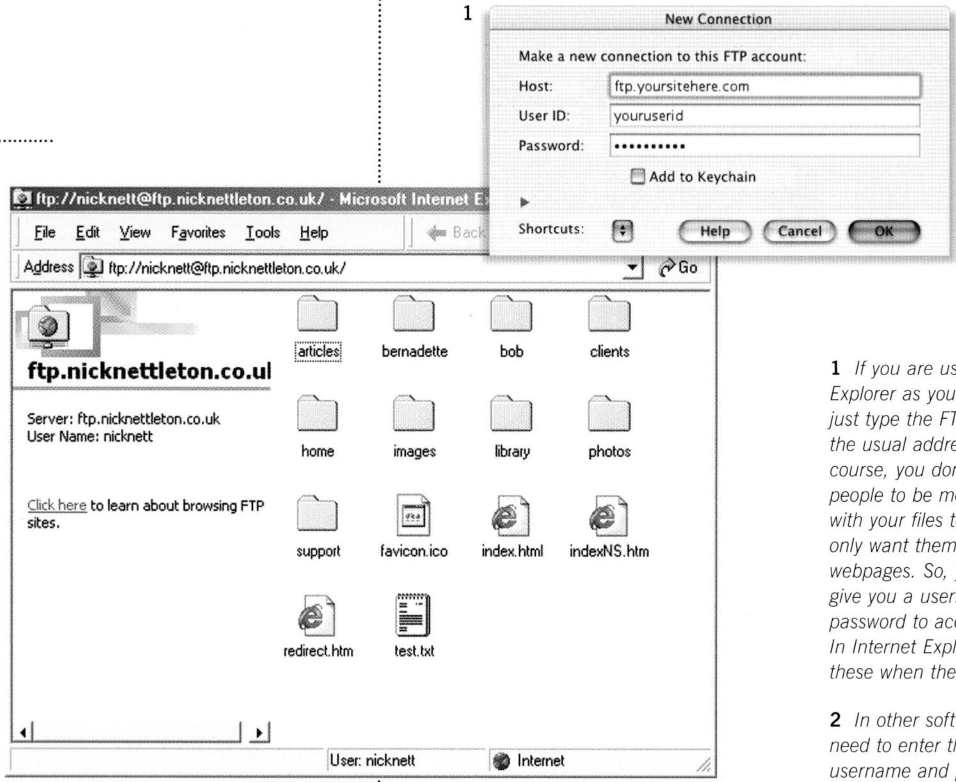

1 *If you are using Internet Explorer as your FTP client, just type the FTP address in the usual address bar. Of course, you don't want other people to be messing around with your files too – you only want them to see the webpages. So, your host should give you a username and password to access the folder. In Internet Explorer, just enter these when the dialog pops up.*

2 *In other software, you will need to enter the FTP address, username and password in a special* Setup *window, like this one in Dreamweaver. In Web authoring software, you'll usually find these settings in the* Site Options *or in the* Settings *dialog.*

USING FTP SOFTWARE

Once you've got a Web address and some space with a hosting company, the next step is to get your site from your computer onto their Web server. In order to do this you need FTP, which stands for File Transfer Protocol. This, like HTTP (HyperText Transfer Protocol), is a standard protocol recognised by computers, but designed specifically for moving files between them, rather than automatically opening the files (as is the case with HTTP).

Using FTP software, you can look directly at your Web space folder on your host's server, and transfer, move, rename or delete files just as you can on your own computer. Usually, all you need is your website folder on your computer showing in one window and your Web space folder on the server showing in another window. Then just drag and drop the whole thing over from your computer to the server – then sit back and relax while it goes down the phone line!

You can often use Windows Explorer as your FTP, although some servers don't allow this. Many Web design applications also have a built-in FTP feature,

2
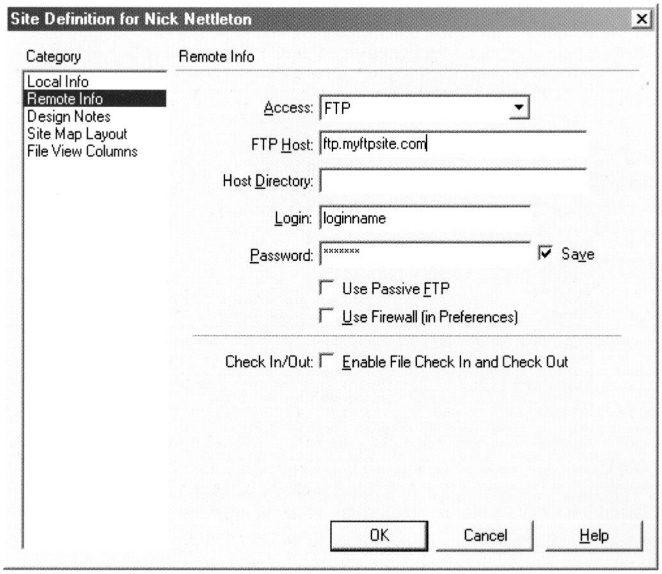

like GoLive's or Dreamweaver's Site Window. Failing either of these options, there are plenty of 'freeware' and 'shareware' FTP clients (as they're known) available. Two of the most popular are CuteFTP – see ***www.cuteftp.com*** – and WS-FTP, which you can get from ***www.ws-ftp.com***. If you have a Mac, try Fetch, ***www.fetchsoftworks.com***.

To see the files in your Web space, you need an FTP address for the folder, which is usually placed in a Setup window. An FTP address is much like a Web address, but it begins with ftp:// rather than http://. Your host may give you a dedicated address.

Of course, you don't want other people to mess around with your files – you only want them to see the finished webpages. So, your host should give you a private username and password too.

Your FTP software probably offers a number of other options, such as Host Directory, Passive FTP, Firewall and so on. Chances are, you won't need to use them, but do check out what they offer.

Once you've got everything set up, just hit the 'Connect' button, wait for the connection to be made and then you should be able to transfer files between your computer and FTP space easily.

3

4

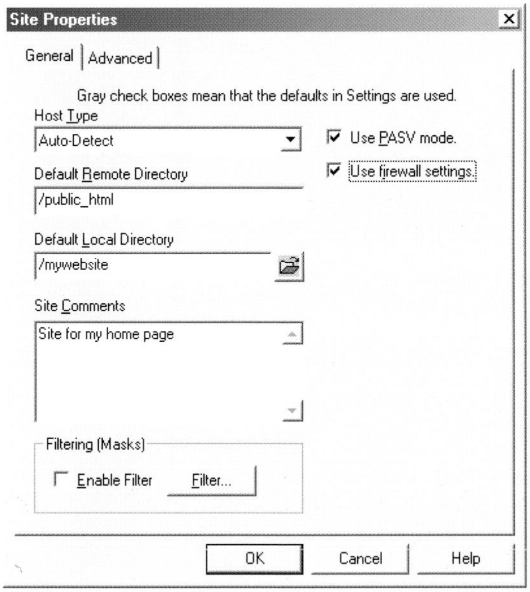

3 *If you are using dedicated FTP software, you will usually find that when opening the application, you come to a window with a list of FTP sites, and a New Site button. Use this to enter your personal FTP settings.*

4 *Your software should offer a number of extra options, such as Host Directory, Passive FTP, Firewall and so on, which can be confusing at first, but don't worry. These will depend on your ISP and personal computer set-up. Most Web hosting companies have detailed instructions for these on their website. Use these as a guide.*

5 *Once you've got everything set up, just hit the 'Connect' button, wait for the connection to be made and now you should be able to transfer files between your computer and FTP space. Experiment with some empty text files, to check that it's all working, and once you're happy, it's time to get going on making your first proper webpage…*

5

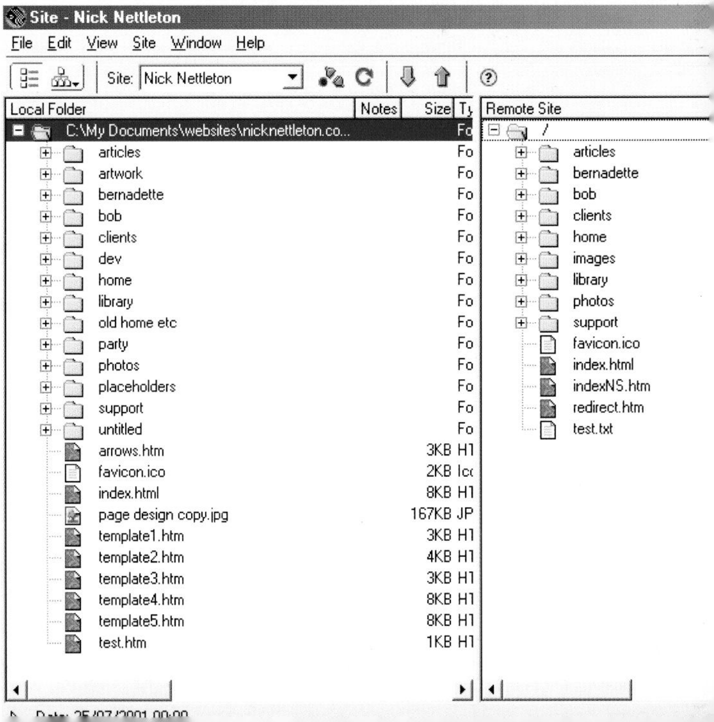

SCANNERS AND DIGITAL CAMERAS

Many computer packages come with a huge selection of free software, add-on tools and bits of hardware, so it can be hard to know where to start. But two of the most useful extras for the Web designer are the scanner and digital camera. If you didn't get them bundled in, don't worry – you don't have to have either, but if you'd like to invest in them prices start at less than £100.

A scanner is a piece of hardware for getting printed photos, designs, artwork and other flat visuals into your computer. Sometimes a scanner is built into a printer or it may be a flat screen with a cover, like a small photocopier. Either way, you simply put your image onto it and your computer should take care of the rest.

A digital camera is just like a normal camera, but it uses a computer chip instead of film to store the images. The advantage of this is that you can plug it into the back of your computer and, using the software that came with it, transfer the image files from the chip onto your own computer.

The appeal of both of these tools is that you can easily include your own photos in your webpages – whether they're pictures of family and friends, your business products or just art for art's sake.

1

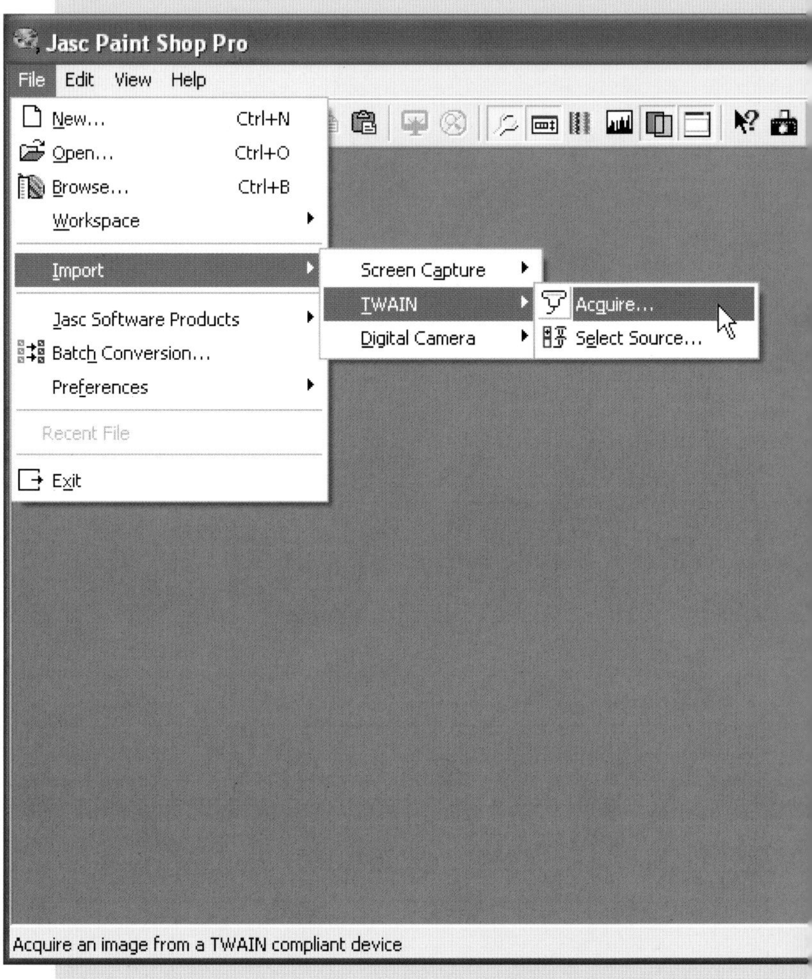

1 *If you're buying a scanner, always look for a USB or Firewire scanner – check first, of course, that your computer supports these. USB and Firewire are simply different ways of getting information into your computer. There will be relevant sockets on the back. It is best to go for these transfer methods because they are much faster than the alternatives. Once you've got your scanner installed, you should be able to open your graphics application and select an option in your File menu called something like 'Import via Twain'. The application communicates with your scanner, and once the image has been scanned (which can take a little while), it will appear in your graphics application. Always scan at the best quality you can, not less than 72 dots per inch.*

Read reviews

Always read reviews in magazines of cameras and scanners before you go out and buy one. The quality that you get for your money varies enormously, and often the best product isn't the one inside the biggest, brightest box.

2 *Digital cameras work in much the same way, also via Firewire and USB, but you may have a hundred images to deal with rather than just one. As soon as you plug in and turn on your camera, a dialog should appear, offering you options to transfer all or just some of your images directly into a folder on your computer.*

2

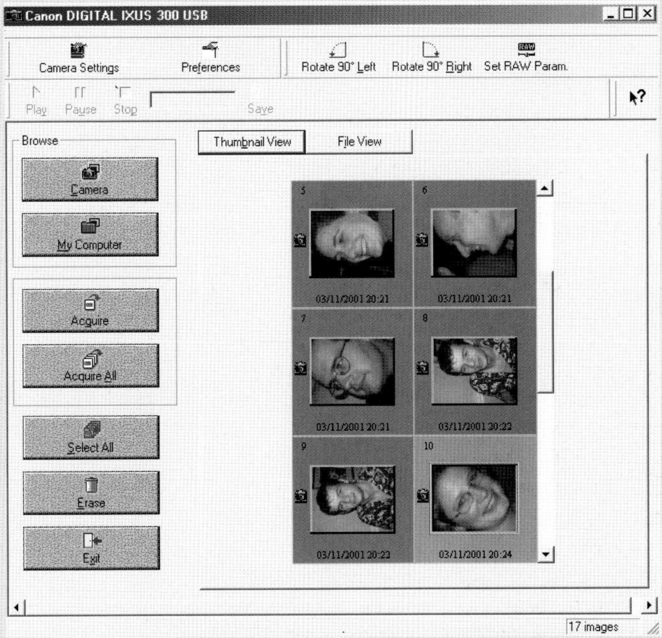

3|4

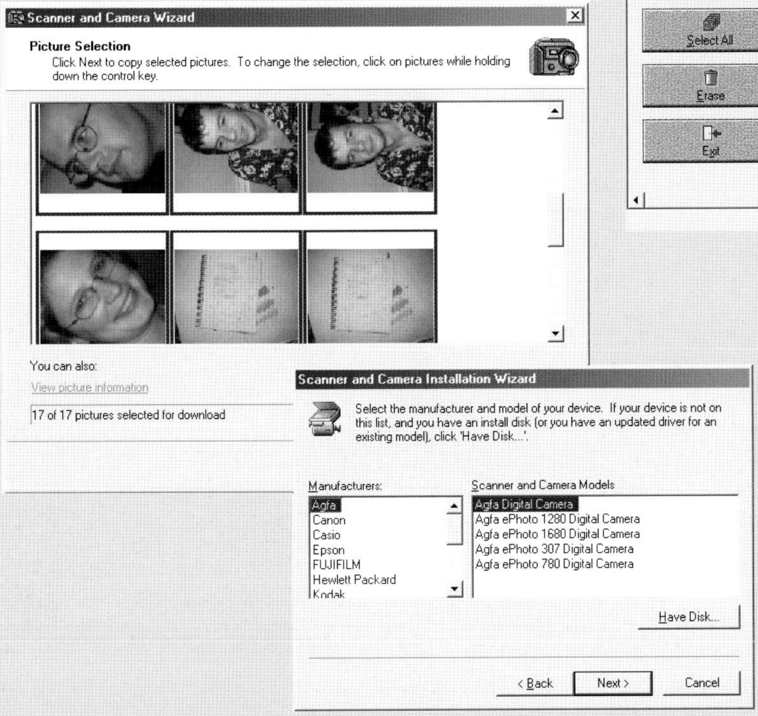

3|4 *If you are using Windows 2000 or ME, select* Scanners and Cameras *from your* Control Panel, *or the* Scanner and Camera Wizard *from your* Start menu Accessories *folder. This helps you to set up a variety of imaging devices and get them all working efficiently.*

5 *On a Mac, you can browse your camera directly from an icon on your desktop – just like a CD – or in OS X by using the* Image Capture *tool that is shown here.*

5

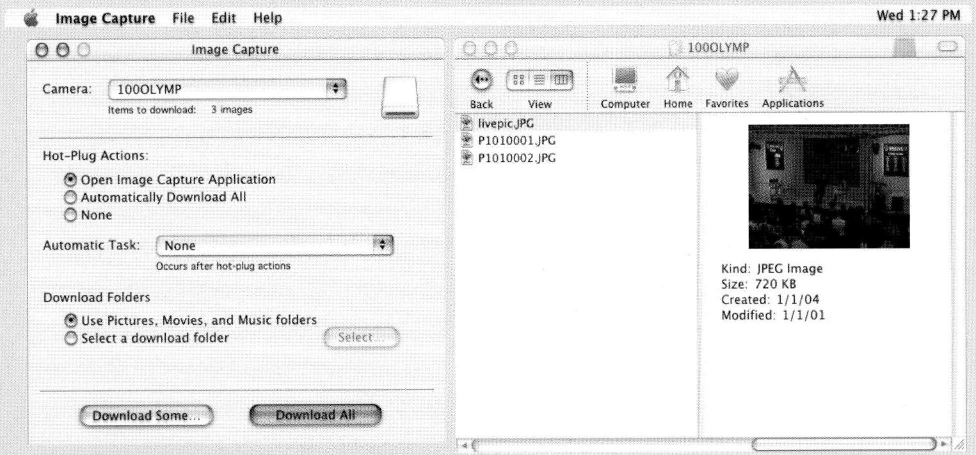

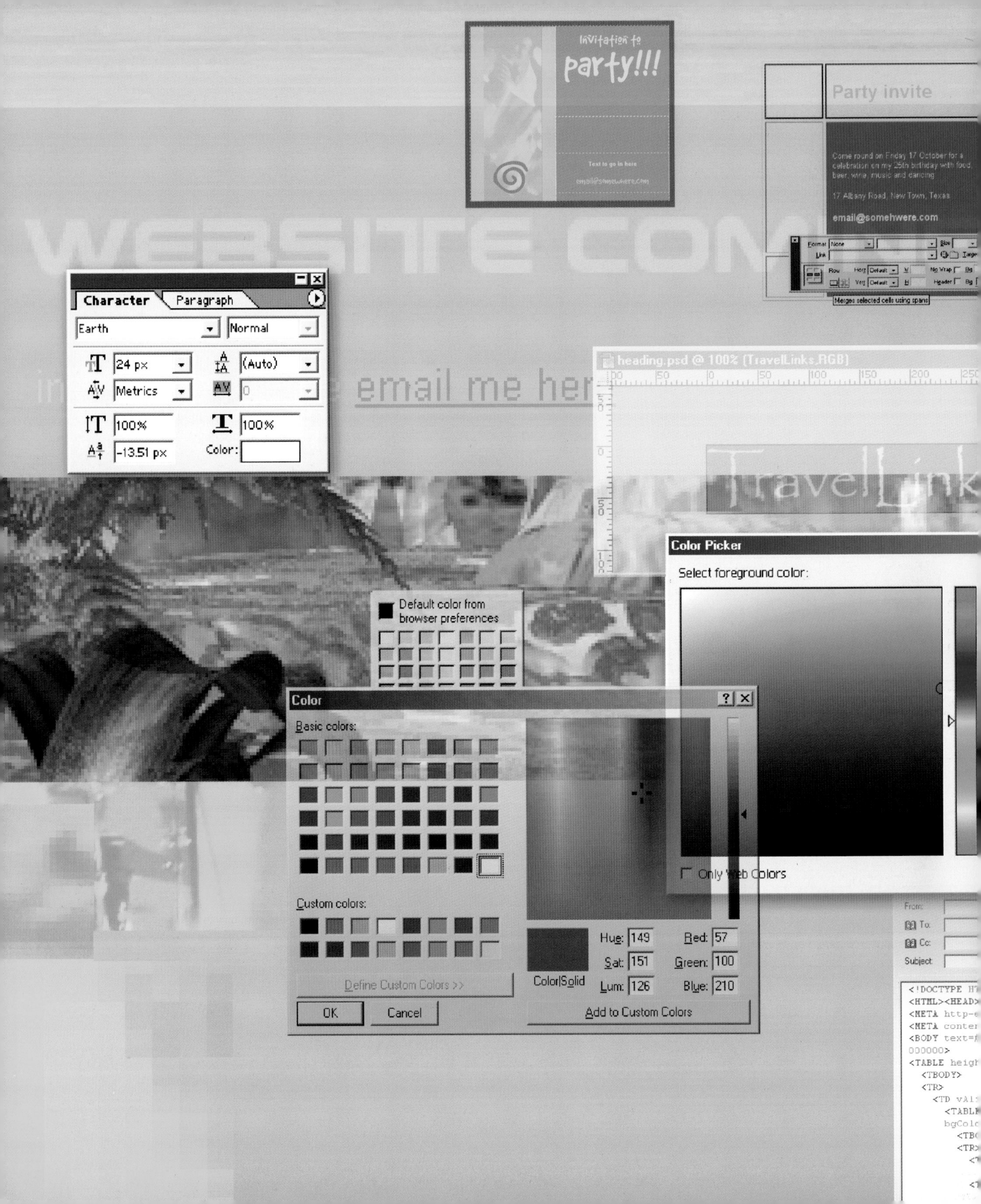
Invitation to
party!!!
Text to go in here
email@somewhere.com
Party invite
17 Albany Road, New Town, Texas
email@somehwere.com
Merges selected cells using spans
Character
Paragraph
Earth
Normal
24 px
(Auto)
Metrics
100%
100%
-13.51 px
Color:
email me her
heading.psd @ 100% (TravelLinks,RGB)
TravelLink
Color Picker
Select foreground color:
Only Web Colors
Default color from browser preferences
Color
Basic colors:
Custom colors:
Define Custom Colors >>
OK
Cancel
Color|Solid
Hue: 149
Sat: 151
Lum: 126
Red: 57
Green: 100
Blue: 210
Add to Custom Colors
From:
To:
Cc:
Subject

CHAPTER 2

Basic Techniques

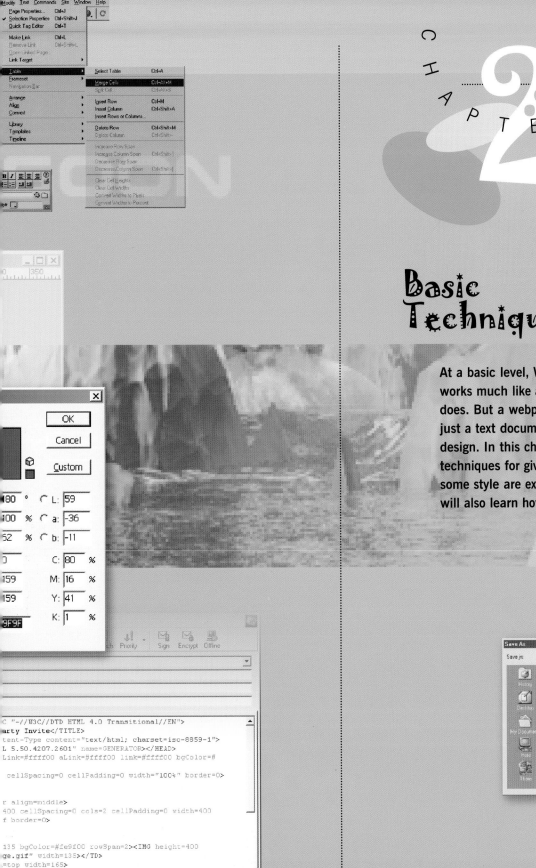

At a basic level, Web software works much like a Word processor does. But a webpage is more than just a text document so it needs a design. In this chapter, the basic techniques for giving your pages some style are explained, and you will also learn how to link them up.

PROJECT 1
KICK OFF

Here's how to make your first simple webpage...

Before you start you should create a new folder on your desktop called 'my webpages'. Make sure that when you save your pages you save them in here, to keep them all together in one place.

Next, open your Web design or authoring application, such as Dreamweaver, FrontPage Express or Netscape Composer. If you haven't already got a new document window open, then choose *File* > ***New***.

The obvious place to begin is with your words. You can type these directly into your Web design application in just the same way as you do with your word processor. But if you're planning on a lot of words, it might be a good idea to write them with your word processor first and then just *Copy* (*Control* or *Apple* + *C*) and then *Paste* (*Control* or *Apple* + *P*) the whole lot into your new webpage when you are happy with it.

It's a good idea in Web design to break your text up into small chunks. Use lots of subheadings, so it's easy for your viewers to skim onscreen and quickly locate the bit they're interested in. First impressions count, and you don't want to scare people with an intimidating, dense wall of prose. The next few pages show you how to make sure your first webpage is both attractive and appealing.

1

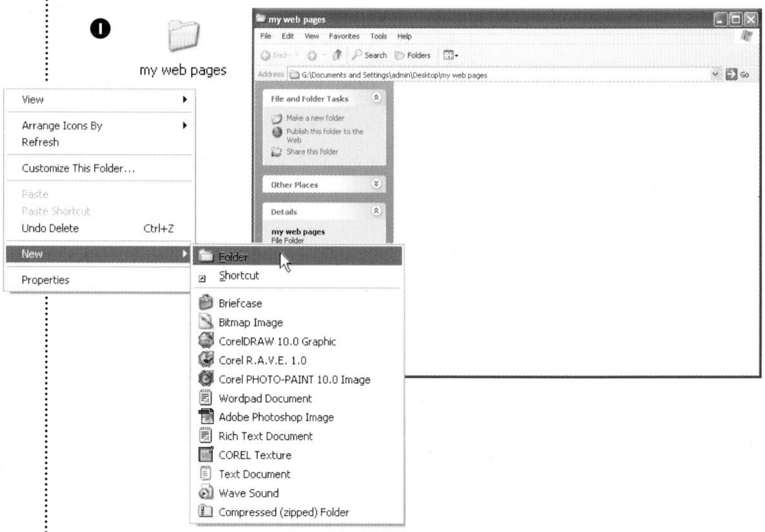

2

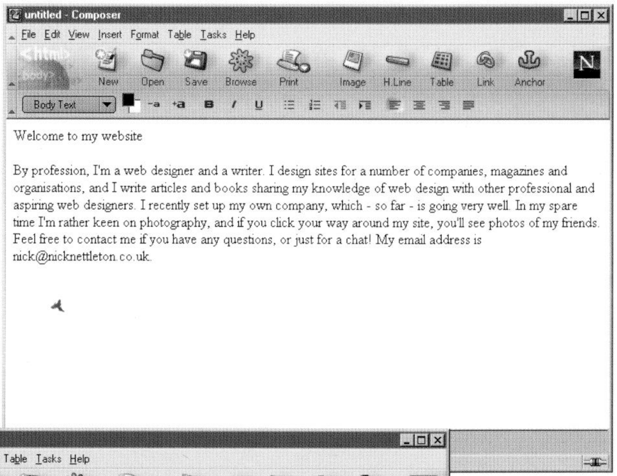

3

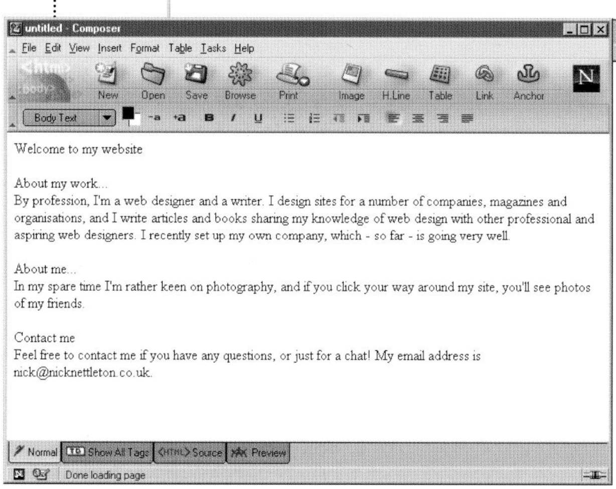

4
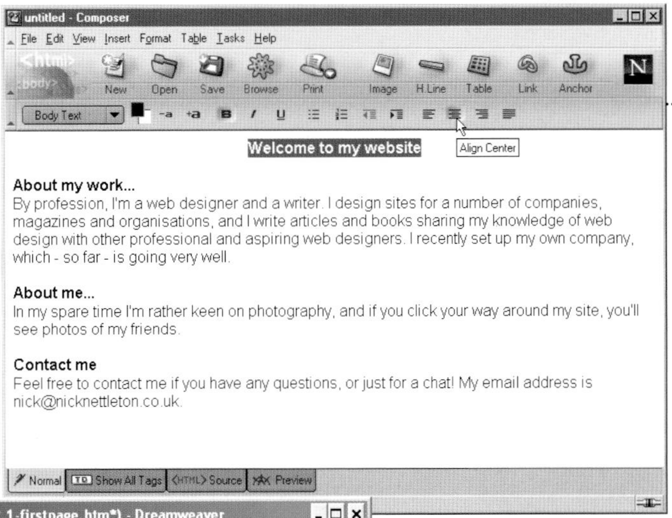

5
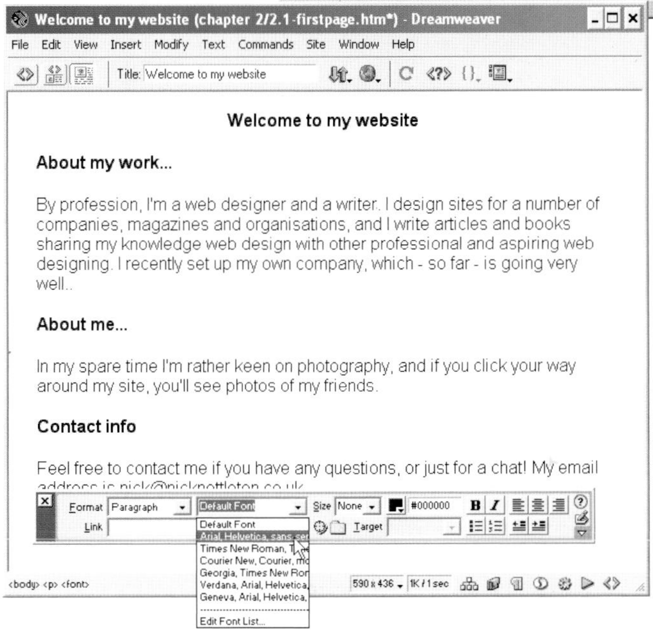

6
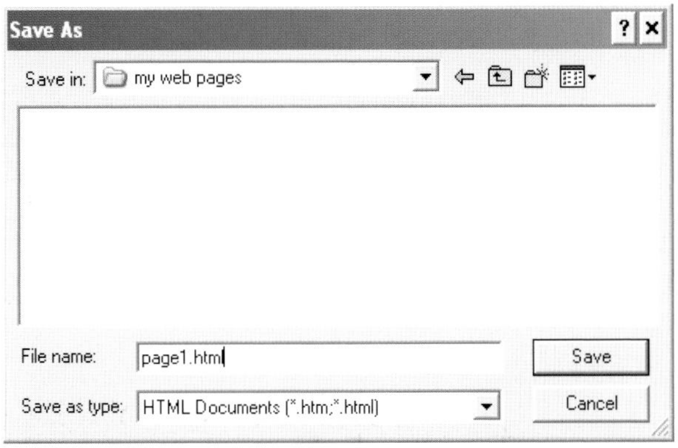

1 Start by creating a new folder for your webpages – and make sure you keep them all in there from now on.

2 Open your Web design software, such as Netscape Composer (shown here), then start a new document and either type in your text directly or *Copy* and *Paste* it from your word processor.

3 It's a good idea to break your text up into short paragraphs, and to use lots of subheadings. This is because reading on screen is quite difficult, and often people just want to scan a page and pick out one or two specific bits of information rather than wade through the whole thing.

4 Next you should choose a font for your text, and make your headings look like headings. In most applications you will find buttons on the main toolbar that will make your text bold, change font sizes, centre headings and so on. Just select the words and click the buttons to apply your styling. Here, the font Arial has been used.

5 If you're using Dreamweaver, you'll find these settings in your *Properties Inspector*. If you can't see it, choose *Window menu > Properties* from the menu bar.

6 Before you move on, save your page into the folder you created at the start.

Choosing colours

❼ Design is all about making your webpages attractive and easy to read; you want people visiting your site to think it looks great. Colour is one of the best places to start for this. You should find a colour menu in your software – usually right by the text formatting tools. Note: not all colours will display exactly the same on Macs and PCs.

❽ First try selecting all your text (using *Control* or *Apple* + *A*) and give it a deep blue hue. Then individually select your headings and give them colours too. It's a good idea to make sure that all your headings of the same weight have the same colour (and other formatting). This helps all the parts of your design 'gel together'.

For the same reason, it's important to make sure your colours work well together. Many people have tried to create rules for this, but ultimately it comes down to good taste, personal preference and common sense. If you get stuck, a good rule of thumb is to stick with two or three colours close together in your picker or colour chart. But here is a general tip: some coloured text is hard to read against other coloured backgrounds, such as black text on blue, or blue text on dark red, which creates a clash.

❾ If you can't find enough colours you like in your colour menu, there should be a button you can click to open a complete colour picker. These might look a bit complex, but all you have to do is click in the window until you find the tone you're after.

❼

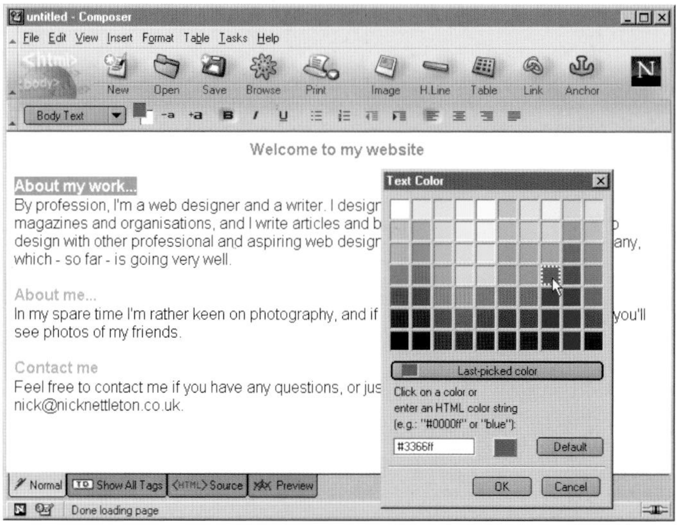

❽

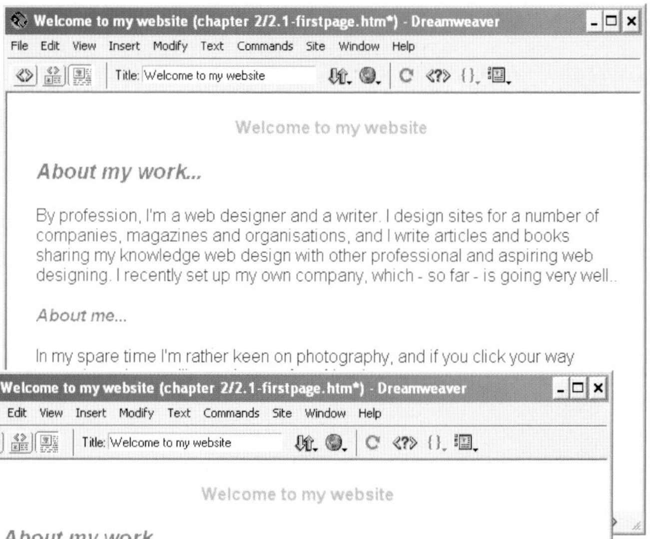

❾

10

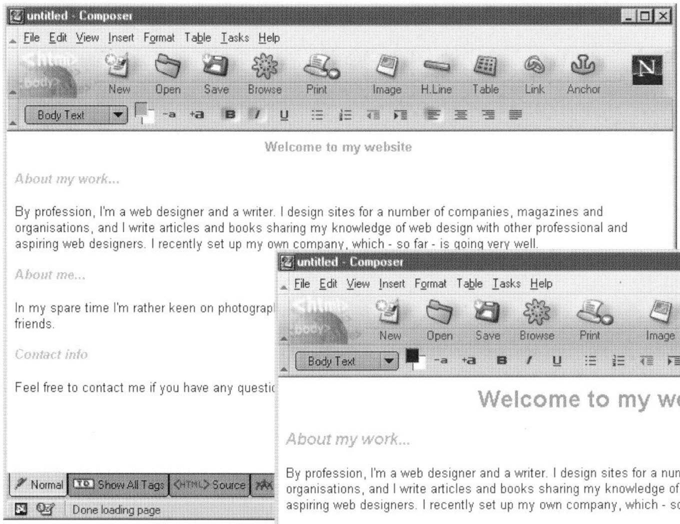

11

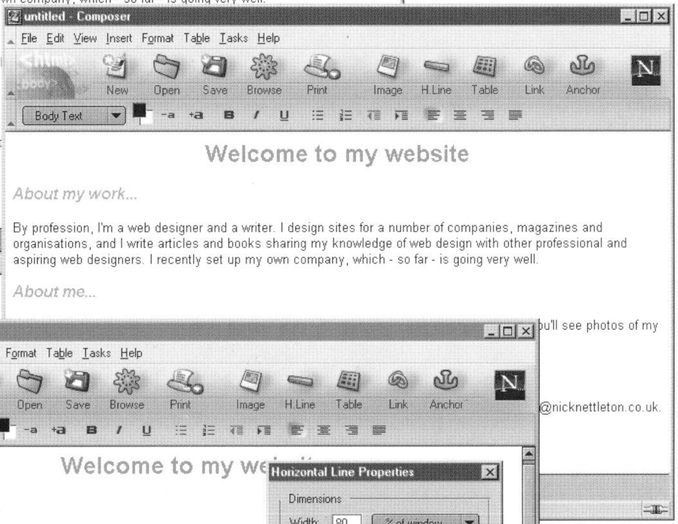

12

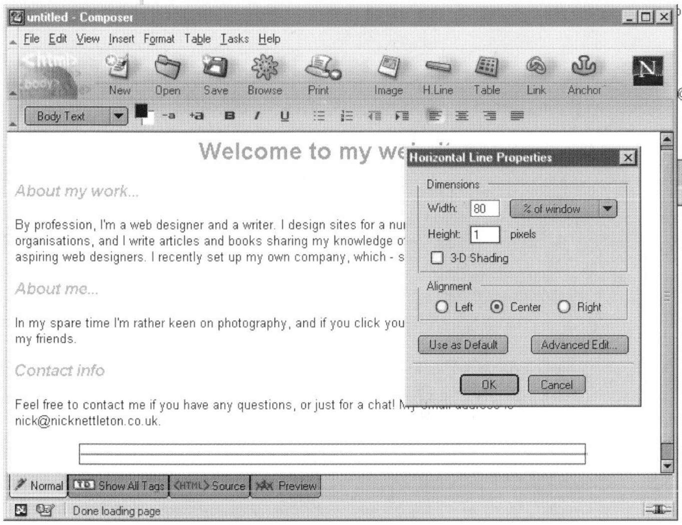

13

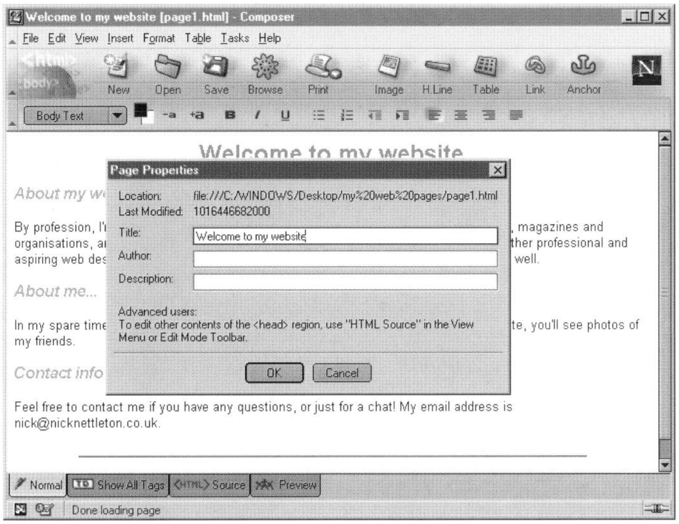

Shape and size

10 This page still looks a bit scrappy, but there are a number of things that can be done easily to improve it. The first is to look at the sizes of the fonts (typefaces): they're almost all the same. A dynamic range of type sizes really helps a design to work. Don't pick too many, though, because your design will look cluttered. Select your main text blocks and take the size down a little.

11 This looks much better, but there's more that can be done. Look in your *Formatting* toolbar or *Properties* and you should see a menu with settings like ***Heading 1*** and so on in it. Experiment with different settings for these on your main and subheadings – go for something big for the main.

12 It's good to have a Horizontal line ruling off the bottom – look for *H Line*, *Horizontal Rule*, or *HR* on your toolbar. In Dreamweaver it will be in your *Insert* menu. You can change the rule's appearance too. If you can't see options for this in your software interface, doubleclick or right click on the line.

13 There is just one more thing to do. Look for *Page Properties* in your menus (or for *Page Information* or *Page Colors and Background*). Here you can add a title for your page, to appear in the top bar of the browser. You can also choose a background colour. Make sure this works with your existing colours!

Finally, save your page, then find the file in your webpages folder, and doubleclick on it to see it in your Web browser.

PROJECT 2

LINKED UP

What really defines a webpage and what makes it different from a Word document? One answer is the links, which are what make the Internet go around. After all, if there were no links, every time you wanted to go to a new page you'd have to type in its specific address, rather than just simply clicking on a link. In fact, that's one definition of hypertext: text that carries live links to other texts.

Remember that each webpage is a different HTML file. In most Web design software, creating a link is easy: you simply select the linking text, and tell it the address of the new file or website that the browser should go to when you click on the link. Try looking at any of the major Internet portals, such as Yahoo! or MSN. Just click on the underlined text (perhaps coloured blue or purple, depending on your browser preferences) and you'll quickly get an idea of how your own page should work (see overleaf for examples). Each link takes you to a page which has its own address, probably something like /news.htm, added onto the end of the main website address. When you use search engines such as Google to research stuff online, you will be presented with pages of links that might match the subject you're looking for.

If you want to link to a page in your own site, though, you don't need to give the whole address like this. Take the page you created in the last project. Alongside this create a new page which contains your contact details, for example, and save it in the same folder, calling it contact.htm. To open this, all you need to do is give the link name – contact.htm. This is called a relative link, which simply means 'Open the file in the same folder with this name'. While you are creating the pages on your computer, you can click the links between them and see how they work, without having to put your whole site on the Internet first.

1

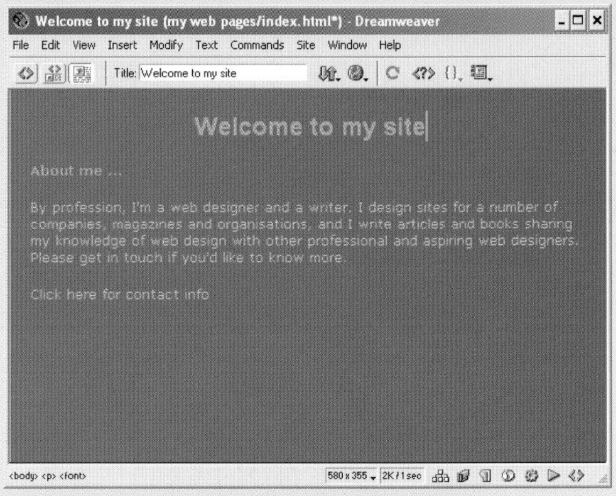

2

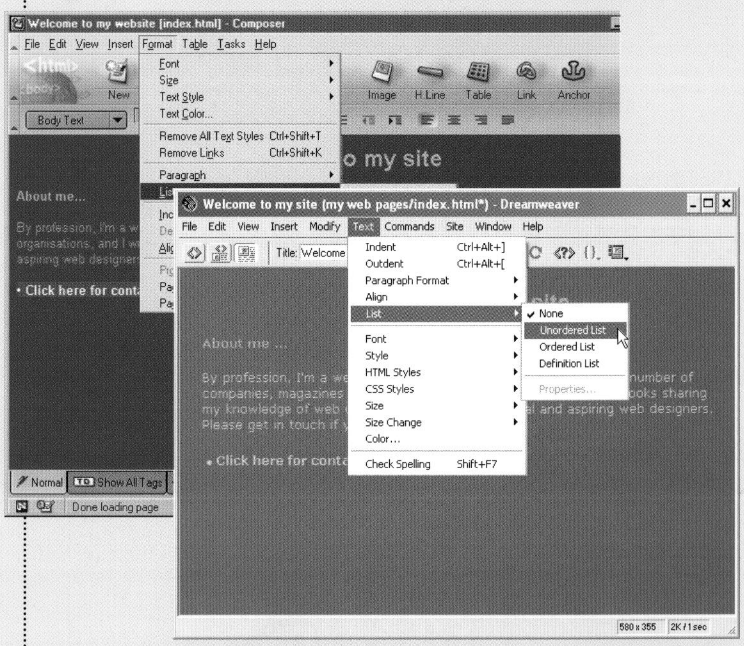

3

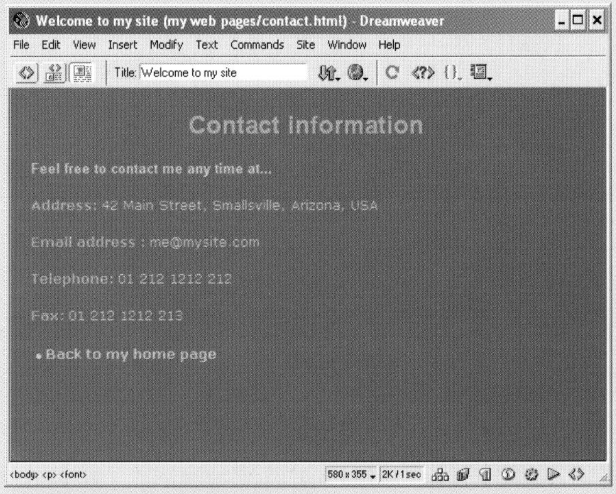

❹

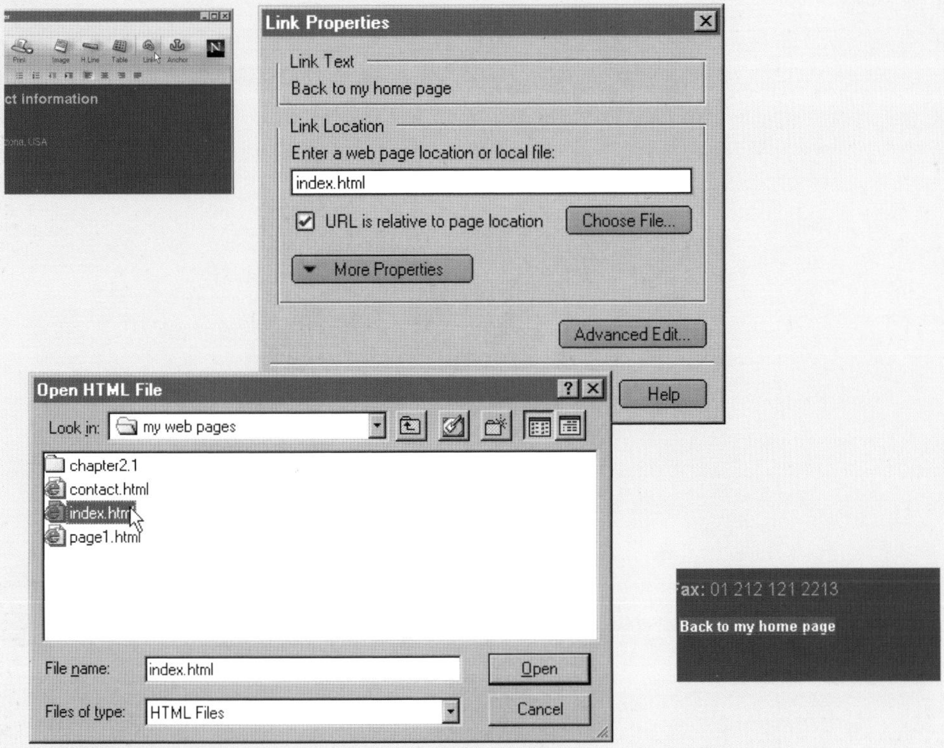

❺

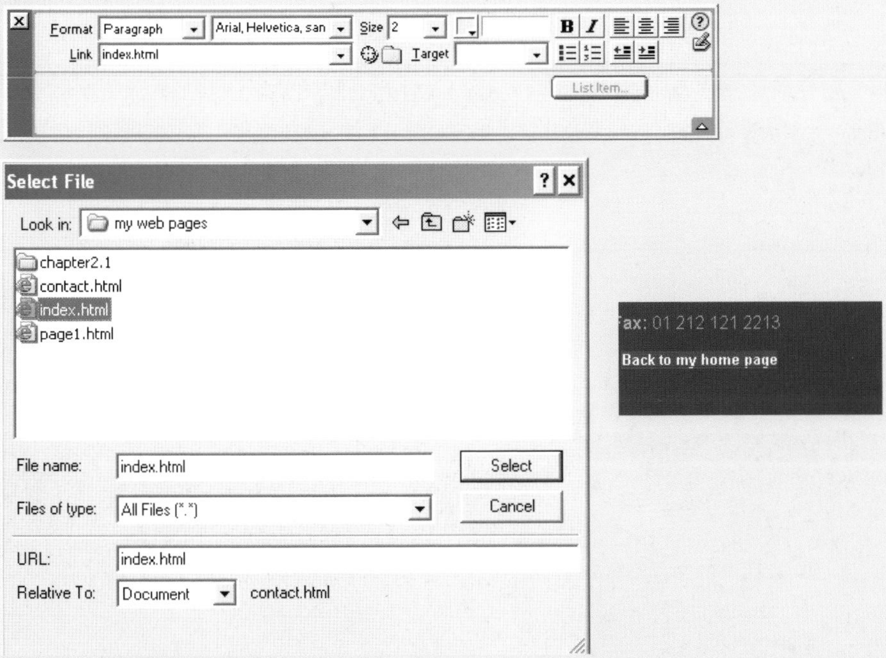

❶ Create a page like the one you made in your first project – or just use the same one – and save it as index.html. Remember, this is what you should call your homepage anyway, because it's the page that opens automatically when someone types in your Web address. Include a line that says 'Click here for contact info'.

❷ Now you can link this sentence to the next page, so you might want to make it stand out. Here it's been made bold and set as a *List* item, which creates a bullet point. You'll find this tool in your text formatting options – in Netscape Composer and GoLive it's in your *Formatting* toolbar and in Dreamweaver you'll find it in the *Text* menu.

❸ Now create a second page for your site, including your contact details and related information. Put your e-mail address in here too, so you can make that an active link, and also add some text to link back to the main page. Save this page as contact.html, in the same folder.

❹ Add a link by selecting your linking text and pointing your Web design software to the page that you want to open with the link. Some applications have a toolbar button you can click to open a dialog where you browse down until you find the file you're linking to, or just type in its name.

❺ In other software, you'll see a link space in the *Properties Inspector* or another palette (in Dreamweaver, it's the picture of a folder). Either way, just choose the file you want to link to, and the link will be set up for you automatically.

❻

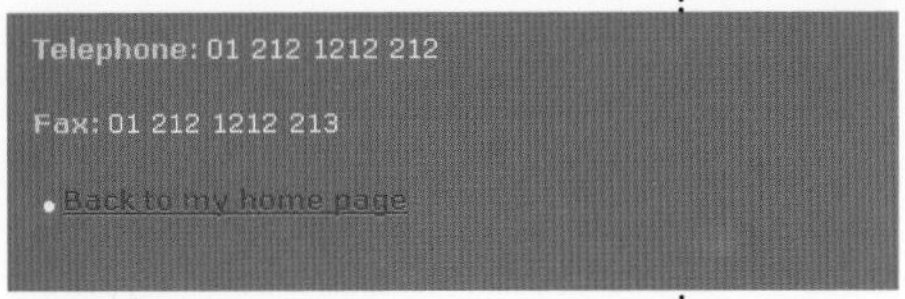

❼

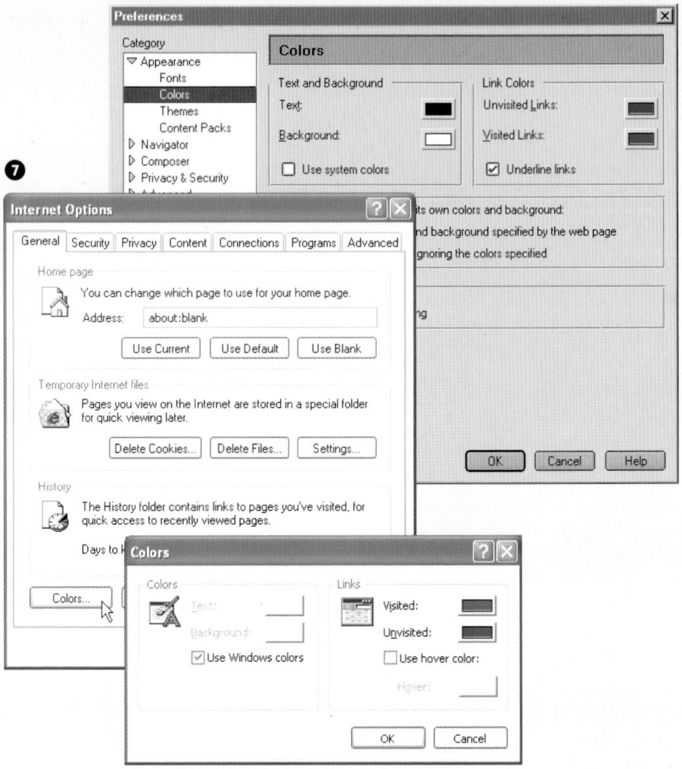

Colouring links

❻ Once you've made a link, it is automatically underlined. This tells your visitor it is a link. In this example, your visitor has clicked on the link, and it has changed colour. This is called a 'visited link'. Unfortunately, it is now very hard to read. You can set the colour of visited links as you wish (see below), or you may choose to leave them the same colour. You'll also find a setting for active links, which sets the colour they turn when you click on them.

❼ When you set up your links, you'll find they take on colours according to your viewer's browser preferences. Usually these are blue and/or purple, unless they've been changed, but you can never be sure.

❽ Therefore, it's a good idea to choose your own link colours that match your designs. Head to the *Page Properties* or *Page Colors and Background* menu item for your webpage, and you'll find a dialog like one of those pictured (from Dreamweaver and Netscape), where you can choose your link colours.

❾ Whatever colours you choose, just make sure they match your page colours well, but are distinct from your main text, so your viewers can quickly see where the links are.

❽

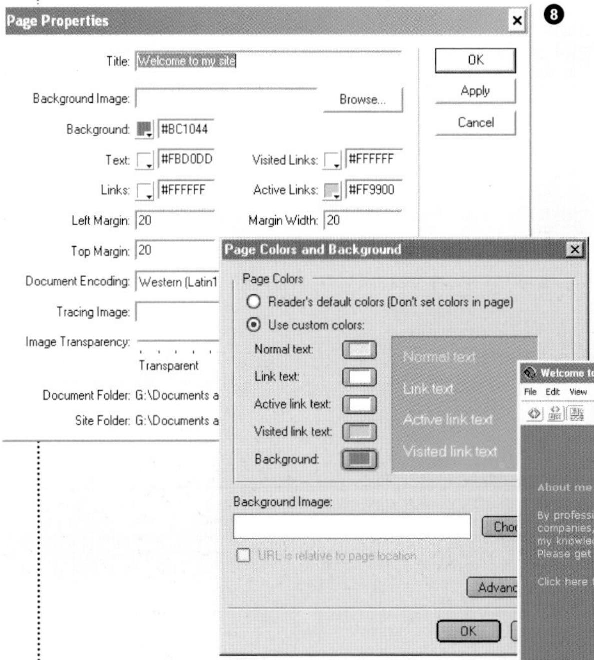

❾

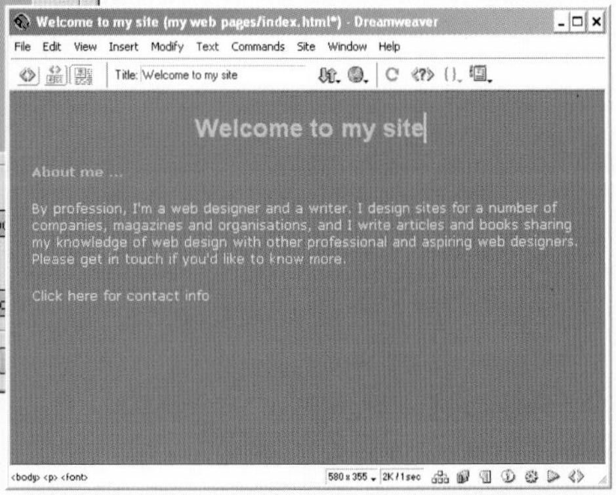

10
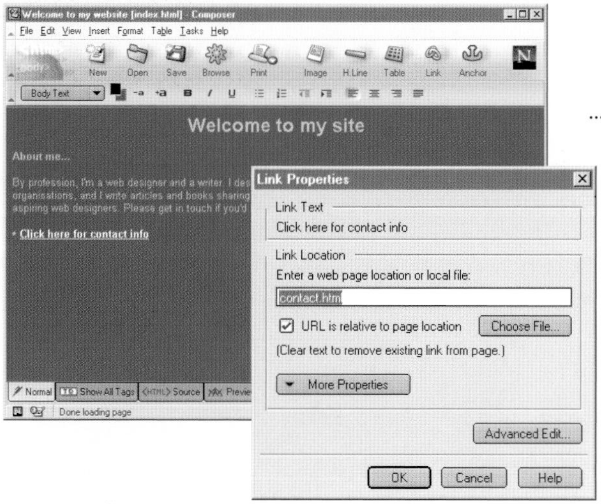

11
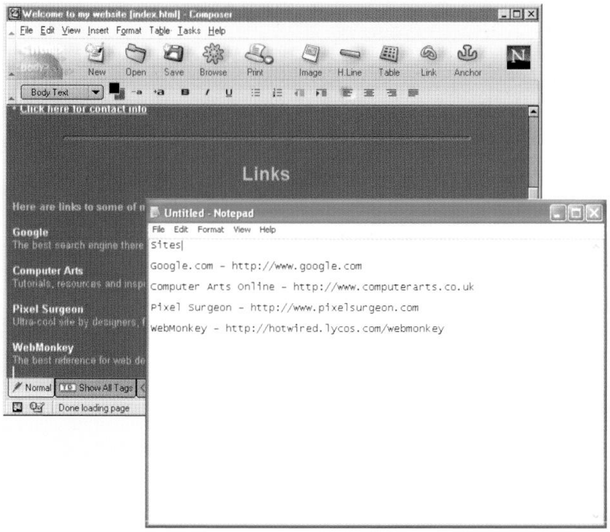

12
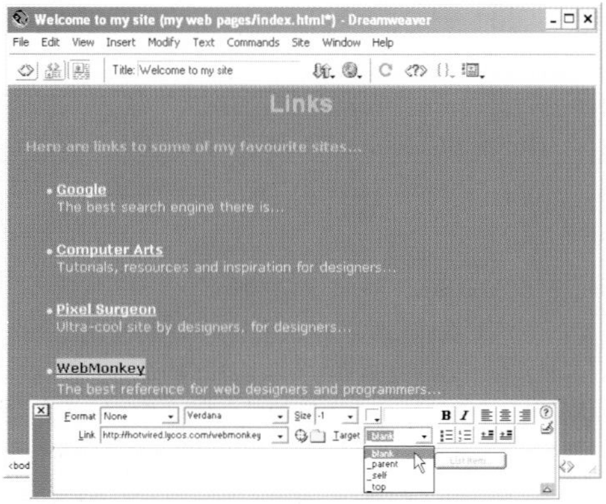

10 Now you've seen how to create a simple link to another page in your site, you can open your index.html page and create the link from there to your contacts page, as well as set up the link colours again (shown here in Netscape). But you can also link to pages in other sites or set up e-mail links.

11 To do this, add a new section called Links to your main homepage, index.html, and choose a few webpages that you would like to put in there. Make sure you get their full Web addresses as you go, just as they appear in your browser's address bar. You can set up these links in almost the same way as the earlier links you did; the only difference is that you can't browse to the file. Instead, just copy and paste the whole address into your link field – not forgetting the http://

12 Because you're linking to another site, you might want it to open in a new page. Most Web design software gives you a *Target* option next to your link field (although in Netscape Composer, the *Target* option means something else). To make your link open in a new window, set the *Target* option to '*_blank*'. You don't need to worry about any other options.

Finally, set up your e-mail address on the contacts page to be a live link. Some applications include an option in your link dialog, or have a special *E-mail Link* tool in your toolbar. If so, use this and just type in the e-mail address. If not, create it like a normal link but type it into '***mailto:***', add your e-mail address, and that's all there is to it.

1

FONT TROUBLE

2

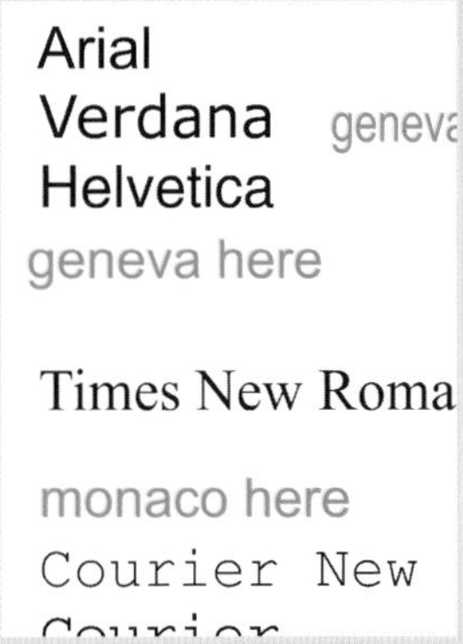

It's really important to use interesting and distinct typefaces (fonts) and styles in your webpages, to help them look attractive and unique. Without them, every site on the Internet would look pretty much the same – apart from the colours that have been selected, of course.

So you might have been tempted, as a designer, to experiment with different font faces in the webpages you've already created. You may even be wondering why all the example screen shots in this book use such similar faces.

The problem is, when you set a font in your Web authoring software, it doesn't include the font file in the HTML. Instead, it just adds a line of code saying, 'Use this font if the viewer has it installed on their system'. If the user doesn't have it, then he or she will just see your page in a standard font, like Arial, Helvetica or Times New Roman. To see this, try creating your page with a cool font, then uninstall the font from your system. You'll see how disappointing the result is.

So what is the solution? In short, the best answer is to use a graphics application…

3

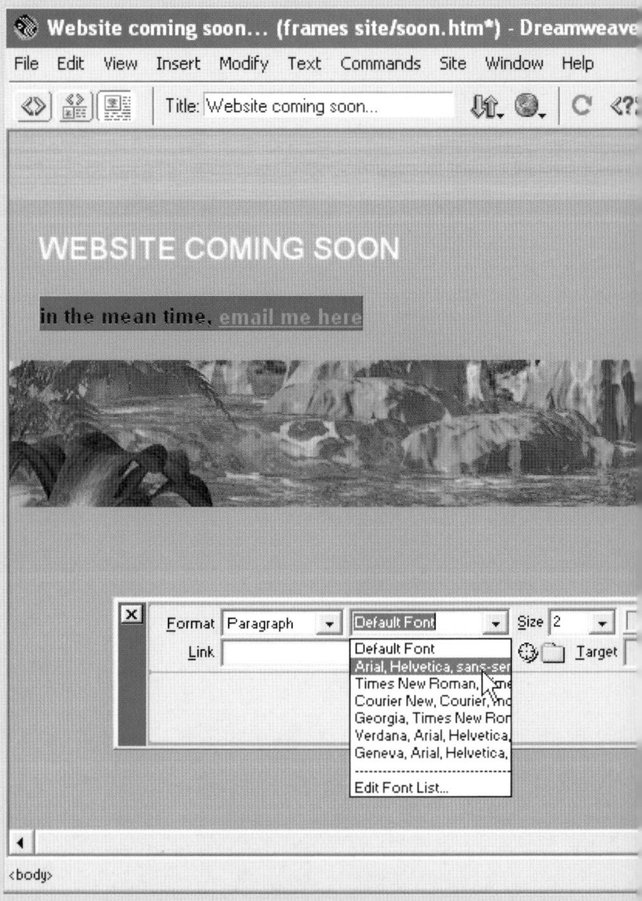

TIP

Which fonts to use

Stick with standard fonts in your Web authoring software. When you want to use more exciting fonts, it is best to use a graphics package instead…

1 *If you create your page in your Web authoring software using lots of exciting fonts, you'll be very disappointed when you see it on friends' computers if they don't have the same fonts installed. This is because the font isn't included, or embedded, in the HTML page – there is just a reference to use it if it's available on the recipient's computer.*

2 *The most common fonts include Arial, Times New Roman, Verdana, Courier New and Comic Sans on the PC. On the Mac they include Helvetica, Geneva, Times and Monaco. Many more Internet users have PCs than Macs, so you're safest to stick with the PC options.*

3 *Better Web design software, like Dreamweaver, FrontPage and GoLive, allows you to specify several different fonts in order of preference, which the user's browser can choose from depending on the fonts they have installed on their system.*

4 *For more visually exciting parts of a webpage, designers almost always use a graphics application, because these save exact information about the form and appearance of a design within a graphics file format. Before you create your graphics, or image file, you need to plan where it will go in your HTML page, what it will look like and how it will fit in with the overall design.*

5 *After you've designed and saved the graphic, open the HTML page in your Web authoring application, then add and position the image files one by one.*

4

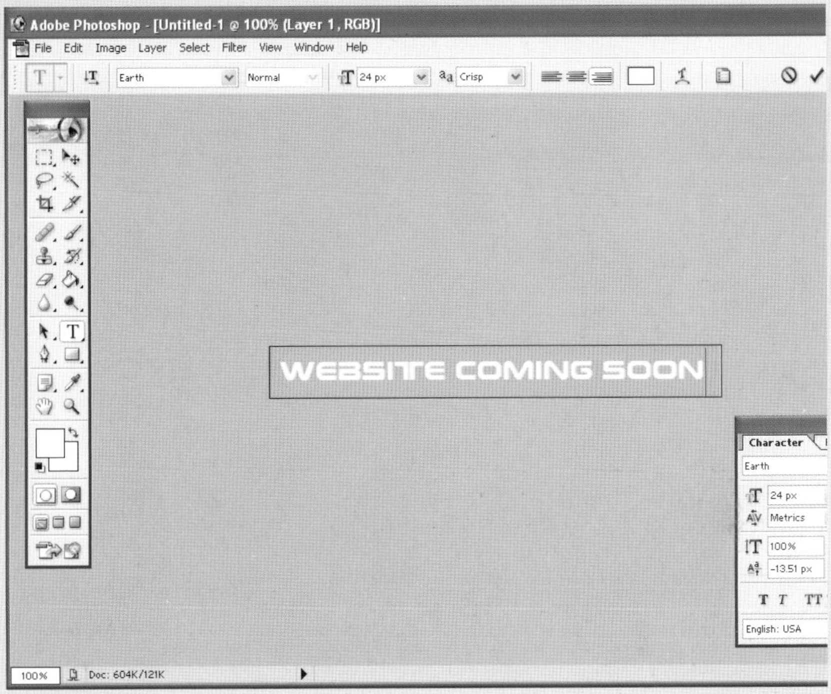

5

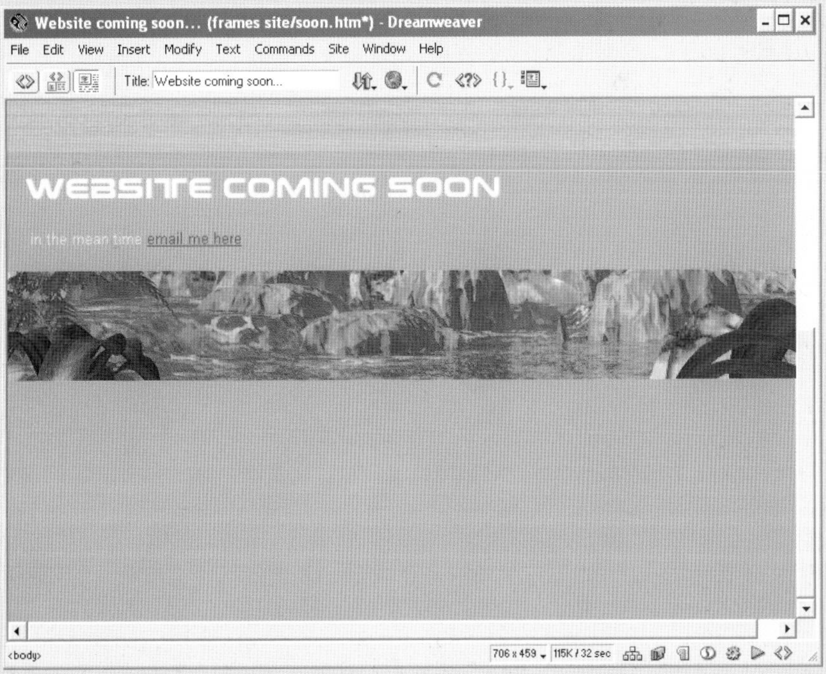

PROJECT 3
SITES TO SEE

For the next project, you are going to create a small, visual links directory of websites on a particular topic. You will include some graphics for the headings and links, to make the page more interesting and compelling.

Before you start, think about what sort of websites you'd like to include. The example shown here covers travel topics, but you can choose anything you like. Then go on the Web and find 10–20 websites and input their names and Web addresses in your word processor. It is a good idea to write a short description of each site, just to let your visitors know what to expect. Alternatively, you can group the sites under subheadings.

Once you've done that, you can get going on the design. First you need to mock up a simple webpage in your Web authoring software, just as you've done before. Think about the basic colours – why not see if you can get them to match the themes of your links?

You now need to decide where you want the main graphics to go – this often works well as a heading at the top of the page. Also consider where and how big your subheadings should be. Create them in a graphics application, such as Paint Shop Pro, Photoshop Elements or Corel Photo-Paint, save them, and add the images to the webpage. This may sound a little complex, but it's easy once you know how. Follow the steps on page 39 and you'll have a great webpage at the end...

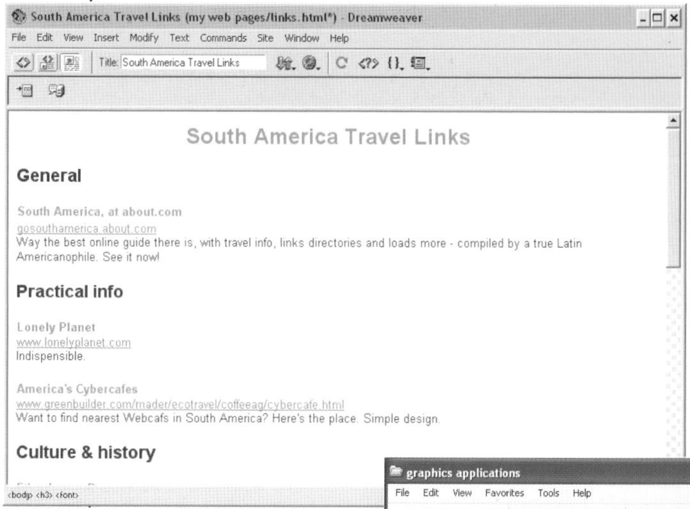

1

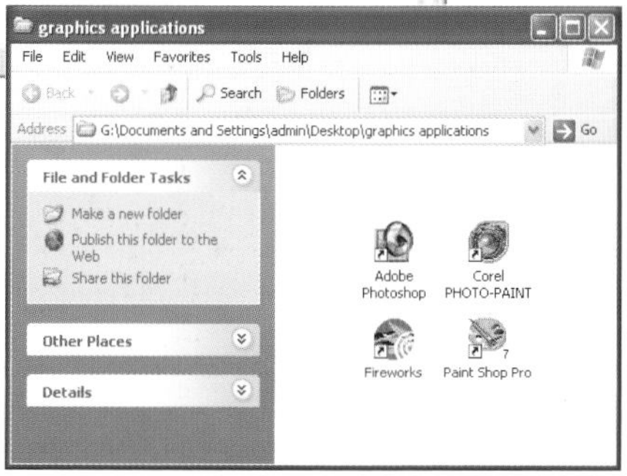

2

3

4

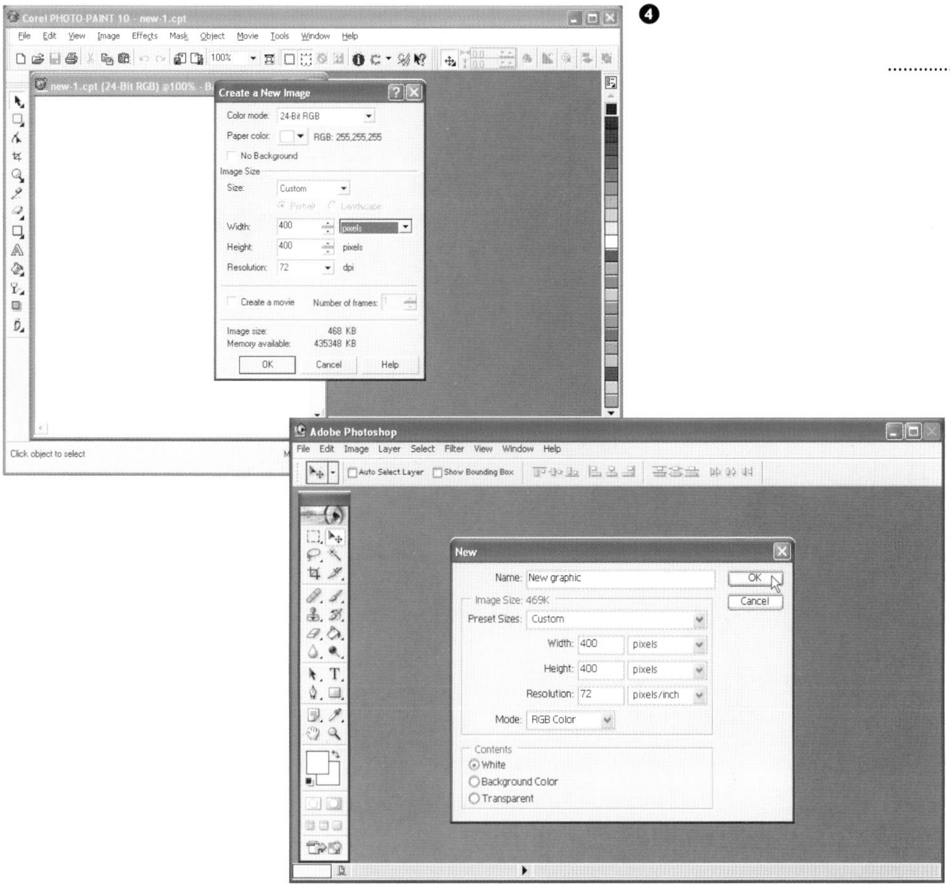

5

1 Start by setting up your webpage as normal: get a new document, copy and paste in your links and other text, and set up the links to make them active. Keep your background white for the time being, but don't forget to set your link colours, and lay out the font sizes in an attractive, easy-to-read style. And remember to give your page a title!

2 You are now going to create a simple but attractive graphic for the main heading and subheadings, so that you can use more interesting fonts and effects instead of the plain text you've got at the moment. For this you need to open your graphics application…

3 Graphics software, like Photo-Paint and Paint Shop Pro, works differently from Web design applications like Dreamweaver. For a start, you can get much more control over the exact style and appearance of what you're working on, although in return the software tends to be a little harder to get to grips with at first.

4 Create a new image that is about 400 x 400 pixels in size. If you have a resolution option, set this to 72dpi, and set the background colour to white to match your webpage. Here you can see Photo-Paint and Photoshop *New Image* options.

5 Resolution in this context simply describes the number of points of colour, or pixels, per inch of your image. A pixel is the smallest area of a single colour that a graphic can have – you can see this by zooming in on an image (the blocks are pixels). The standard resolution for Web graphics is 72 pixels per inch, or dots per inch.

Graphic headings

6 To add text to your new graphics page, you need to use the *Type* tool in your toolbar or box, which usually has a letter A or T on it. Select the tool, and then click in your page and type away. Here you can see this being done in Photo-Paint.

7 8 Once you've done this, choose a font, colour and size for your text. You might find these in your main toolbar, or in a *Character* or *Type* palette, depending on your software.

In some packages, like Paint Shop Pro (PSP), you are given a dedicated text window that you can type in and adjust the settings for your text.

9 If you've got a longer heading, it's often a good idea to break it into phrases on different lines, with different font colours and sizes.

10 Next you'll probably want to add in some effects, to make your headings more interesting. Most graphics software comes with quick-and-easy effects, of which drop shadows are by far the most popular – shown here in Photoshop and PSP.

How you create and apply your effects depends largely on the software you're using, so you should take a look at the *Help* files if you get stuck. In Photoshop, to apply effects you right-click on a layer; in PSP you use the *Effects* menu, while in Macromedia Fireworks you use your *Effects* palette.

Keep the effects simple for now. Once you're happy with your heading, save it, but keep the file open as you add the heading to your webpage.

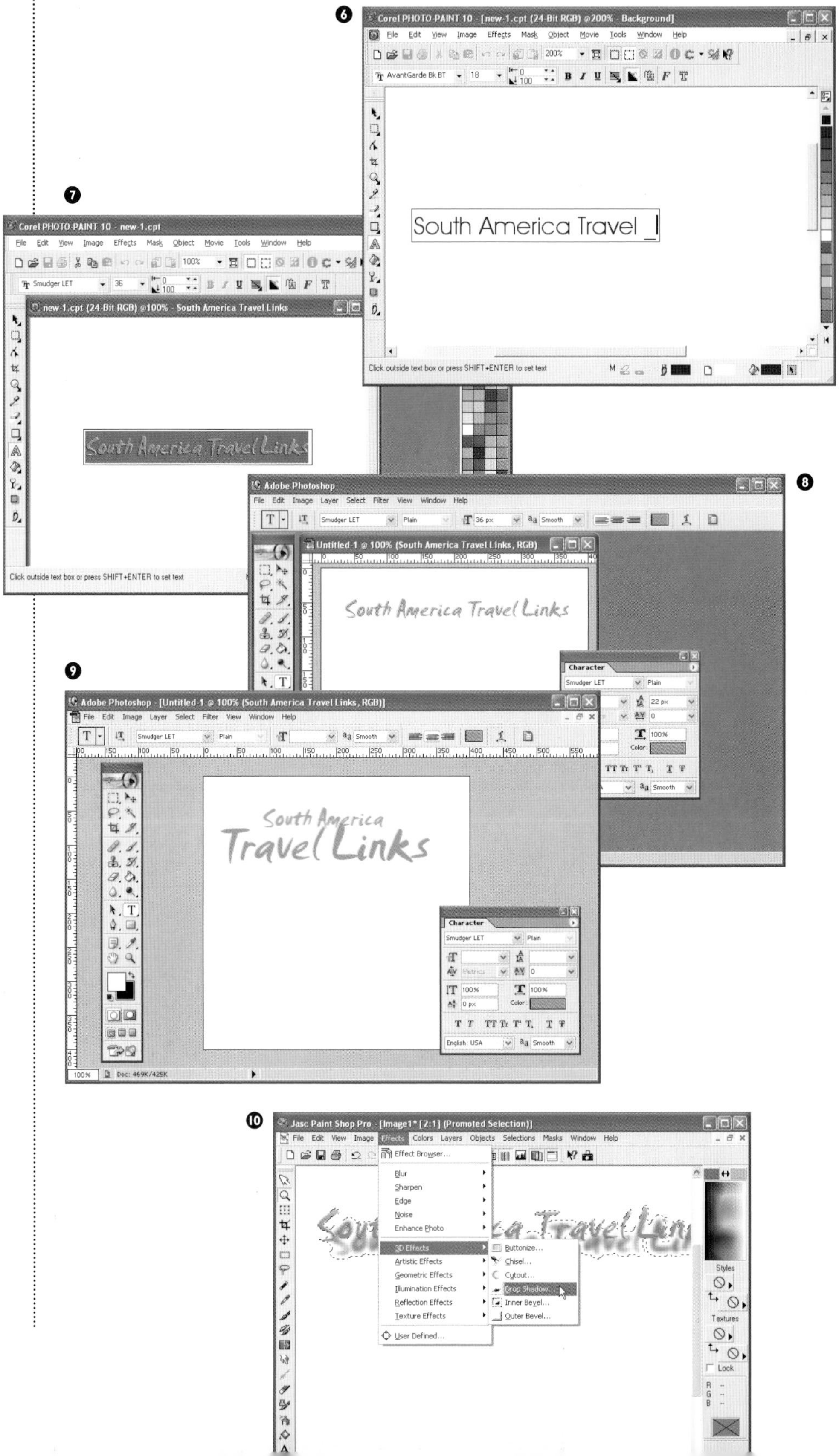

⓫

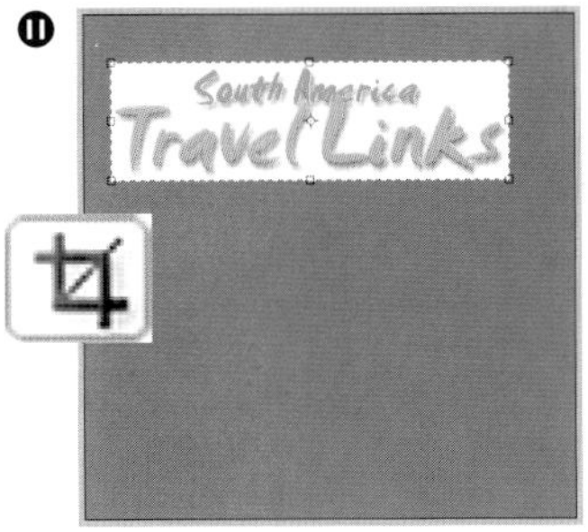

⓬

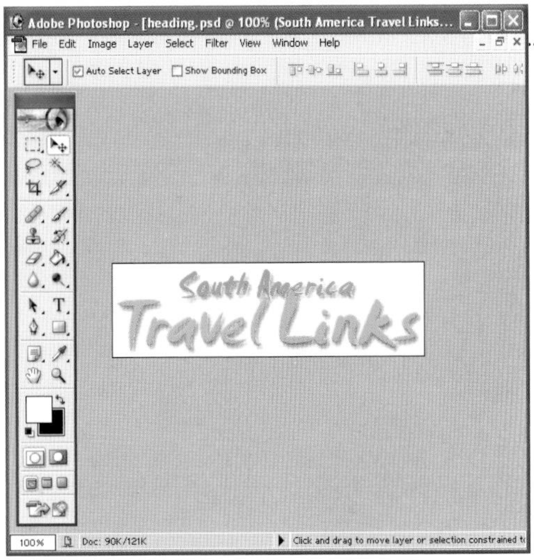

⓭

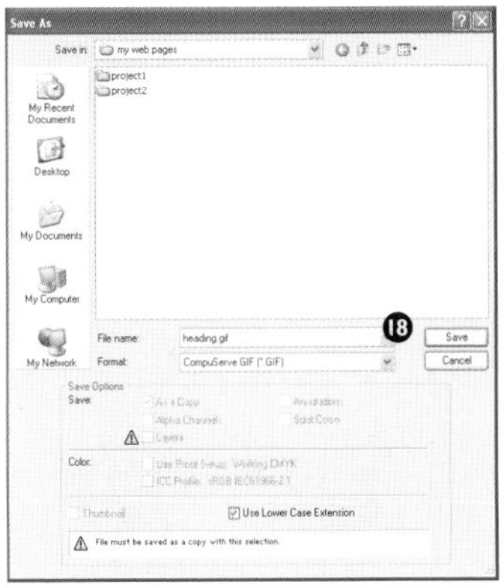

⓮

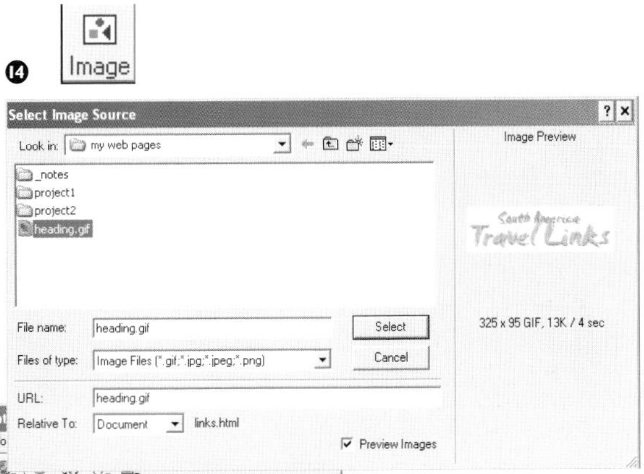

⓯

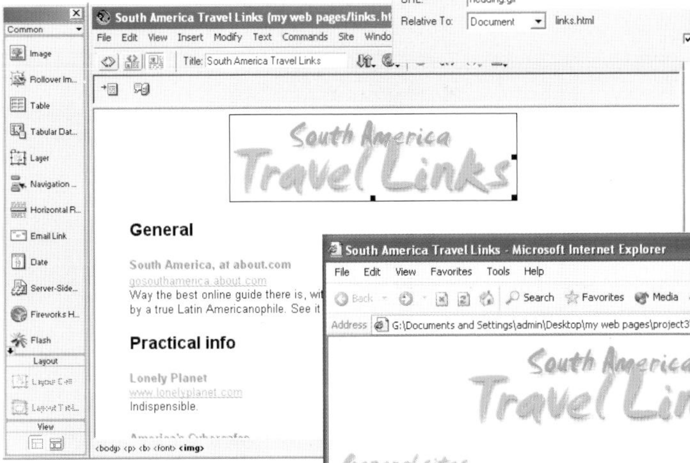

⓰

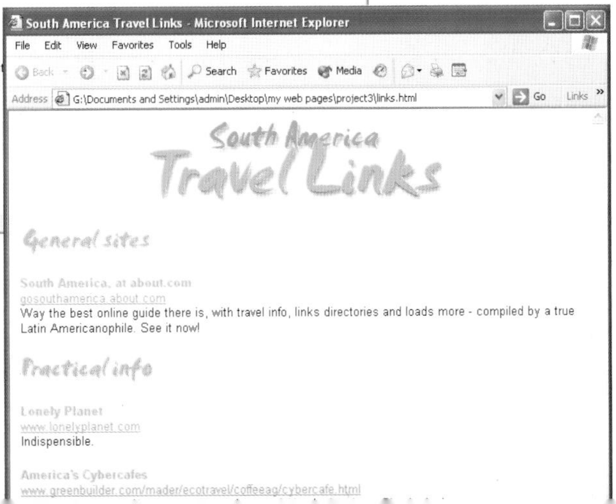

Adding a graphic to your webpage

⓫ At the moment the size of your graphic is 400 x 400 pixels, which is far bigger than the heading itself. This will create a lot of strange space if you add it directly to your webpage as it is. First, you need to crop the image tight around the edges using your *Crop* tool...

⓬ To do this, select the area you want to keep, and doubleclick to complete the crop. Next you need to save the image in GIF format, which is sometimes called CompuServe GIF. Choose ***Save As*** from your File menu, and select the option for the format menu. Save your image in the same folder as your webpage.

⓭ You may see some options like those pictured here, including options for the number of colours and so on. If so, just leave them as they are for the time being.

⓮ Now go back to your Web design application and open your *Links* webpage to delete your main heading. Find the *Image* button in your toolbar, toolbox or *Objects* palette, and use the browsing option to find and open the GIF image you just created.

⓯ And now your heading will be centred and in place.

⓰ You may also want to make smaller graphics for each of your subheadings. Here's our final page as seen in Internet Explorer...

TABLE TRICKS

Just by adding a simple fun graphics heading, you made the link page so much more attractive and appealing to read. But it could still do with a bit of background colour, and, at the moment, everything just goes straight down in one long line of content. Wouldn't it be good to break it up a bit, say, into two columns, to give the page a sense of horizontal as well as vertical movement? This also gives the reader twice as many options on what to read. But how do you do that?

The answer is to use what Web designers call tables. In the old days of the Web, when pages were always simple because design was unimportant and information was all that mattered, a new technology was added to HTML so that people could display information in a tabular format, like a spreadsheet, chart or database.

1

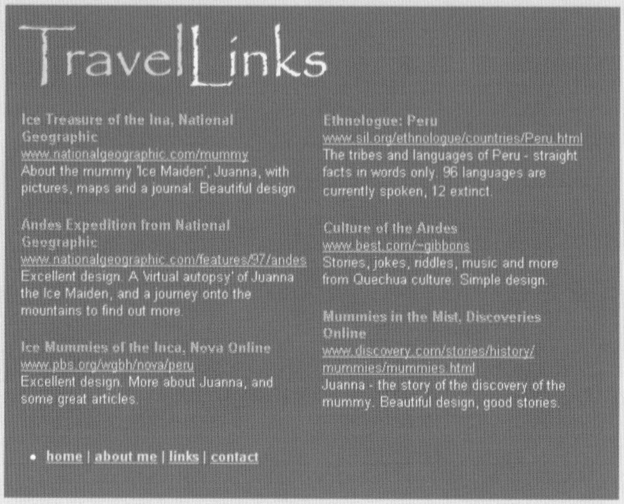

1 *To really get the design going, you need to break your pages up and get away from the obvious one-column style of design. You've added in a soft, attractive background colour, but the real coup is breaking the text into two shorter columns, making it much easier to read as well as more interesting to look at. This also means that your viewers are more likely to reach the end of the page and see the links or whatever other information you have there.*

2 *To create two columns you use a table. Tables in Web design are just like those in your word processor or a spreadsheet.*

2

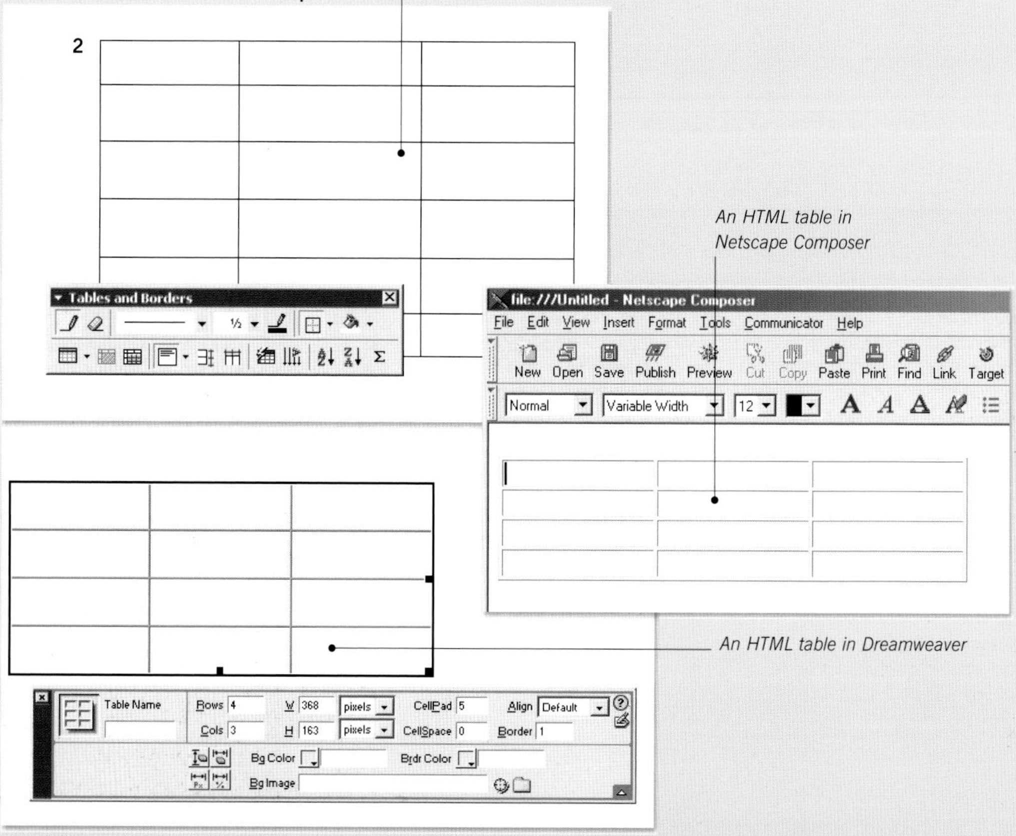

A table in Microsoft Word

An HTML table in Netscape Composer

An HTML table in Dreamweaver

3

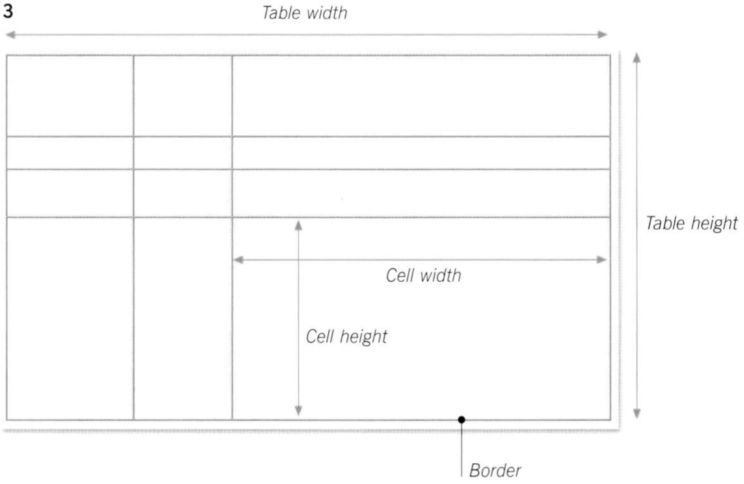

4

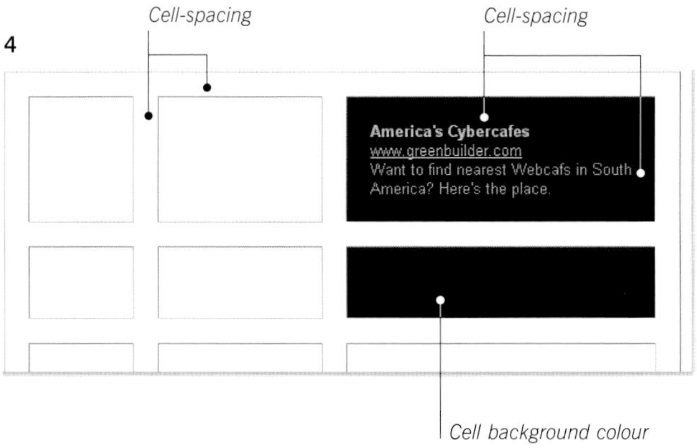

Just like a spreadsheet, tables in Web design have a certain number of rows and columns going down and across, which make up individual cells in which you can put text, images and other webpage content. Just by having a one-row, two-column table, you can put two sets of content side-by-side, rather than always having them come one after the other, which makes for much more attractive and easy-to-read webpages.

In fact, there are so many different things you can do with tables that they have become the undoubted cornerstone of Web design for laying out a page and giving it what is called 'shape' (more than just one long wide column of information).

5

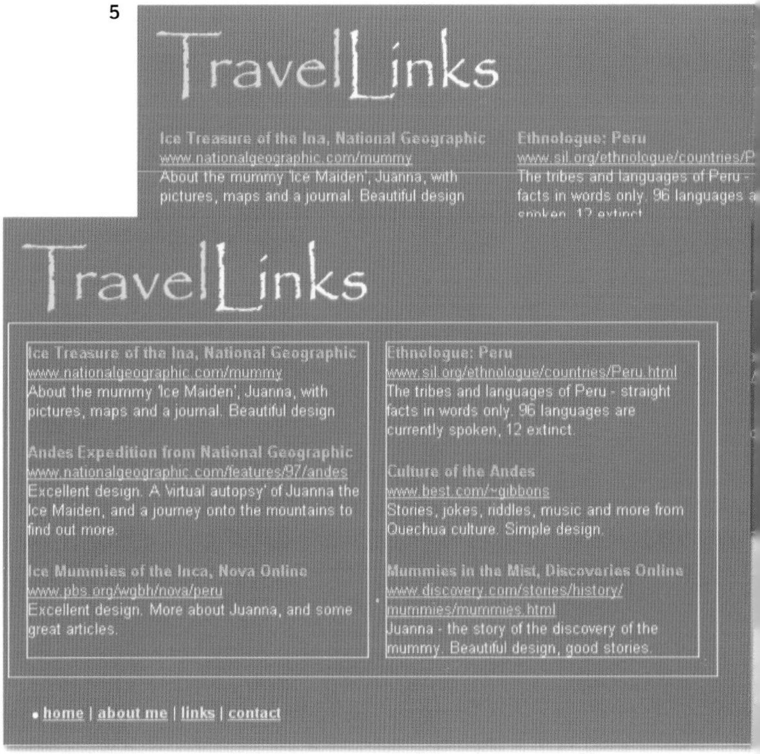

3 You can control most aspects of the appearance of a table, including the width and height of each cell, and how big the borders are (most designers usually set this to 0, so that they are invisible).

4 You can also control how much space is within each cell, which is called cell padding, and how much space there is between each cell, called cell spacing. You can also give particular cells different background colours and apply general background colour to the whole table.

5 Here's our two-column design, which you're going to create in the next project. It is shown here with and without borders, so you can see how we used a simple table with cell spacing to improve its appearance quickly and easily.

COLOUR TRICKS

Before creating the new tabular layout, let's take a moment to look at colour. You may have already found that choosing colours and getting them to look just right in HTML is a bit tricky – that's why we stuck to a white background in project 2. Yet it's so important to get your colours right as they really do influence the overall mood. While there's no right or wrong in Web design, there is good and bad style; and you miss the mark at your peril, with so much good design out there.

Even just choosing a single colour, and keeping it constant through your different files, can be difficult, because the tools for choosing colours tend to be a bit awkward. Both Windows and Mac OS have built-in standard colour palettes, but many software developers incorporate different tools in their software and, as a result, working with colour is rarely the same from one bit of software to the next. Another complication is that Windows and Mac operating systems do not share all of the same colours in their standard palettes.

And as if that's not hard enough, there are several different code schemes you can use to pinpoint exactly which colour it is you want. And, if you want to make your colour the same in one file as it was in another, you often need to find out what its code is by looking at the numbers in your colour mixer. But don't worry. There are a few key techniques for dealing with colour that will make the whole process much easier…

1

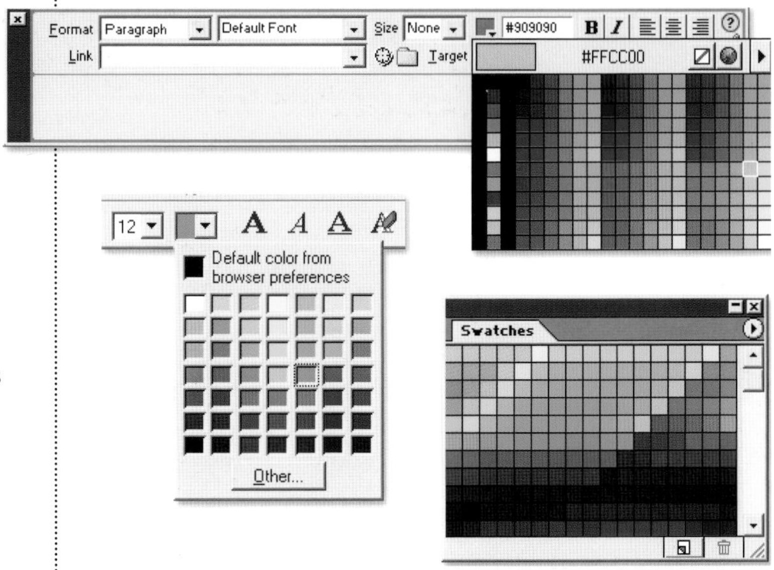

1 *Most design software offers a quick-access palette of pre-set colours, sometimes called a* Swatches *palette. But you'll soon tire of these and want to get a bit more experimental. There should be a* More *button you can click.*

2 *In Windows, you can use the standard Windows Color Picker. Click the* Define Custom Colors *button if you can't see the whole palette. Focus on the rainbow colour area and the slider to the right: you can use the rainbow to pick hue and saturation (or intensity), and the slider to set its luminosity.*

2

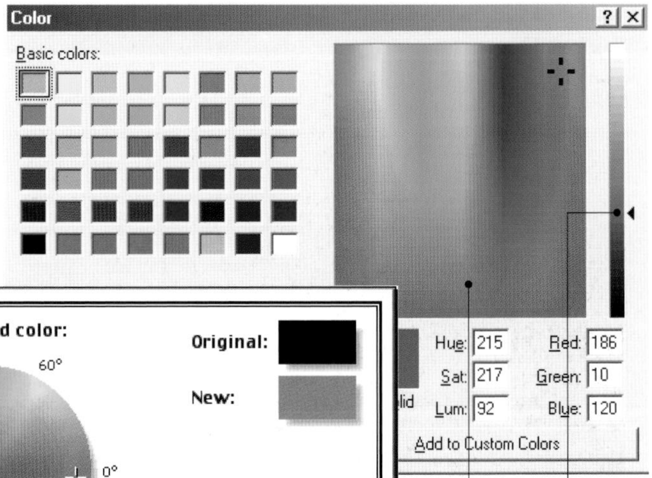

3

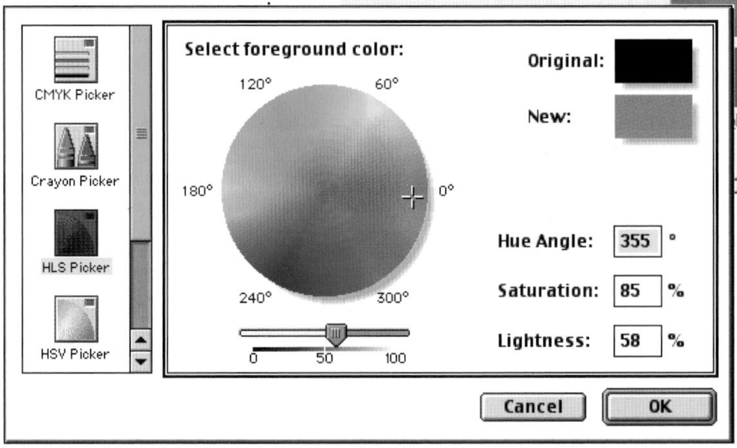

3 *The Mac Color Palette gives you several pickers all in one, using the icons on the left. The HLS Picker works like the Windows equivalent; choose your hue and saturation using the colour circle. The slider on the bottom controls luminosity.*

4

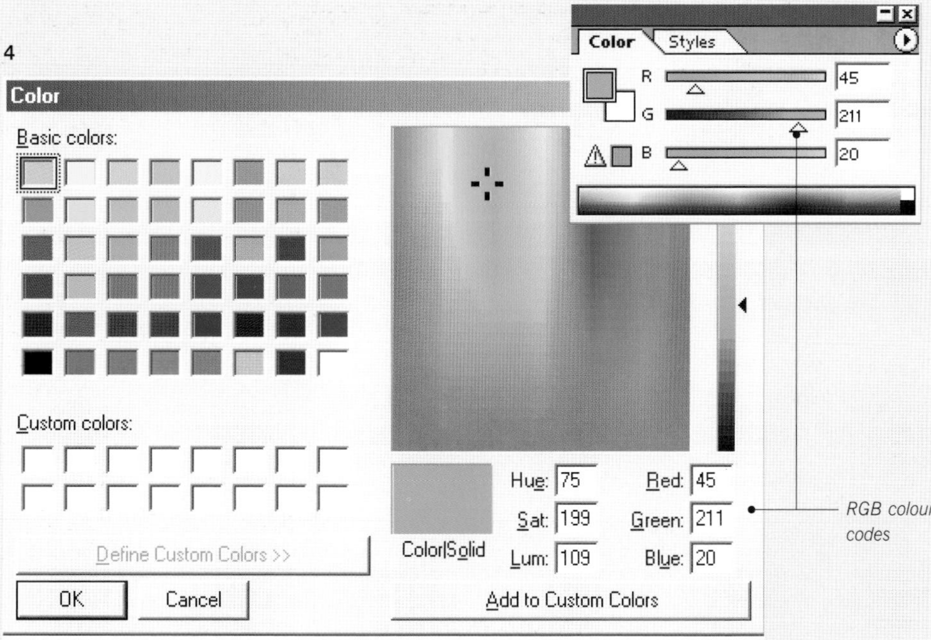

5

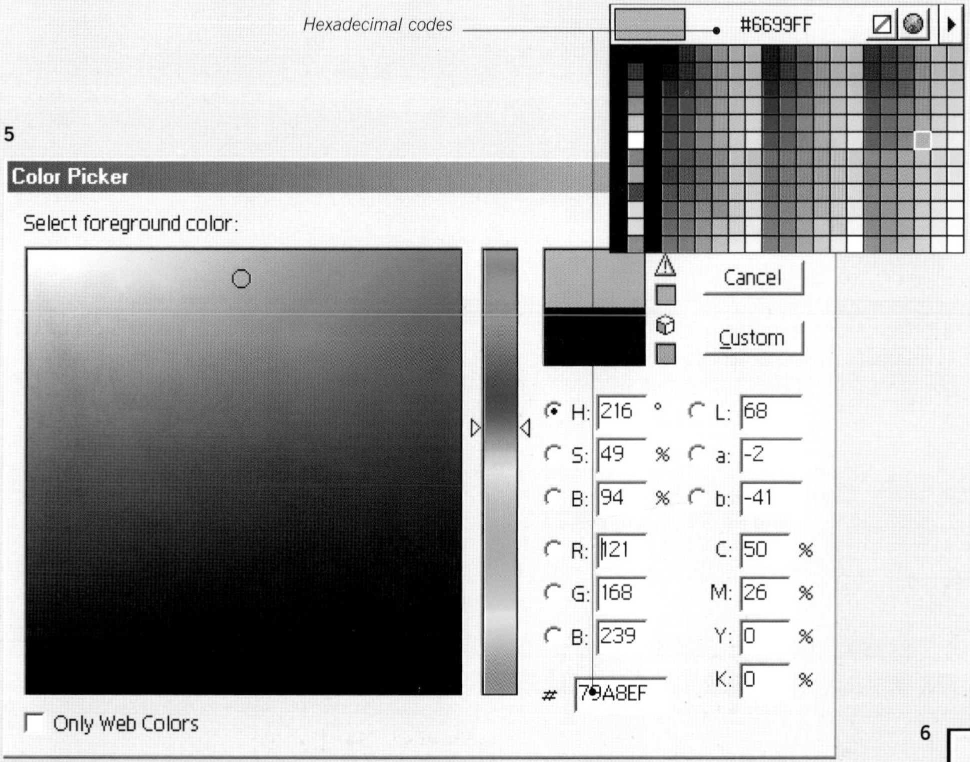

6

4 *In Web design, there are two important colour-coding schemes. The first is RGB, (Red, Green, Blue). An example of this is 255,0,0. These numbers say how much of each hue is used to mix up your chosen colour.*

5 *The other scheme is called Hexadecimal, and this is written as #FF0000. The six letters are actually three pairs; each pair indicates how much of the hues Red, Green and Blue are mixed in. This is the colour format that is used in HTML, and often you'll need to make a note of the #-reference, as it is called, for the colours you're using.*

6 *Usually the easiest way to get a particular colour is to open the file and use an Eyedropper tool to copy the colour, if your software has one. But if this isn't possible, you just have to look in one colour palette, write down the colour code and then type it into your other colour palette. It doesn't matter which code scheme you use for this.*

PROJECT 4
LAYOUT CONTROL

Now let's make a tabular links page...

❶ Start by creating a new page, give it a title (say, links2.html) and set its background, text and link colours. We've used the background colour #009F9F (0,159,159 in RGB). The text is white and the links are #FFEFB0 or 255,239,176.

❷ Next, create the graphic for your title. Use the same colour background as you did for your webpage. Try giving the two words different colours.

❸ Crop and save it as a GIF, and add it to your webpage using the *Image* button.

❹ Now you're ready to add your table beneath. The method depends on the software you are using, but you should have a *Table* button in your toolbar or *Objects* palette. Here you can see the *Options* as we set them in Netscape Composer...

❺ Here is Dreamweaver. Whatever software you're using, you need to create one row and two columns with a border set to 0, cell spacing to 15 pixels and cell padding at 0. Set the width to 80 per cent. This means the table is 80 per cent as wide as the window.

❻ Here's how it should look. The dotted border is there for preview, and shouldn't appear in your browser.

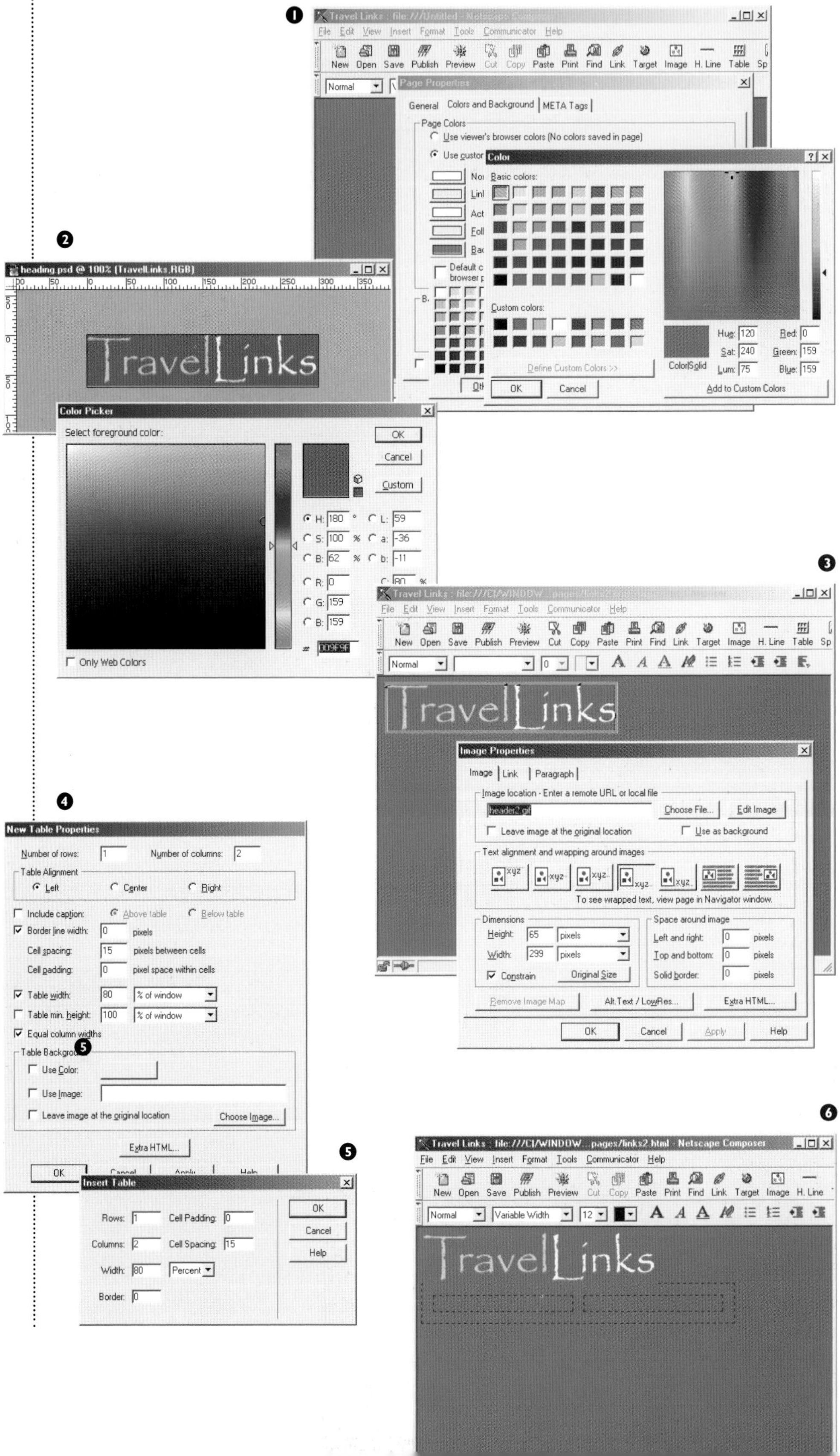

7

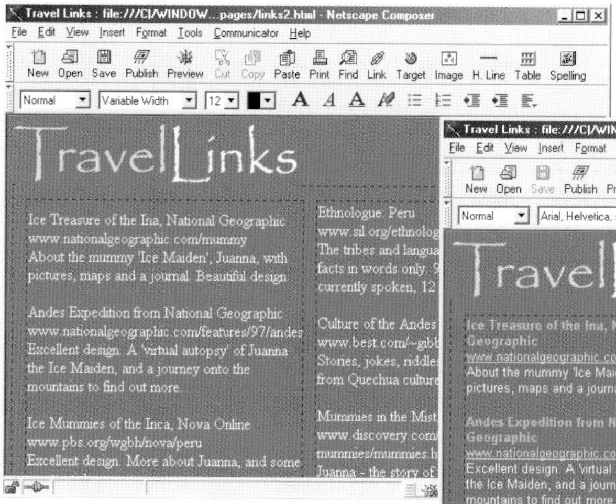

8

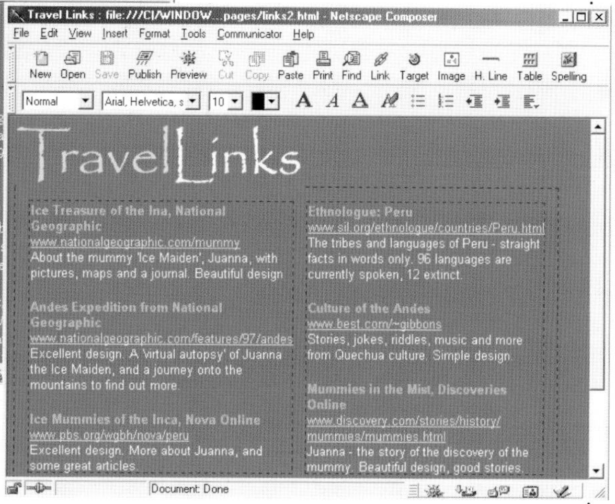

9

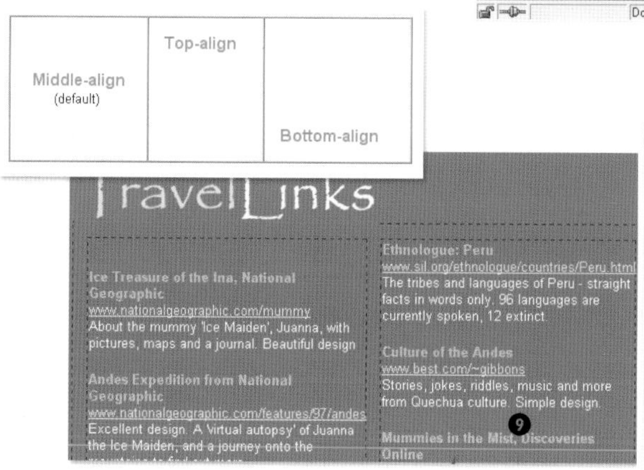

10

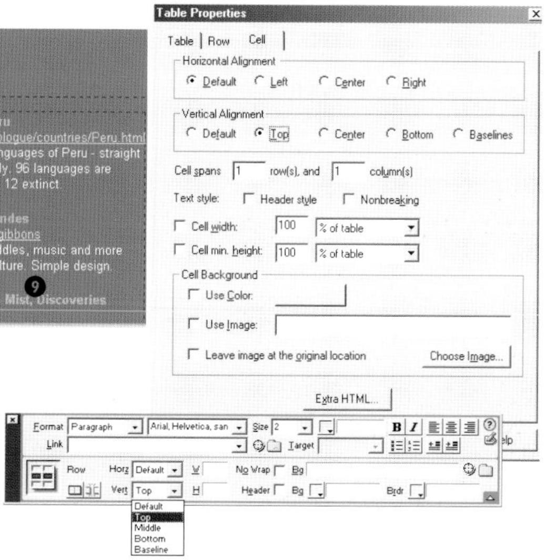

11

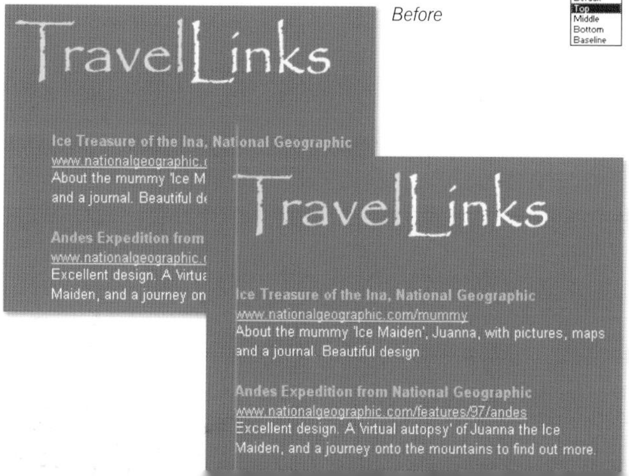

Before

After

7 The next stage is to add your content to the table, and then you can go back and tweak anything as necessary. Divide your list of links into two roughly equal chunks, and copy and paste them into the columns. Unfortunately, you can't get them to flow in automatically, like you can in a word processor.

8 Next set the fonts, sizes and colours for the text. Remember to vary these a bit to break things up, and stick with a standard font that many people will have on their computers. If you're having trouble with double spaces when you don't want them, try hitting *Shift-Return* instead of just *Return*.

9 If one of your columns is longer than the other, even slightly, you might find that they're not lining up at the top. This is because content is automatically centred vertically in HTML table cells. You can easily change this by changing the properties for the cell...

10 To do this, look in your *Properties* palette, or doubleclick or right-click a table cell to view its properties. There are lot of options here that you can experiment with; *Valign*, or *Vertical Alignment*, is the one you want to fix this problem – set it to Top.

11 You should now preview your page in a Web browser. Because of the cell padding, it'll probably seem as if the heading is too far over the left. The easy answer is to add some Non-breaking spaces in before it. If just hitting the spacebar doesn't work, try your *Insert* menu or toolbar for this option.

Finally, add in some links to your other pages at the bottom.

PROJECT 5
AN E-MAIL PARTY INVITE

One of the great things about Web design is that you can use it for almost anything. An HTML page doesn't have to be part of a website, and it doesn't have to do the sort of things that most webpages do. You could, for example, create a really radical ad to send by e-mail. Why pass on your information with boring old text when you can jazz it up a bit to make it more effective?

Here you're going to create an invite for an imaginary birthday party, which you can then send by e-mail. Once you've got the idea, you can adapt the design in thousands of ways for different kinds of parties – Christmas, New Year's Eve or Hallowe'en – or even for marketing your business or anything else.

You have seen over the last few pages some of the things that you can do with tables, but that is just a small taster. Many designers take years mastering the art of HTML tables. To be honest, however, once you know the tricks you've got a head start and can create designs you never imagined in the first place.

The two new tricks we're going to look at here are merging cells and nesting tables. The first simply means combining two or more cells into one, so that you've got a less rigid space. The second means putting one table inside another to get even more control over your layout.

Merging cells and nesting tables

1

1 Here is the party invite you're going to create, which uses some new layout techniques with tables. Can you figure out how it was done?

2 As you'll remember, a table is basically a grid with all kinds of features, which you can use to control where your content goes. But it can seem a bit rigid and limiting...

2

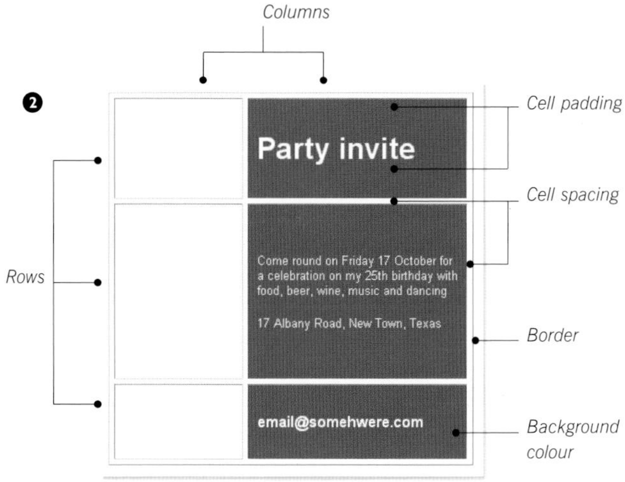

3

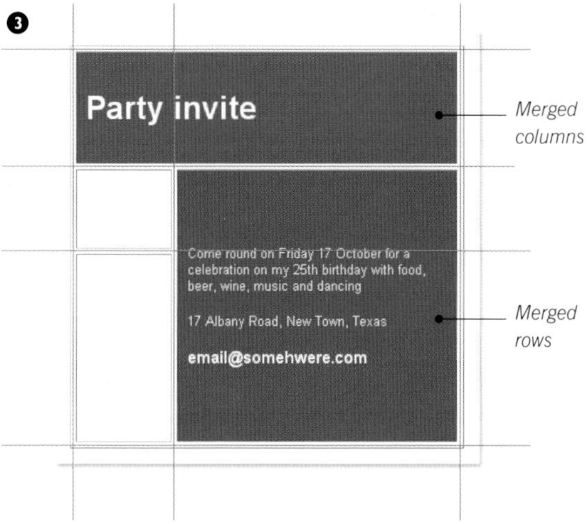

4

5

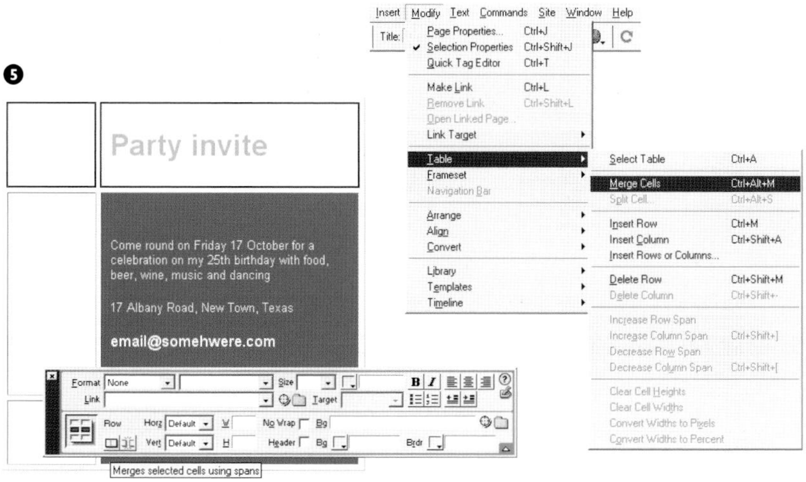

6

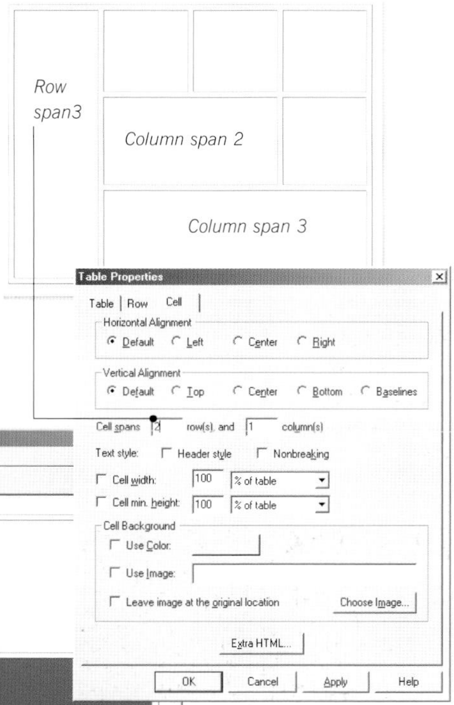

7

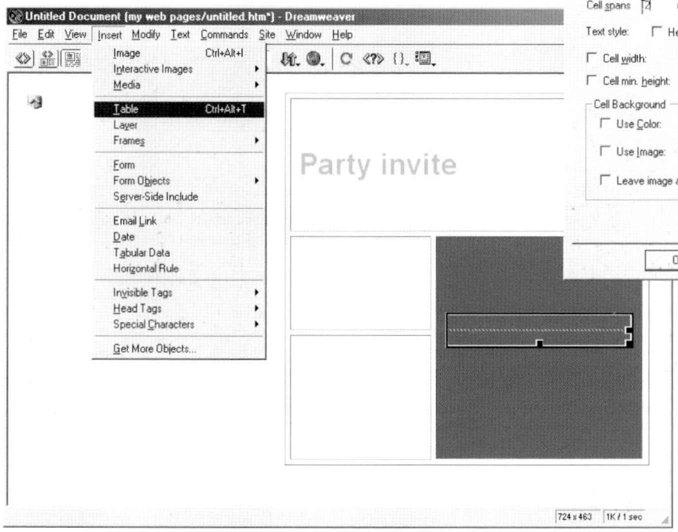

❸ If you want a subheading to go the full width of the table, say, you can combine the columns. Or you can combine rows to create a long, vertical space. You can see where the grid would be from the blue guidelines.

❹ You can also put more tables inside cells, which is called nesting, to get tighter control of spacing and alignments. Remember that line and space are the most important aspects of layout design.

❺ How you merge cells depends on the software you are using. In most applications, you can just click-and-hold in the first cell, and drag to select the cells you want to merge. Then you just find and click your *Merge Cells* button or menu item. This is how better Web software works, including Dreamweaver.

❻ In other software, you may need to manually set what are called column spans and row spans. If a cell is made from two cells that have been merged horizontally, it has a column span of two, because it is two columns wide. If it is merged from three cells horizontally, it has a column span of three. If it is merged from three cells vertically, it has a row span of three, because it is three rows deep.

❼ Nesting tables is much easier: you just put your cursor inside a cell and insert your new table in the normal way…

Preparing the layout

8 You are going to create your invite as an exact square, smack bang in the middle of a spacious black background. To do this, create a new webpage in the normal way, giving it a black background. Then add a new 1 x 1 table and set its width and height to 100 percent. This means that it will fill the full width and height of your viewer's browser, whatever the window size.

9 By setting the horizontal and vertical alignment of the one cell to centre and middle, you can add and nest a new table in here that appears right in the middle of the window. Make this table 400 x 400 pixels with two rows and two columns. By using pixels rather than per cent, you will ensure that its size is exact and does not change according to the browser window. The background colour here is #BB006F, while the padding and spacing are 0.

10 Merge the two cells in the left-hand column, and set the background colour to #FE9F00. Then set the alignments in the bottom right cell to centre bottom, and in here add a new 1 x 1 table with padding set to 15. You are doing this in order to create space around the text at the bottom. Your page should now look like the one pictured.

11 Next you need to create the graphics. You should do a little planning here to make sure the widths of your left-column graphic and heading aren't more than 400 pixels. We've gone for 165 pixels for the heading, which leaves 135 for the column.

8

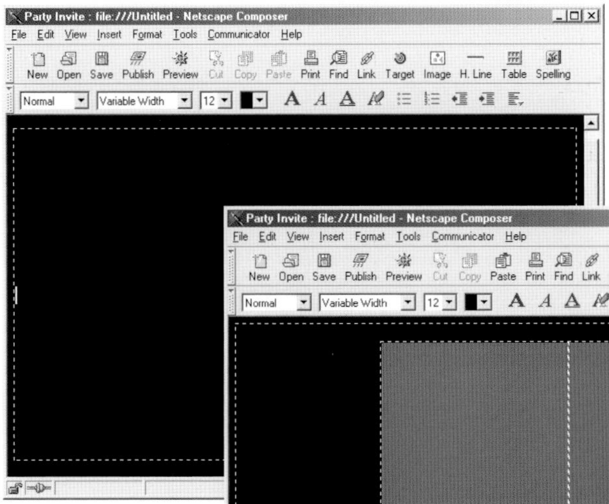

9

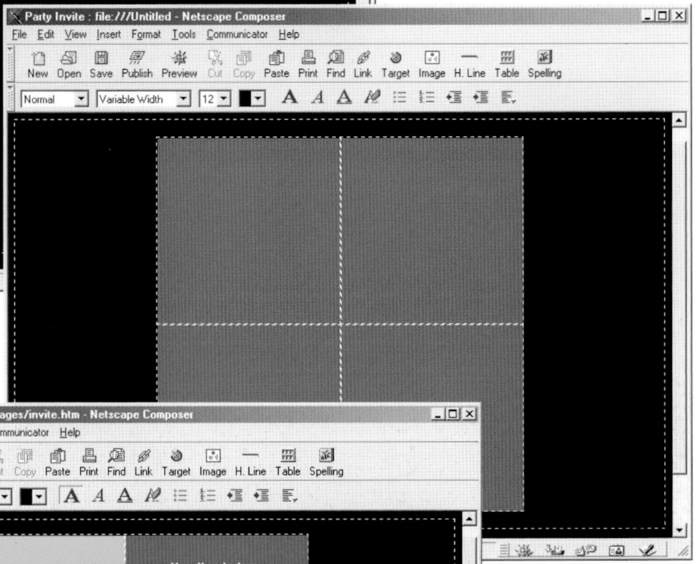

10

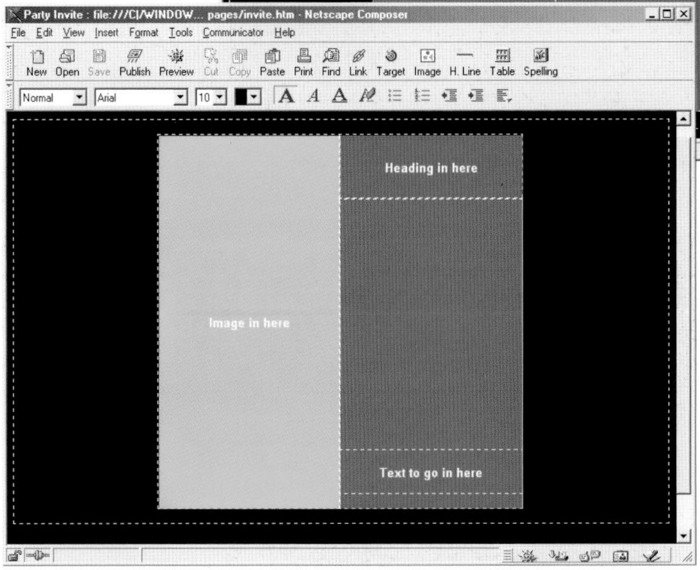

11

12

13
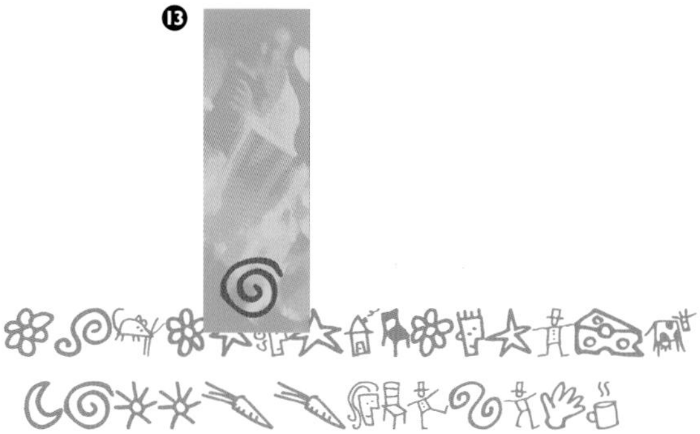

14

15

16
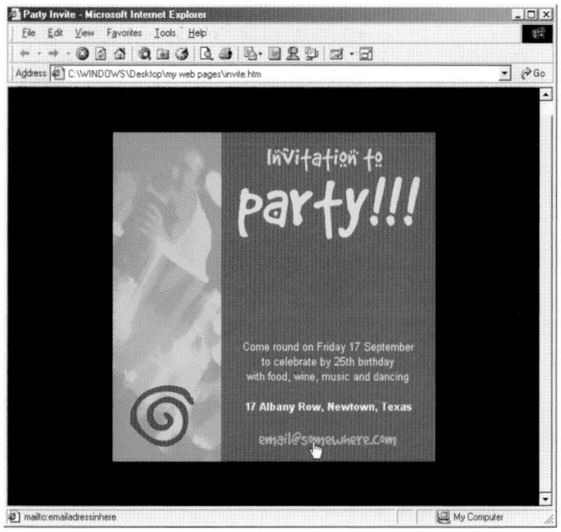

Fitting the graphics together

12 Create your heading first, and make it nice and big. We've used a font called Cool Dog for the heading, and the colour is #FEE900. Don't forget to make the heading's background colour the same as your main background colour – #BB006F in this case.

13 We created the graphic for the left-hand column by squashing a photo and using effects to adjust the colour; the swirl comes from the Good Dog Bones font. We'll show you more about how to create these effects in the next chapter. Don't forget to make sure your graphic is exactly 400 pixels high.

14 And don't forget to create your e-mail address graphic, which will then be turned into a link…

15 Now head back to your webpage and add in the graphics. When you add the heading, set the vertical alignment of the cell it's inside to the top, and when you add the big graphic, set its cell width to the same as the image's width. You should find everything fits perfectly. If it doesn't seem right, check it in your browser first – perfectly good webpages can sometimes look squiffy in Web design applications.

Select the e-mail image, then add a link to it just as you did with the earlier text, typing 'mailto:' followed by your e-mail address to make it into an e-mail link, and set the image's border to 0. Finally, type in your main text for the invite.

16 Here's the finished page.

Sending a webpage by e-mail

❶ So how do you get it into an e-mail to send to your friends? In Netscape it's easy. First, open your page in Composer, and then click *Control* or *Apple* + *A* to select everything, and *Control* or *Apple* + *C* to copy it.

❷ Then create a new message in the normal way and click *Control* or *Apple* + *V* to paste your webpage into it. You'll have to update the background and text colours, but apart from that you can just send your page as usual.

❸ The process is easy in other e-mail clients, in Outlook Express on a PC, for example. First, find the *View Source* option for your Web design software, where you can see all the code. This might seem scary, but don't worry about it. Just select the whole lot and hit *Control* or *Apple* + *C* to copy it.

❹ Now open Outlook Express and create a new message. Make sure your Format settings are on Rich Text or HTML, and click the Source tab at the bottom of your message window. Delete everything in here, and then click *Control* or *Apple* + *V* to paste your entire HTML in instead.

❺ Now if you click back to your *Edit* view, you'll see the images are missing. This is because you need to place them right into the e-mail…

❻ To do this, right-click on the missing images, select *Properties* and browse to where the files are on your computer.

❼ Your webpage is ready to e-mail. Here's how it will look.

❶

❷

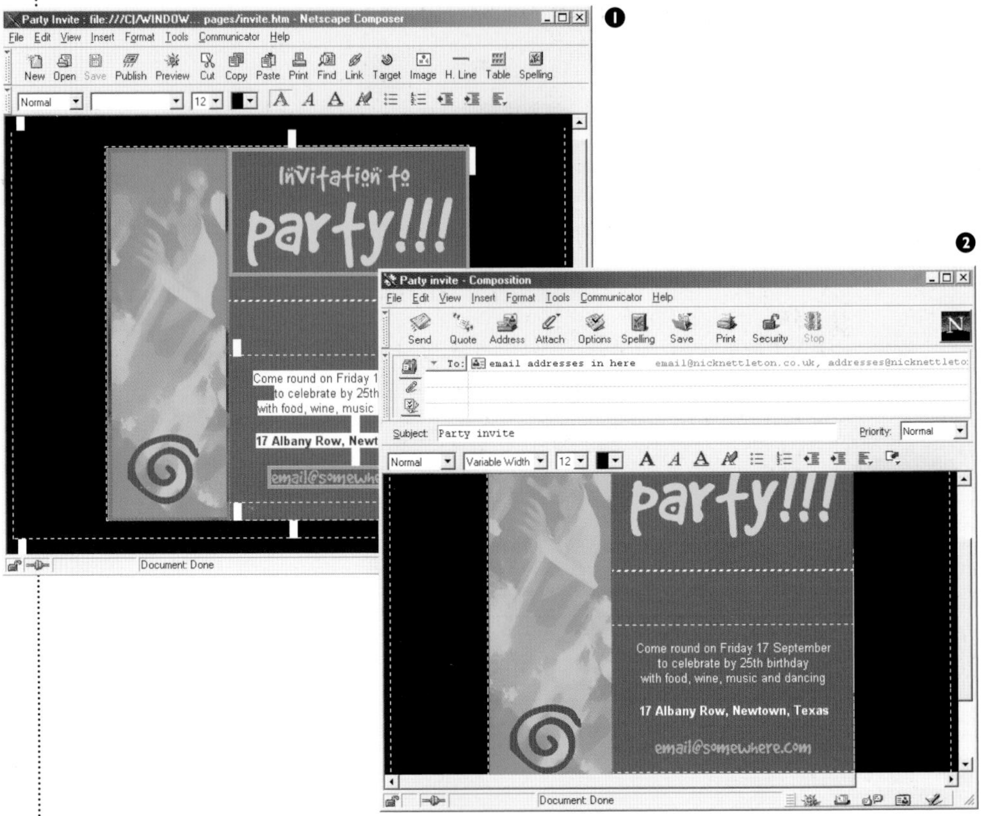

❸

❹

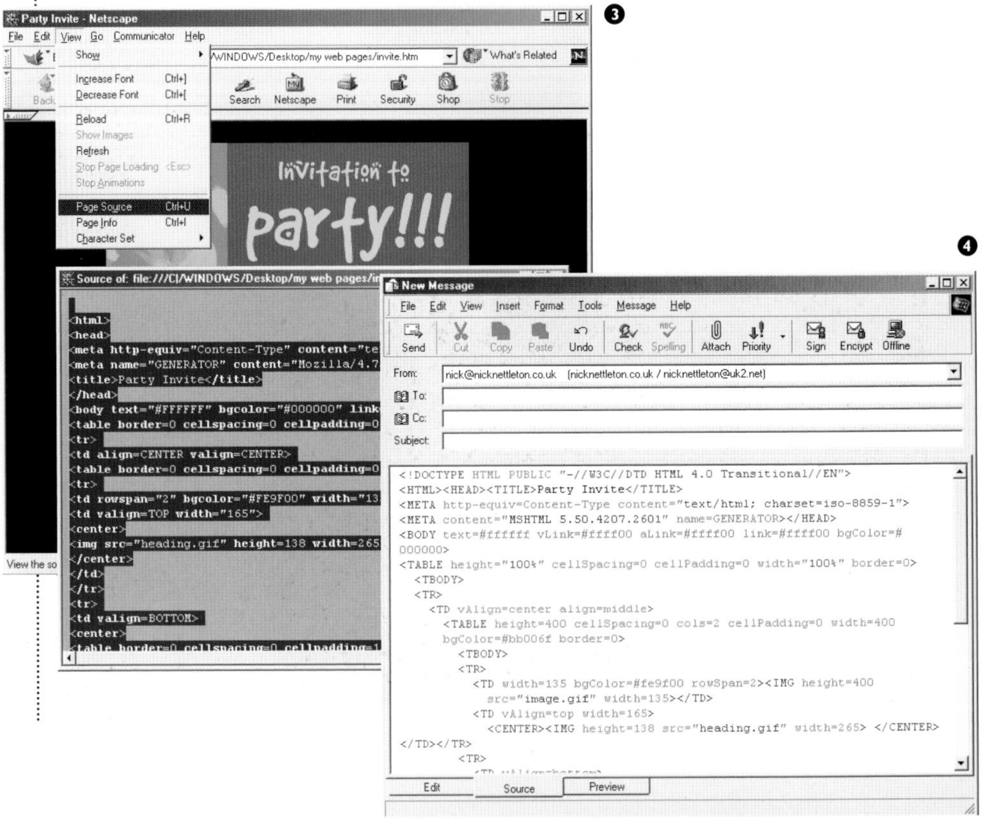

5

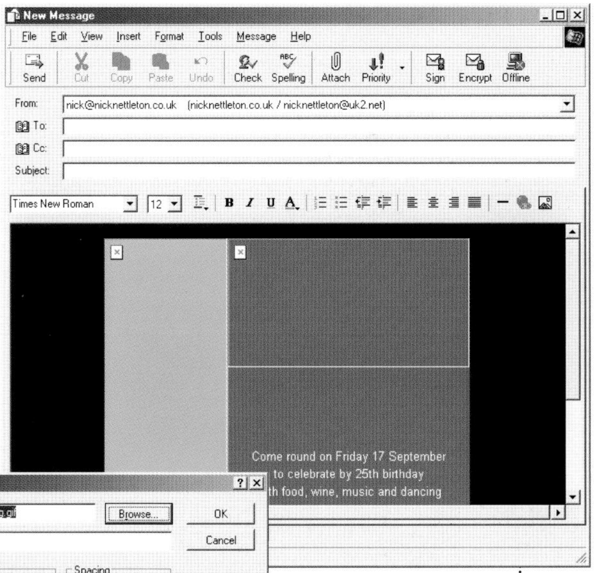

6

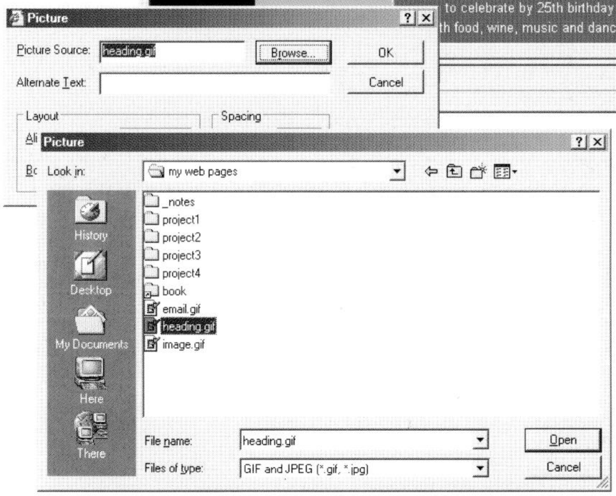

7

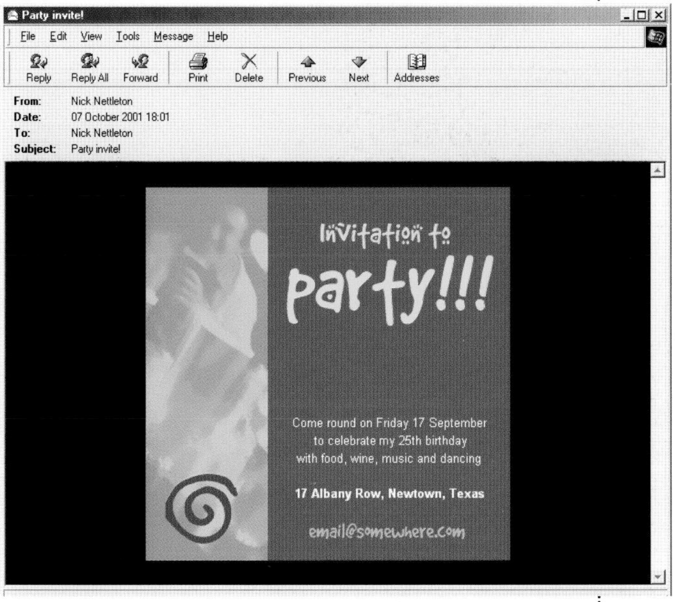

WEB DESIGN CHECKLIST

We've covered an awful lot already and you're probably thinking there's too much to remember. But don't panic – every Web designer gets the same feeling, and all you need is a checklist. So here's one for the information covered so far. You'll get others at the end of every chapter so that you can use them as reference points whenever you create a new webpage...

Ten things to remember

✓ **1 Give your page a title**
This appears in the 'to' line of the Web browser.

✓ **2 Set its background colour**
Even if you're sticking with white do set the background, because some Web browsers show unspecified backgrounds as grey.

✓ **3 Set your link colours**
You never know how someone else's computer is set up, so it is important to specify these.

✓ **4 Save your homepage as index.htm or index.html**
Most Web hosts automatically open this file when people visit a site.

✓ **5 Use standard fonts for your main text**
Remember that unusual fonts show only if your viewer has them installed, unless they're in graphics files.

✓ **6 Font sizes**
Use a dynamic range of sizes for your text – it makes webpages easier to browse and read.

✓ **7 Colour schemes**
Stick with just a few colours for your scheme, and make sure they match. Use different colours for headings and links, so that they stand out.

✓ **8 Are your colours consistent?**
Graphics should be on the same background colour as your main page, otherwise they look like an afterthought.

✓ **9 Use tables where possible**
Break up the content and give your page shape and space whenever you can to make it more interesting and accessible to your viewers.

✓ **10 Check all your links**
It's easy to get a link wrong and a dead link is worse than no link at all, so always doublecheck every link in your site.

BUGS AND BROWSERS

One of the eternal difficulties in Web design is that the same webpage may not look exactly the same when seen in different Web browsers, and might look different again when you view it in your Web design application.

This really is frustrating, and it means that you must doublecheck your work over and over in the most popular browsers – Internet Explorer and Netscape Navigator – and don't rely on just one or other, or what your design software shows you. In fact, if you're putting in a few hours work, you should doublecheck what you've done every hour or so. It's always easier to go back and fix problems soon after they appear.

You really must ensure that you have recent versions of both the leading browsers installed on your computer. And if you are working on a Mac, you should borrow a friend's or colleague's PC from time to time to check how things look on there.

2

Invitation to
party!!!
Come round on Friday 17 September
to celebrate by 25th birthday
with food, wine, music and dancing
17 Albany Row, Newtown, Texas
email@somewhere.com

1

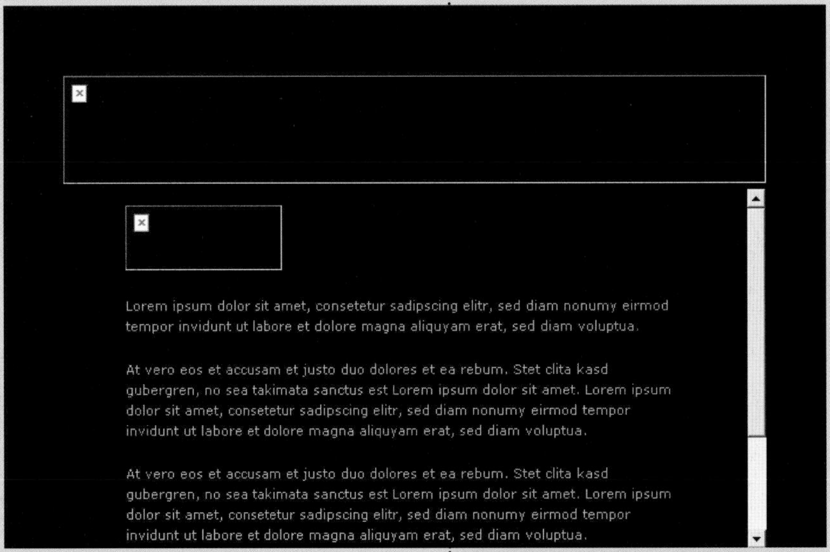
Lorem ipsum dolor sit amet, consetetur sadipscing elitr, sed diam nonumy eirmod tempor invidunt ut labore et dolore magna aliquyam erat, sed diam voluptua.
At vero eos et accusam et justo duo dolores et ea rebum. Stet clita kasd gubergren, no sea takimata sanctus est Lorem ipsum dolor sit amet. Lorem ipsum dolor sit amet, consetetur sadipscing elitr, sed diam nonumy eirmod tempor invidunt ut labore et dolore magna aliquyam erat, sed diam voluptua.
At vero eos et accusam et justo duo dolores et ea rebum. Stet clita kasd gubergren, no sea takimata sanctus est Lorem ipsum dolor sit amet. Lorem ipsum dolor sit amet, consetetur sadipscing elitr, sed diam nonumy eirmod tempor invidunt ut labore et dolore magna aliquyam erat, sed diam voluptua.

1 My images or links are broken
This is the most common error on the Internet, so check your pages well. First, make sure that the images or other pages are within the same folder as the current page, and ensure filenames don't include spaces (this causes errors in Netscape). Then set up the links again. If you have an option for Relative Links, *use this.*

2 My horizontal lines and table borders are grey
Versions of Netscape 4.x or less don't apply colours properly to table borders and lines. The solution will be covered later.

3 My tables don't line up
This is another common problem. Usually, but not always, it's worse in Netscape. The solution is to open your page and set exact widths for all the cells in your table, ensuring the content within them fits. If your tables still don't line up, doublecheck that the cells' different row and column spans add up to the right number in total, and that you've set their various spacing, padding and other properties correctly. Remember that if you have 10 pixel padding in a 200 pixel wide cell, then you don't have room for a 200 pixel wide graphic – only 180 pixels.

4 I've got missing background colours in cells
This is a problem in Netscape 4 or less. If a cell is empty, the background colour doesn't show. The answer is to put a nonbreaking space in the cell, which you should find in one of your menus.

3

4

Otherwise you might get a nasty shock. The same is true for PC users, who should borrow a Mac.

It's worth bearing in mind that in the 'dot com' Internet boom of the late 1990s, many commercial websites failed to work across different browsers and/or PC or Mac platforms. This was one reason why many of them went bust. Even today, problems remain. Don't make the same mistake, or you too could lose vital visitors. And once they've gone, they usually don't come back!

Most errors will be obvious, even if their cause is less so. But you should also be sure to doublecheck links, images and so on for any bugs. The examples on these two pages illustrate the most commonly encountered problems…

Original
Optimized
2-Up
4-Up
2020:VISION
Stroke
Basic
Soft Rounded
Tip:
Texture: Grain
Times New
abcdefghijklmnop
Arial
Gill Sans
abcdefghijklmnop
Helvetica
Franklin Gothic
Syntax
Barmeno
Generation Got
Eurostile
Goudy
Garamond
Clearface
Courie
Andale Mono
Serpenti
Bauhaus 93
CONTACT INFO
Fireworks - [Untitled-1.png @ 100%*]
File Edit View Insert Modify Text Commands Xtras Window Help
Original Preview 2-Up 4-Up GIF (Document)
CARTOON WORLD
Effect
Stroke Fill Info Effect
Untitled
Drop Shadow
48%
Knock Out
None
Use Defaults
Adjust Color
Bevel and Emboss
Blur
Other
Shadow and Glow
Sharpen
Eye Candy 4000 LE
Inner Bevel
Inset Emboss
Outer Bevel
Raised Emboss
Text
MICKEY
Bear
Mister Earl
Tombats Smilies

CHAPTER 3

Creating Graphics

You can only do so much with HTML alone: if you want inspiring fonts, logos, shapes or even a vertical line, you need to use graphics, which means different software and new techniques. Graphics are the really creative side of Web design, and in this chapter you will discover how to get the most out of them...

GRAPHICS TOOLS

Graphics software can be divided broadly into two types: bitmap and vector graphics software. The basic difference is that with vector software you can continually resize and edit your designs without losing the quality, because all the information is stored as mathematical shapes and formulas. Bitmap software just remembers the colour of each individual pixel, so you need to avoid enlarging anything by more than about 25 per cent, if at all, otherwise you will get a blurry, 'pixelated' result. On the plus side, bitmap software usually offers much more in the way of effects, tone and lighting control, and painting tools. Vector graphics tend to have a cartoony, flat-colour style.

Bitmap software is, in general, more popular with designers and includes Photoshop, Photo-Paint and Paint Shop Pro. Meanwhile Adobe Illustrator, Macromedia FreeHand and CorelDraw are all vector design applications. Macromedia Fireworks combines tools of both types into an excellent and easy-to-learn interface. It's also dedicated entirely to Web graphics, and, as such, it's an excellent option for the Web design beginner (and many pros too). For more details about the different graphics software you can get, and information on where to buy them, refer to chapter 1 (see page 16).

Because bitmap software is the most popular, that's what we'll focus on throughout this chapter. You can easily follow the projects and create the same graphics in a vector design application, however, if that's what you have.

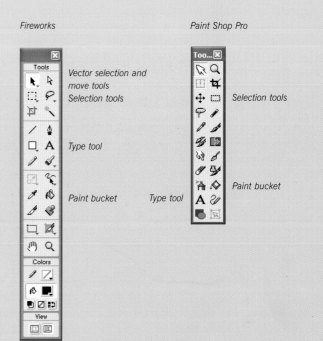

Photoshop

1

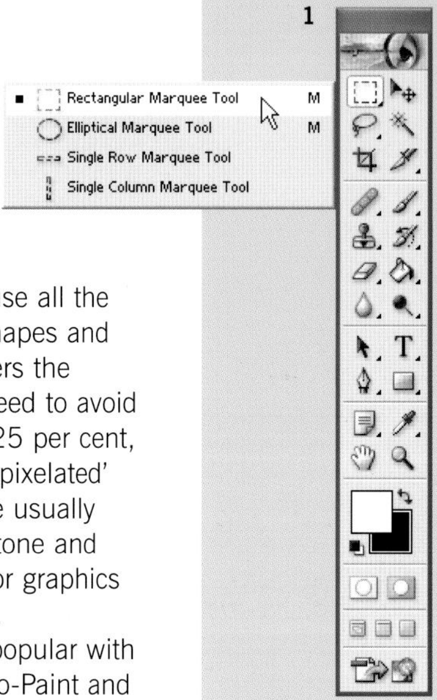

Move tool

Selection tool

Paint bucket

Type tool

Photo-Paint

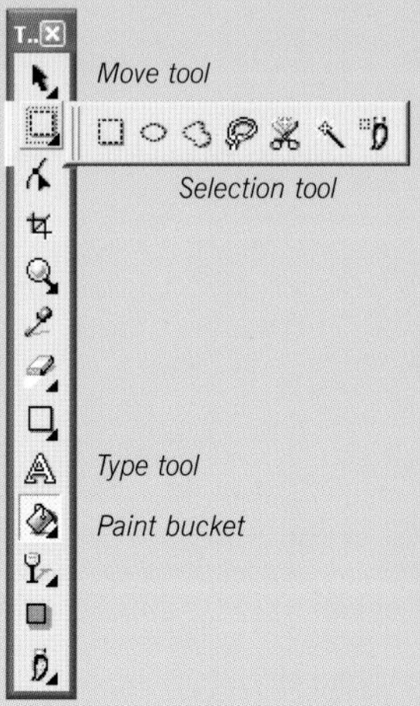

Move tool

Selection tool

Type tool

Paint bucket

Fireworks

Vector selection and move tools

Selection tools

Type tool

Paint bucket

Paint Shop Pro

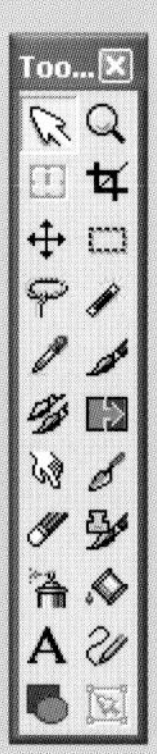

Selection tools

Paint bucket

Type tool

1 *Most graphics software works in broadly the same way and, although the interfaces may look different, you'll find you've got most of the same tools. Your most important tools are the* Move *tool, the* Marquee *or* Selection *tool, the* Line and Rectangle *tools, the* Paint Bucket *and the* Type *tool. In vector software, like Fireworks, you'll also find you've got palettes for* Fill and Stroke *(or* Line*), where you can change colours and apply effects. Read the Help files to understand how these work in your particular application.*

2 *You also need to find the* Layers *or* Objects *palette. This enables you to keep different parts of a graphic separate or on different layers. You can also quickly change what appears above what by moving their order around.*

2

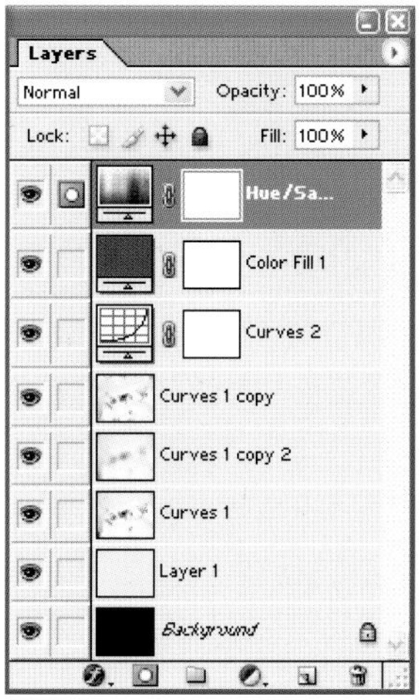

3

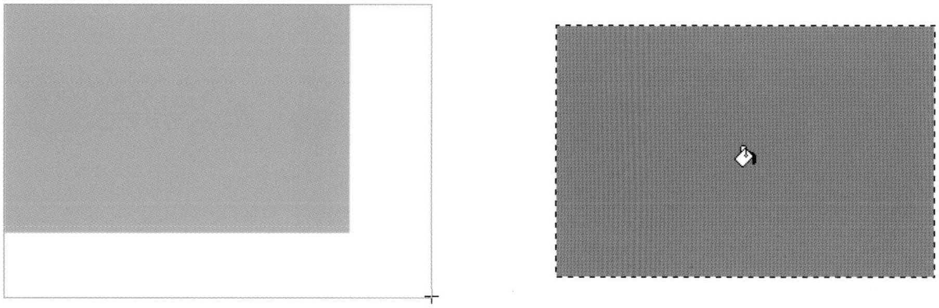

4

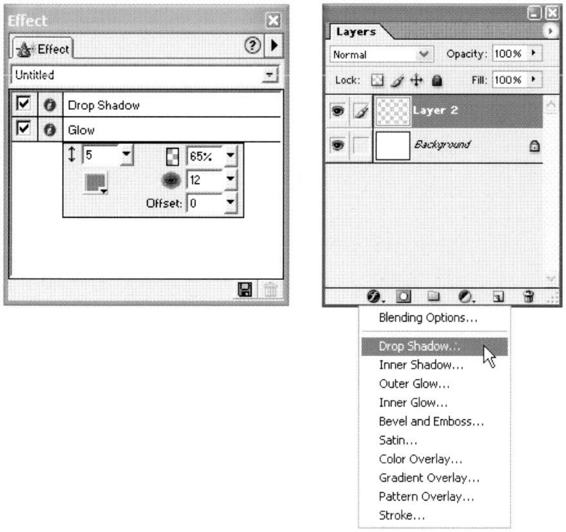

3 *To create a rectangle in vector software, you just need to use the* Rectangle *tool and draw its size. However, with bitmap software like Photoshop you usually need to create a new layer. Use the* Marquee *to draw its size and then use the* Paint Bucket *to fill it in with colour – rather like you do in Microsoft Paint.*

4 *You also need to find out how to apply effects in your software. In some cases you have an* Effects *palette (in Fireworks, for instance), an* Effects *menu (in Photo-Paint), or an* Effects *dropdown menu at the bottom of the* Layers *palette (in Photoshop). Experiment with these to get the hang of how they work.*

WHICH FONTS?

Text is the easiest place to start with graphics, because the words themselves govern the shape and form of your design and you don't have to do any drawing if you don't want to. However, the key to making text graphics work is to get an interesting, attractive and appropriate font. There are literally thousands of fonts out there, many of which you can get for free, noncommercial use, as shareware or freeware over the Internet. In fact, it can all get quite overwhelming. Use some of the ideas over the next few pages to start you off.

The important thing is to consider the topic and character of your webpage. If it's about sci-fi films, go for something slick and futuristic. If it's about grunge music, go for something with a deteriorated or scrawled look. Or if it's quite serious, choose a more traditional font – but this doesn't have to mean it will be dull. It's important that your type should show some real character, rather than appear just the same as everyone else's.

It's also important, with so many different and exciting fonts available, not to get carried away and use too many. Typically, a one-page design will use just two or three fonts and no more: one for the heading, a very simple font for the main text, and maybe one other for what is called page furniture – navigation buttons, side-headings and so on. If you try to use too many, your designs will appear chaotic and will also lack a clear identity. Also remember that in Web design, the main body font needs to be a standard that will display on most people's computers. But you'll quickly learn the principles of good design – look around you for good examples.

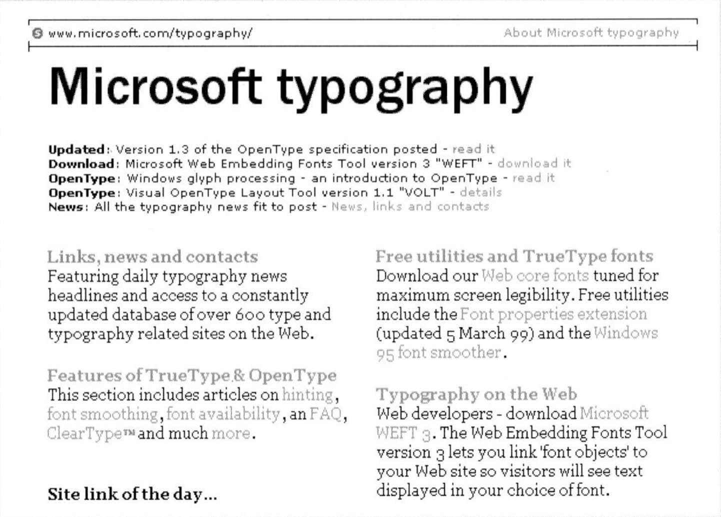

www.microsoft.com/typography/
About Microsoft typography
Microsoft typography
Updated: Version 1.3 of the OpenType specification posted - read it
Download: Microsoft Web Embedding Fonts Tool version 3 "WEFT" - download it
OpenType: Windows glyph processing - an introduction to OpenType - read it
OpenType: Visual OpenType Layout Tool version 1.1 "VOLT" - details
News: All the typography news fit to post - News, links and contacts
Links, news and contacts
Featuring daily typography news headlines and access to a constantly updated database of over 600 type and typography related sites on the Web.
Features of TrueType & OpenType
This section includes articles on hinting, font smoothing, font availability, an FAQ, ClearType™ and much more.
Site link of the day...
Free utilities and TrueType fonts
Download our Web core fonts tuned for maximum screen legibility. Free utilities include the Font properties extension (updated 5 March 99) and the Windows 95 font smoother.
Typography on the Web
Web developers - download Microsoft WEFT 3. The Web Embedding Fonts Tool version 3 lets you link 'font objects' to your Web site so visitors will see text displayed in your choice of font.

1

2

All fonts
New fonts
Categories
Antique & Gothic
Brush & Marker
Calligraphic & Script
Computer & Electronics
Decorative & Display
Drop Caps
Funky Décor

Handwriting

Music, Film & TV
Seasonal
Symbol & Dingbat
Typewriter
Alphabetical

Name search

Welcome to the Font Paradise where you can download thousands of free fonts! Before you start, take a moment and read about Font Paradise and our cool ActiveFont technology. The latter allows you to install fonts directly from our web site into your computer - all you must do is find the right font and click on its image! But of course you are not forced to use our installation technology since ordinary font download links are also provided.

Where to get fonts

1 *You can get many fonts for free on the Internet, at some of the sites listed below. The best fonts, however – those that have a well-refined appearance, good spacing and so on – usually cost a little. (This is rarely more than £100, and more usually around £40.) The first port of call, if you're on a Windows PC, is* ***www.microsoft.com/typography****, where you can pick a pack of standard and varied Web fonts for free, via download. You might also want to install the font smoothing application.*

2 *For absolutely thousands of free fonts, one of the best sites to visit is* ***www.fontparadise.com****, where you get a preview of every typeface before you choose which to download, and you can install them directly over the Web too. Other vast, free font archives include* ***www.acidfonts.com****,* ***www.fontfreak.com*** *and* ***www.1001freefonts.com***

3

4

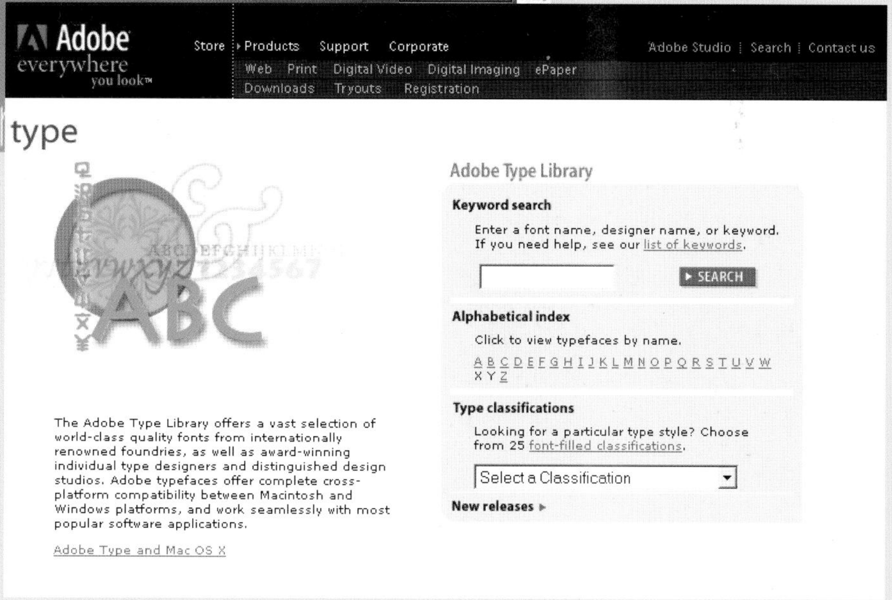

3 *Sometimes professional type designers offer just a few fonts for free on their own sites, and these are usually of far better quality (and are often more crazy). Some of the best of these include* ***www.antidot.de, www.fontmonster.com*** *and* ***www.fonthead.com***

4 *For better quality fonts – and especially traditional, easily readable faces – try out a few commercial fonts sites, such as* ***www.fonts.com, www.myfonts.com*** *and* ***www.adobe.com****. All of these include some brilliant features for you to browse or experiment with to get professional results.*

Traditional fonts

Fonts are roughly divided into two groups: those with 'lips', or serifs as they are known, and those without – sans serifs, or just 'sans' for short. The most famous serif font is, of course, Times or the newer Times New Roman, which is pictured here. Arial, meanwhile, is perhaps the best known sans typeface, if only because of its status as the bog-standard MS Windows font.

More modern design tends to revolve around sans-serif typefaces, but you rarely see Arial in serious design, because, although it is eminently readable at small sizes, the shapes of its characters do not have the elegance of more classic sans faces. The most famous of these by far is Helvetica. Other favourite sans faces include Gill Sans, Futura, Franklin Gothic and Foundry.

You can also get sans faces that have a more distinct character but which will retain the forms and readability of the classics, such as Barmeno, Generation Gothic and Officina Sans.

There are also, of course, a number of classic and popular serif typefaces apart from Times, and these include Garamond, Goudy and, on the more modern side, Rockwell, Clearface and Cooper.

Finally, don't forget the mono typefaces, of which Courier is the best known. These can be sans or serif, but are spaced so that each character has exactly the same space – like an invisible box – around it. In normal fonts, spacing between each character is set individually. In most cases, though, character spacing can be manually adjusted. Two types of space adjustment procedure are 'kerning' and 'tracking', which are best carried out in page layout programs. They are usually in the domain of professionals, but by all means experiment.

TIP

Getting fonts

You can get most of the above fonts in the free fonts archives, but if you're having trouble locating something specific, try a search at *www.google.com*. More traditional fonts may come already installed on your computer. If not, it really is worth forking out a few pounds for those that you like best.

Times New Roman
abcdefghijklmnopqrstuvwxyz

Arial
abcdefghijklmnopqrstuvwxyz

Gill Sans
abcdefghijklmnopqrstuvwxyz

Helvetica
abcdefghijklmnopqrstuvwxyz

Futura
abcdefghijklmnopqrstuvwxyz

Franklin Gothic
abcdefghijklmnopqrstuvwxyz

Foundry Journal
abcdefghijklmnopqrstuvwxyz

Syntax
abcdefghijklmnopqrstuvwxyz

Myriad
abcdefghijklmnopqrstuvwxyz

Barmeno Medium
abcdefghijklmnopqrstuvwxyz

Generation Gothic
abcdefghijklmnopqrstuvwxyz

Officina Sans
abcdefghijklmnopqrstuvwxyz

Eurostile
abcdefghijklmnopqrstuvwxyz

Benguiat Gothic
abcdefghijklmnopqrstuvwxyz

Goudy Old Style
abcdefghijklmnopqrstuvwxyz

Garamond
abcdefghijklmnopqrstuvwxyz

Rockwell
abcdefghijklmnopqrstuvwxyz

Clearface
abcdefghijklmnopqrstuvwxyz

Cooper Black
abcdefghijklmnnpqrstuvwxyz

Courier New
abcdefghijklmnopqrstuvwxyz

Andale Mono
abcdefghijklmnopqrstuvwxyz

OCRA
abcdefghijklmnopqrstuvwxyz

Fun fonts

Of course, you will not always want to use a classic or simple font: sometimes you just want something that is a little bit more crazy or descriptive. And for this, you have no shortage of options – although you should take care not to go too far.

Bauhaus 93, Pump, Stop and Serpentine (which looks good in italics) all offer solid, rounded and blocky shapes excellent for big fat headings.

For a futuristic look, try Luggage Round, Federation, Earth or House3009. Westminster, on the other hand, has that 1970s retrofuturistic style.

Other typefaces offer an inky or calligraphic, handwritten appearance, which is great if you want to give your site a spontaneous feeling. Some of the best are Grunge, Smudger and Fatboy Slim. Papyrus gives a more eastern look.

But don't get too carried away. In most cases, non-traditional fonts are best used in moderation, or as a design feature. They can sometimes be difficult to read over a long piece of text – they probably weren't designed for this purpose – and this risks turning your visitors off.

Some fonts are specially designed for comic book and cartoon work, such as Bear, Mighty Tomato (which is all in capitals), Mister Earl, Beesknees and the ludicrous Ravie.

Finally, many fonts include only symbols, not letters, and these are particularly useful for little graphics, icons, arrows and nonstandard characters. These are called dingbats, and can include anything from quick hand-drawings to mathematical and technical signs. You'll use some of these later; the ones shown here are called Tombats Smilies, Good Dog Bones, Wingdings 3, Almanac and Arial Alternative Symbols.

PROJECT 6
CARTOON AND FUTURISTIC TEXT

Text is the basis of much design, and it's often the starting point for your headings and buttons. It's also the easiest way to get to grips with graphics, because you've already got the shapes in the fonts that you choose, so you don't need to worry about drawing anything.

But, by the same token, it's easy to be a bit boring, because anyone can get themselves a fancy font, make it blue or orange, and stick it on a webpage. What you want to do is give it a special character, a visual identity all of its own.

Colours and gradients are a great place to start. By the time you're putting together your graphics, you've probably already chosen a colour scheme for your page (although there's nothing to stop you from changing it). So choose a colour for your graphic that goes with that, and you're off to a fantastic start!

Gradients simply describe where you have two or more colours blending gradually into each other. This is dead easy to do in most modern graphics software, and can be used to great effect. Another, similar effect is to fill your text with a texture or an image, instead of a solid or gradient colour. You might also want to include some warping or distorting, which we'll look at later.

The important thing is not to go overboard: there's nothing worse than an overwhelming mishmash of arbitrary graphics effects. And try to choose effects that enhance the character of your graphic in line with the topic or identity of your webpage.

1

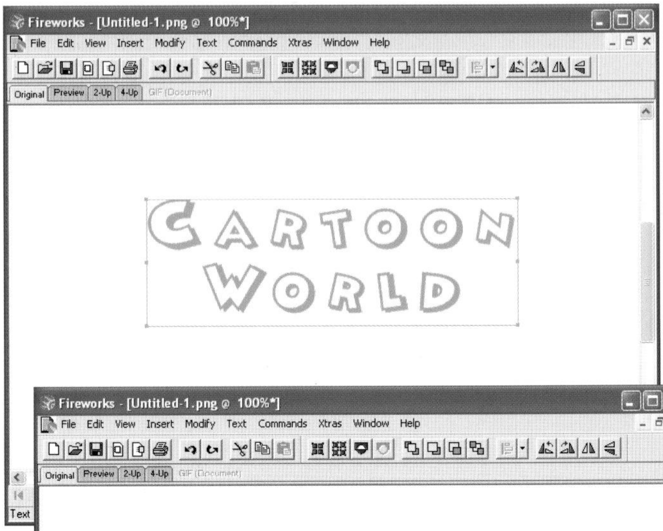

2

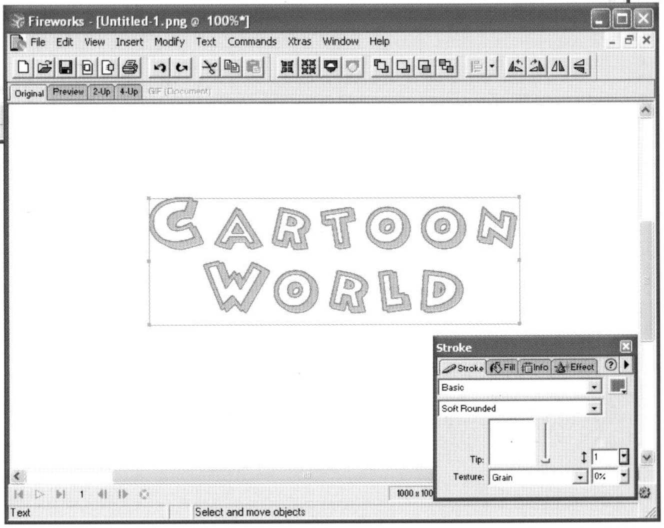

3

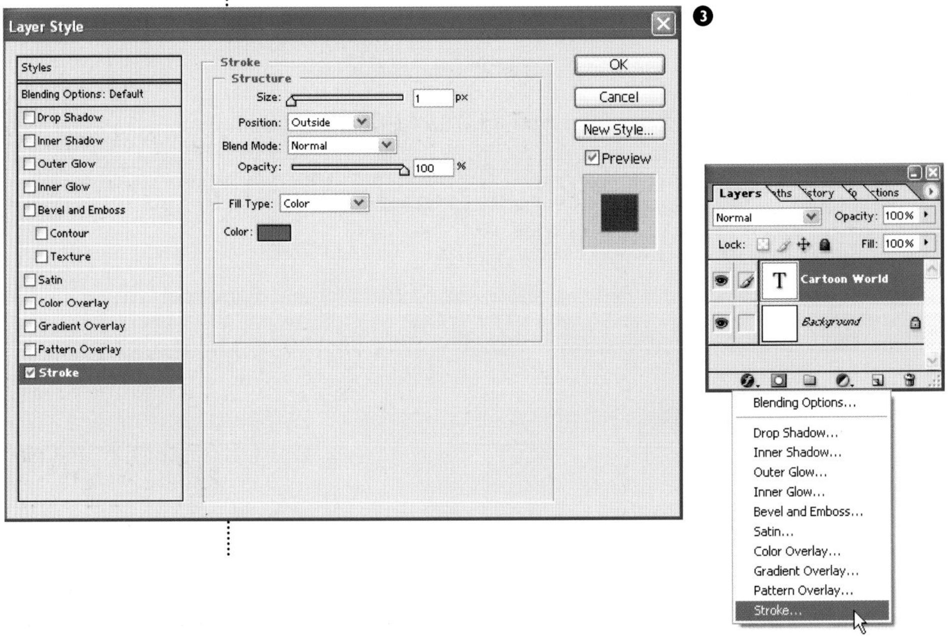

❹
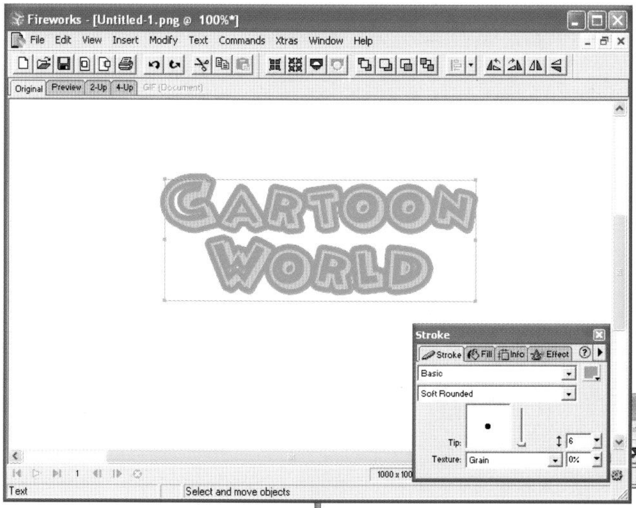

❺
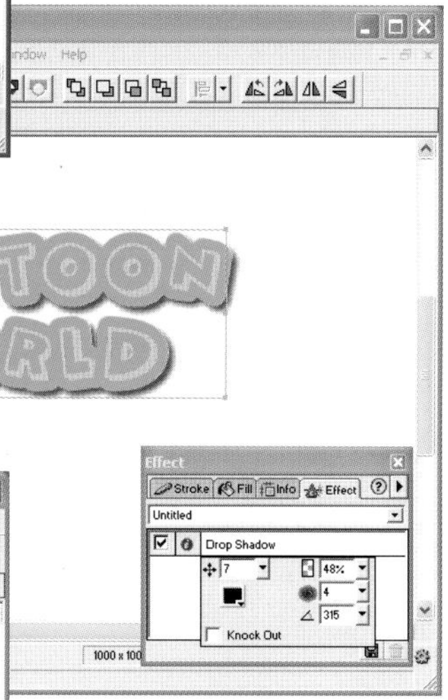

❻
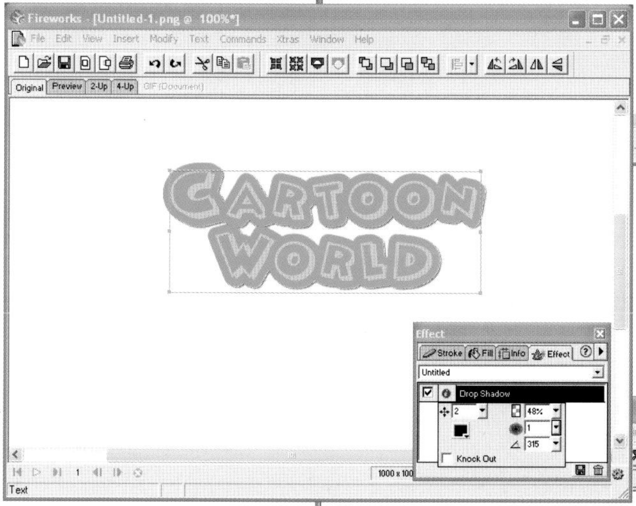

❼
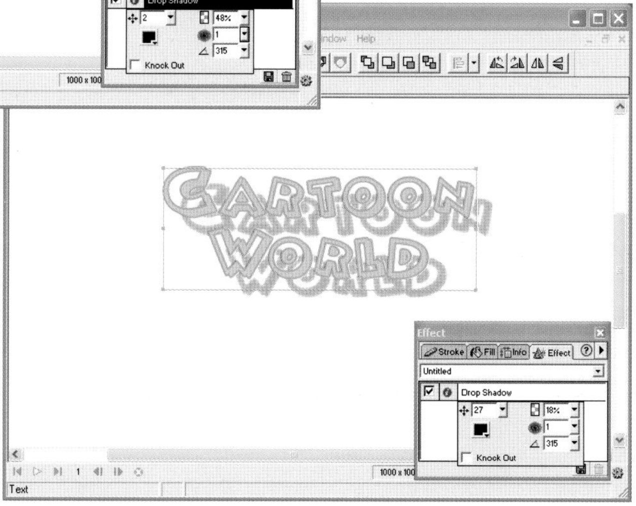

Colours and shadows

❶ The easiest way to make your headings more exciting is to choose a cool font, with a style that relates to what your webpage is about, and then to beef it up with a nice bright colour. Mickey would be an ideal font for a site about cartoons. It has been used here in Macromedia Fireworks.

❷ This colour is called a *Fill*; in most software you can also easily apply a *Stroke* – this means a line around the edges of the *Fill*. Look for a palette or menu option called *Stroke*.

❸ In newer versions of Photoshop, Stroke options are in the *Effects* menu at the bottom of your *Layers* palette. In older versions, you need to *Control* or *Apple* + click on your text layer, then create a new layer and select *Edit* > ***Stroke*** to create your outline.

❹ You don't have to use the settings as they are: experiment with giving your text a really chunky border, so that it looks even more cartoonlike. Here, eight pixels have been used.

❺❻ Next, use your program's drop-shadow effect to add a shadow to your text. Drop shadows are everywhere on the Net, so avoid using them 'as is', and find a unique look. Try setting the distance and blur, or spread, of the effect to be very low – about one or two pixels, so your shadow is very tight.

❼ Alternatively, if you've gone for quite a thin font or stroke, set the distance high, at say 50 pixels, and the blur and transparency low (about 20 per cent). This will give it a floating look.

Using gradients

❶ Flat colours with sharp lines are great for pulp-style art with a fun look, but sometimes you want something softer, more natural or metallic – and this is where gradients come in. Choose a solid, futuristic font for this steel effect, and use a black background.

❷ First, set the *Fill* to a mid-grey, then give your text a drop shadow, but set its colour to white and if there is a *Mode* option set to *Multiply,* change this to *Normal*.

❸ Next, make the shadow blur 0, distance 2, and set its *Transparency* or *Opacity* to 100 per cent. Also, turn the angle right around, so you've got a 3D-highlight effect instead of a shadow.

❹ Now change the *Fill* type of your text to a linear gradient. In Fireworks you do this in your *Fill* palette. In Photoshop it's easiest to use *Gradient Overlay* in your *Layer* palette *Effects* menu, and set the overlay mode to *Normal* and *Opacity* to 100 per cent. In Paint Shop Pro, you use the little *Fill* pull out menu in your *Text Editor*.

❺ Next, you need to create a metallic-style gradient. You may already have some in your software, but if not you can create one. The idea is to use lots of shades of near-white, grey and near-black, perhaps with a slight bluish or orange tinge (for rust).

❻ Exactly how you create and edit a gradient depends on your software: in Photoshop, doubleclick the *Gradient* preview in your *Gradient Effects* palette to edit the gradient.

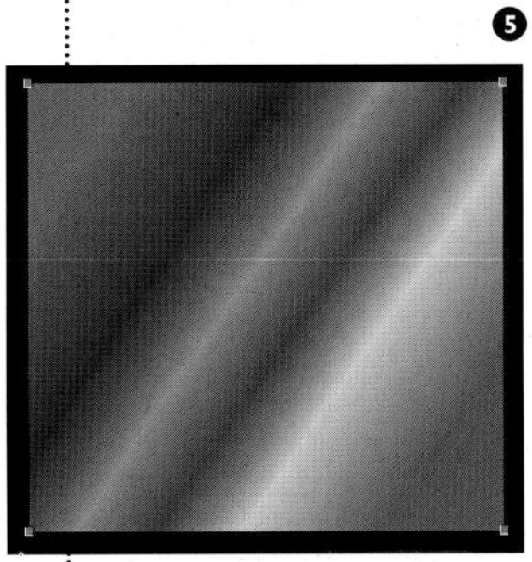

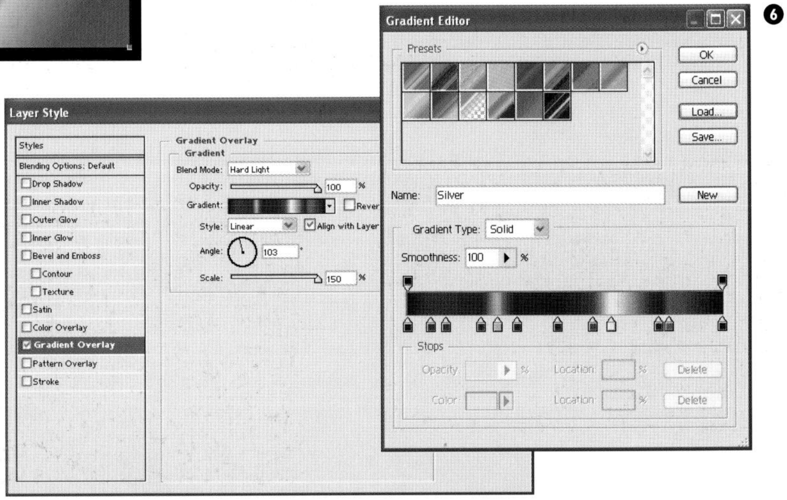

7

8

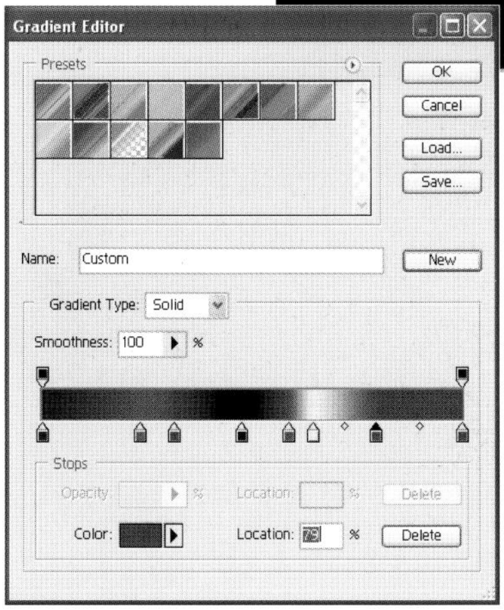

9

10

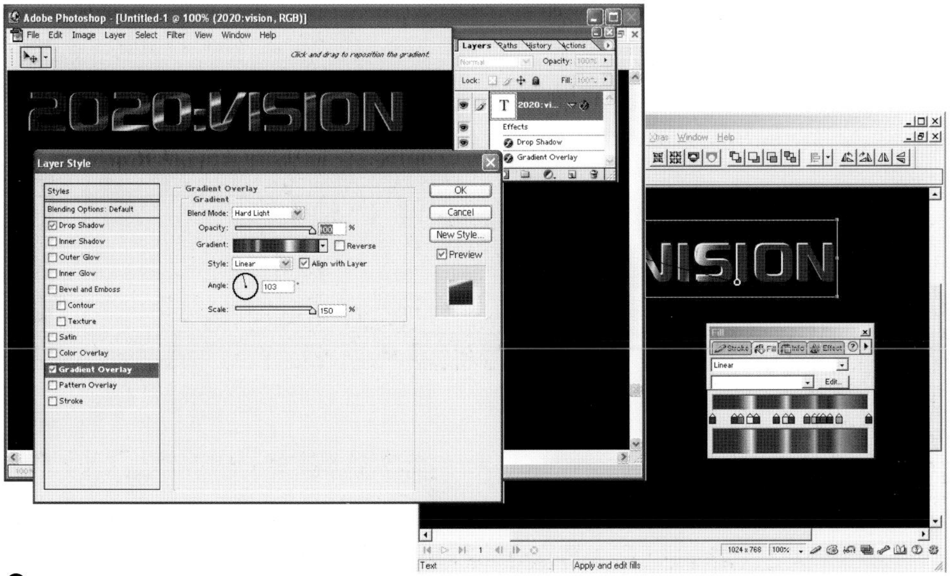

11

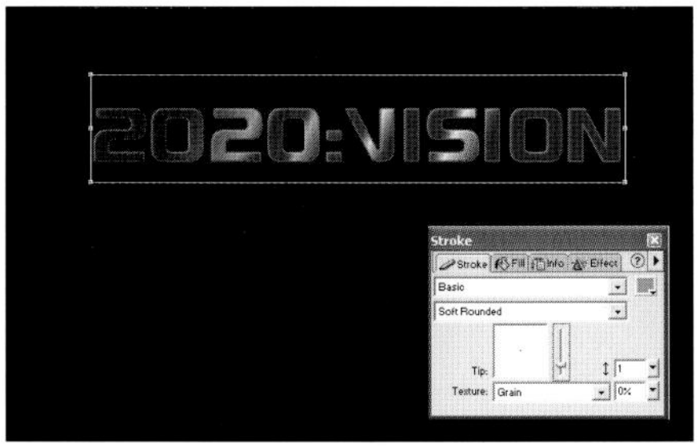

12

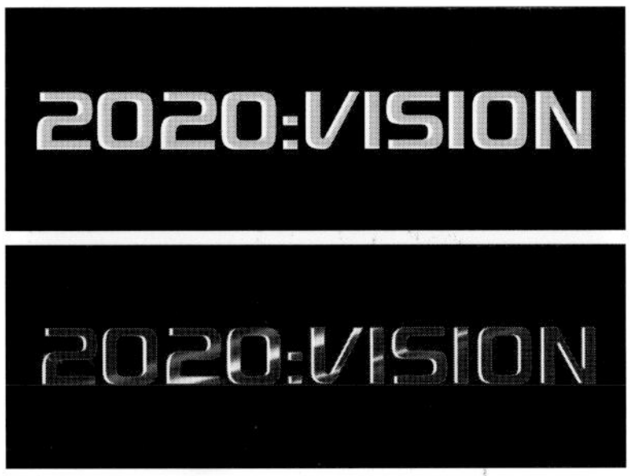

❼ In Fireworks, you just click the *Edit* button in your *Fill* palette.

❽ The next bit works much the same in all standard software: you have a gradient colour bar, and by clicking along the bottom you can create new tabs, or colour points. By double-clicking the tabs, you can set the colour for that point, and you can single-click and drag to slide it along and vary the widths of colour areas in your gradient. To remove a tab, just drag it away from the bar.

❾ You want to get a good variety of tones, from near-white to near-black – and be sure to get some very thin, sharp white streaks in there…

❿ Develop your gradient until it looks as much like metal as you can get it, and set it on a steep angle. In Fireworks, you'll need to select the text, click your *Paint Bucket* and use the gradient widget to do this.

This is getting pretty close now – although it looks great just as it is. There is only one more touch to add.

⓫ It would be good to give the appearance of slightly rough edges, so add a very thin and, if possible, transparent mid-grey stroke to your text.

⓬ And that's it: a fantastic, easy-to-create metallic style heading. You can also experiment with further effects in your package – like texture fills, satin overlays and so on. You'll be shown more about these later…

PROJECT 7
ANCIENT EFFECTS

The futuristic look is always appealing, but it's not right for every project. In fact, more often than not the space-age look probably isn't what you want. The techniques you used to create the metallic 2020:VISION graphic, however, work just as well if you want to create an old, historic-looking graphic, perhaps for a site about a vacation in Egypt, or the former Persian Empire.

You will use colour and gradients again to get the right look, but this time will add some textures in too, to make the text look a bit old and battered. This is great fun, because computer graphics and websites tend always to look terribly clean, pristine and perfect. Of course, the real world isn't like that, and by 'dirtying up' your graphics you make them seem much more real.

How textures work depends, as ever, on the software you're using. Often you can use a tile, which is a graphic designed to repeat across and down a page without the seams being visible. These are very useful in Web design, and most graphics software comes with a range of texture tiles bundled in. You can also download them for free from many websites (you will make your own later on in this book).

1

2

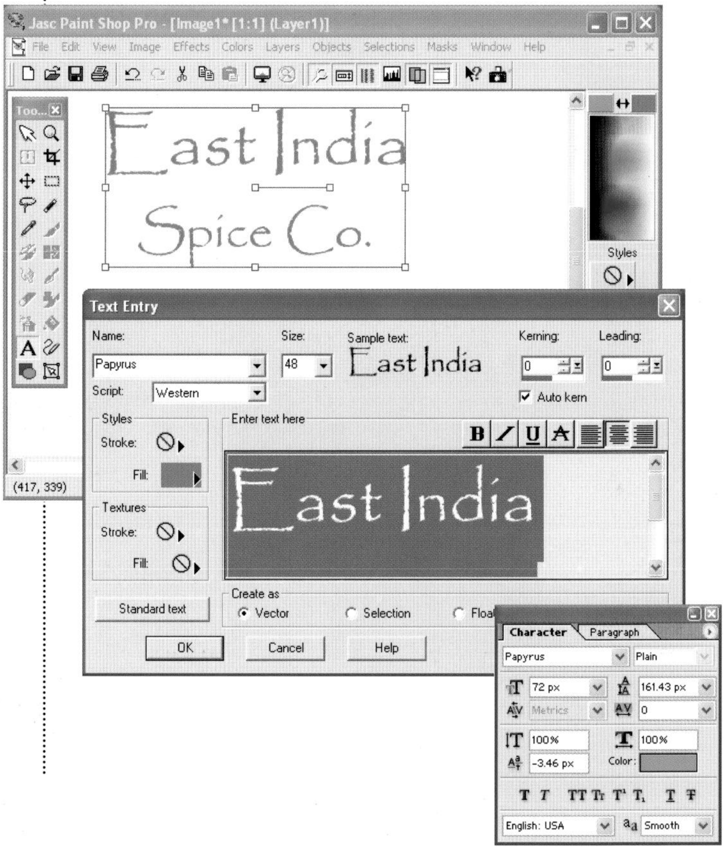

TIP
Free textures

You can download many textures and tiles for free over the Internet, for many different purposes. Head to sites like ***www.arttoday.com*** and ***www.melizabeth.com,*** where you can browse and choose from hundreds, and get links to other sites too.

3

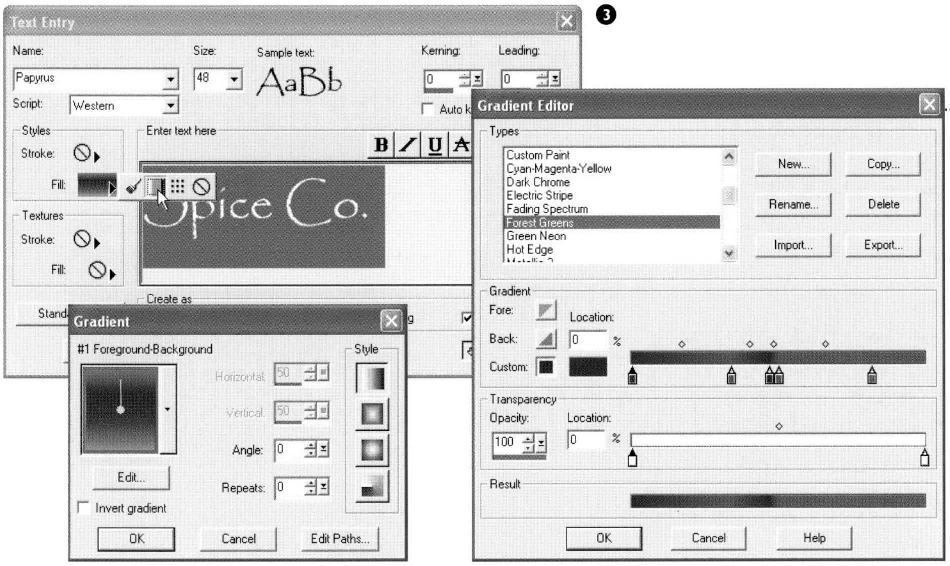

4

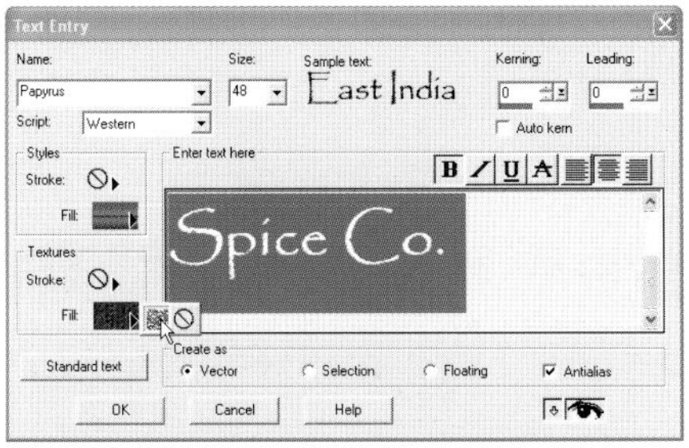

5

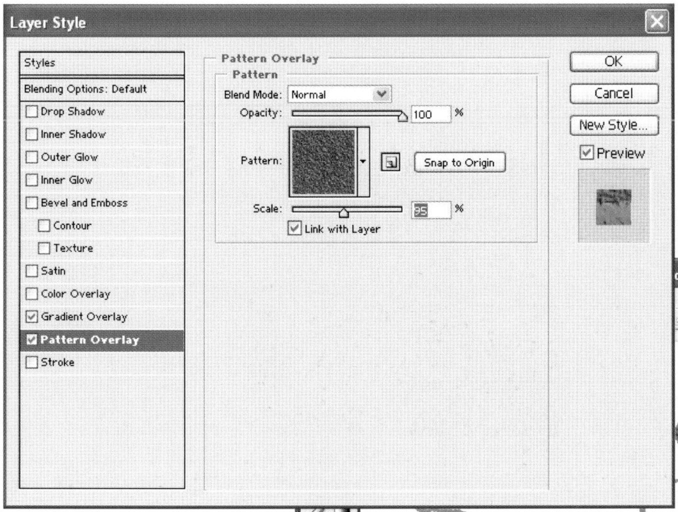

6

❶ First you need to choose a font that is right for the task. Papyrus (top left), Parchment (bottom left) and Runic (right) all have a good, 'ancient' feel. Go for Papyrus here, which has an Eastern flavour and is well textured around the edges already. Also choose a deep, spice-green colour.

❷ When you add your words, you might want to adjust the spacing of the text. Experiment with *Kerning*, which is the spacing between characters, and *Leading*, which is the spacing between lines. Sometimes these options are in your *Text* dialog, as they are here in Paint Shop Pro. In Photoshop, they are in your *Character* palette.

❸ In Paint Shop Pro (PSP), you can quickly create a gradient by clicking-and-holding on the little *Fill* arrow, choosing the gradient option and then clicking the colour patch and choosing the *Edit* option in the *Gradient* dialog that appears.

❹ You can choose a *Texture Fill* in PSP in the same way, from the *Texture* options. In Fireworks, use your *Fill* palette.

❺ In Photoshop, the easiest way is to create a *Pattern Overlay*, in the same way as you did a *Gradient Overlay*. You can load new pattern sets using the little *Corner* menu by the pattern preview.

❻ Here we've gone for a Stucco pattern with a *Normal* blending at 100 per cent *Opacity*, and a warm browns-to-green *Gradient* overlay with an *Overlay* blending at 100 per cent. You should experiment with the different blending modes yourself.

PROJECT 8
DISTORTING, WARPING AND 3D

Some of the most fun things you can do with text involve distorting and warping. There is no reason why your words should always go direct from left to right in a straight line, when you can squeeze and squash, stretch and skew, rotate and reflect! You can have your text going from top to bottom, or right to left as part of a mirror effect. Or why not go the whole hog and have it curve around a circle, or sit on a wavy line? You can even distort your letterforms to get a 3D effect, receding into the distance or rushing towards you.

Most graphics applications have tools for doing all of these effects and more. The most important of these is the *Transform* (*Control/Apple + T* in most applications), which allows you to scale, squash or stretch, and rotate. Most software also has a *Transform* submenu in one of the main menus, where you can choose options like *Flip Horizontal* or *Flip Vertical*, which are the same as reflecting. If you click-and-hold or doubleclick your *Transform* tool, or use it in conjunction with the *Control*, *Shift*, *Alt*, *Apple* and/or *Command* keys, you'll find you have even more options to experiment with. These include *Skewing*, which sheers your selected graphic as a parallelogram, and *Free Distortion*.

Your *Text* options should give you the choice to have your text running left to right or top to bottom, while you may also find an *Attach* or *Fit To Path* feature. This allows you to draw a shape and then make your text follow the curve of its edge. Photoshop offers an *Envelope* menu in your *Text* options as an alternative, while in Paint Shop Pro and Photo-Paint, you can use a variety of distortions from the *Effects* menu.

Follow the next few pages for some inspiration and techniques for making the most of these tools.

❶

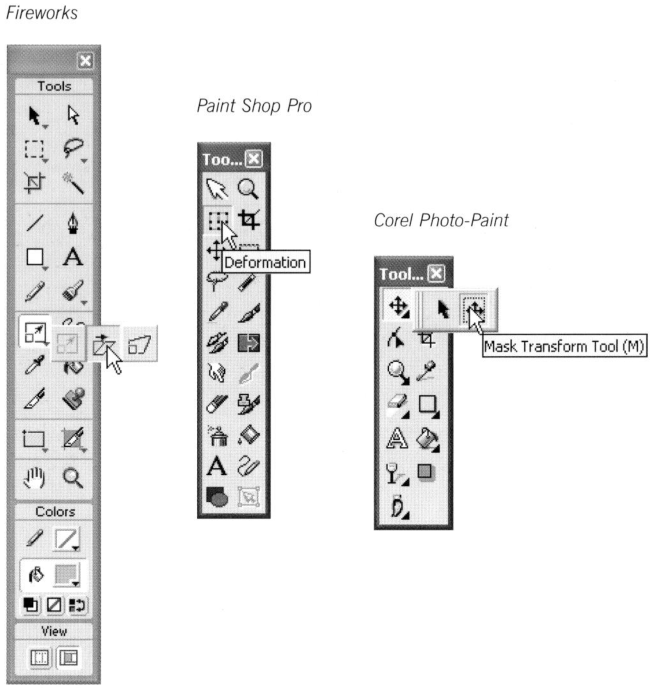

❷

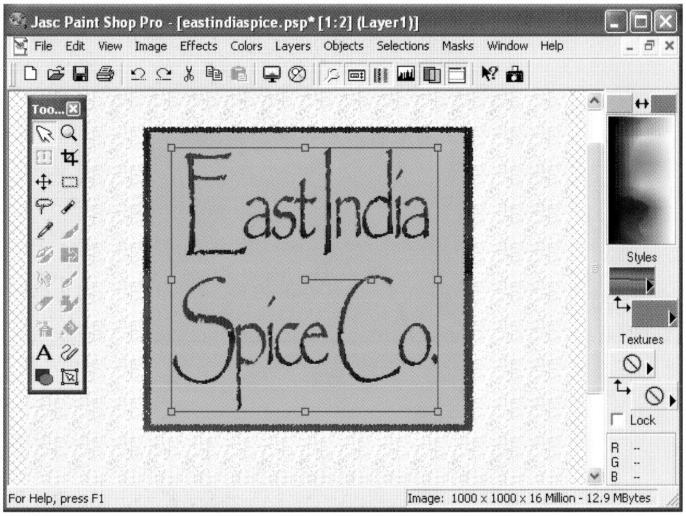

3

4

Simple distortions

1 The simplest distortions involve using your Transform tool, which may be in your toolbox, or you can usually access it using *Control* or *Apple* + *T*. With some vector software, you can just use your normal *Point*, *Select* and *Move* tool. When you want to transform something, don't forget to select it first, with your Marquee if you have one (the tool with dotted lines or 'marching ants' as they are known), or just with the *Point and Move* tool, depending on your software.

2 Here's a simple squash and stretch in Paint Shop Pro using the heading from the last project. This was done to fit it into a square-ish textured background with a fat stroke.

3 Skewing involves sheering a graphic into a lozenge-shaped transformation. This works particularly well with futuristic graphics. In Photoshop, click *Control/Apple* + *T*, then use your Control or apple key with the *Transform* tool to create this effect. In Paint Shop Pro, use your *Shift* key, or in Fireworks click-and-hold your *Transform* tool, then choose the *Skew* tool that appears.

4 To rotate your text, hold your *Transform* tool close to the corner of your selection and when you see a little *Rotate* cursor just click and drag. You can get some great, almost-3D effects by combining this with a skew. Here we've added in a transformed, gradient-filled ellipse too.

Warping

❶ The real fun in distorting text comes with warping. You'll probably find your software already has some filters and effects for quickly warping text, such as *Punch*, *Pinch*, *Twirl* and *Ripple*. Sometimes these are great, but by and large they're hard to control and unless you exercise skill and restraint, they can easily turn out to look like cheap effects rather than skilful design work.

❷ You may find you have to 'Rasterize' the type before you can apply the effects, which means converting it from vector letter forms to a bitmap. Right-click on the type's layer and choose the *Rasterize* option.

❸ A more controlled option for creating 3D or warped text is to apply free distortion with your *Transform* tool, by holding down *Control* or *Apple* (Photoshop), or *Shift* (Paint Shop Pro) as you use it; or in Photoshop, select the *Free Transform* subtool, like the *Skew* tool. Now you can pick individual points on your *Transform* rectangle, and drag them to new positions.

❹ To create a controlled 3D effect, just move the two points that you want to appear 'far away' closer together, to give the illusion of perspective, and then squash, or foreshorten, the whole thing. If you get stuck, then picture two lines converging into the distance, and use your natural instinct to get the ratios right.

❶

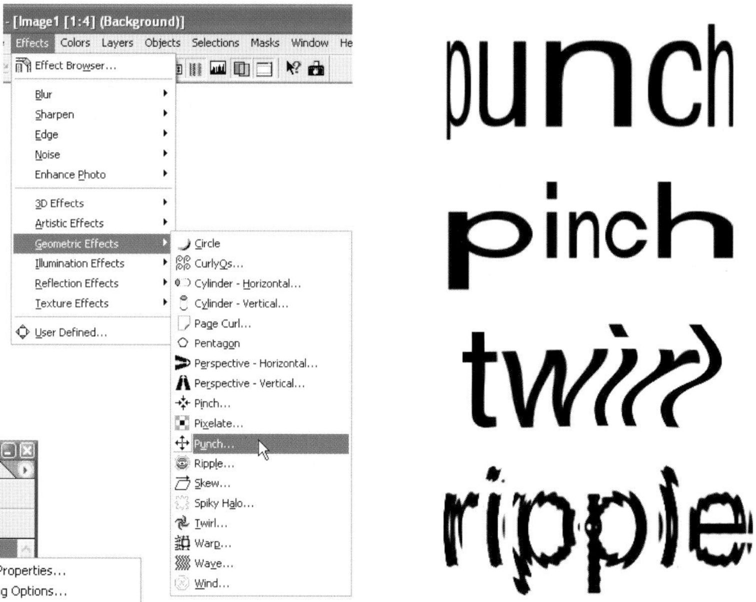

❷

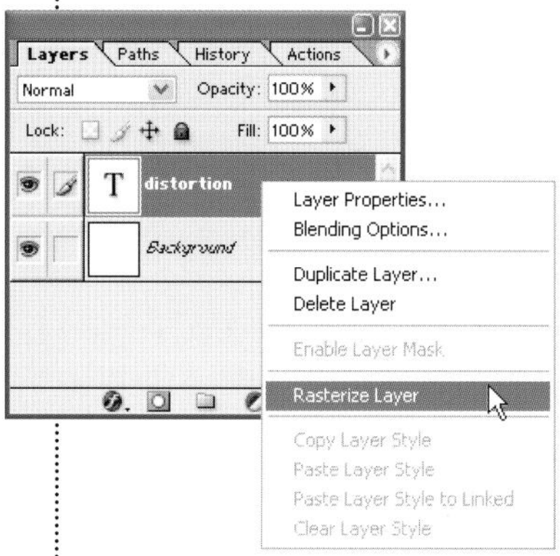

❸

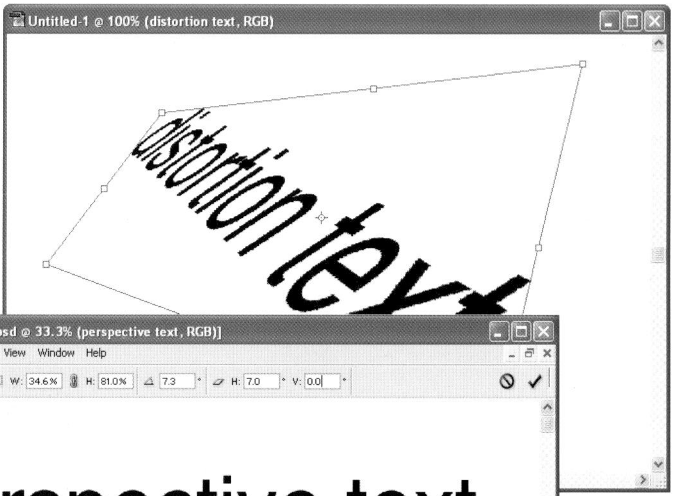

❹

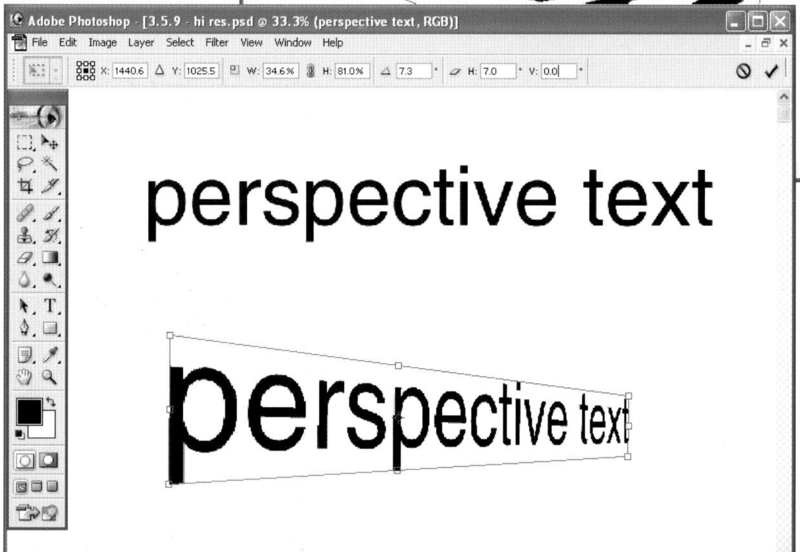

2

1 3 4

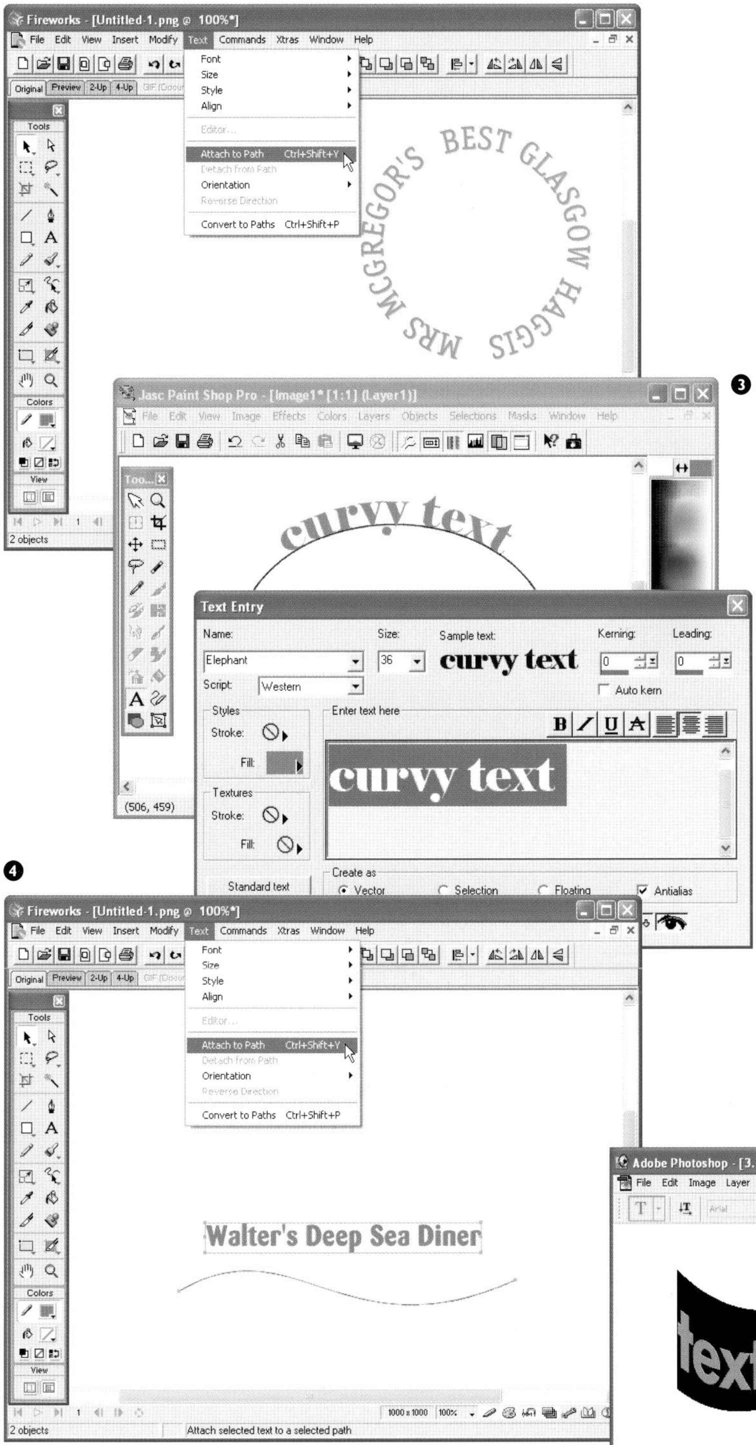

Paths and envelopes

1 You can spend ages experimenting with these techniques. But there's another great technique for distorting your text: fitting it to a path.

2 A path is an editable line, although it needn't be visible. (More accurately, it's the boundary that defines the form of a vector object.) To set your text on a path, first draw the path, using any of your usual drawing tools: pens, pencils, circles, squares, lines, etc.

3 In PSP the next step is easy: select your *Text* tool and hold it close to the edge of your path. You'll see your cursor change to the letter A at an angle, which is the *Text on a Path* tool. Just click, enter your text in the usual way, hit OK, and that's it.

4 In Fireworks, create the text in the normal way, then click-and-drag to select both the text and the path you want it to follow. Now choose *Attach To Path* from your *Text* menu.

5 Photoshop 6 onwards has a *Text Envelope* feature for applying curves and warps to text graphics. Just add your words as normal, then click the T button with the curved shape.

5

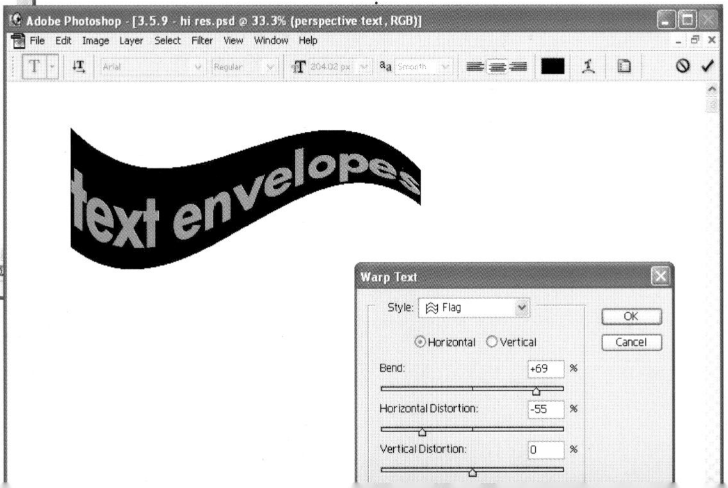

PROJECT 9
DESIGNING BUTTONS

So far the focus has been on headings and text effects, but what about buttons? Every webpage needs buttons. The good news is that you can use all the same techniques that you've already learned for your buttons, and more. In fact, it's a particularly good idea to make sure you do use the same or similar techniques for your buttons as you have for other graphics in your webpage, because, like colour, you should aim to keep styling consistent throughout a site. This helps to reinforce the look that you're going for, which should tie in with what your site is about. If you go crazy and try to use too many different techniques, you (and your visitors) will get a headache.

There's something about buttons, though, that separates them from headings and other graphics, and you've got to convey this in the design. They're there to click, and you want people to know that as soon as they see them. You shouldn't need to say 'click here' if your design is good.

If you've spent any time surfing the Web, then drop shadows and button-like 3D bevel effects will be familiar to you. Like underlined links, people already know and expect graphics like this to be clickable, so much of your work is already done. But there are numerous other techniques too: you can use arrows, boxes, graphics suggesting movement, and other pointers...

TIP

Button style

You need to design only one or two button styles for a whole website so, to save time, create just one button first, then reuse the same design with a different label elsewhere...

1

2

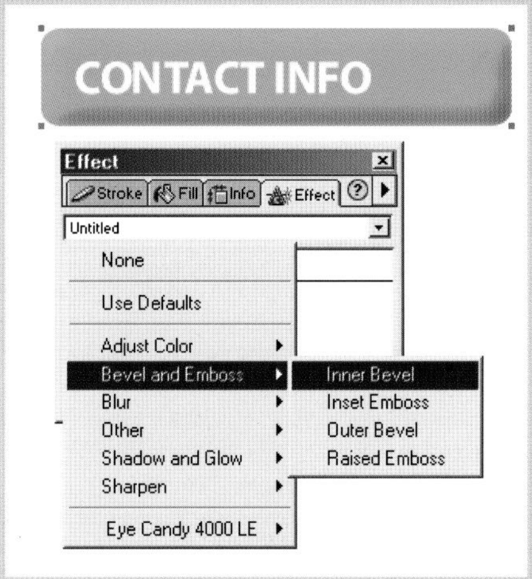

3

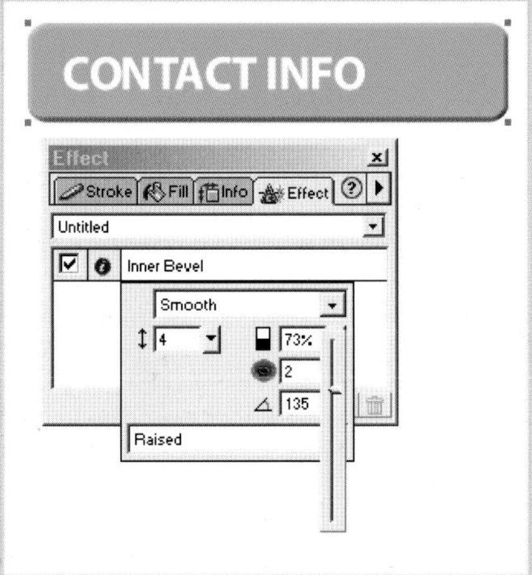

4

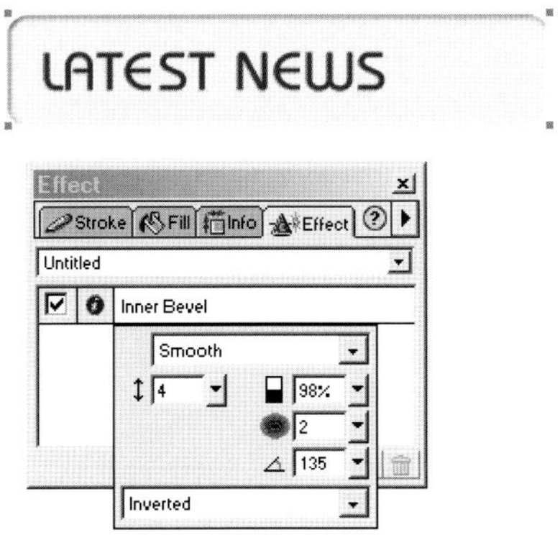

5

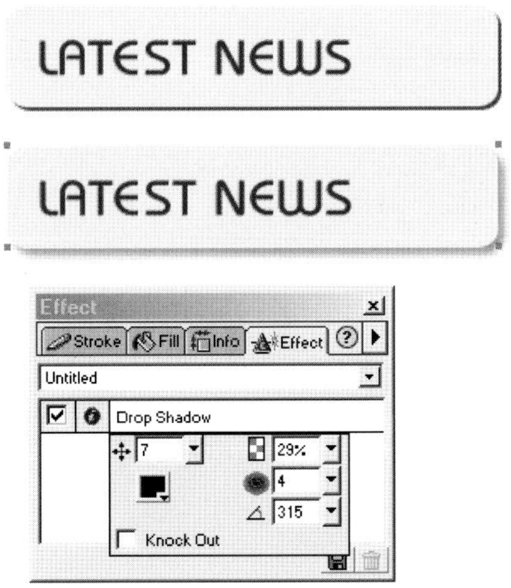

6

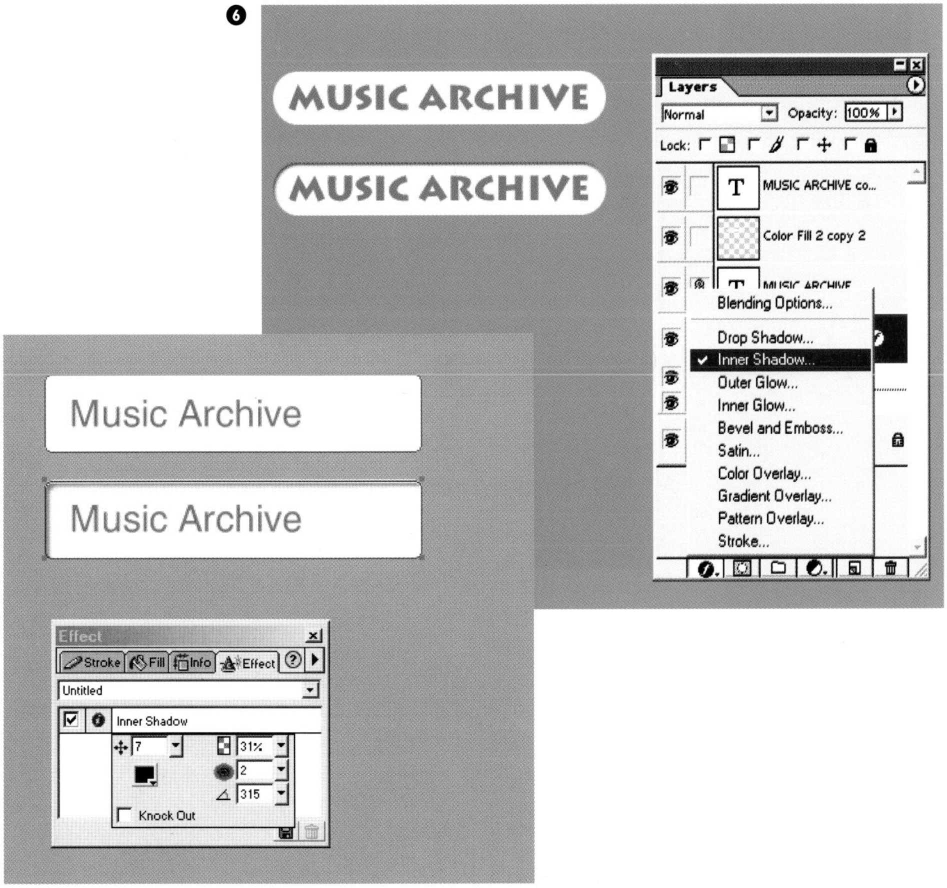

The basic button

1 The trick with buttons is to mark them out from the rest of your page. One of the easiest ways is to put labels for them in a box. Use your graphics package's *Rectangle*, *Marquee* or *Ellipse* tool, and apply a *Fill* or *Stroke* colour to work with your overall webpage.

2 3D effects are popular with buttons. You should find a *3D Bevel* option in your normal *Effects* palette or menu.

3 You'll have a variety of options for your bevel, such as whether to raise it or inset it, how deep the bevel is, the opacity of the highlights and shadows, and how soft the graduation is. Here we've used a shallow, raised effect with 90 per cent opacity and some blur.

4 This is almost exactly the same effect, but inverted and with a different fill colour. Inverted effects can be especially effective.

5 Drop shadows also help to lift buttons out of the page and have similar options to 3D bevels. It's always good to experiment with the settings, and not just use the standard shadow you see everywhere. The first of these has a very tight, opaque shadow with the colour changed to a dark blue. The second is a very soft, transparent shadow, at a greater distance.

6 You may also have an *Inner Shadow* effect, which is good for making buttons look 'punched through', and works well in white over a coloured background. Here you can see before and after examples.

Label-out buttons

The buttons shown are looking predictable. What else can be done to them?

❶ One technique is to put the label outside the part that looks like a button – although you still want the label to be clickable in the webpage. There are infinite ways you can develop the idea. Here, the button acts like a bullet point.

❷ You need to think about sizing and spacing to get this to look right. A good rule of thumb is to set the block to the same height as a letter H. If you make your rulers visible in your View or Window menu, you should be able to drag Guides from them, which will help you size and position elements.

❸ Make the spacing between the block and the start of the word about the same as a single space between words.

❹ Here we've just added a slight gradient to the *Fill* for the block, to make it look more refined, alongside the existing subtle drop shadow.

If you decide to use a circle, you can make it about the same size as a letter O, but set its middle to align with the middle of a letter H.

❺ It's also good to use triangles, arrows and other pointers, which will help create the idea that this graphic is going to take them somewhere. The easiest way to create a triangle is to type the letter U in Wingdings 3 font (free from www.microsoft.com), or Mac users should try an S in Zapf Dingbats, and spin it 90°.

❶

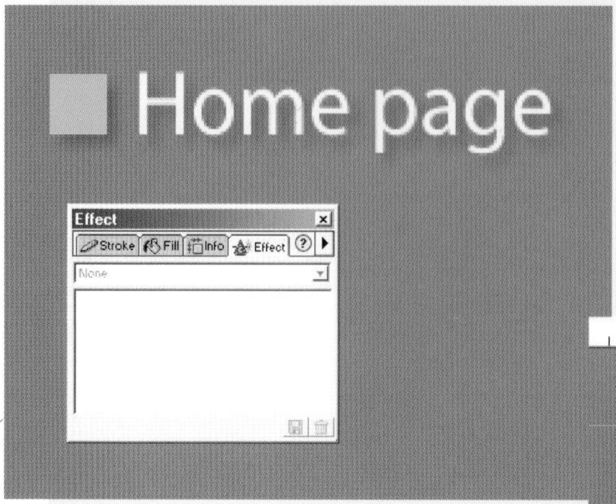

❷

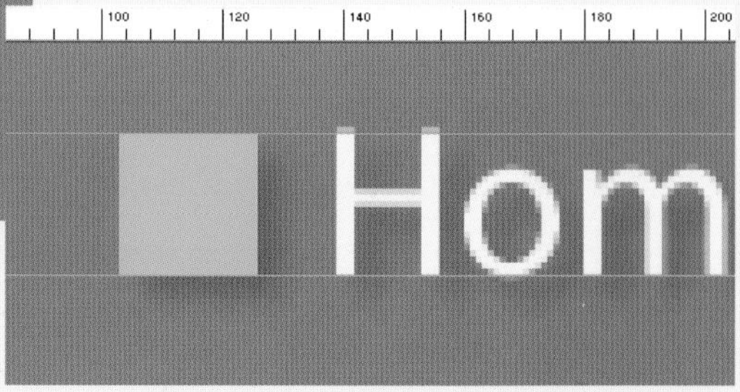

❸

❹

❺

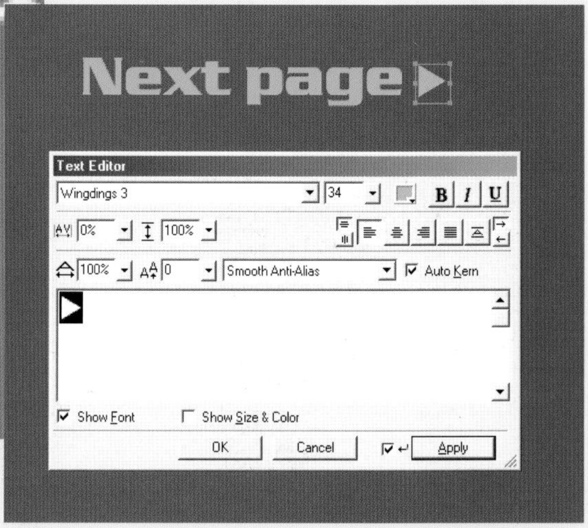

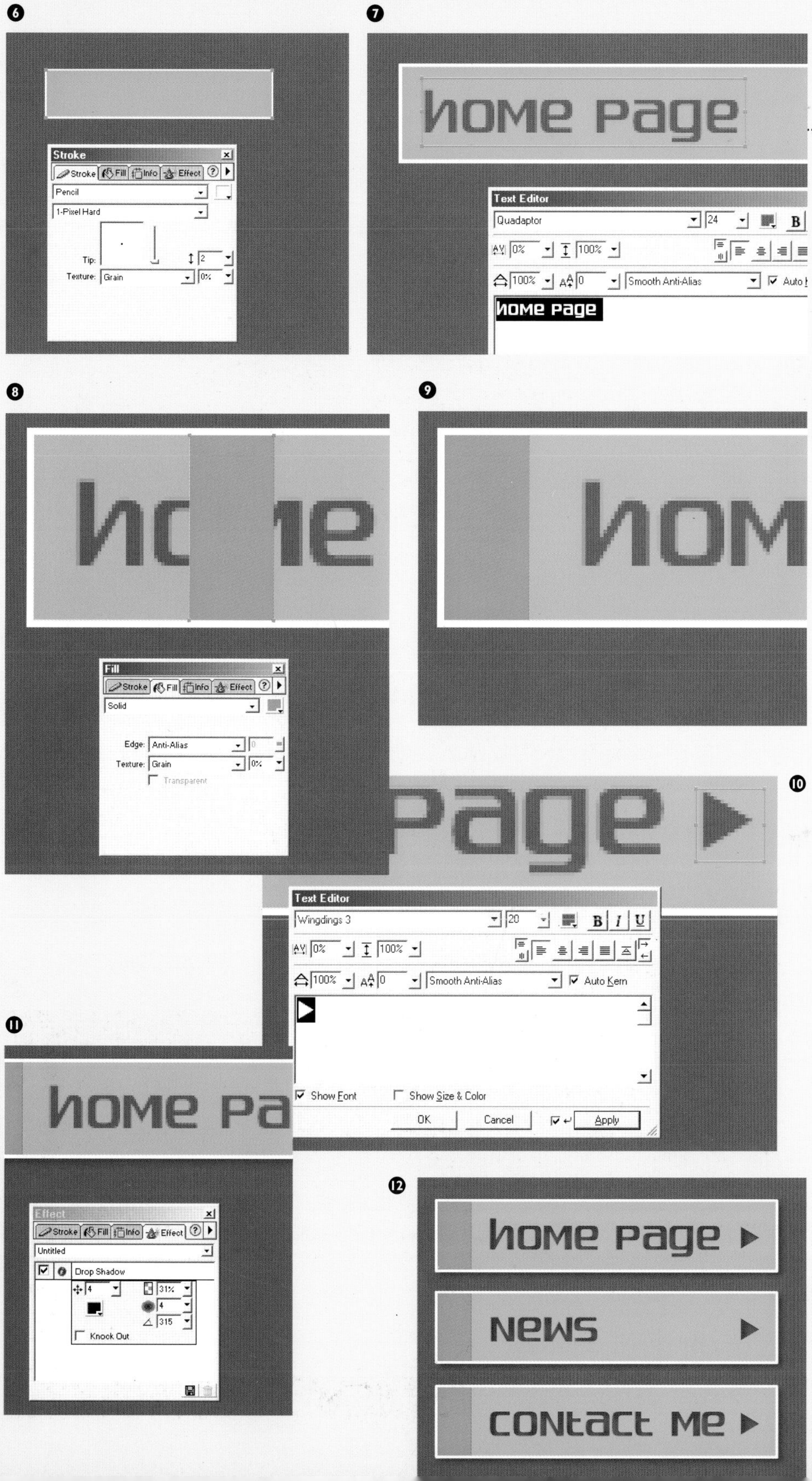

Combined techniques

6 It's good to experiment as much as you can, combining techniques together. For example, start with a deep, rich canvas colour like this (#056C90). Then draw a brighter rectangle on it with a two pixel white border.

7 Next, type in the text with a solid, chunky font. We've used Qadaptor, which you can get at many of the free sites (see page 60). Use your *Eyedropper* to give it the same colour as the background.

8 Now zoom in and (on a new layer if you're in a bitmap package) draw a rectangle that fits exactly into the height of the button box, but not over the white border and about half as wide as it is high. We've used the colour #FF0066 here.

9 Still zoomed in, move this rectangle over to the left edge of the box, and then select the text and use your arrow keys to nudge it to the right, until it's about a one-space width away from the rectangle.

10 Scroll so that you can see the end of the rectangle, and add a triangle pointer here. You want it to be a little smaller than the height of a letter x, and again about a space-width from the right end of the box.

11 Now zoom out and apply a simple, tight drop shadow to your main button box.

12 Finally, apply an inner shadow to the label and the triangle with similar settings. Now you have a simple but great button, which you can use throughout your site.

PROJECT 10

BRAINSTORMING AN OVERALL LOOK

The importance of giving your Web design an overall look has already been discussed. This will make sure all your buttons, graphics, colours and so on work in harmony. It will support and enhance the main topic and character of your site and will also ensure that it has a recognisable, distinct visual identity that people will remember.

This can all seem quite daunting to begin with. After all, there are so many different elements to design. And coping with the different software you need and getting it to do what you want can become so all-consuming that you barely have any mental or creative energy left to deal with what actually comes out at the end. However, it's not really that difficult, and you don't have to be a genius to create something impressive. In fact, with a few good techniques, the whole process becomes easy, and, better still, great fun.

Think of it as decorating a room to a particular theme, or working out an outfit for a costume party – these employ similar kinds of creative thinking. Or imagine you're devising a set for a play: the topic of your site and what you want to say are the script and the actors. What sort of backdrop do you need to make it all seem more real? After all, this is a lot of what design is about. Here are some essential techniques for helping you on your way...

❶

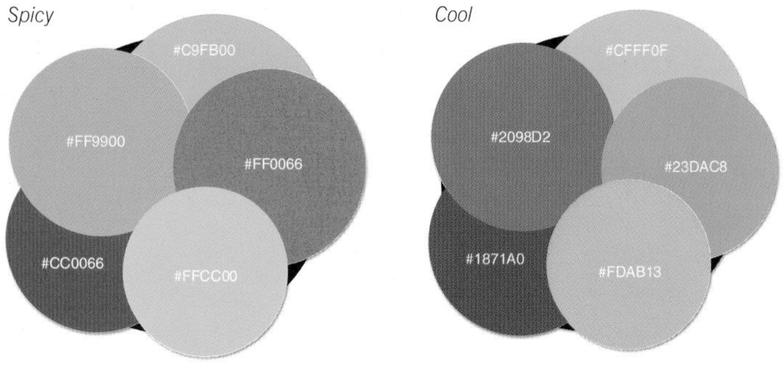

❷

❸

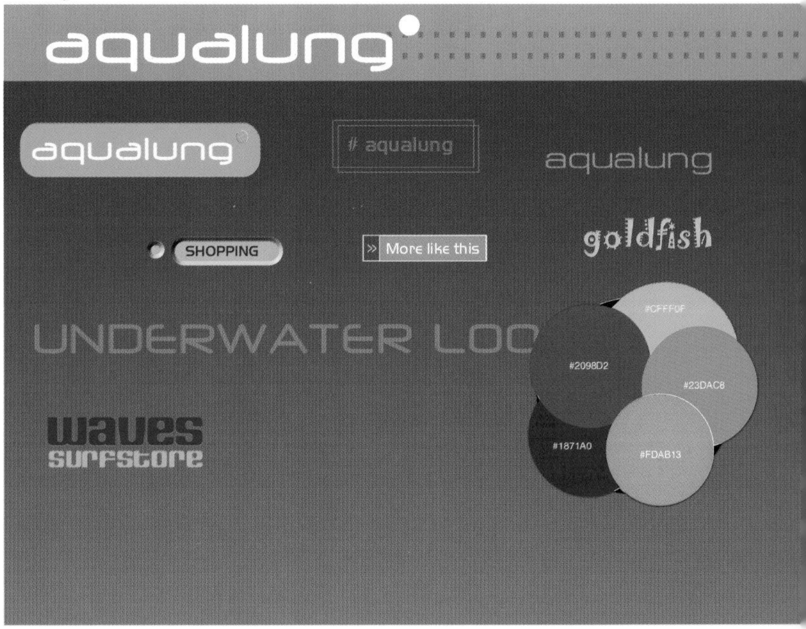

❹

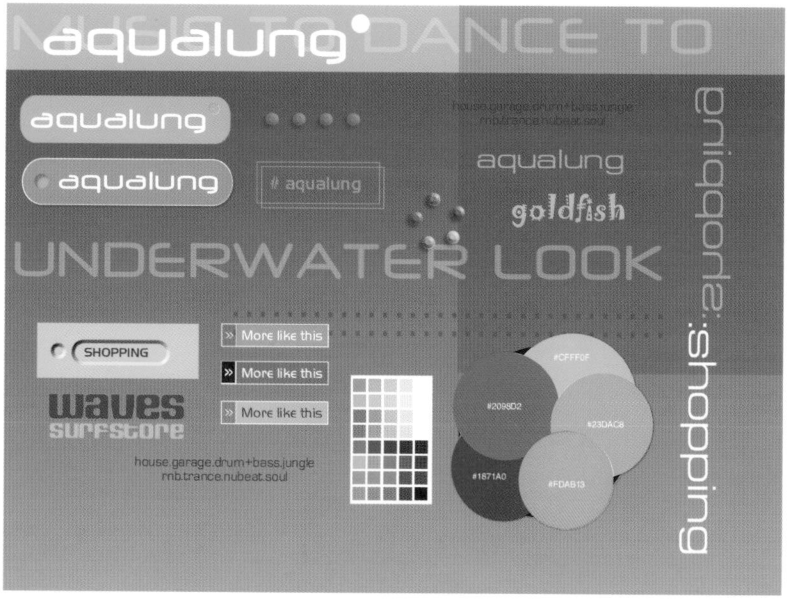

❺

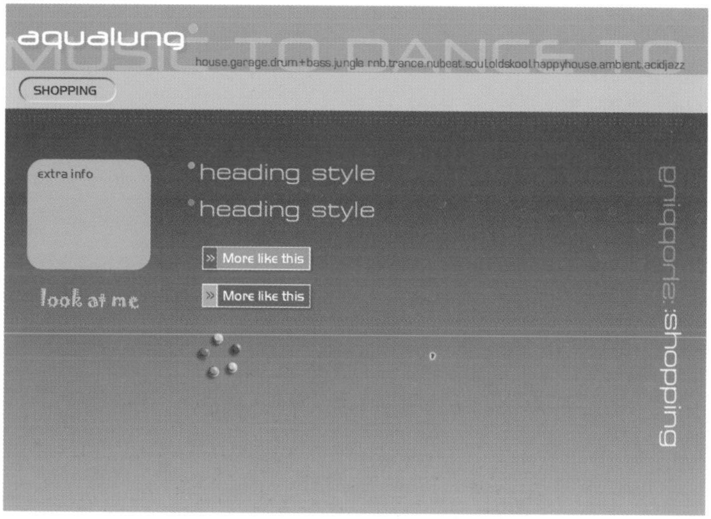

❻

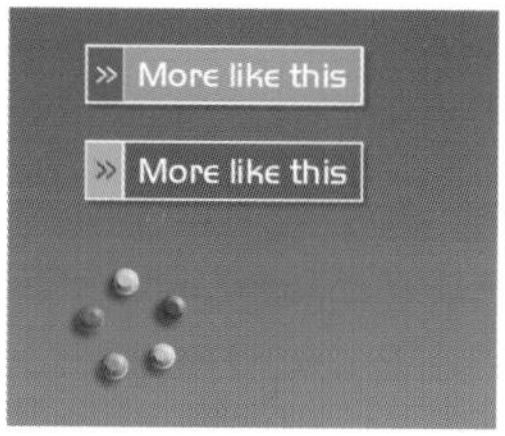

Leave your computer alone for a while, grab a pencil and a pad of paper, and sketch and write down anything that comes into your head to do with what your site is about. Be descriptive, connect things together and cross out things that you are not happy with…

❶❷ When you've honed your scribbles to a top 10, open your graphics application, create a new document as big as your screen, and draw four or five big overlapping circles on separate layers. Experiment with changing their colours until you've got a colour scheme.

❸ Search your font collection and the Internet for typefaces that match your brainstorm ideas, and use them to write big text words describing what your site is about on the same graphics page.

❹ Now experiment with heading and button styles. You're creating a sketchbook, but on a computer instead of on paper. By doing all this in the same document, you can see how your ideas work together.

❺ Use *Copy* + *Paste* a lot, to reuse similar graphics, just changing them slightly. Don't delete any ideas!

❻ Once you've got plenty of ideas, take a copy of the file, and start to slim them down to include just the very best. Leave yourself one or two heading styles, one or two buttons and so on. Move them around the page to create an overall shape, and you should begin to see your design coming together.

Add details to enhance your design, and you are ready to turn it into a proper webpage!

EXPORTING AND OPTIMIZING GRAPHICS

You've probably got a head full of ideas now. This is a good time to start placing the graphics you've designed into a proper webpage, so that you can see how it all looks and make any changes before you put in too much effort.

If you followed chapter 1, you'll know there are several things you need to do: first, take each individual graphic and crop it down to the smallest size possible. Then you need to save it in one of two main file formats – either GIF or JPEG – which are understood by Web browsers. You can't just put a Photoshop PSD or Paint Shop Pro PSP file into a webpage and expect it to work.

File size

There's also another step you need to take. You've probably noticed when you surf the Web that sometimes webpages take forever to download, especially if you're using a modem, and this is really frustrating. This is because all the different files – the HTML, graphics and anything else – have to download onto your computer. And the larger these files are, the longer they take to download.

To make sure your webpage downloads quickly, you need to compress, or optimize, your graphics, which literally means squashing their file size down as small as possible. This is an extremely important process and, fortunately, most graphics applications include *Optimize* or *Save For Web* features that help you to do this. Also, the GIF and JPEG file formats both include particularly good technology for reducing graphics file sizes, although this often results in a loss in the overall quality.

❶

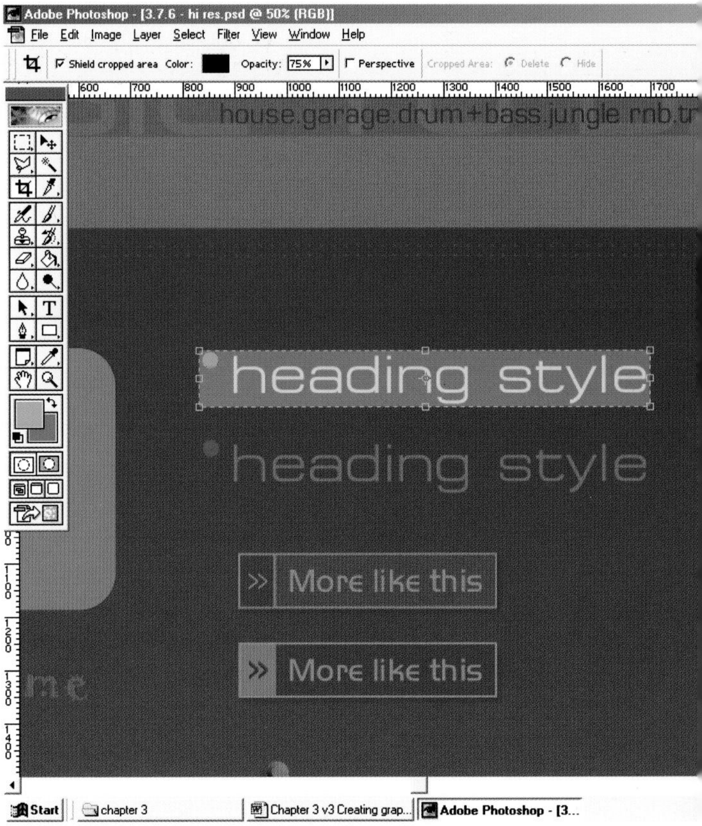

❷

❸

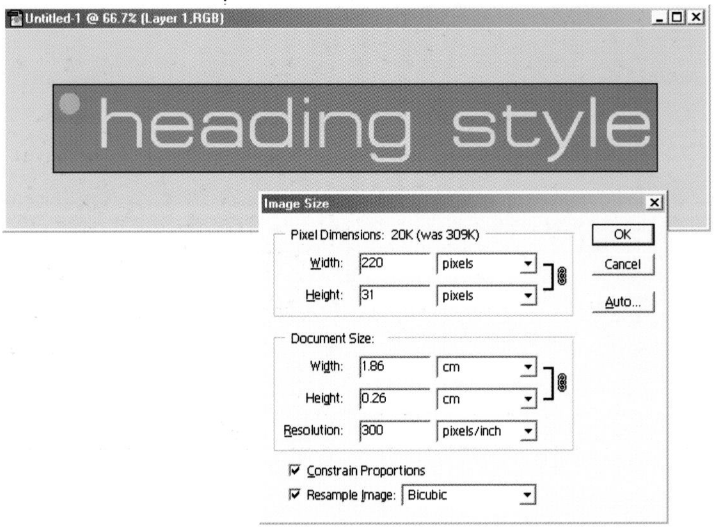

4

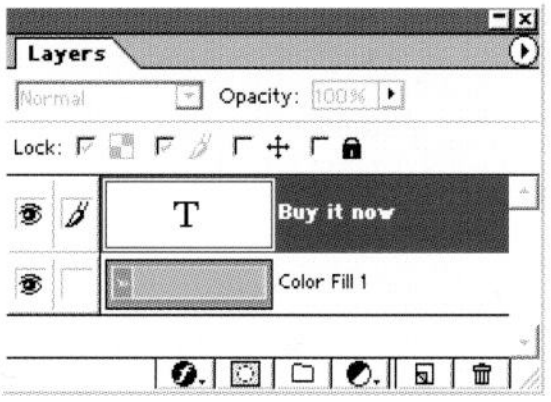

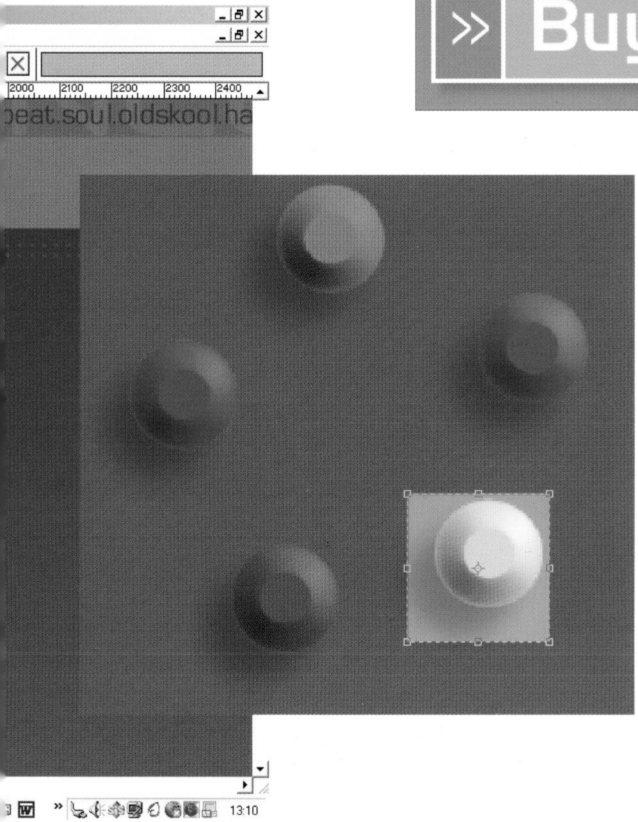

5

6

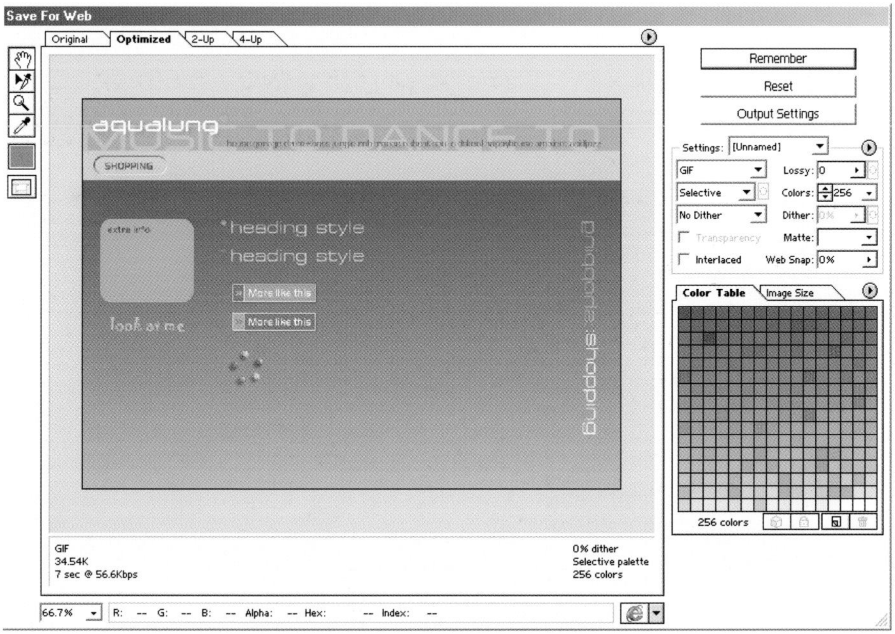

Adding graphics

❶ When you're ready to start adding your new graphics to a webpage, you need to save each one as an individual file. Take a copy of your design, then open the copy and use your *Crop* tool to isolate it from the others in your sketchbook.

❷ If this causes it to run very slowly on your computer, you can select individual graphics, then copy and paste each one into a new document, and crop that way. If you're using a bitmap package like Photoshop, you'll need to flatten your layers first, using the *Flatten* command in the *Layers* menu.

❸ Don't forget to resize your graphic to the exact size you want it to appear!

❹ For buttons and headings, you probably just need one file for each style you've created. Use it and just change the text as and when you need to.

❺ Smaller graphics have smaller file sizes, so they download faster. Use small graphics effectively whenever you can. Crop them as close as you can around the edges. You might be tempted to create your whole page as a single graphic, so that you don't have to do much in your authoring application. You can do this, but it creates a slow download. Do it only if you can't recreate the same look in HTML.

❻ Finally, you need to use your graphics software's *Save For Web*, *Optimize* and *Export* features to compress each graphic, and save it in your website folder. Refer over the page to see how this is done in your own software.

Optimizing in Photoshop

❶ Photoshop is still the world's most popular graphics software among Web designers and, although originally created for print designers, recent versions include an excellent and easy-to-use *Save For Web* feature, which you will find located in the *File* menu.

❷ It features one or more *Preview* windows, where you can see how the graphic will look after compression. This is because optimizing graphics generally changes their appearance or quality. However, you can usually get away with a lot of optimization before this becomes really noticeable.

At the top are tabs where you can choose how many previews you want, in order to compare different settings.

On the right is the important bit: settings for the file format you want to use, as well as how much compression you want to use and how you want it to work. We'll look at what all these settings do in detail in the next section (see page 88).

Also important, at the bottom of each preview you can choose the file size of the compressed graphic. You should try to get this as small as possible.

And finally, you have a *Save* button – save your compressed graphic into your website folder. (But don't forget to keep a copy of the uncompressed original too, just in case you need to change it later).

❶

❷

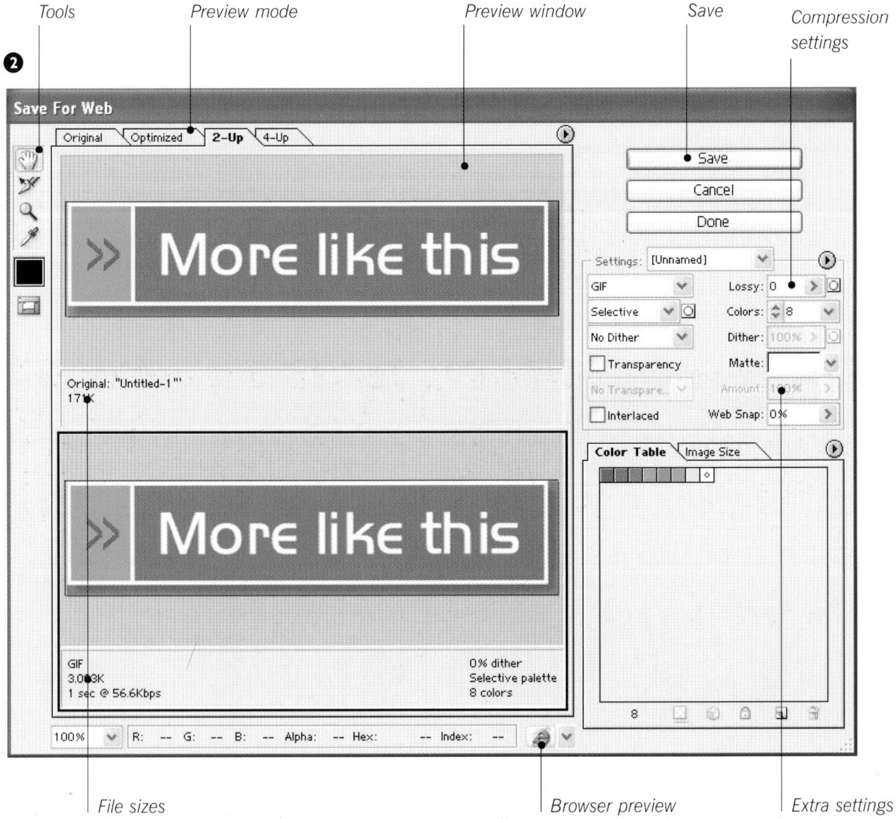

❶
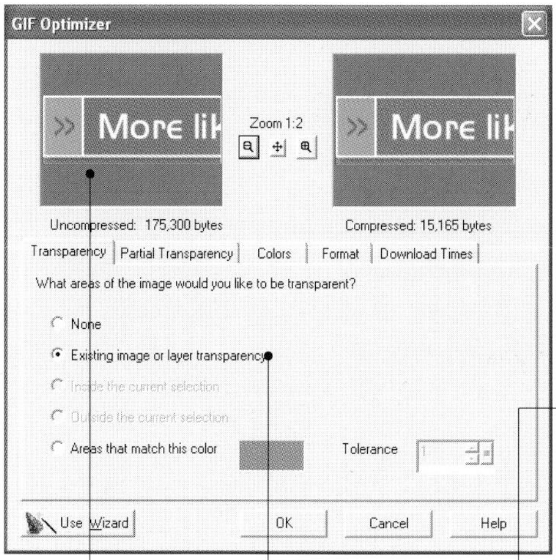

❷
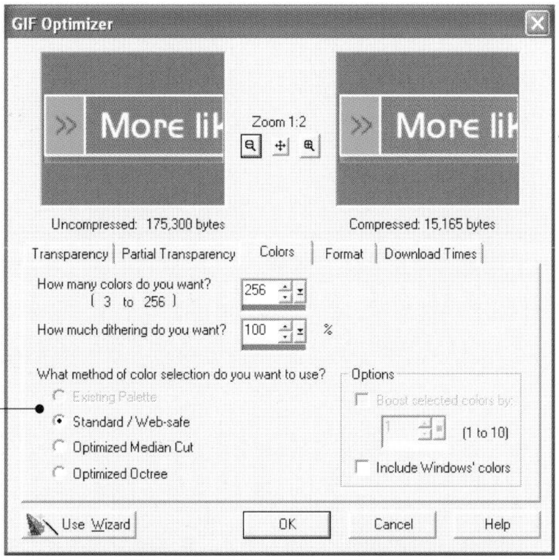

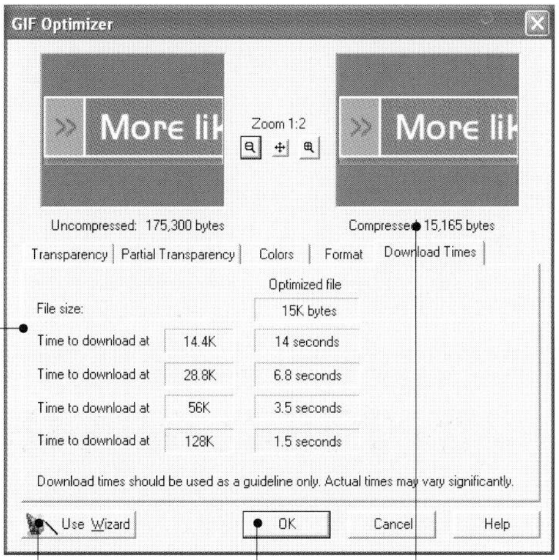

❸

❹
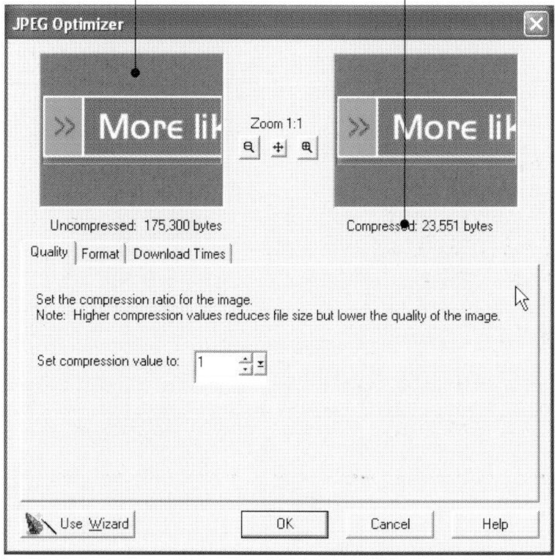

❺
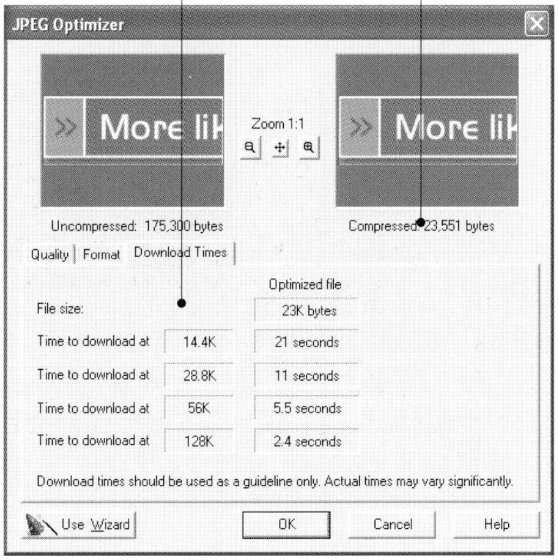

Optimizing in Paint Shop Pro

❶ Paint Shop Pro also includes useful features for optimizing Web graphics, via the *File > Export* menu. You have to choose which format you want first, but in the next section we'll show you the differences so you can quickly make a choice (see page 88).

❷ Paint Shop Pro's GIF *Optimizer* offers before-and-after previews, and under these, tabs for different settings.

❸ This opens to the *Transparency* section, which you can use to make areas of your GIF file see-through.

More important is the *Colors* section, where your main compression settings are, and one or two items in the *Format* section.

A handy *Download Times* section helps you work out if you've reduced the file size enough. It also gives an indication of the file size.

❹ The *JPEG Optimizer* is very similar, but includes no *Transparency* tab because the JPEG format doesn't support transparency. Instead you should begin at the *Quality* tab, which is the main compression setting, alongside *Format*.

❺ Again you have a useful *Download Times* tab, together with before-and-after file sizes, under the *Preview* windows.

Both *Optimizers* also have a *Wizard* (automatic help) that you can use if you're stuck. However, you'll almost always get much better results if you use the main dialogs.

Optimizing in Fireworks

❶ Fireworks has some of the best compression features of any graphics software, and they're easy to use too. In this case, you can do the preparation in your main window, using the *Optimize* floating palette.

❷ You use a series of tabs along the top of your normal workspace to flick into a *Preview* mode, which includes two- and four-up options for comparing different compression settings against your original. You can also easily flick back to the main mode to make any last-minute changes.

At the top, next to these tabs (or below the preview in two- and four-up modes) you can see the file size for the compressed graphic, together with an estimate of how long it will take to download, depending on your user's connection speed.

All your compression settings are in the *Optimize* palette, which includes a *Settings* menu where you can quickly choose from the most common compression settings. It offers a large variety of file formats, not just GIF or JPEG. For instance, there is WBMP, which you would use for a WAP site, to enable people to look at material via Web-enabled cell phones.

To save your compressed graphic, choose *Export* from the *File* menu, or click the *Export* button in your toolbar.

Fireworks also includes a sophisticated *Export Wizard* in the *File* menu if you need help.

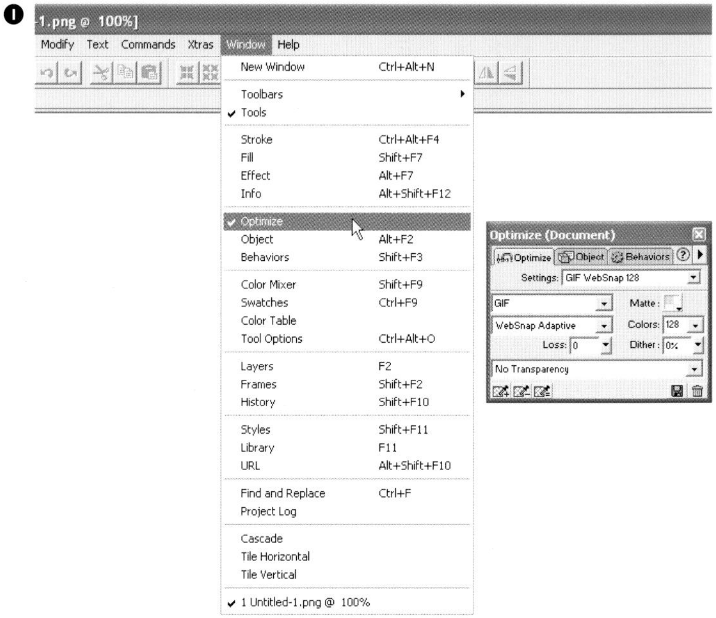

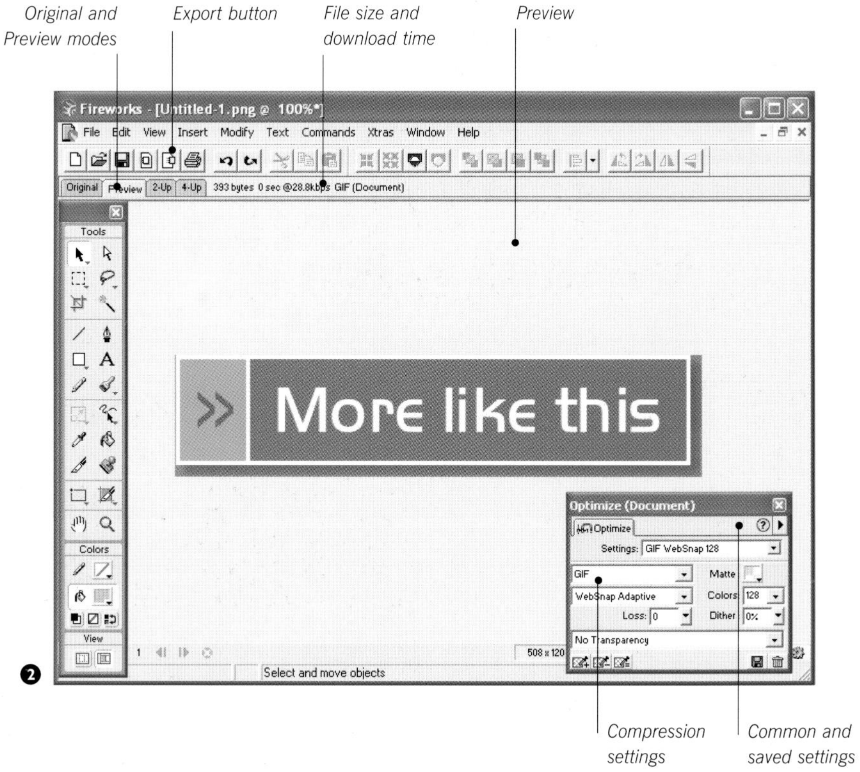

1

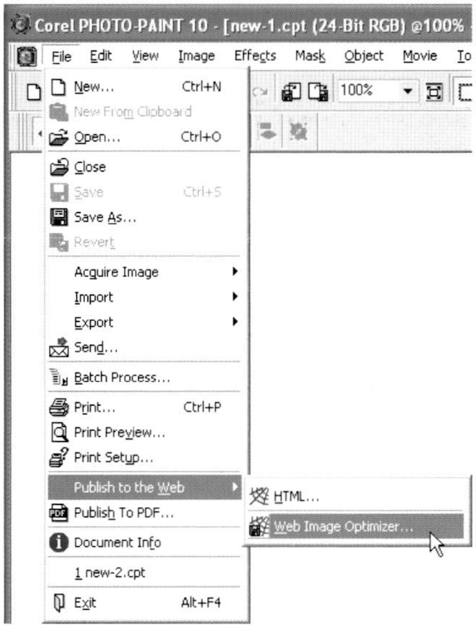

2

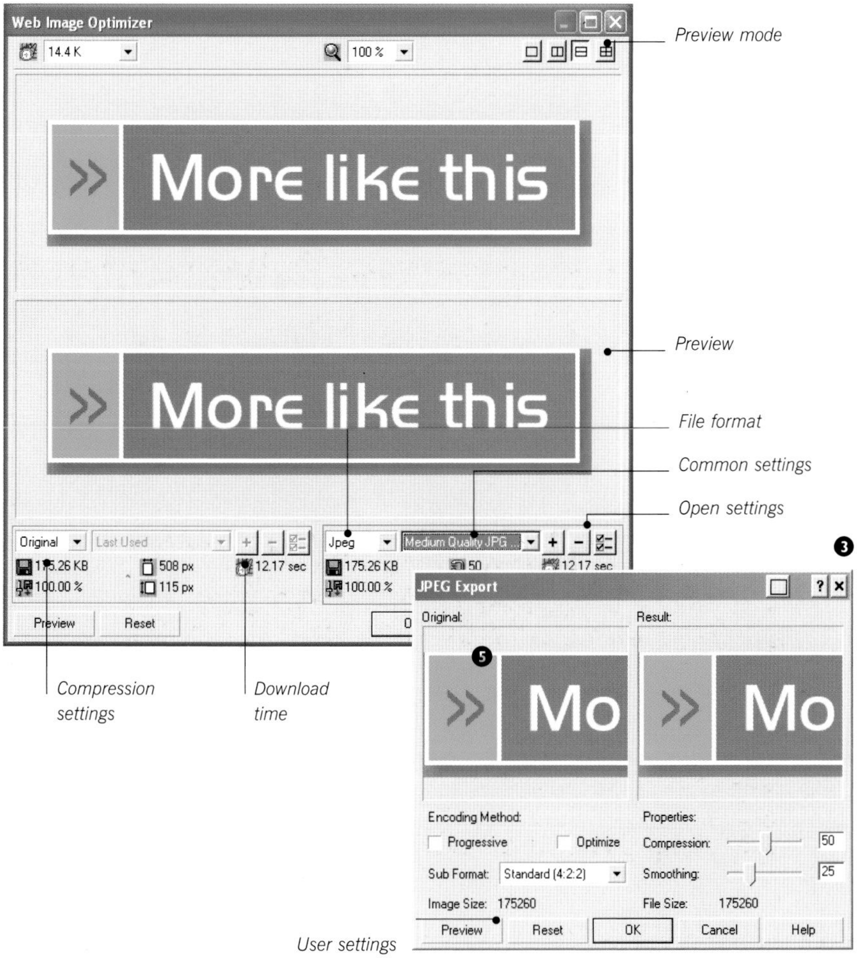

Optimizing in Photo-Paint

1 Corel Photo-Paint includes a *Web Image Optimizer*, very similar to that in Photoshop and Fireworks. You access it via the *File* > ***Publish to the Web*** menu…

2 Here, you have a selection of *Preview* modes, including two-up horizontal or vertical, and four-up, for comparing different settings. You choose your mode using the icons at the top right of the dialog.

In boxes below the previews, you choose your file format, and next to this you have a menu of the most common settings for that format…

Below these menus you also have an indication of the final file size of your compressed graphic, and an estimated download time based on the connection speed you choose in the dropdown menu at the top of the window. The most important speed to look at is 56K, since this is by far the most common of the modem speeds. And if your graphic is fine on 56K, then it will be great for ISDN, ADSL and other fast connections.

3 To manually select your own compression settings, you need to click the far right icon in the box, which opens a dialog depending on the format you've chosen. These look rather complicated, but in essence they're the same as the options in the other packages, and we'll look at exactly what they all do in the next two sections. (See pages 88–91.)

Finally, hit the *OK* button to save your compressed graphic.

GIF AND JPEG

When you compress an image for the Web, it usually (although not always) means a loss in quality, depending on how much compression you apply. For example, the edges become less sharp, or you get 'blocky' colour areas. But for the most part the reduced file size and the benefits this brings – allowing your webpage to download much more quickly – far outweigh the loss in quality. Just ask your visitors!

But exactly how this compression works, how badly it affects the image and how many kilobytes you can trim off all depends on the format you choose (GIF or JPEG) and the image itself. To get the best overall quality along with a manageable file size, you need to use the right compression format for the right image. And it really does make a huge difference.

So how do you know which one to use? In all the applications covered in the previous section (apart from Paint Shop Pro), you can preview and compare GIF- and JPEG-compressed images side-by-side before you choose which format to use. This means that working out which you prefer is simply a matter of trial and error as well as personal taste.

It is helpful to know how the formats work since you'll usually be able to tell instantly, without needing to experiment, what format you want to use for a particular image. Because both GIF and JPEG formats offer a variety of options, this will help you get much better results overall in choosing not just which format to use, but how much and what type of compression to apply.

❶

❷

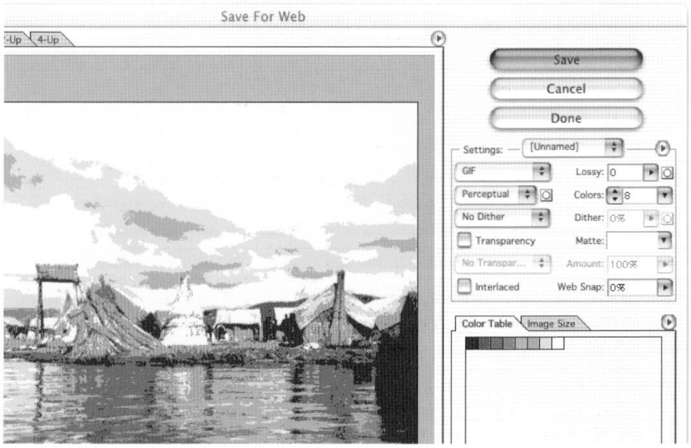

❸

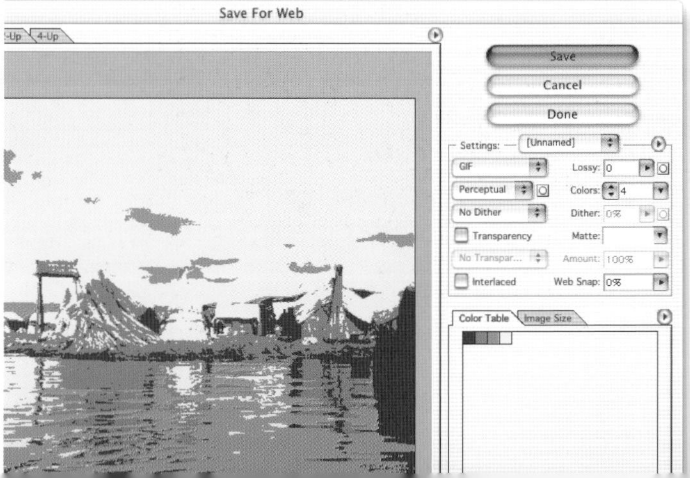

4

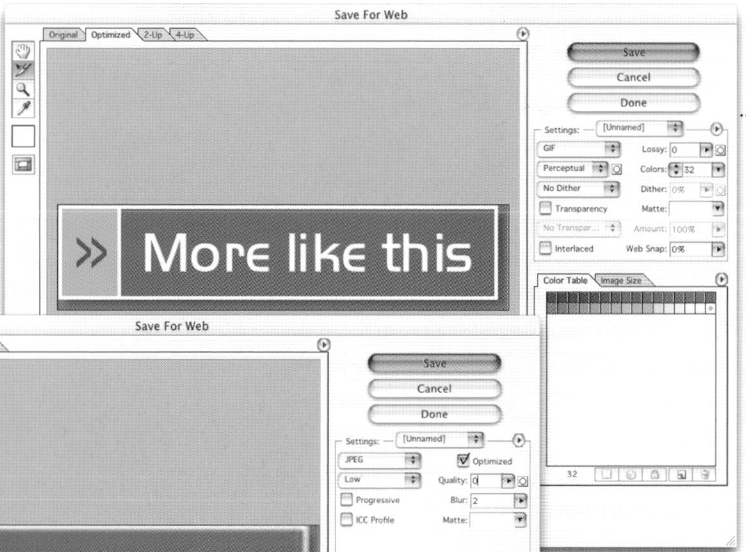

5

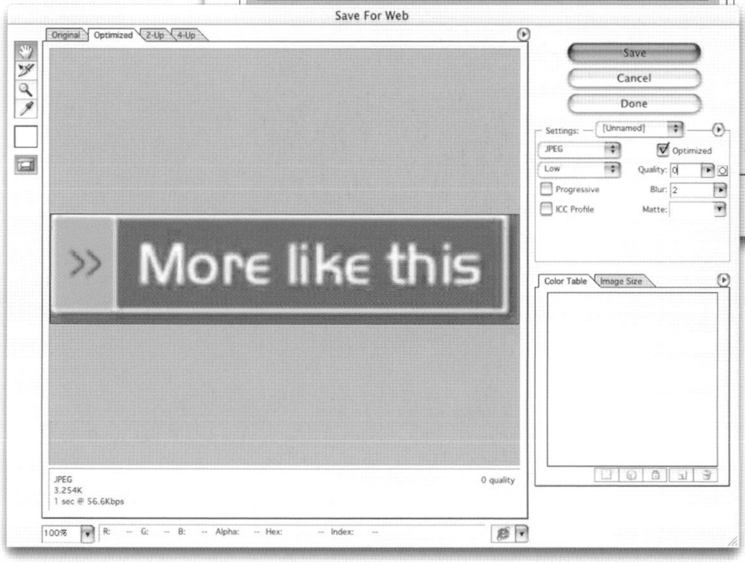

6

GIF or JPEG?

❶ More than anything else, the GIF format saves on file size by reducing the number of colours in an image. The easiest way to see how is by using an extreme setting. Open a colour photo and, using your GIF options, set the number of colours to just eight…

❷❸ You should see the effect instantly – your image flattens out. Now reduce the number to four, and finally two. In this image, the original file was 540K, and it has been compressed to 16K, 10K and 5K respectively: a huge saving.

❹ The trouble is, unless you particularly want this effect, it pretty much ruins your photos. But the technique is ideal for flat graphics that have only a few colours, like those you've been creating. Here we used 32 colours, and reduced the image from 171K to just 4K.

❺ A JPEG, on the other hand, always contains 16.7 million colours. It trims off the fat by getting 'sloppy' about detail. It blurs edges, muddies colours and creates 'artefacts' – blocky visual aberrations.

❻ This looks awful in flat-colour images, where crispness is essential. But it works well with photos where you want to keep the full range of colours, since the muddying just blends in with the natural noise. This image has been compressed from 520K to just 16K.

It also works with images including gradients, where the blurring becomes hardly noticeable.

Compressing GIFs

So a GIF works by reducing the number of colours, but what are all those other settings? Whatever your interface looks like, it should have all, or most of these options.

❶ The most important, initially, is the number of colours…

❷ …and second, is dithering. This is a process by which you can create the appearance of a colour that isn't there by combining tiny dots of colours that are. This makes your GIF look less blocky, but it also massively increases the file size.

❸ *Transparency*, which is only available in the GIF format, allows you to have some completely see-through pixels. But you can't have partially transparent areas, so you need to say which colour should be mixed in instead – and this is called the *Transparency Matte*.

❹ The colour conversion settings control what type of process is used to work out which colours should be used in the image in the reduction process – and whether they should be 'Web-safe'. This is an old term that relates to when many people had only 256 colours on their monitors, and the PC and Mac had only 216 of these in common, so it is often called the Web 216 palette. This is less of an issue today since most people have 16.7-million colour monitors.

❺ *Web Snap* refers to the same process, where colours similar to Web-safe colours are substituted for the safe version.

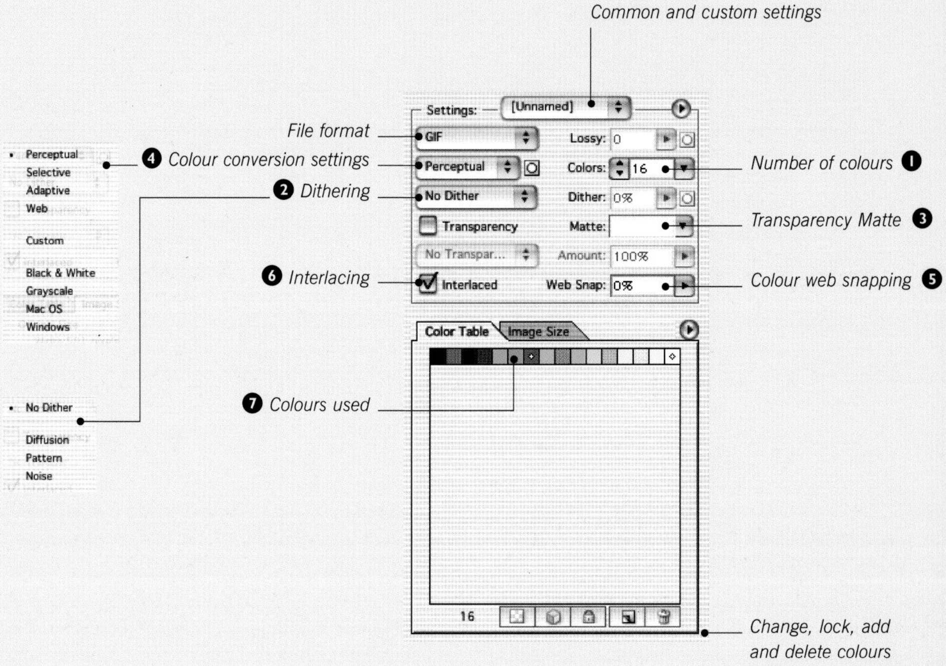

❻ The *Interlaced* check box controls whether your GIF downloads completely before displaying, or displays in low-resolution first, and then increases the details.

❼ The *Color Table* gives a preview of which colours are being used in your GIF, and you can edit and change these according to taste.

Compressing JPEGs

JPEGs are much simpler than GIFs because they have fewer settings, although it can be harder to get an attractive result in return for a small file size with this format. Your main setting is the quality (or compression) option, which draws a straightforward trade-off between file size and quality. In most applications, the higher this figure, the bigger the file (and better the appearance). As a guideline, use between 30–50 in Photoshop, 40–75 in Fireworks, 10–50 in PSP and 10–60 in Photo-Paint.

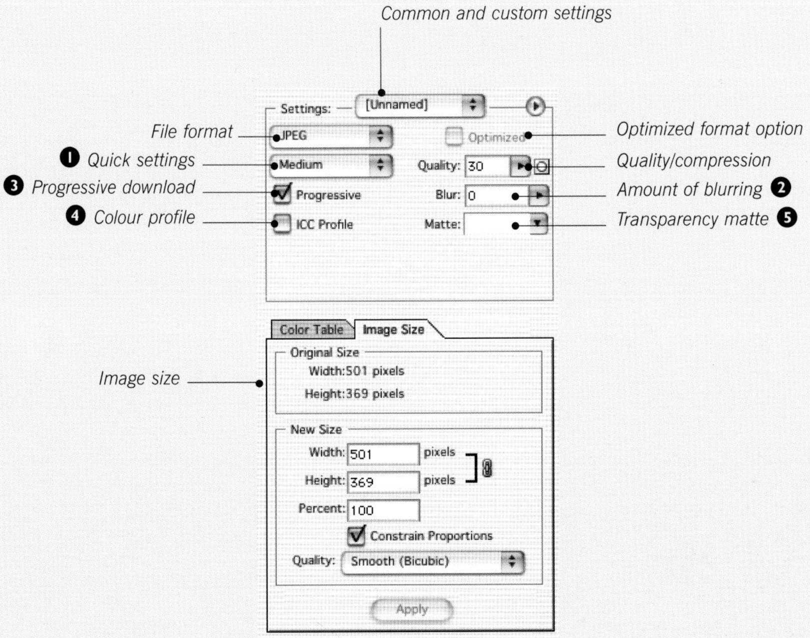

❶ Most applications offer a menu of quick settings, such as *High*, *Medium* and *Low*, which you can use as a guideline.

❷ The *Blur* setting, sometimes called *Smoothing*, blurs the image, which usually helps to reduce the file size. This is very useful if you don't need the image to be sharp. It should be used with care on ordinary images, however.

❸ *Progressive* download for a JPEG is similar to interlacing in a GIF file. Select this if you would like your image to appear as it downloads. Or, leave it off if you'd prefer the whole image to load before it appears.

❹ Some applications allow you to include an ICC profile in a JPEG. This provides extra information that describes exactly how the colour should appear. This is not usually necessary for Web work, however, because you're never quite sure about your viewer's monitor settings anyway.

❺ You can't have transparency in a JPEG. However, most applications give you a *Matte* setting, where you select the colour that appears instead if you have any transparent areas in the original image.

PROJECT 11
A COMPLETE WEBPAGE

You will have created a lot of graphics by now, and looked at a huge range of styles and techniques that you can use to create impressive designs with a minimum of fuss and bother. Hopefully, you've got more ideas than you know what to do with. Maybe you feel a bit frustrated that you can't get them out quickly enough, or to look the way you want. Don't worry, it will all come with practice.

It's important at this stage not to go wild, because you've still got to turn your designs into a proper webpage. This can be tricky because getting things to look the way you imagined them in HTML is not always easy. If you master the right techniques, though, and bear in mind as you design what you can and cannot do with your Web authoring package, then you'll find it much easier. And as you go through this book, you'll pick up more techniques to put you, rather than the software, in control of the final result.

You're now going to use the underwater-style design you created earlier, to speed things up a bit, with a just few tweaks here and there. (You'll find you always want to tweak your designs, especially when you take a fresh look at them a few days later – although at some point you do have to stop!) You will individually export and optimize the graphics, then prepare a template webpage including these graphics, which you could use for an entire site.

1

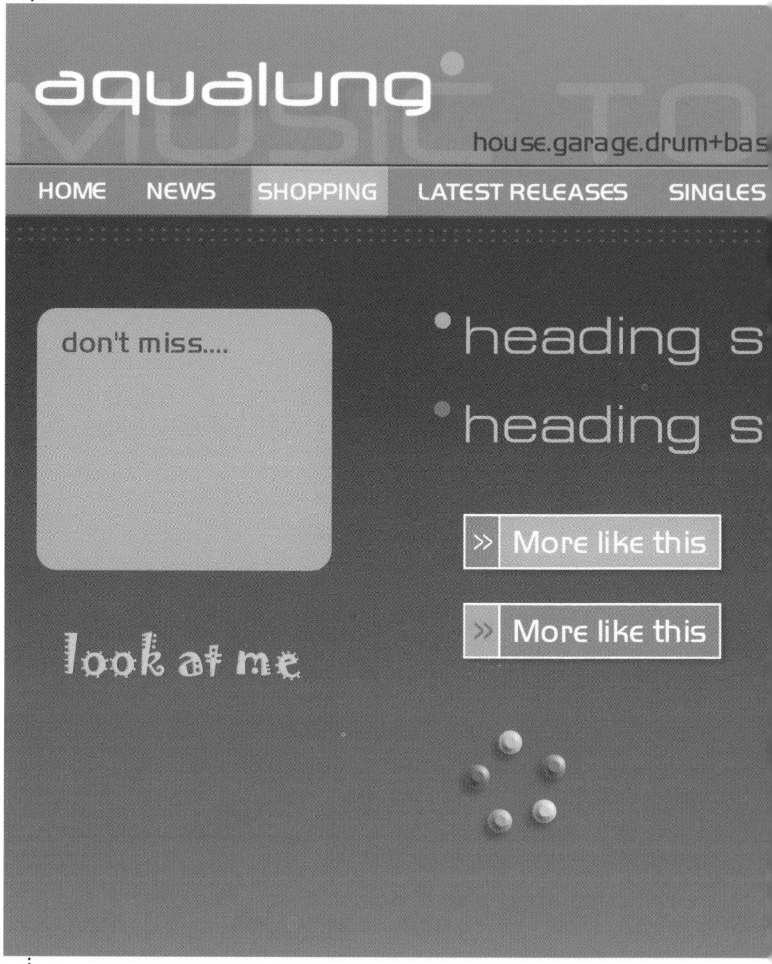

2

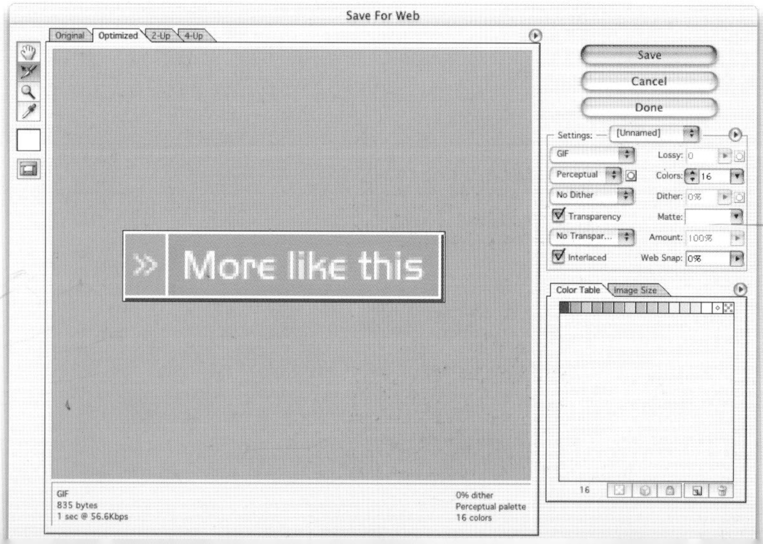

3

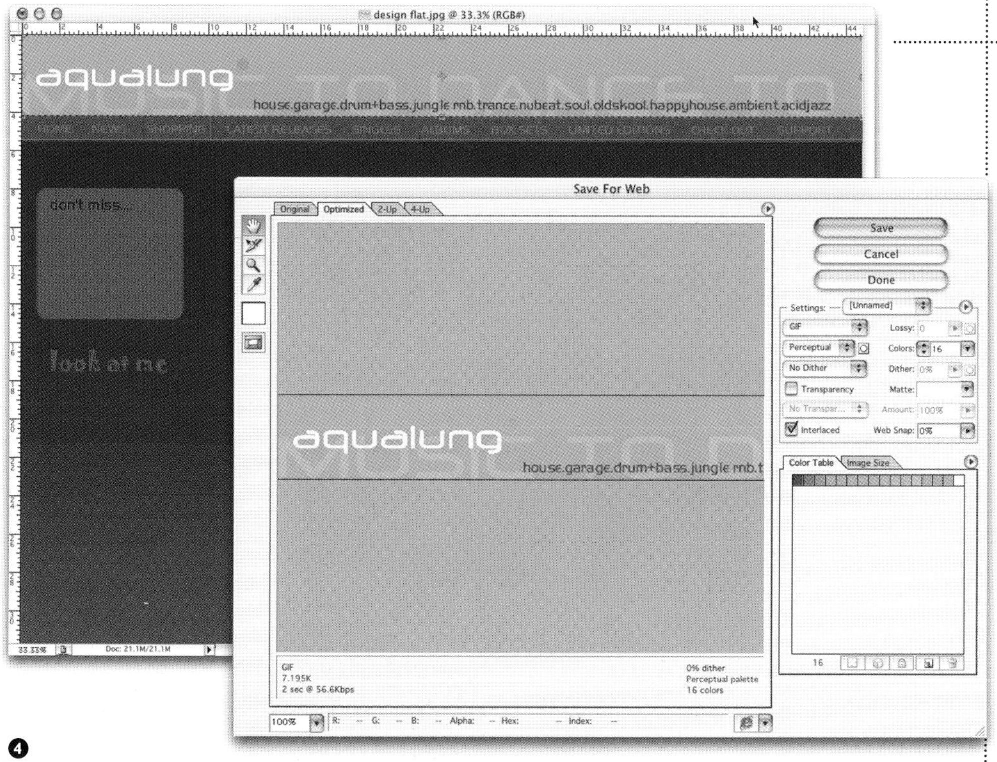

4

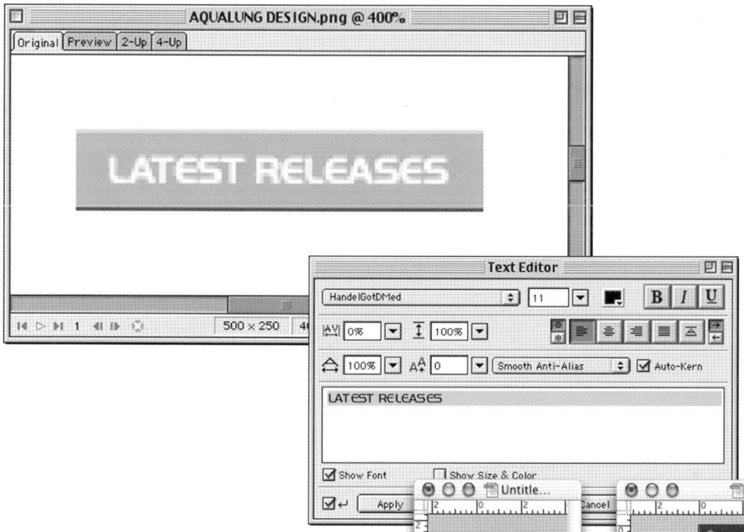

5

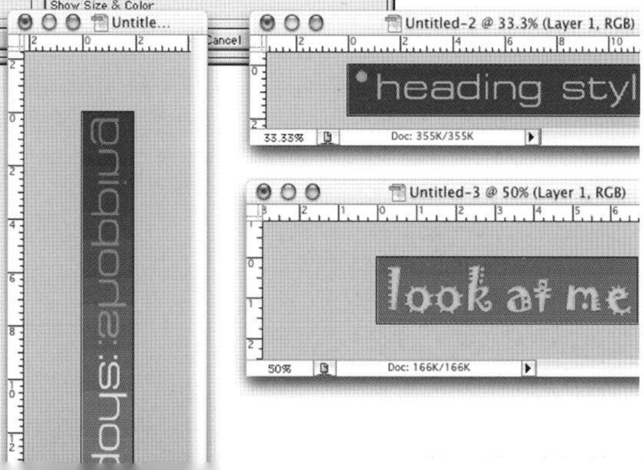

Preparing the graphics

❶ Here's the design you're going to use, which you created in Project 10, with just a few changes. All the techniques that you will use have been covered in this chapter.

❷ The easiest place to begin is with the buttons. It's a good idea to copy these into a separate file, so that you can just open it and change the text for whatever button you need. This is exported as a 16-colour GIF, which comes out under 1K. Don't forget to save this in your website folder.

❸ Next, work on the heading area, saving it as one big graphic. You can either copy this section in a new file, or save the whole document as a new file and crop it to the exact area. It may look as though it's going to be a huge file, but because there are just a few flat colours it will be fine as a 5K, 16-colour GIF.

❹ Next save the links across the top. Aim to save these in a file where you can easily update the text. But remember to keep the overall design tidy because you'll want to have exactly the same space on either side of the text – five to ten pixels is good. So that you've got enough width for the background, you should make the file as wide as your longest link, then you can crop it for the smaller ones. You'll also need a thin, blank one to go in the gaps.

❺ Finally, copy, crop, save and export your other graphical elements in the same way, all into the folder where you're going to create the webpage…

Creating the webpage

6 Use your Web authoring software to create a new document and save it in the same folder as your graphics. Set a page title, background colour (we've gone for black here) and so on, and set all the page margins to two.

7 The design suggests that you need four main rows: one for the header across the top, one for the links or navigation, one for the space directly below this, and one for the main content area. So add a table with four rows, and set its width to the width of your page. In this example, 760 pixels have been used.

8 Add your heading file in the top row – the size should match – and set the background colour of the whole table to the colour you want your page to be.

9 In the next row, add another table, this time with one row, as many columns as you want links in your navigation, and 100 per cent width. Keeping the new table selected, find the setting for its background image, and navigate to your blank button.

10 Like textures, background images in Web tables always tile, repeating themselves across and down throughout the table.

This means that now, when you add a link graphic in each of the cells of this table, you don't see empty spaces between them. To get the spacing right, set the horizontal align of the cells to *Center*.

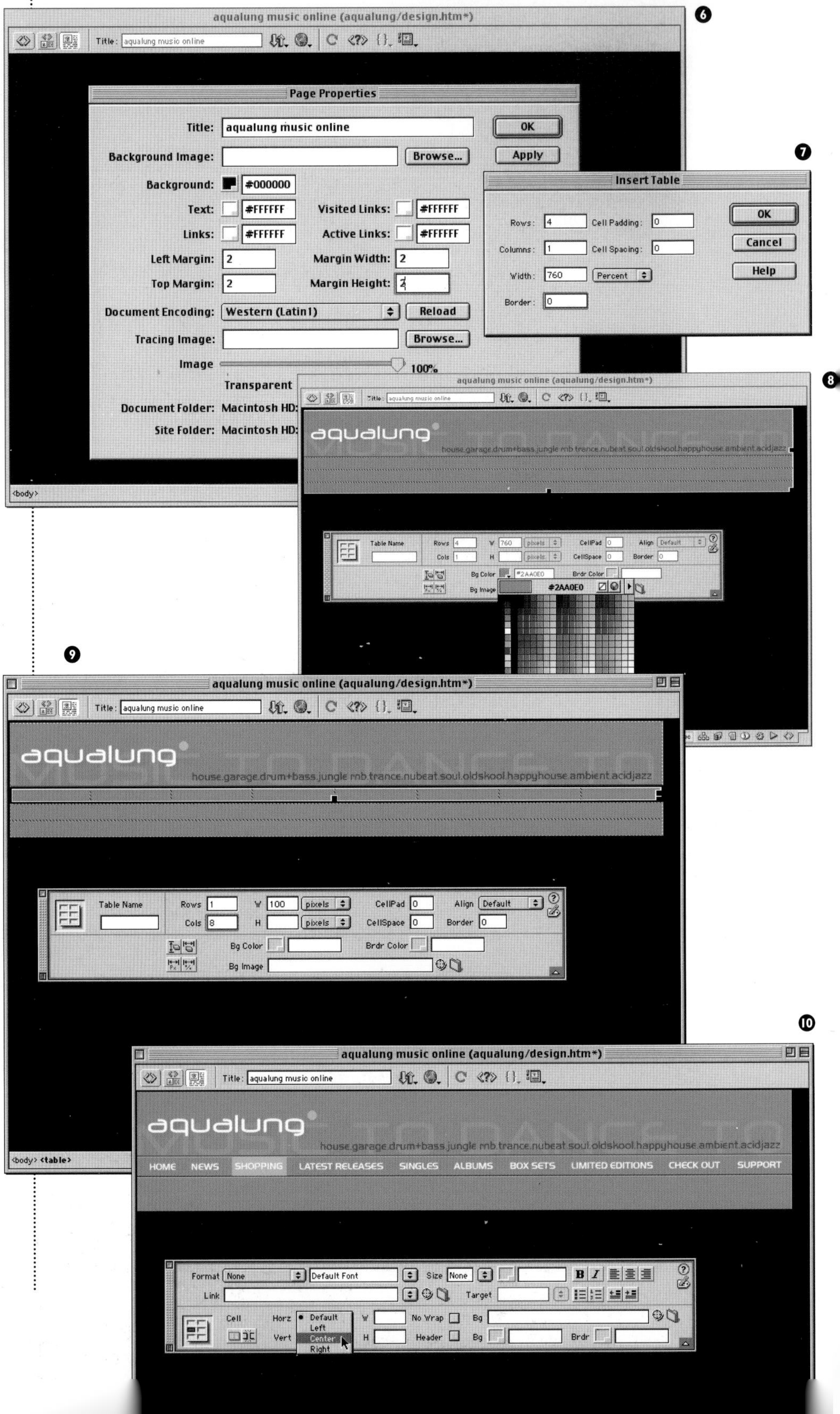

⓫

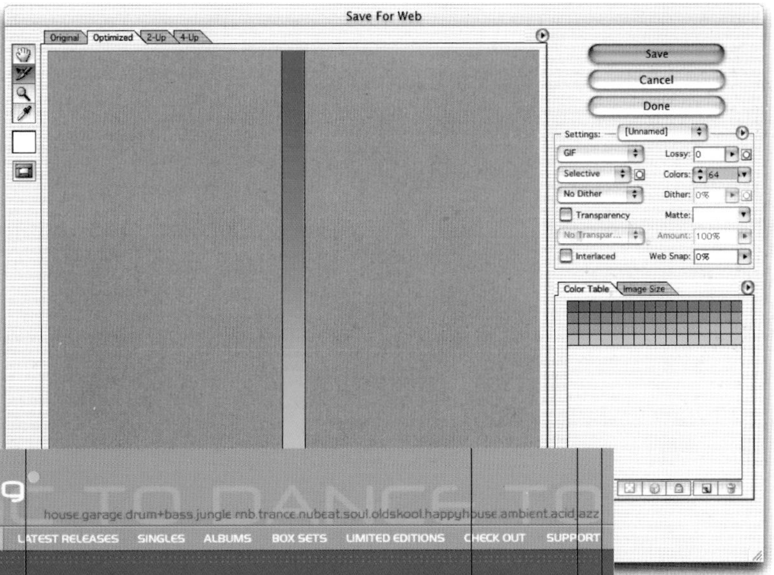

⓬

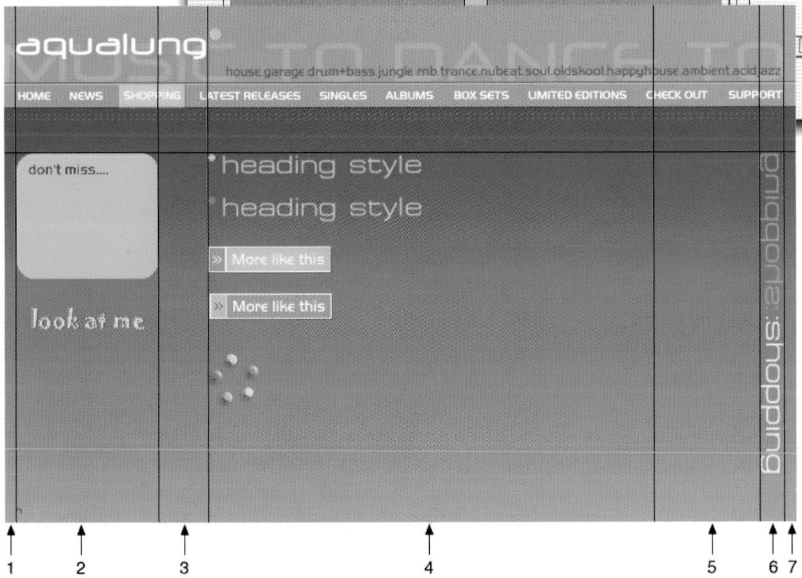

⓭

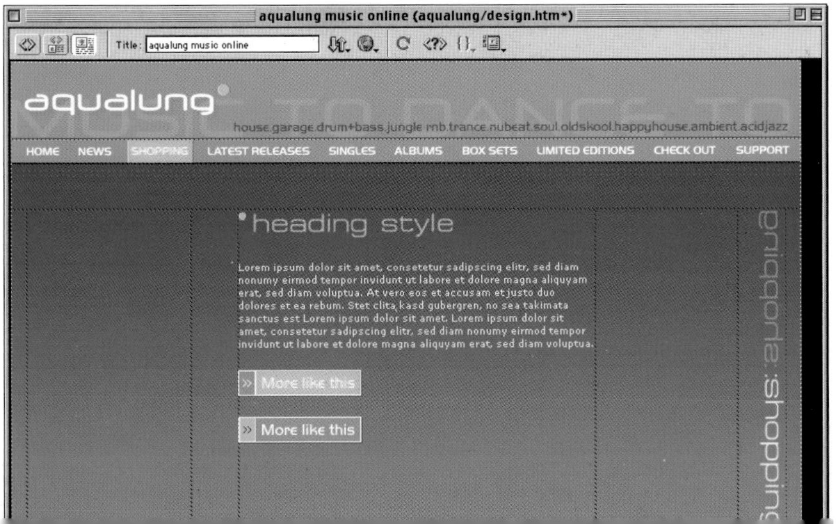

⓫ Set the height of the next row to create the space before the main content – about 40 pixels is good here. You can also put a background image in a single cell, and here we've added a subtle, dotted graphic as a background. The tiling effect saves on the file size.

To create the soft gradient effect for the main background area, use another, very long, thin tiling background graphic cut out from the main design. This is the background for the bottom row of the webpage.

⓬ In this cell, you need to add another table with seven columns and 100 per cent width (to fill the whole containing cell), as you can see from the diagram. Use your software to roughly set out the column widths, and set the vertical alignment to *Top*.

⓭ Add all the remaining elements to your page except the green box on the left. Add in some dummy text too, and make sure you set its size, colour and font.

To add the box in, first export the heading part as a complete image, and then add the curved footer to it.

Next, create a simple three-row, one-column table with the same background colour and width as your graphics. Then add the graphics into the top and bottom rows.

Finally, add yet another table in the middle row of the box, this time 1 x 1, 100 per cent wide and with a 10-pixel cell spacing, to create a margin. Paste some dummy text in here.

Check your page in a browser and tweak accordingly.

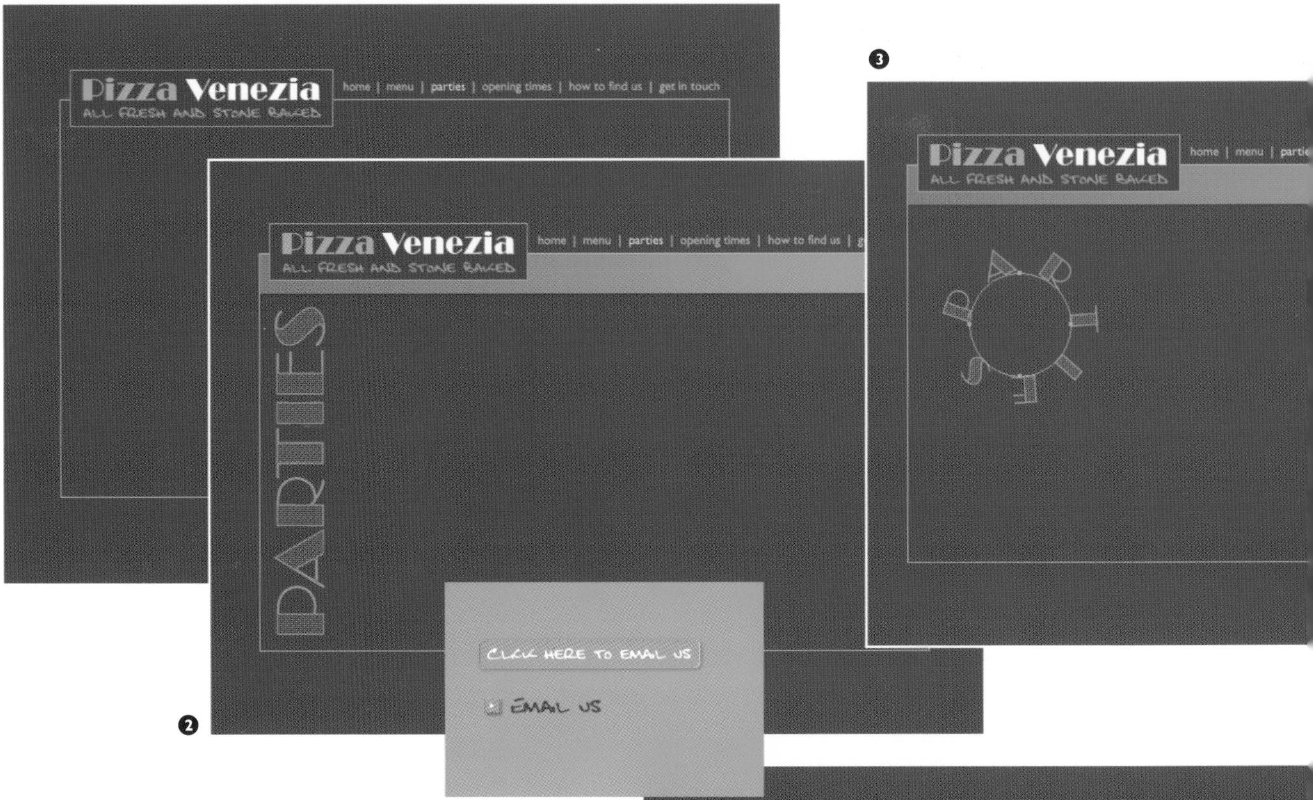

1 2 3 4

EXPERIMENTING

A great deal has been covered in this chapter, from simple type graphics through to heading and button designs, as well as creating a complete webpage design. If you're feeling a bit overwhelmed, take it easy, go back over some of the pages and give the projects another go. The key to making the techniques your own is to experiment, see what you can do with them yourself and adapt them in ways that work well for you. You'll quickly discover tricks of your own that haven't been covered here, as well as styles and effects that are unique to you.

Because Web design is at heart a creative process, this book can only shine a light in the right direction and point out the technical issues you need to know. It's up to you to work out what you like and don't like. Nevertheless, there are various established techniques that Web designers use, and, although they're not the only, or 'right', way to do things, they work effectively – and that makes them a useful (and easy) place to start. These are the things you've learned in this chapter and here's a quick graphics checklist to help you remember.

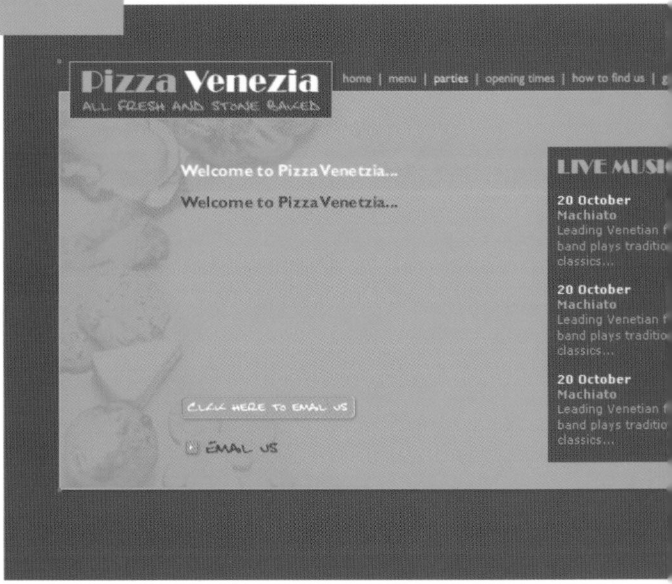

5

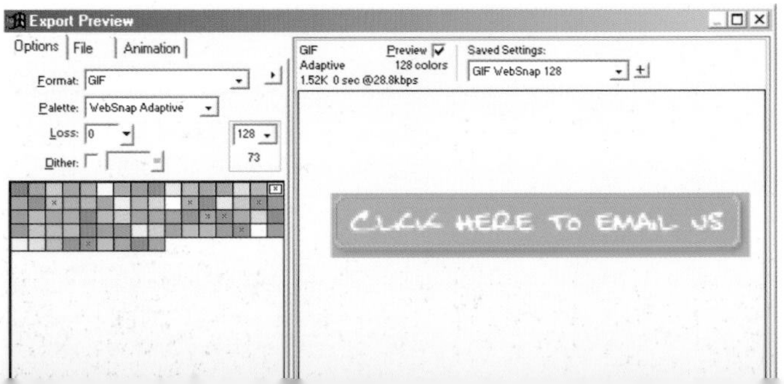

6

❼

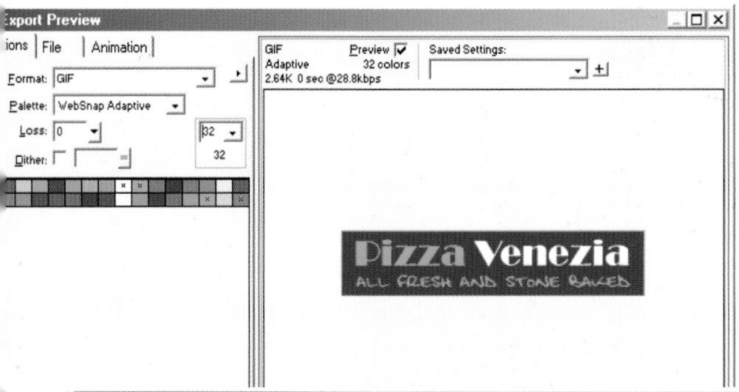

❽

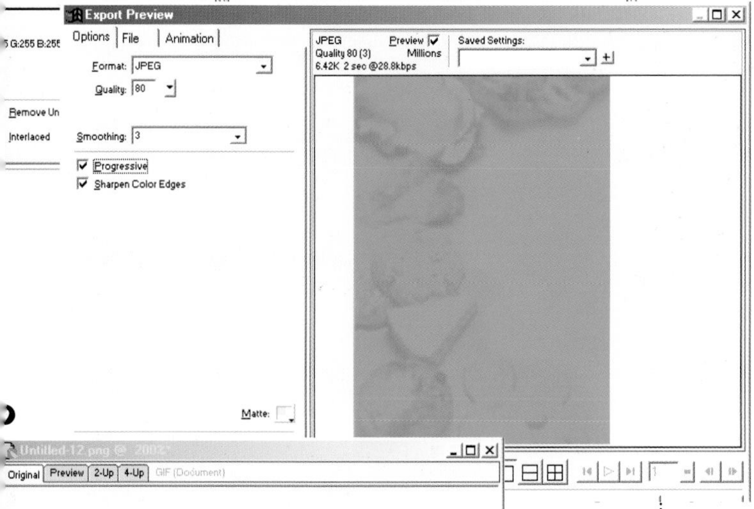

❾

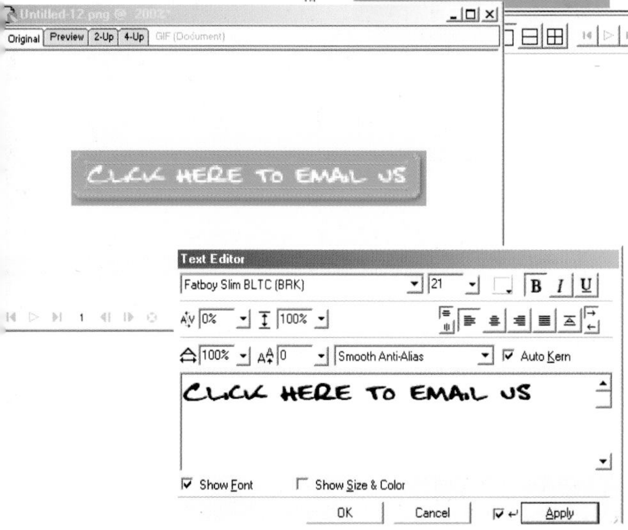

❿

GRAPHICS CHECKLIST

There's a lot to remember when you're creating graphics, and you might want to start with just one or two techniques. Use this checklist as you go along as a source of quick ideas, and to make sure you haven't forgotten something important:

❶ Fonts
You can really go to town with heading and button fonts. Choose carefully and stick to one or two, however, so your design looks professional, rather than flashy and cheap.

❷ Fills and edges
Use simple or exciting gradients, textures and edge colours to create interesting and different effects for your text graphics.

❸ Distortion
Distort, warp, stretch and squeeze, rotate and reflect your text – or set it to follow a curvy path. Experiment!

❹ Buttons
Buttons need to be clearer than headings, so it's quick and easy for people to see what they say. They also need to look like something that should be clicked on. Try using shadows and bevels, but steer away from crude or overdone effects.

❺ Getting an overall look
You need to make sure all your graphics and visual ideas work well together. Get one big page in your graphics software, design everything on that, and then start cropping bits out for your individual graphics files.

❻ Optimizing
Always optimize, or compress, your graphics files before you add them to your webpage, so that they download quickly.

❼ GIF format
The GIF format should generally be used for graphics files with areas of strong or flat colour, sharp edges and those using a limited range of different colours.

❽ JPEG format
The JPEG format should generally be used for photos and graphics with lots of colours, gradients and blending effects, and if you are trying to create a soft, blurry appearance.

❾ Save time with one file
For buttons, headings and so on, save time by creating just one main file in each style, then simply change the text before you optimize to make each button and heading you need.

❿ Background graphics
Use tiles as background images in webpages to create the appearance of a big graphic. Because it's a tile, you need only a single small file, which downloads quickly – but looks good.

Fill: Foreground
Mode: Normal
Corel PHOTO-PAINT 10
File Edit View Image Effects Mask Object Movie Tools Window Help
36%
Brightness-Contrast-Intensity
Brightness:
58
Contrast:
100
Intensity:
100
Preview
Reset
OK
Cancel
Help
Text Editor
Tombats Smilies
Smooth Anti-Alias
Auto Kern
Show Font
Show Size & Color
OK
Cancel
Apply

CHAPTER 4

Designing with Images

Whether it's a photograph or an illustration, an image adds instant visual impact to a design, and with modern software there is almost no limit to what you can do. In this chapter, you will experiment with a whole range of quick, fun and impressive techniques that you can use to beef up your webpages.

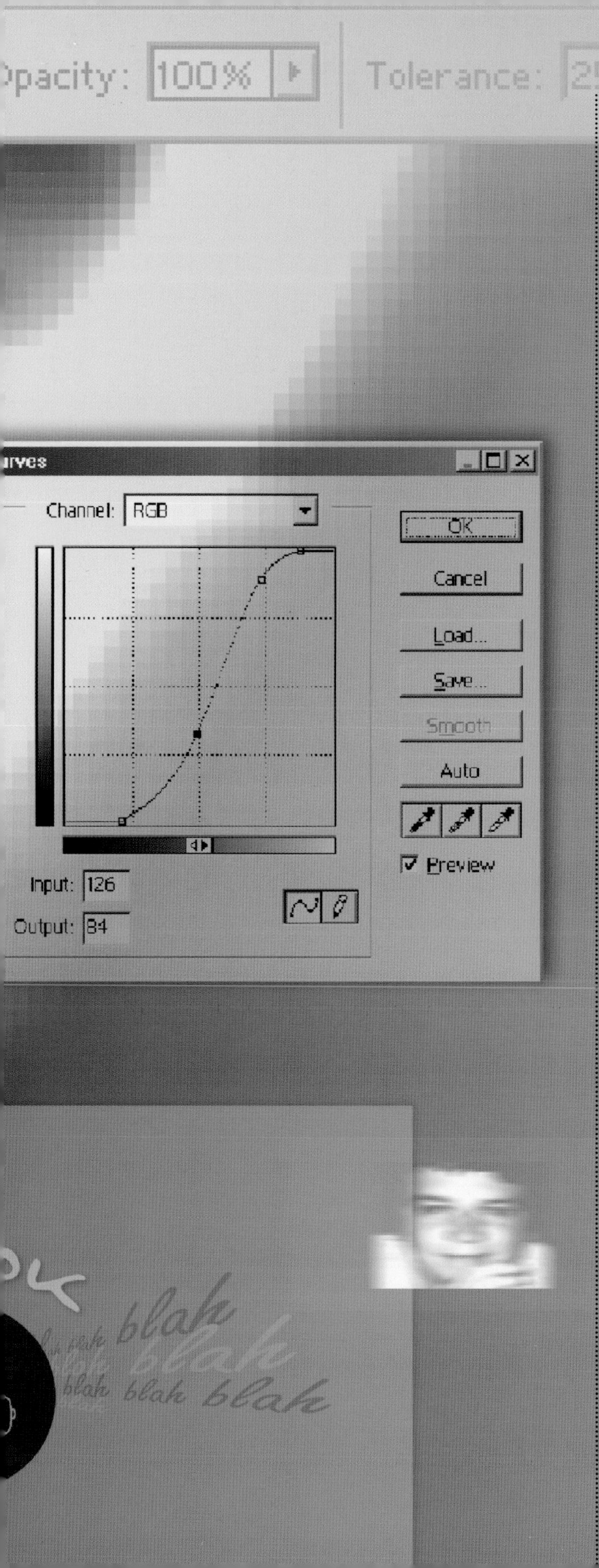

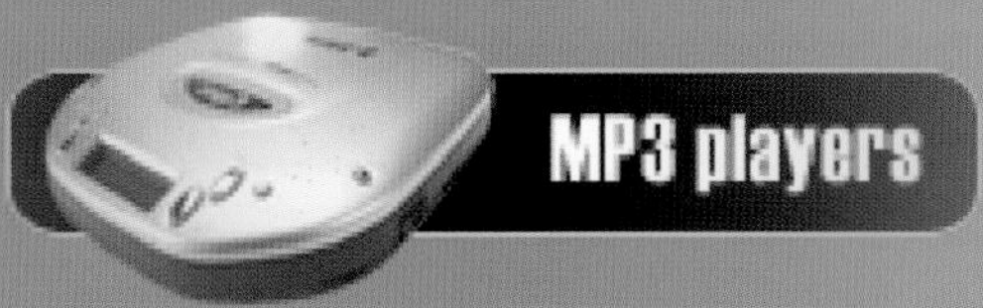

PHOTOS

Working with photos is creative and exciting, it also adds a whole new dimension to your Web design. A single photo will add something tangible to a webpage, while a whole series of photos can tell a unique story.

And, moreover, there is so much more you can do with a photo than just stick it on your webpage the way it is. You can enhance it, effect it, distort it and completely change it, if you want to. You can combine it with other graphics, montage it with other photos, or develop it into an abstract graphic all of its own. But first, you have to get some photos onto your computer...

Digital cameras

By far the easiest way to get photos onto your computer is to use a digital camera. True, these can be a little more expensive than a lot of ordinary cameras, but prices are coming down fast as the consumer market catches on.

The advantage of a digital camera is that you can just plug it into the back of your computer – usually via USB or Firewire – and if you have Windows XP, ME or a Mac, you can just browse and transfer the image files on your camera.

Because your images are already in digital format, you save yourself a great deal of time and trouble scanning them in, and you'll most likely get much better results. If that's not enough to convince you, consider that you'll never need to pay for processing again, and that you can see a photo straight after you've taken it: if there's something wrong with it, all you have to do is delete it and take another shot.

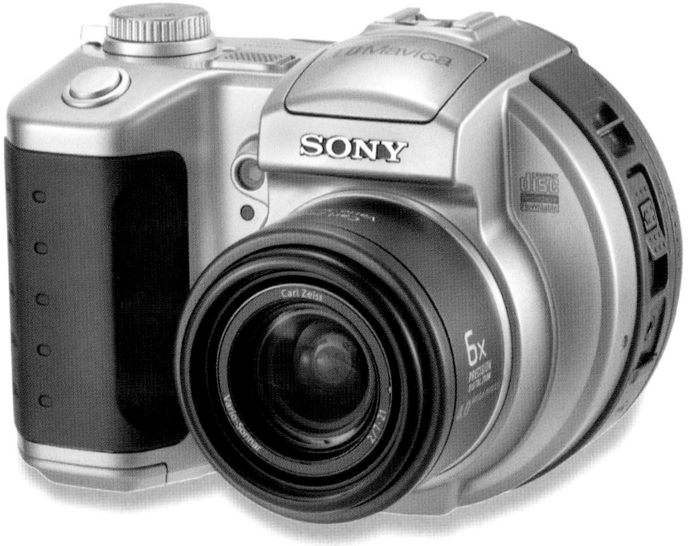

One of the numerous digital cameras currently available – this mid-range example is a Sony.

An Olympus automatic SLR (single-lens reflex) camera, with motorised zoom. Even non-digital cameras are often fully automated to get the best results.

A Umax flatbed scanner. It is used to scan any hard-copy image, such as a photographic print or transparency.

Non-digital cameras

If you're not prepared to spend a lot of money on a digital camera, you can still avoid the hassle of scanning. Many film-processing services today will offer you a CD-ROM containing digital files from your film, or they will put them on the Internet in a password-protected area that only you can access. You'll most likely get better results than you will by scanning, but you've got to pay for every image you want developed and you've got to wait for them.

Scanner

If you're still determined to go down the scanning route, or it really is the only option, then be aware that not only is it a slow and boring process – particularly if you've got 30-odd images to scan in – but cheap equipment means cheap results. And these really are noticeable. You'll probably never be able to get a decent image out of a poor scanner, unless you want to go effects-heavy, or make a Blair-Witch-style gritty feature out of the poor quality. Nevertheless, there are techniques you can use to improve things, which are detailed on page 103.

A top-of-the-range Sony Vaio desktop, set up as a multimedia workstation.

Creating an image library

Make a folder on your computer called 'Photos', 'Scans' or something similar. Keep all your images in sub-folders within this one.

2 It's useful to have an image browser too, so that you can quickly see what the images are without having to open them all. On a PC, you can use the *Thumbnail* mode in Windows Explorer. In some versions of Windows, you can also customise folders with an *Image Preview* template.

3 In Mac OS X, you can use the *Column View* located in Mac Finder.

Using a digital camera

4 When you take photos with a digital camera, you should always use the highest resolution and best image quality you can: you'll get much better results, and you can resize and compress the images afterwards.

5 To transfer files, just plug the camera in according to the manual's instructions. If you're in Windows ME, or higher, you'll get an automatic *Wizard* dialog – use this to transfer your images. Or you can browse the camera from your *My Computer* icon.

6 On a Mac, an icon for the camera should appear on your desktop. Doubleclick on this to browse the camera's image files and transfer them across. In OS X you can use the *Image Capture* tool.

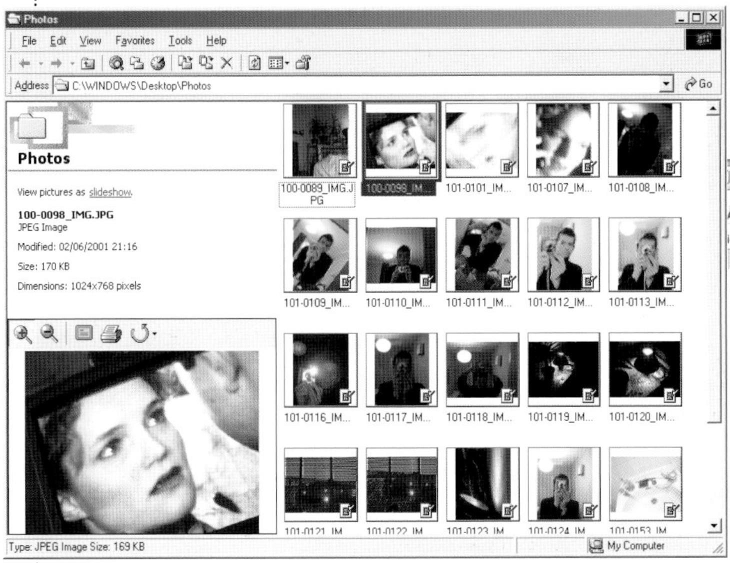

2

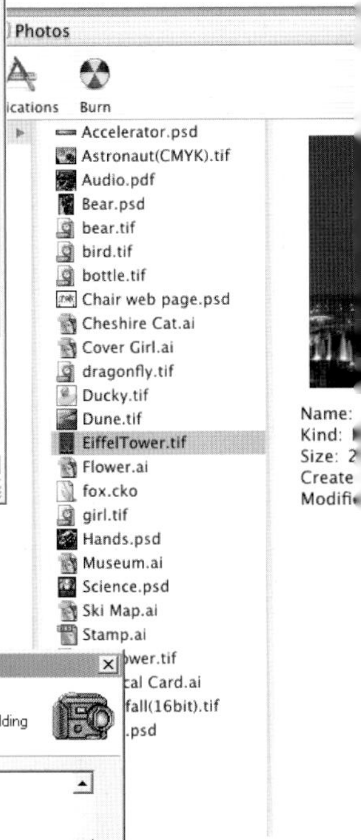

3

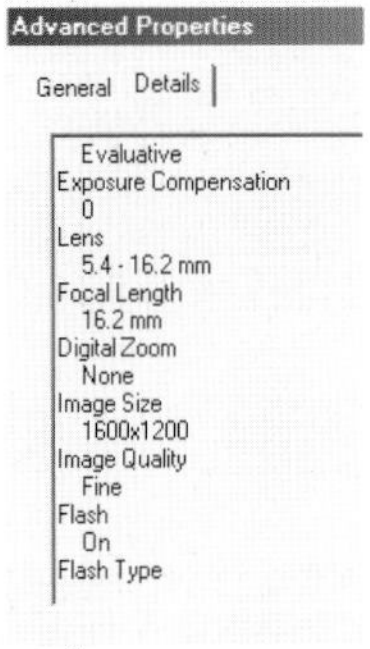

4

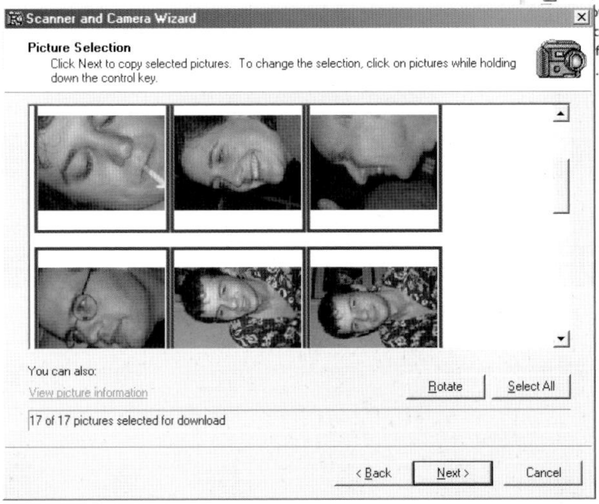

5

6

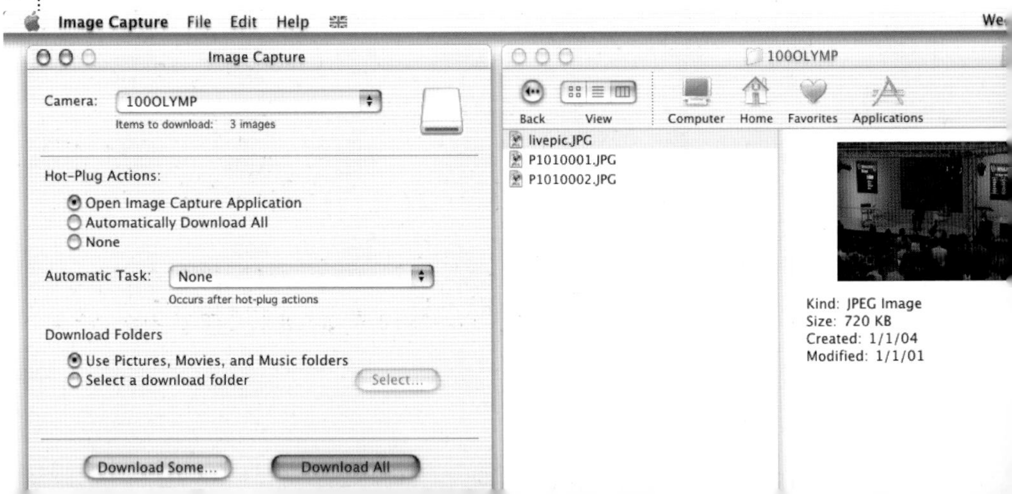

1

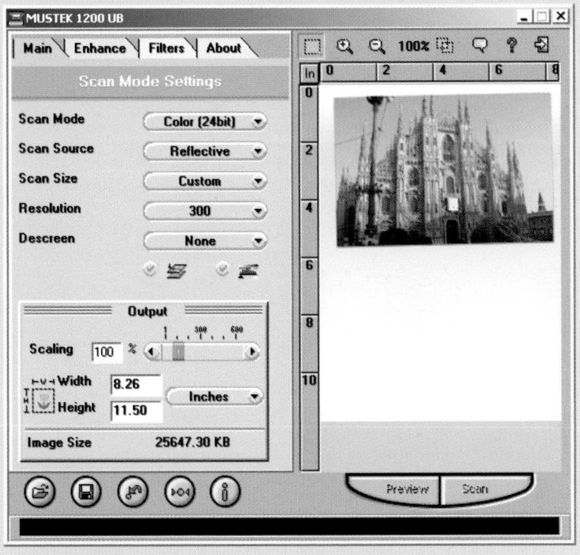

2

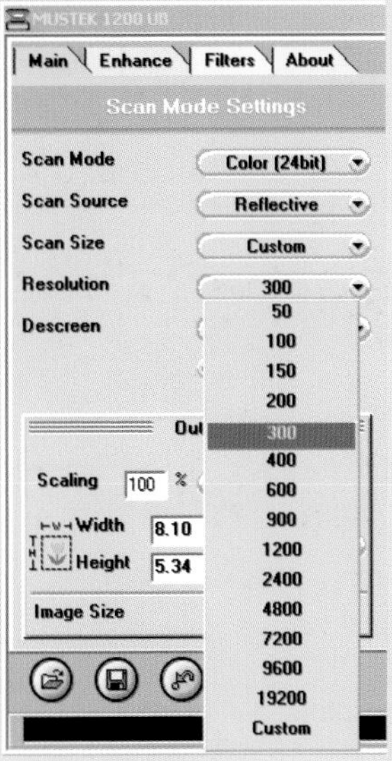

3

4

Using a scanner

1 Scanning is the bane of graphic design: it's difficult and expensive to get high-quality results, but you can get workable image files from your home equipment if you spend time on it.

2 Ideally, you would always scan your images at the highest possible size, resolution and colour depth. But this can take ages and also creates huge files, which are not practical to work with. So, as a guideline, make sure your scan is at least twice the size in pixels as the size you finally intend to use it. This gives plenty of room for error and loss in quality, and allows you to experiment or change your mind.

3 Wherever possible, avoid scanning from printed material like magazines, books and so on. Not only will this raise copyright issues if you reproduce them online, but you'll also get terrible results. Printing is done with tiny dots of colour, not solid colour, and these are impossible for a scanner to interpret properly. The result may be 'interference' or 'moiré' patterns in the scanned image – in the form of stripes or swirls across the image. Ordinary photos, however, are fine.

4 Always go for a preview scan before finalising the real thing. This may seem like a bore, but you can use it to check you've got the colour and size settings right, and that you've got your scanning material aligned properly. You can also opt not to scan empty space. All in all, you'll get a better result and save time when scanning the real thing.

ESSENTIAL TOOLS FOR EDITING PHOTOS

In its simplest form, adding a photo to a webpage is just like adding any other type of image. Use your graphics software to get it to the right size, then optimize and export it (usually as a JPEG in the case of photos), and add it to your webpage in the normal way. But with just a few quick tricks, you can dramatically improve almost any photo and give it the appearance of a professional, darkroom-developed masterpiece. This is extremely good news because, as a Web designer, you're aiming to achieve impressive and appealing visual quality for your website, and that includes photos. In addition, unless you are a supreme photographer with fine equipment and a perpetually superb source of light, it's hard to produce consistently good images with a camera alone.

Most bitmap-based design software comes laden with features for the photographer, including Photoshop (and its cheaper, stripped-down versions LE and Photoshop Elements) Photo-Paint and Paint Shop Pro. These can be baffling at first, but the developers of most of this software have had the foresight to include a range of autofeatures to make the whole process much easier. Until you become an expert, you'll probably be happy with the results you can get using these, perhaps with just a manual tweak here and there to get things precisely the way you want them.

1

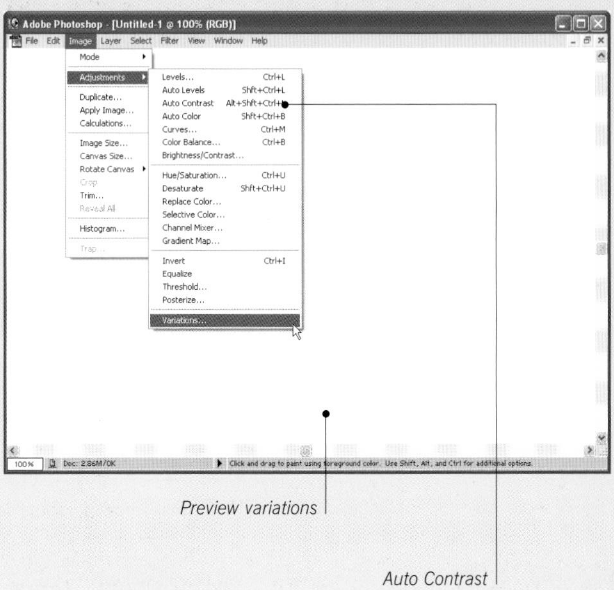

2

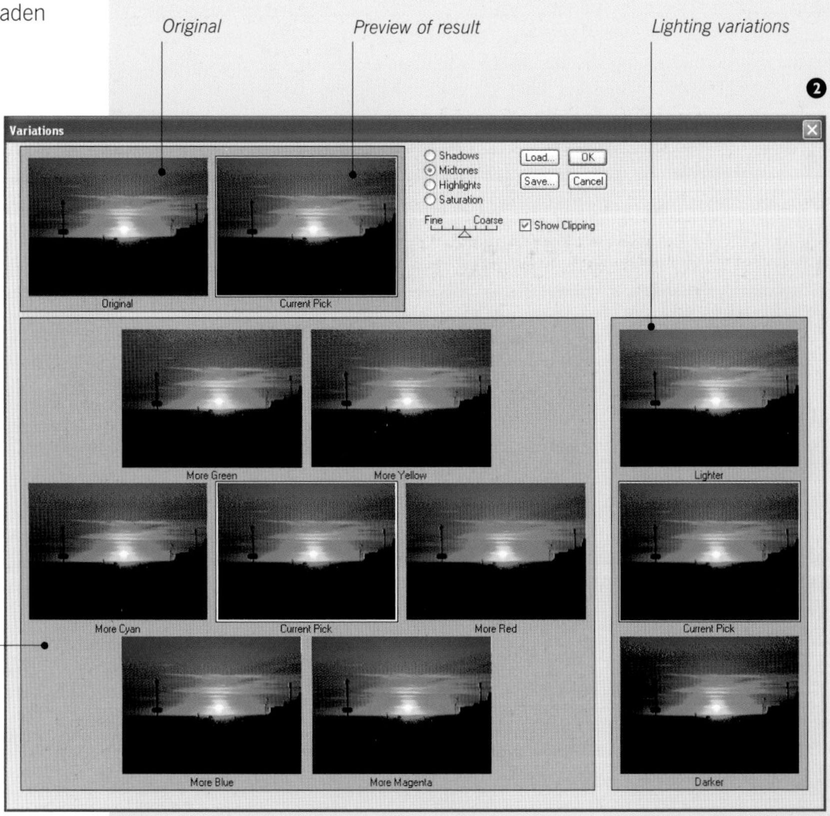

❸

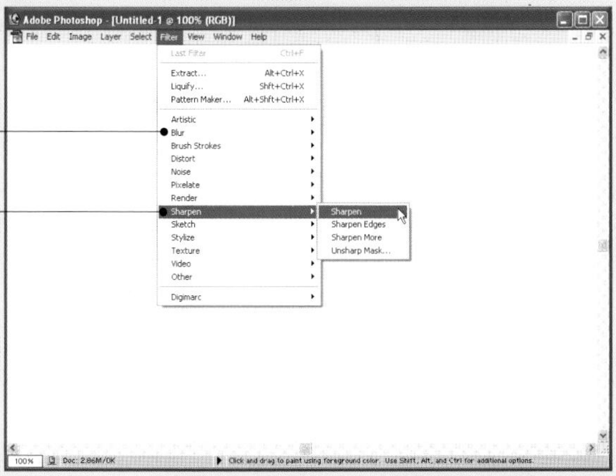

❹

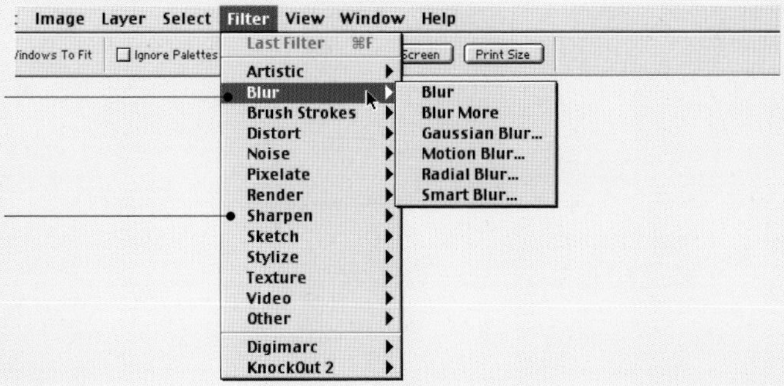

❺

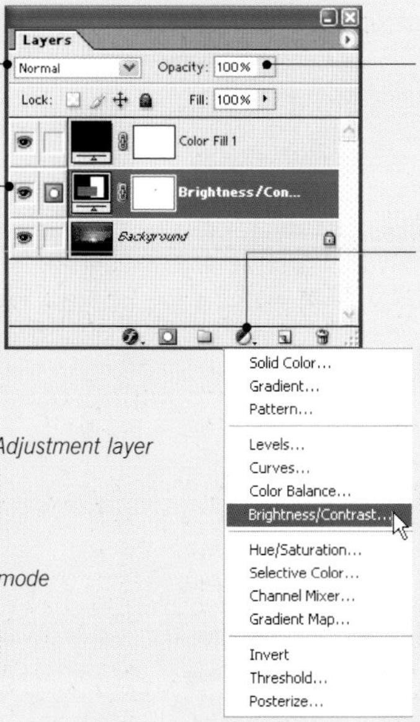

❻

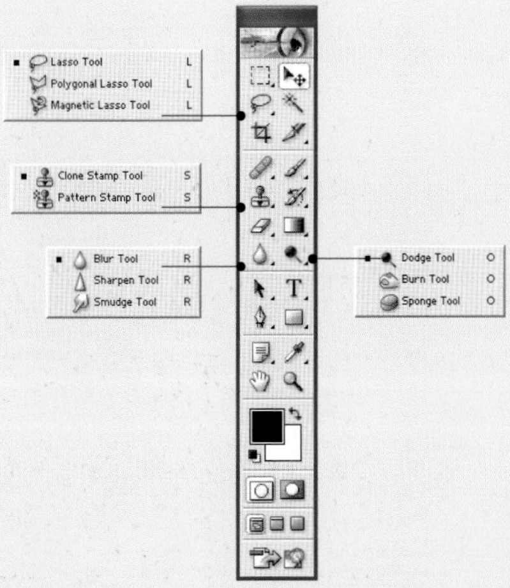

In Photoshop

❶ Photoshop remains the most popular professional-level software. It's pricey, but its cut-down, cheaper LE (Limited Edition) and Photoshop Elements versions include the key features you'll need at this stage. The main image-processing commands are in the *Image* > ***Adjust*** menu, including *Auto Contrast*, *Auto Levels*, *Curves* and *Variations*. Another option in the menu is manual, which gives you control over lighting and colour balance in the current selected layer.

❷ The *Variations* option can improve an image quickly. It gives you a range of previews of colour and lighting adjustments, and you choose the one you want by clicking the preview in the current layer.

❸❹ You'll also find the *Blur* and *Sharpen* commands very useful. These are in the *Filter* menu and also only apply to the current layer.

❺ The *Layers* palette includes features specifically for photos. Using an *Adjustment* layer, you can *Contrast* and make other adjustments to all layers. *Blending mode* and *Opacity* control how a layer blends with the one beneath it.

❻ Your toolbox also hosts some important features, including *Lasso* and *Marquee* tools for making selections; the *Cloning* tools for copying areas of the image; *Blur*, *Sharpen* and *Smudge*, which do just what they say; and *Dodge*, *Burn* and *Sponge*, for recreating darkroom effects. Keep an eye on the messages in your status bar for more detailed information.

In Paint Shop Pro

❶ Paint Shop Pro has many of the same features for photo-editing as Photoshop, although they are not quite as easy to use. The most important lighting and colour features are in the *Colours* > ***Adjust*** menu. These include *Brightness* and *Contrast*, *Colour Balance* and *Levels*, which are like a sophisticated version of lighting and colour balance all rolled into one feature.

❷ To make things easier, though, head for the *Effect* > ***Enhance Photo*** menu, where you'll find *Auto Contrast*, *Auto Colour Balance* and similar features. Unlike Photoshop, you get a small (well, tiny) preview of the result, which you can manually tweak in a simple interface before choosing it.

❸ Like Photoshop, Paint Shop Pro has a *Layers Palette*. If you can't see it, right-click on your main toolbar and open it from the menu that appears. You can create *Adjustment Layers* by right-clicking on any other layer, and you can also adjust *Blending Modes* and *Opacity* on the right-hand side.

❹ *Sharpen* and *Blur* tools are located in the *Effects* menu, just above the *Enhance Photo* options.

❺ To get the most out of Paint Shop Pro's toolbox (or *Tool Palette*, as it is called), you need to have the *Tool Options* palette open, which you can do by right-clicking on the main toolbar. In here you'll find an abundance of different options for each tool. Your main photo tools are the *Freehand*, with which you can draw selections, as well as the *Cloner* and *Retoucher*.

❶

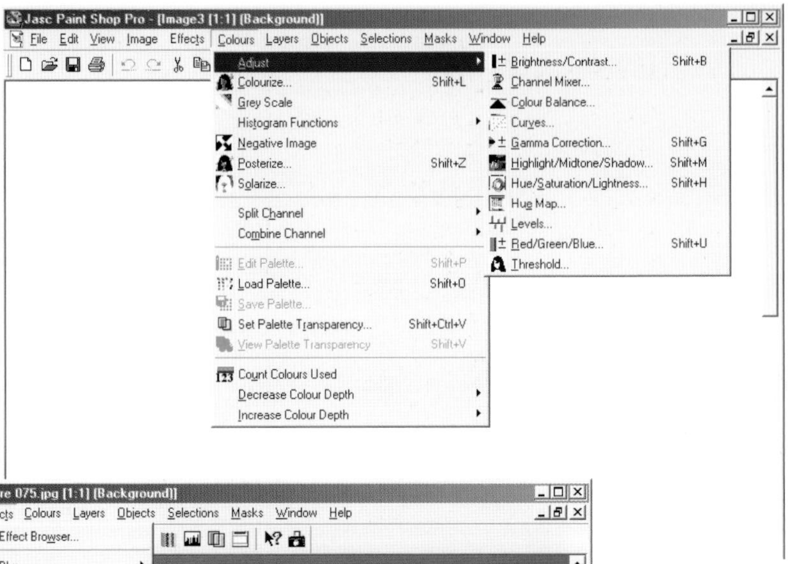

❷

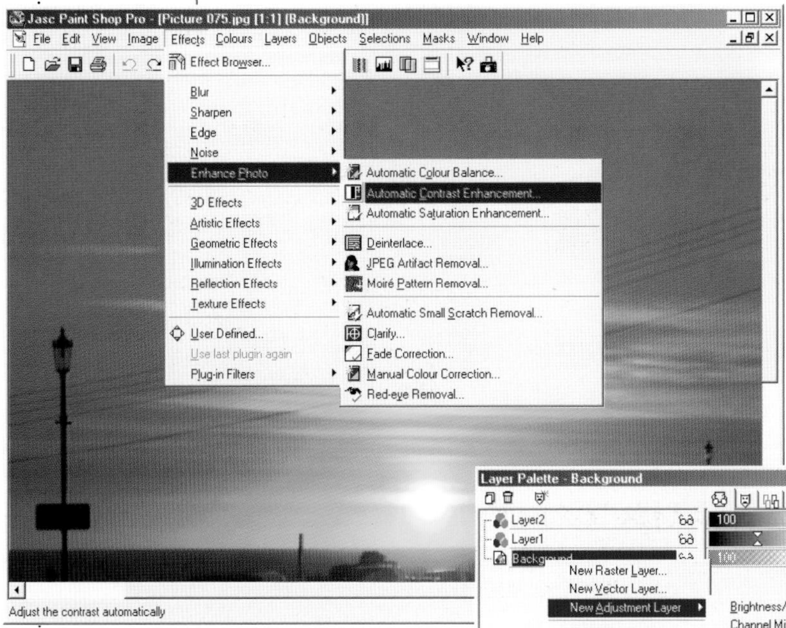

❸

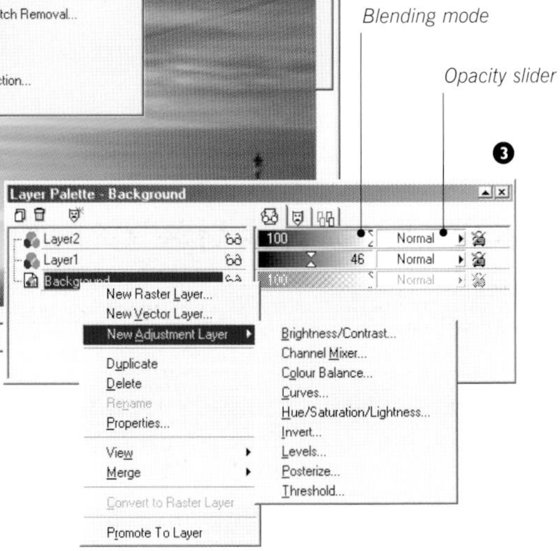

❹

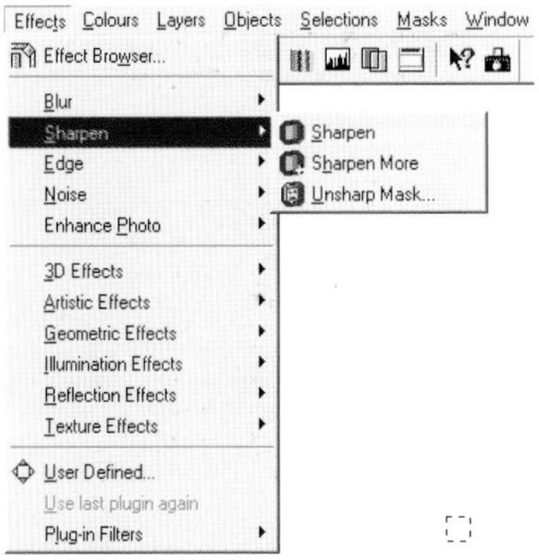

❺

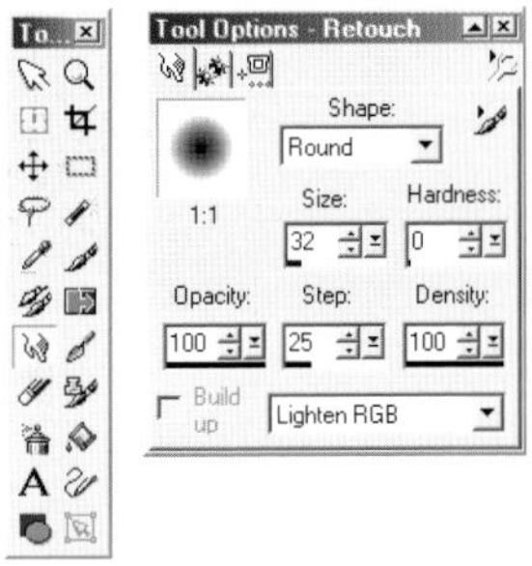

❶
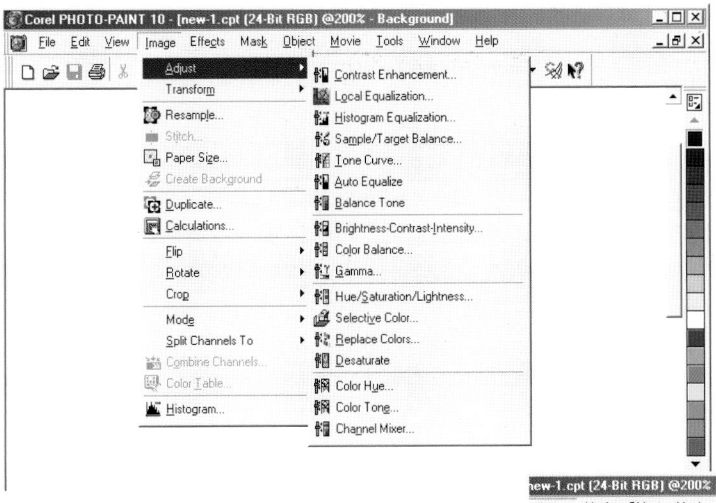

❷
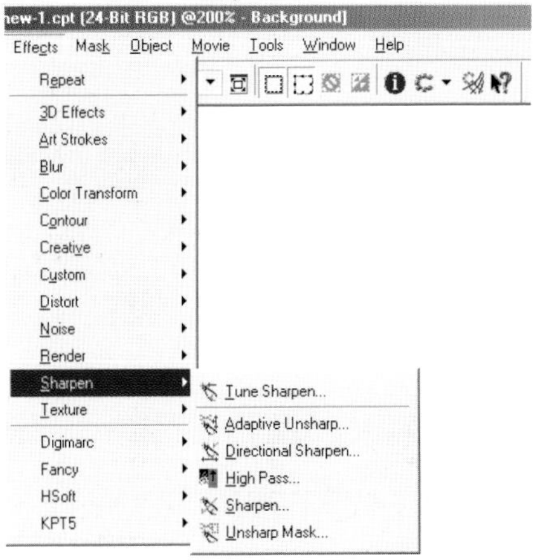

❸
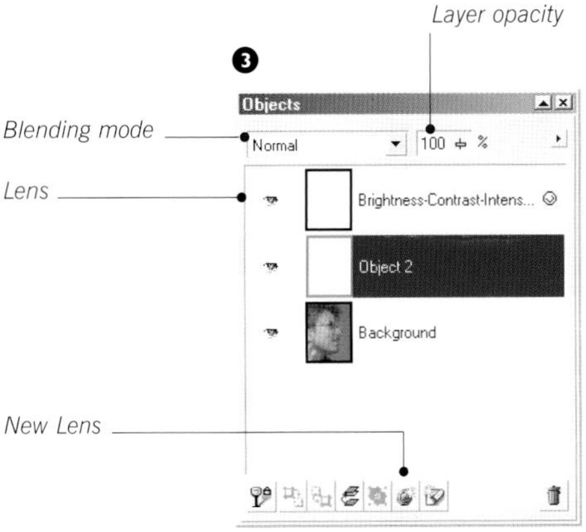

In Photo-Paint

❶ Corel Photo-Paint's image-editing features are more like those in Photoshop than Paint Shop Pro. You can find just about everything you need and more – including the core lighting and colour-adjustment options – in the *Image* > *Adjust* menu.

❷ You'll find *Sharpen* and *Blur* in the *Effects* menu, while the toolbox has similar tools to Photoshop and Paint Shop Pro. You can access a complete *Cloning* toolbox by right-clicking anywhere on the main interface.

❸ Photo-Paint uses *Objects*, (similar to *Layers*), and has an *Objects* palette where you can apply blending modes. And instead of *Adjustment Layers*, here you use *Lenses*, which work in a similar way.

❶
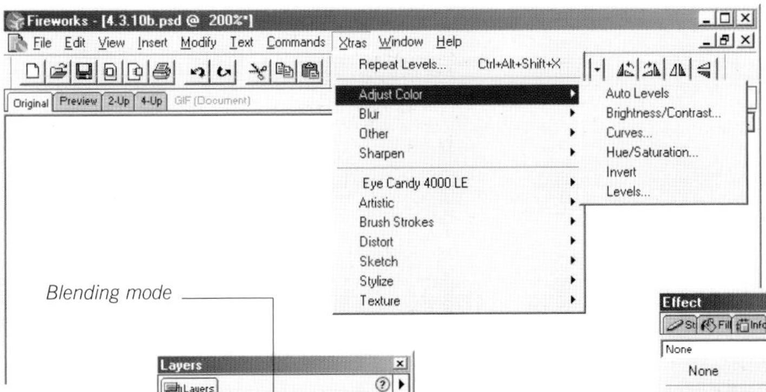

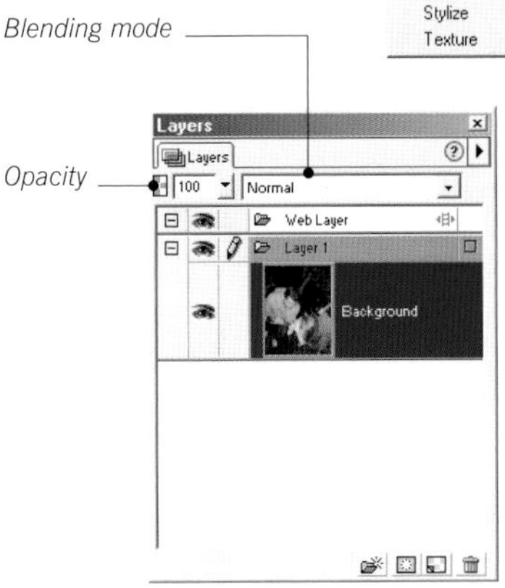

❸

❷
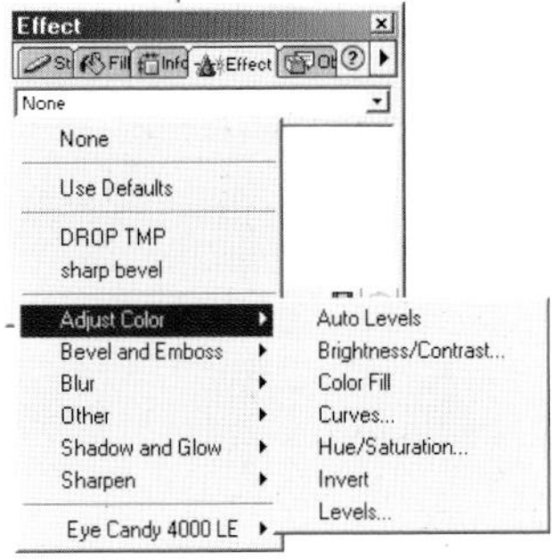

In Fireworks

❶ Macromedia Fireworks has simpler photo-editing tools than the other applications, but for the most part you'll find them more than adequate, and perhaps less baffling. The colour adjustment features, as well as *Blur* and *Sharpen*, are all in the *Xtras* menu.

❷ You'll also find the settings in your *Effect* palette menu, where you can apply them alongside bevels and buttons for quick, easy working and, like the *Adjustment Layers*, you can go back and edit at any time.

❸ Fireworks' *Layers* palette also has *Blending Modes* and *Opacity*, which you can apply on a per-object, rather than per-layer, basis.

PROJECT 11
PREPARING AN IMAGE

So those are the tools and features you need to prepare your photos, but how do you actually use them effectively?

If there are only three things you experiment with in a photo, they should be lighting, colour and composition. You don't need to go overboard, but it's difficult to get these right in just a few short seconds through a viewfinder. You're often better off to worry about getting them right in your computer and let the modern software take control. In the field, just focus on capturing the moment and getting a sharp image.

The more practice you get, the quicker and easier it becomes to get your photos looking just the way you want them. You'll also find that your visual perception of colour, lighting and so on, becomes more acute. What once took an hour will soon take just five minutes. But to help you on your way, there are some established techniques.

Go gentle on the processing. This is a subtle art and most of the changes you need to make will be slight, unless you're looking for an extreme effect. Moreover, too much effort in your digital darkroom can reduce the overall quality of your image, as well as making it look cheesy.

The examples here are in Photoshop (viewed in Mac OS X).

❶

❶ Here's the image you're going to work on. Remember, start with an image that's much bigger than the one you plan to end up with – twice as big is good. This helps to minimise distortion from processing in your final image.

❷

3

4

5

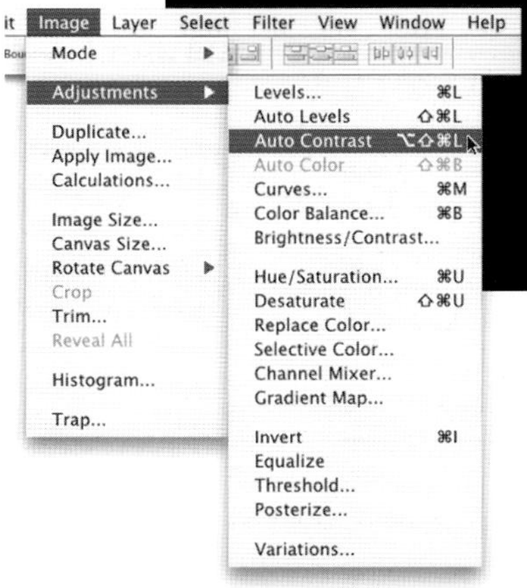

6

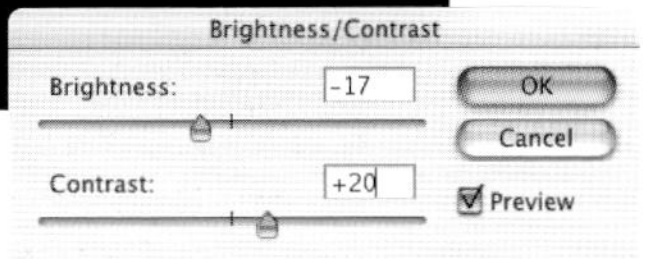

2 Before you do anything else, and especially if your image is a scan, you need to get it straight. Use your design software's guides feature to place a guide near an obvious straight line in your image, then *Select* > ***All*** and use the *Transform* to rotate everything else to match this.

3 Then use your *Crop* tool to tidy up the edges. Remember that you can click-and-drag sides and corners to adjust them after you've roughly drawn the main area. Once this is done, you're ready to work on the image itself, starting with the lighting.

4 Contrast is important. Most images look better if you can give them a complete, dynamic range of tones from dark to light, with the majority of the tones well balanced between the two extremes. The trouble is, it's not easy to achieve this with a camera, and most professionals use either software or darkroom tools to make up the difference. You should too.

5 Start with the *Auto Contrast* tool in your software, if there is one, and see if this does the trick. This might not do a lot because *Auto Contrast* features tend to err on the side of caution, especially for Web work. However, there are things you can do yourself.

6 Dig out your manual *Brightness/Contrast* tool, and experiment with this. It should work just like the settings on your monitor or TV. In this image, you can improve things dramatically with a hefty dose of contrast, together with bringing down the overall brightness.

Lighting and colour

❼ It's tempting to take this further, to get really striking lighting – but push it too far and you'll begin to ruin the photo. As you increase the contrast, so the colours become more intense and blotchy. This can make skin tones, in particular, look extremely ugly and unnatural.

❽ Push it further, and the colours separate out. You won't want this, unless you're after a gritty 1980s fashion look.

❾ We decided to stick with something subtler here – but what about colour? One feature you can use to adjust this is the *Hue/Saturation* and *Lightness* tool. This includes three sliders, one for each of these settings. By changing the *Hue* slider, you can shift all the colours of an image 10 or 20 notches, say, around the colour wheel.

❿ The Saturation slider controls the intensity of colours, just like the colour setting on your TV. For example, –100 gives you black and white, while +100 is far too much. It's best to use slight settings to give your image a vibrant but natural look.

⓫ *Lightness* controls the overall lightness of the colours. You shouldn't use this to generally brighten up an image, however, because it washes out the shadows too.

❼

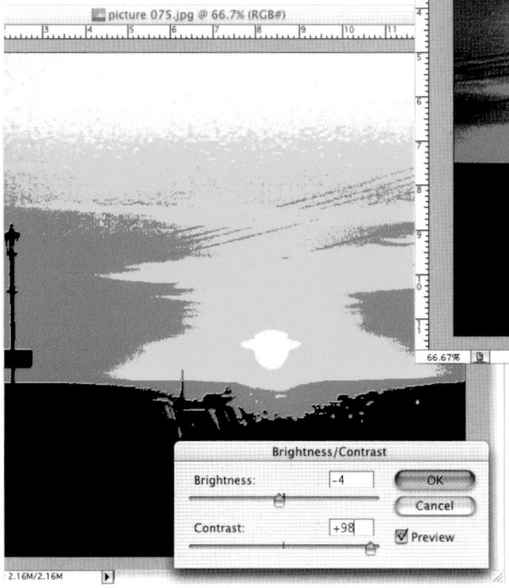

❽

❾

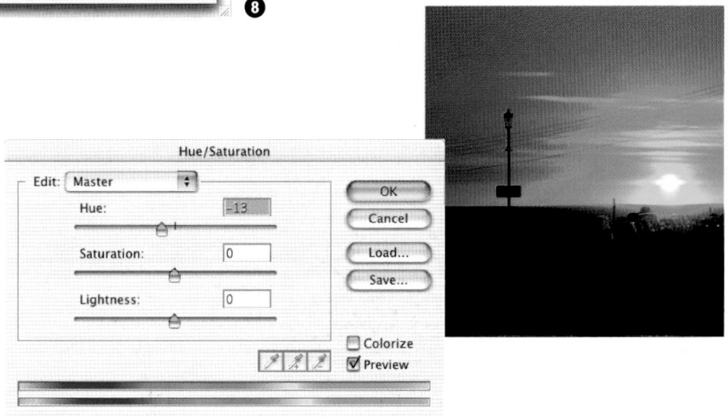

❿

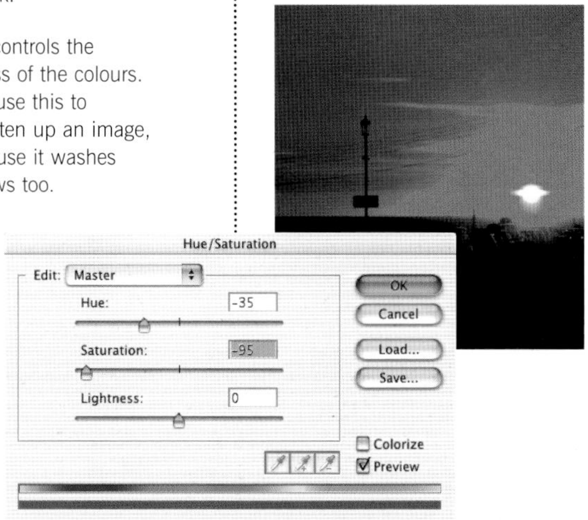

⓫

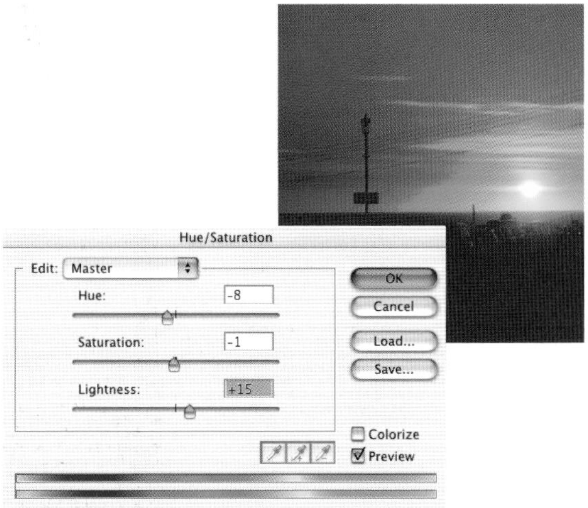

⓬

⓭

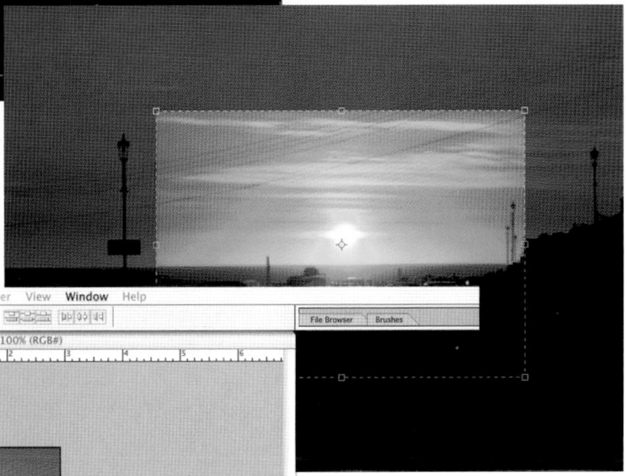

⓮

⓯

⓰

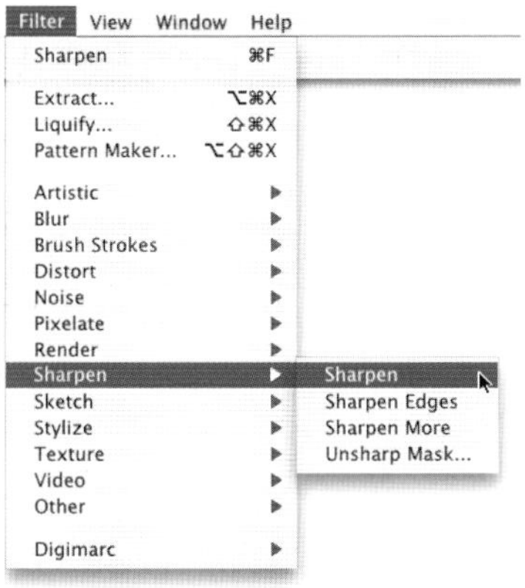

⓱

Finishing off

⓬ Once you are happy with the overall lighting and colour in your image, it's time to look at the composition. This can be hard to start off with because it means cropping your image – and how do you choose which bits, if any, to lose? And because composition is such an abstract, subjective idea, it's also hard to tell what's going to be a great composition before you've seen it.

⓭⓮ The objective of composition is clear: to give your photo a special character or personality through the way the shapes in it relate to each other. Experiment with lots of different compositions: try radical crops and extreme close-ups or try focusing on the least expected bit of the image. See if you can create a sense of drama and space. Find photos by other photographers that you really like, or from magazines you read. The same goes for getting your colour and lighting the way you want them. If in doubt, take inspiration from the greats! (After all, these factors made their reputations.)

⓯ This done, you're ready to resize your image. As with graphics, you need to get this to the exact size you want it in the webpage. (But save a full-size version first, in case you want to go back and change it later.)

⓰ Size reduction almost always helps to sharpen your photo up a bit. It's probably also a good idea to use the basic *Sharpen* command in your software too, for a really crisp image.

⓱ Finally, optimize and save your image as before. You'll usually want a JPEG for photos.

PROJECT 12
COLOUR AND LIGHTING 2

Whole books have been written on the subject of getting the colour and lighting ‘right’ in images. Of course, in a sense there is no right and wrong. But you need to make them look as good as you possibly can.

Most photos will benefit from the techniques that have been covered over the previous pages – but for that professional look you sometimes need more. In particular, *Brightness* and *Contrast* are crude ways to control the balance of light and dark; and you can’t do much with *Hue/Saturation* without taking your photo into the realms of psychedelic fantasy (which you might want, of course).

You’ve probably already found that you just couldn’t get certain images to look right. So what should you do? Most photo-editing tools come with two additional features, *Levels* and *Curves* (*Contrast Enhancement* and *Tone Curve* in Photo-Paint). These are geared towards highly accurate and detailed control over the exact balance of lighting and colour at every level in your image. You can do this for each of the red, green and blue channels, which mix together to make the final RGB colour for every pixel.

❶

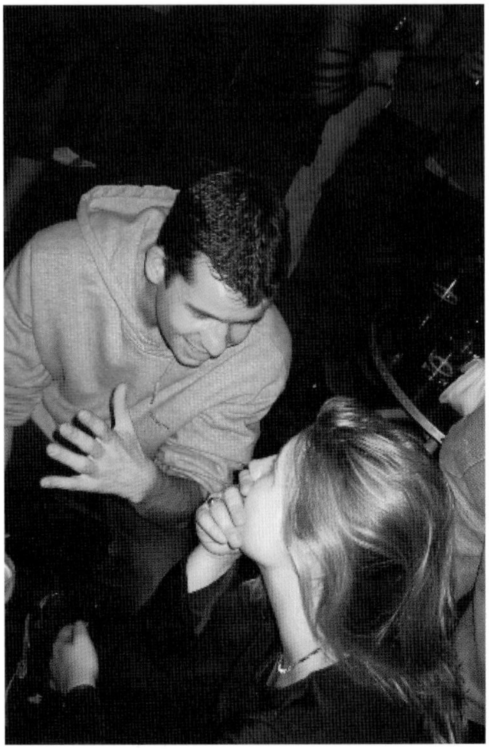

❷

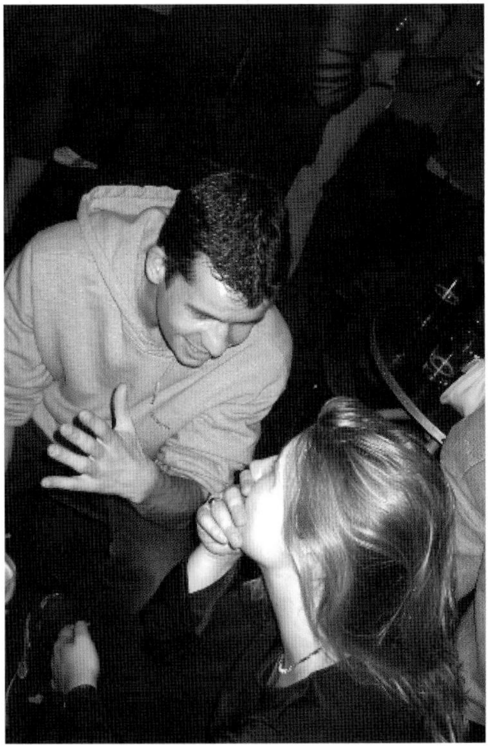

❸

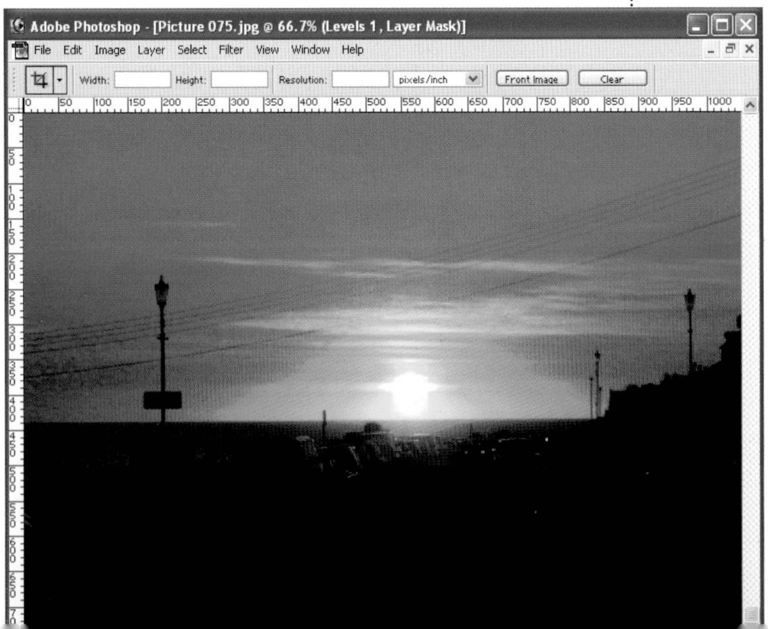

4

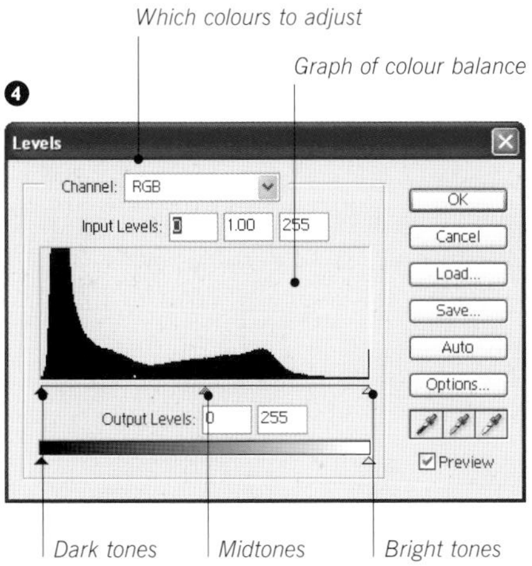

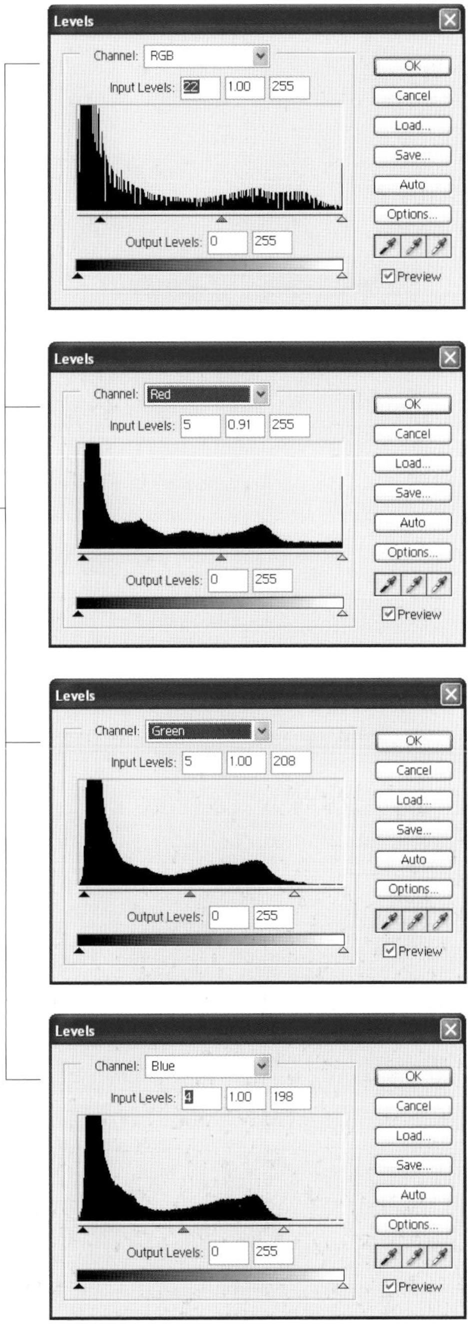

5

Levels

1 As you can see here, it is impossible to get this image right using *Contrast* and *Hue* settings alone.

2 Instead, go back to the original and try applying *Auto Levels* (known as *Auto Color Balance* in some software). It's similar to *Brightness* and *Contrast*, but has individual settings for the different primary colours, as well as an overall setting. You'll see that the auto-feature changes the colour as well as lighting in the image, to create a more even spectrum.

3 In this image *Auto Levels* works reasonably well, although it's not perfect by any means. In some images, though, a more even colour balance is the last thing you want – like the sunset photo from the previous project.

4 *Manual Levels*, or *Contrast Enhancement* in Photo-Paint, make it possible for you to control this process yourself. Dragging the right slider for bright tones inwards increases their brightness, while dragging the left slider – dark tones – makes them darker. The middle slider (or *Gamma* in Photo-Paint) affects midtones – drag left to darken, right to lighten. By choosing different colours, or channels, from the top dropdown menu, you can also adjust these balances individually for the red, green and blue colours.

5 For this image, considerably brighten the blue and green channels, while increasing the overall contrast. This will have the effect of cooling the light tones, while intensifying the shadows and keeping them rich and warm.

Curves and colour

❻ *Curves* are very similar to *Levels*, and achieve much the same job, but provide you with a different visual way of making your adjustments. Here you have a line on a graph and you can click this to create points. Then drag the points to adjust the brightness of light at that particular point.

❼ It's hard to explain, but very easy to use: experiment a little and you'll soon get the idea. Drag the top right point to the left to increase the brightness of the bright tones; drag the bottom left point to the right to intensify the dark tones.

❽ Place a point in the middle of the curve and lift or drop it to increase the overall lightness or darkness of your image.

❾ Like *Levels*, *Curves* have a *Channel* menu, and by choosing different channels in here, you can affect the overall colour balance. Here we've applied a dramatic, sharp contrast in the red channel only.

❿ For subtler colour correction, before you apply any other processing to an image, open *Curves* and then go through each of the channels (except the RGB one) and experiment with dragging the top-right and bottom-left points inwards by different degrees, but not too far. With just the right balance of setting across the channels, you can get superb colour balance and vibrancy. Then go back to the main RGB channel and make any final, overall changes.

❻

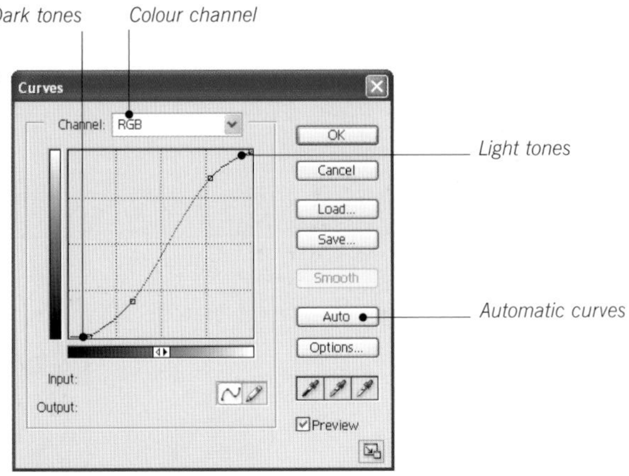

❼

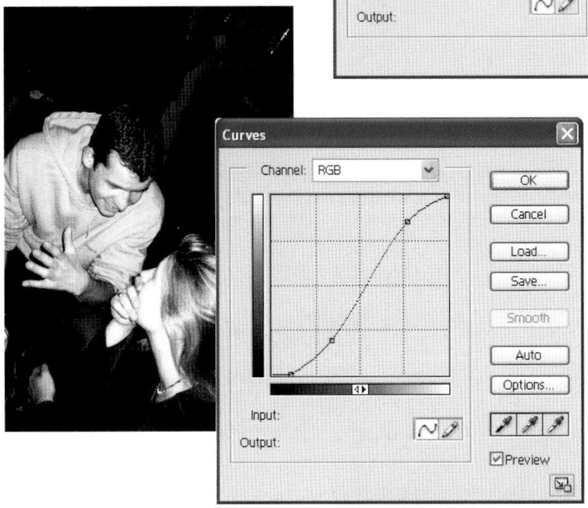

❽

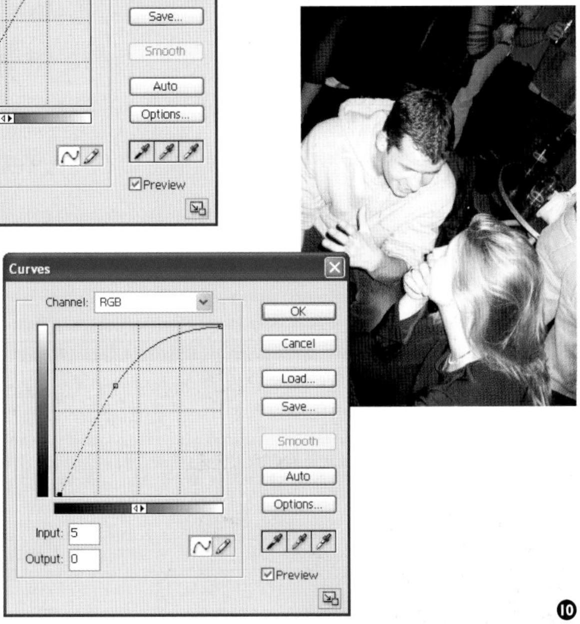

❾

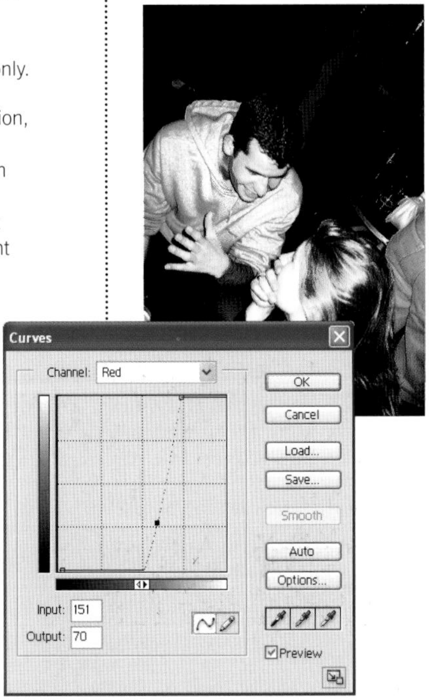

❿

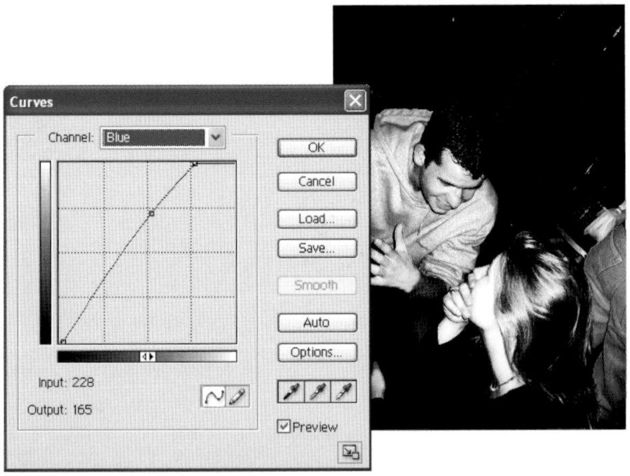

11

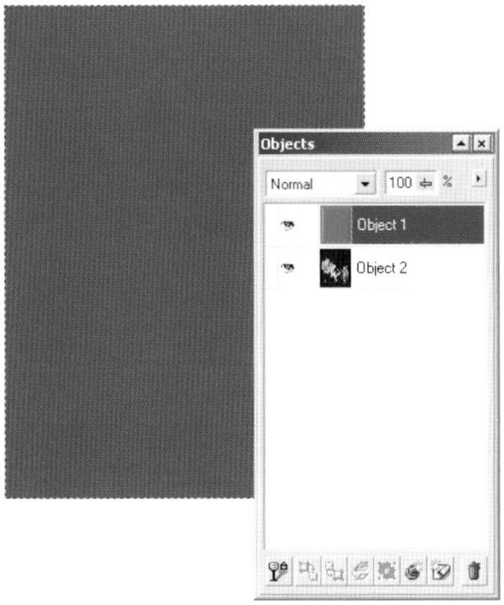

12

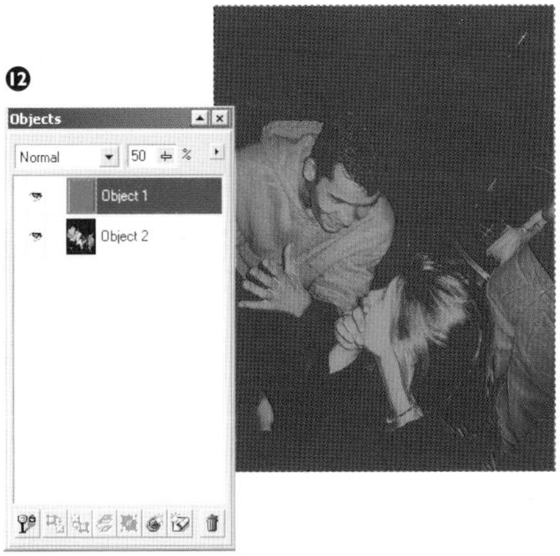

13

14

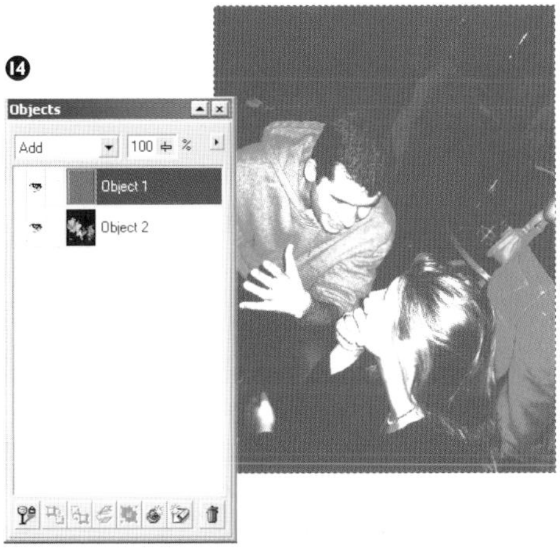

15

16

Blending modes

11 All the main graphics software have layers or objects that you can apply different transparency or opacity and blending modes to. In short, these control how one part of an image combines with the one below it. With *Normal* blending at 100 per cent opacity, it simply blocks it out.

12 But if you reduce the opacity to 50 per cent, whatever is below becomes visible. It's like the first coat of paint you put on a wall.

13 The other blending modes control how the blending is worked out. If *Normal* mode is like applying a layer of paint on a wall, then *Hard Light* is like shining a spotlight on it. Even at 100 per cent, you can see what's below, but the colour is highly distorted.

14 *Multiple*, or subtractive mixing, is like holding different colour films up to the light and overlapping them. Each blocks out different colours, until you end up with black. *Screen*, or *Additive Mixing* (pictured here), is like shining different coloured lights onto a white wall and overlapping them. Each adds more light until you end up with white.

15 The *Hue* (pictured) and *Color* modes are particularly useful in photography for giving an overall tint to an image. Just fill a layer with a solid colour or gradient, and experiment with different opacities.

16 *Dodge* (pictured) and *Burn*, meanwhile, produce striking (but not always great) results.

PROJECT 13
CREATIVE LIGHTING AND COLOUR

We've looked at preparing photos in a realistic way, to get a cleaner and more designed look, but of course you don't always have to go the route of realism. In the same way as we talked in the previous chapter about creating an identity and building a look, you can develop your own distinctive ways of preparing images that enhance this, and complement the overall look of your site. After all, a photo almost always serves to focus your viewer's attention.

How far you want to take the processing is up to you: your imagination is the limit. But over the next few projects we'll look at different ways you can prepare images with a more extreme appearance, and start to build design ideas for your website around them. In this one, we're going to coin a variety of new ideas for applying dramatic colour and lighting changes to an image. (These are also particularly useful if you've got a poor-quality photo, but you really want to use it somewhere).

In the first few ideas, you will work with a black-and-white image and play with different lighting. Black-and-white can have an air of cool sophistication. It's easy to edit, so you can make it moody or bright white. But black-and-white can also be dull: you need to make sure your composition and subject matter are good.

The following ideas build on what you will have done, combining strong tints and dramatic changes to the colouring, to give an image an individual character or style. Finally we look at how you can begin to build a website design style around this…

1

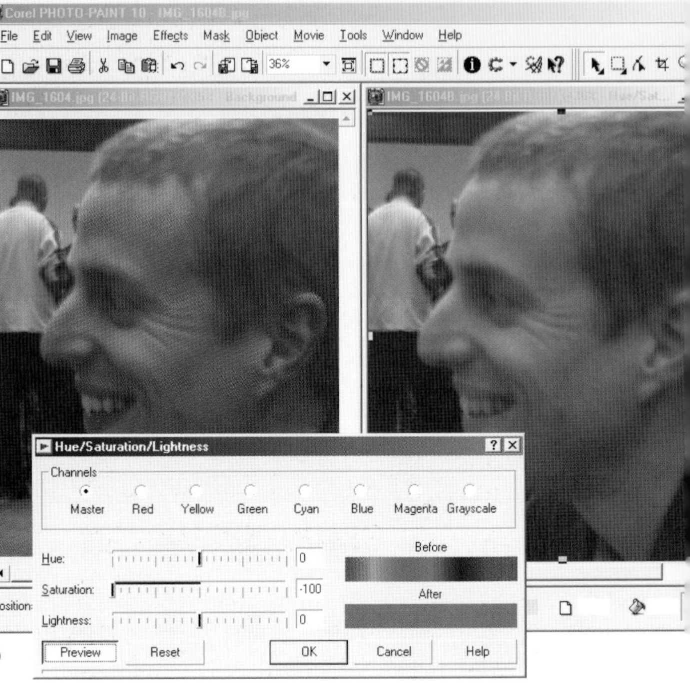

2

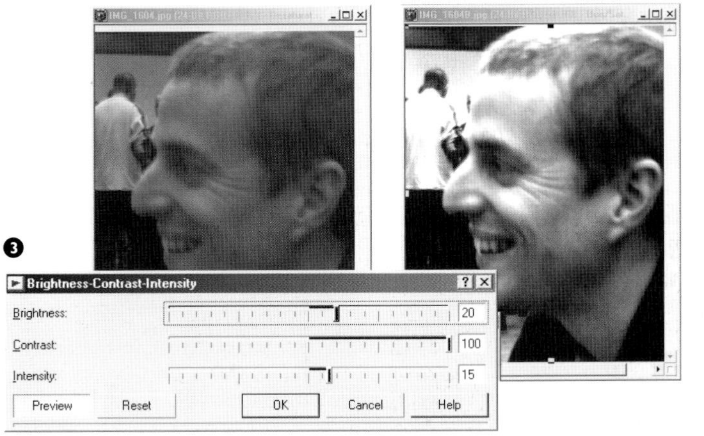

3

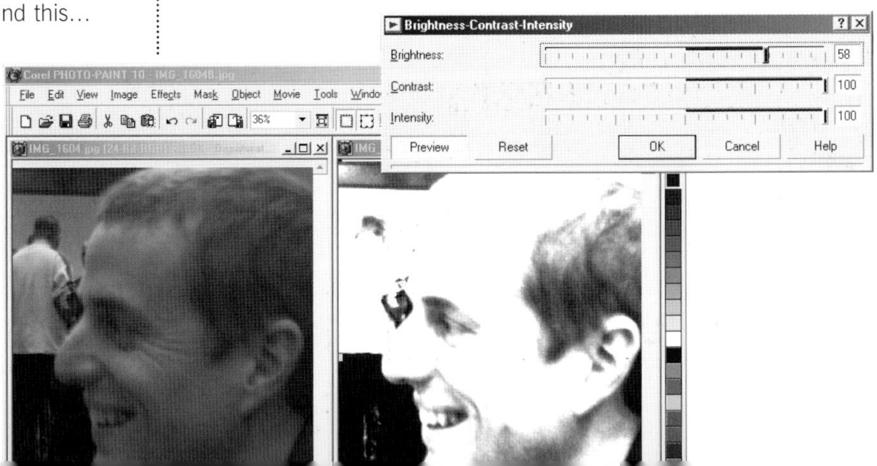

4

Black-and-white

❶ Black-and-white photos are particularly easy to work with, and extremely effective if the form and lighting are good.

❷ Many colour images improve if you make them black-and-white, or desaturate them. If you don't have a *Desaturate* feature in your software, just use *Hue/Saturation*, and drag the *Saturation* slider down.

❸ Next, use your lighting controls to adjust the contrast and brightness of the overall image. Here we've gone for a fairly high contrast, keeping brightness evenly balanced.

❹ Pushing the brightness and contrast up, you start to get a sharp, intense white-space look. Too much for this picture…

❺ …but it looks great here!

❻ Taking the brightness right down, you can create a much moodier look. Note that here we're using *Curves* for more control over the midtones, so we can prevent the darkness from getting out of hand.

❼ You can also achieve good results by making your image *almost* black-and-white, so that just a touch of the original colour shows through.

❽ Or you can use the *Color* dropdown menu in your *Hue/Saturation* to desaturate only certain tones. For instance, we've used red here.

❾ Finally, by applying the maximum contrast possible, you can create a quick, pop-art style, two-tone image, which is great for real impact. But it doesn't work well on all photos.

❺

❻
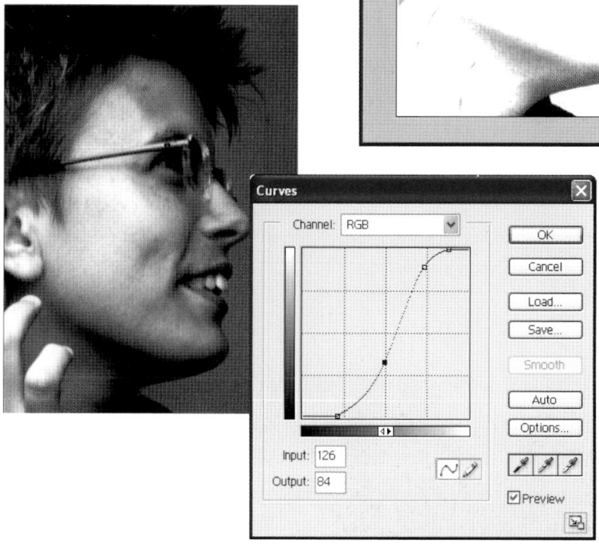

❼
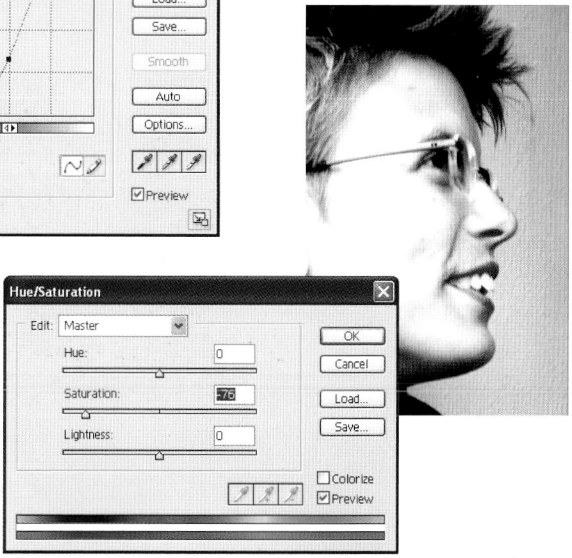

❽
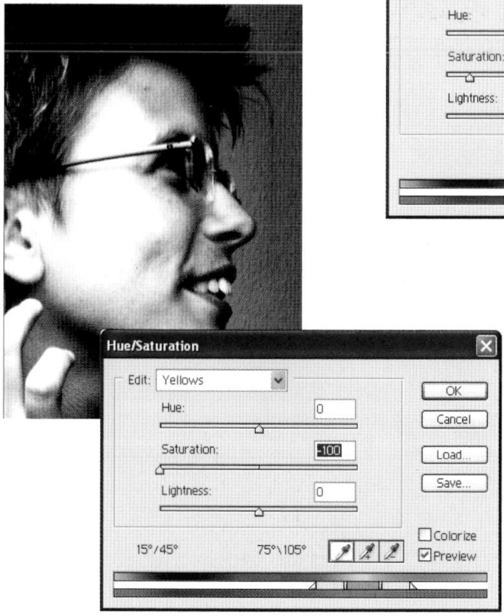

❾

Tinting and colouring

(10) Tinting means affecting the overall colour with a single, or graduated, tone. There are several different techniques you can use for tinting a photo, but one of the easiest is to fill a new layer with a solid colour, and set blending mode to *Hue*.

This doesn't affect the luminosity (amount of light) or saturation of the underlying photo, so it won't work on a black-and-white image…

(11) …for that you need to set the blending mode to *Color*, which affects hue and saturation but not luminosity. The effect can be intense unless you reduce opacity, or use a fairly neutral colour on the tinting layer.

(12) Remember always to experiment. If you've used *Adjustment Layers* or *Lenses* for your processing, rather than applying it directly to the layer or object, then you can always go back and change the settings.

(13) You can also use blending modes other than colour for your tinting layer. In this image we've used a high contrast and set a soft orange tinting layer in *Dodge* mode, which is sometimes called *Color Dodge*.

(14) And here's the same tint, but this time in *Burn*, or *Color Burn*, mode. It gives a gritty filmlike quality to the image, and colours the grey tones of a black-and-white image.

(15) Posterizing is a great effect, particularly on black-and-white images. It reduces the overall number of tones in the image, a bit like a GIF, and you can tint afterwards as necessary.

10
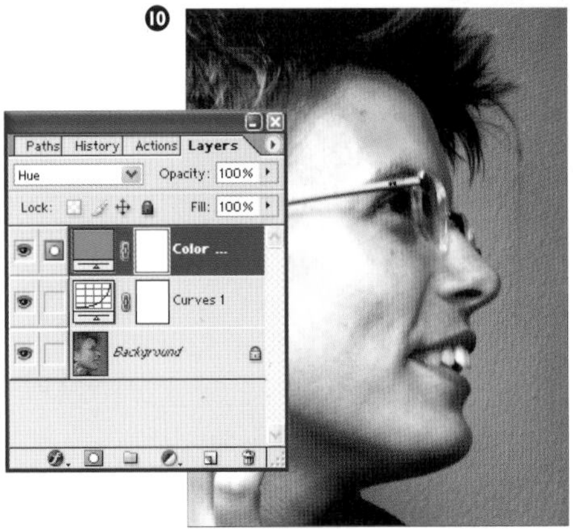

11

12
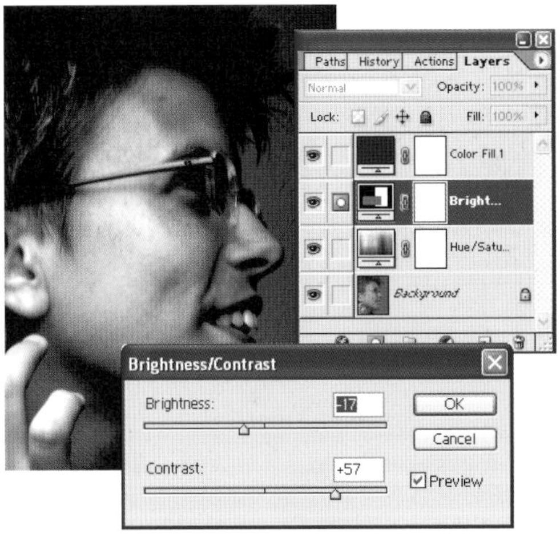

13

14

15
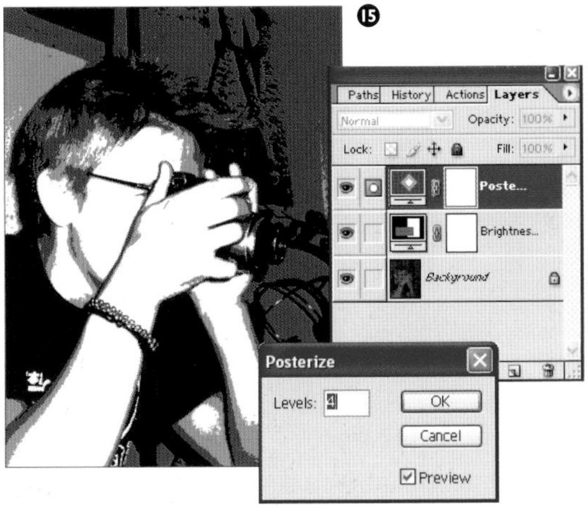

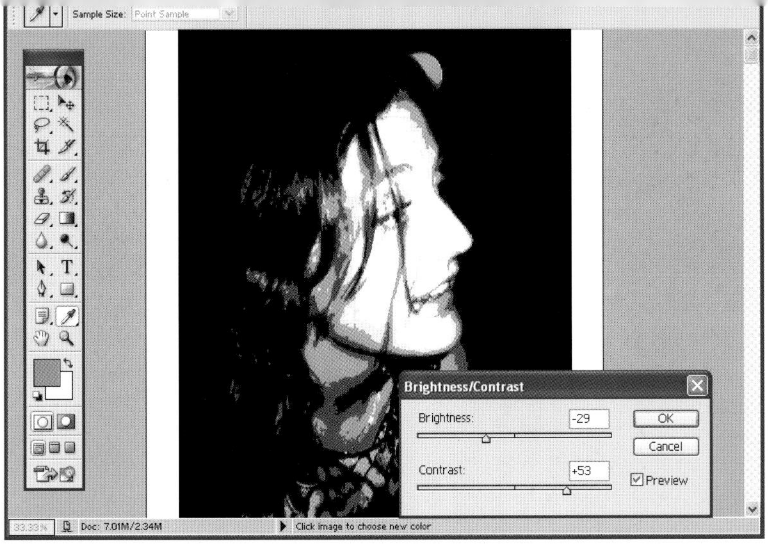

❶

❷

❸

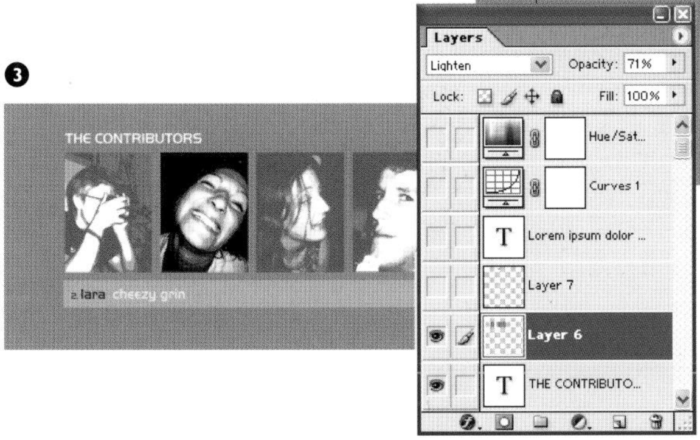

❹

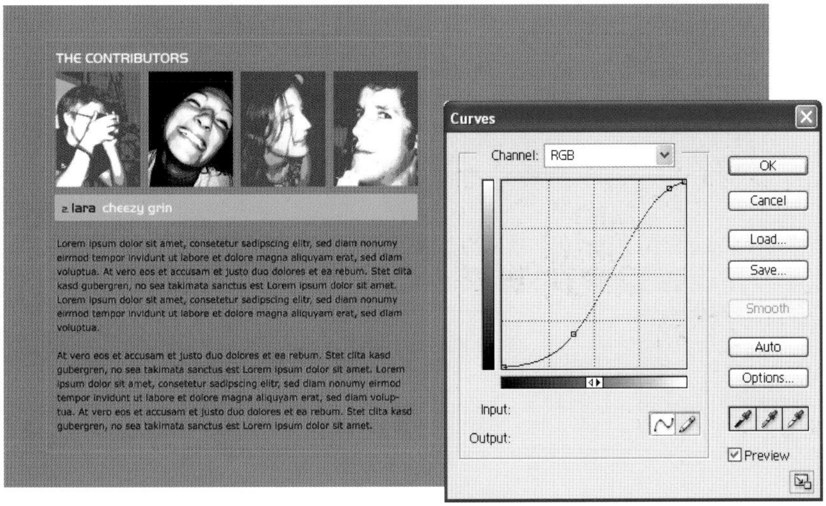

Creating an overall style

If you'd like to edit your photos in a distinctive, graphical way, make sure the style is in harmony with that of your webpages. You may decide to gear the whole look of your site around the photo effects. The easy way to do this is by working in one big file, as in the design on this page for an imaginary online magazine.

❶ Start by taking four photos that have a similar overall character, and apply the exact same lighting and colouring effects. Then tweak the original contrast (in an *Adjustment Layer* or *Lens*) for the individual image.

Next, resize them all to a similar size, then crop each to exactly the same size, and finally save an editable copy, before merging all the layers into one image.

❷ Copy and paste them all into one image, giving them even spacing, and use guides to make sure they line up accurately. Here, background colour was sampled from one photo with the *Eyedropper*, then lightened a little.

Using the same guides, add the main heading, and a box and name space below the images.

❸ To fade the three photos that aren't currently selected, put a 70 per cent opaque background colour over them, with blending set to *Lighten*.

❹ Finally add the text and outline, then apply overall *Curves* and *Hue* adjustment layers to tweak the colour and lighting of the whole image.

PROJECT 14

EDGES AND FRAMING

In real life, we like to frame photos. This isn't an arbitrary obsession to make things more decorative, or to keep them straight. It actually makes pictures look better. A good frame enhances the content of a picture, helping to draw in a viewer's attention. The same goes for images in Web design.

On screen, the way an image borders onto its background – what you do with its edges, in other words – affects the whole appearance of your design and photo. And, moreover, it's a creative opportunity not to be missed.

Framing your image doesn't mean you have to go crazy with elaborate 3D wooden or gilded frame effects with bevels and shadows (although you can if you want to). You may decide not to do much at all. At the most basic, you can add just a simple one-pixel black, white or tinted line around the picture, called a keyline. This is particularly popular in magazines and newspapers.

You can colour your image so parts of it match the background, or you can feather its edges so that it actually fades into the background. You can cut out the main content and sit it directly on the background, rub away edges so it looks like an unfinished painting or distort your picture to give it the appearance of a printed photo in a scrapbook.

1

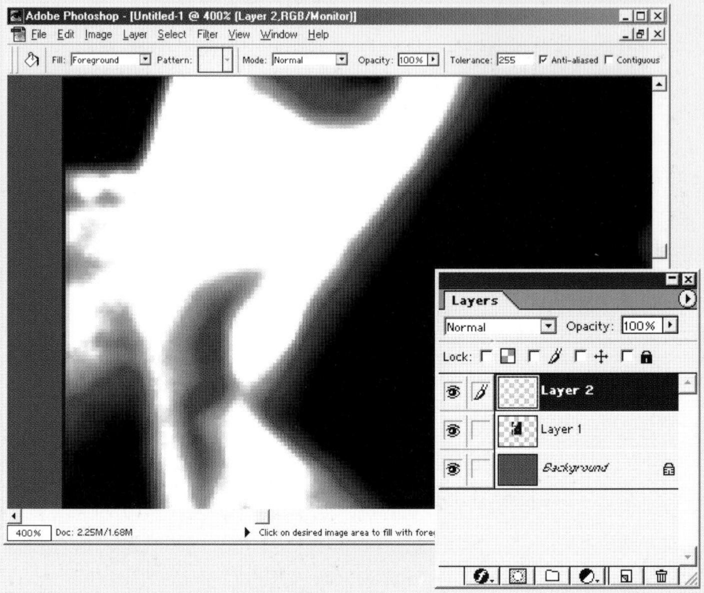

2

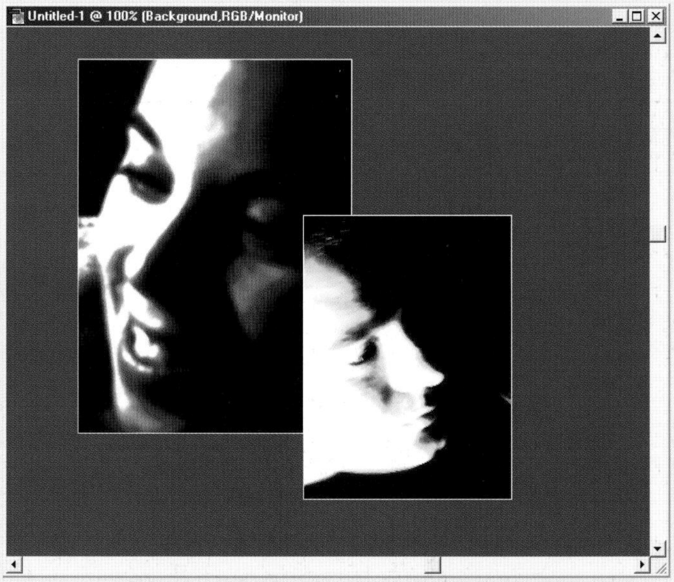

3

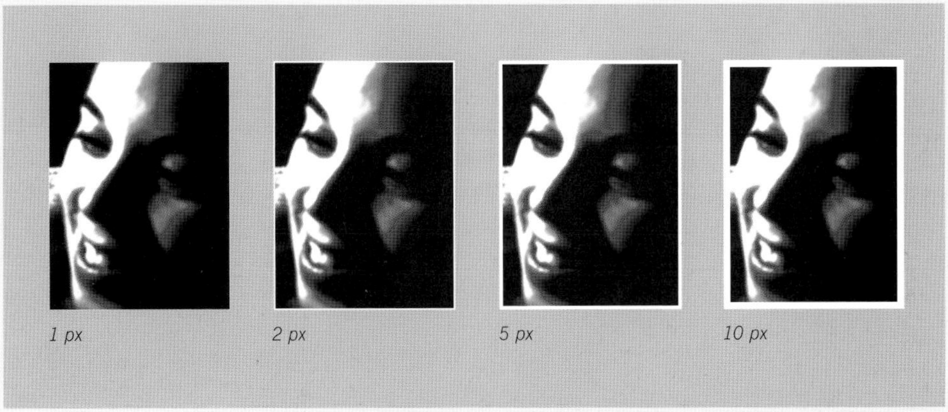

1 px 2 px 5 px 10 px

4

5

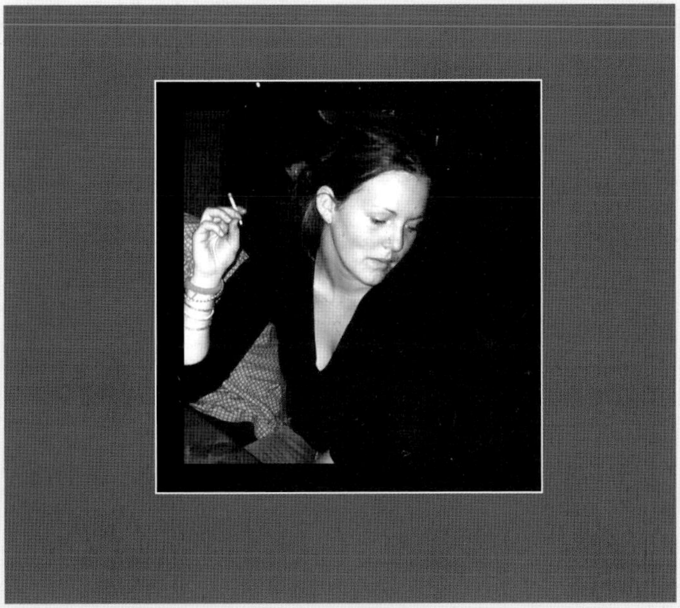

Keylines and borders

1 Perhaps the most popular treatment for photo edges (apart from doing nothing at all) is to add a simple one-pixel black line. In a bitmap package, simply use your *Marquee* to select the area of the photo, and apply a black stroke to the selection on a new layer.

2 Your keyline doesn't have to be black, though, and it doesn't have to be one pixel thick. A white keyline is particularly effective on mid-to-dark backgrounds, or if you want to overlap dark-toned images. You can also use a keyline that is a light or dark tint of a colour within your website's colour scheme.

3 Try experimenting with different-sized keylines. As your keyline gets fatter, the more it begins to look like a proper border. Fat keylines can be really distinctive in Web design, although you might want to tone down the brightness…

4 Here a colour sampled from the photo itself was used as the border colour. Don't forget, you can also experiment with different blending modes and transparencies for your borders if you put them in a separate layer or object, as was done with the second image here.

5 For this image, a massive 35-pixel black border was put around the image, where it blends in all around the right, which is more or less black anyway. A two-pixel white keyline was added around the edge of this border to lift it out from the main page. This looks really sharp.

Feathered edges

6 You can use the blending technique to great effect if you're applying strong colouring or lighting techniques to your images. This image uses colouring effects like those discussed in the previous chapter, with tint colours the same as the chosen background colour. Only parts of the image have an edge, and this breaks up the predictable rectangle.

7 Another option is to feather the edges of your images, which will give them a soft edge. If you select your *Marquee* tool and open the *Tool Options* palette or toolbar, you should see a *Feather* option. (It may be in a dropdown menu alongside 'Hard' and 'Anti-alias'.) Ten is a good setting to start off with.

When you're preparing to crop your photos, leave plenty of space around the main subject so you'll have at least 20 pixels to spare right around after you've resized the image.

8 Do the resizing and sharpening, then use your software's *Guides* feature to place guides 10 pixels in from each of the edges. Next, use your *Marquee* tool to draw a selection fitting against these, copy the selection and then paste it onto a new layer.

9 Now hide or delete the original layer and, below the new layer, create another layer with a solid colour fill for a background. This process feathers edges by ten pixels on the inside and outside of your selection. So, if you use a larger *Feather* setting, remember to leave more space in for this in your original crop.

6

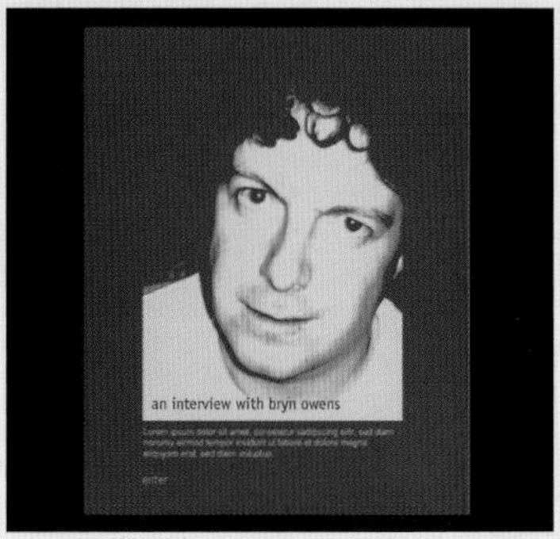

7

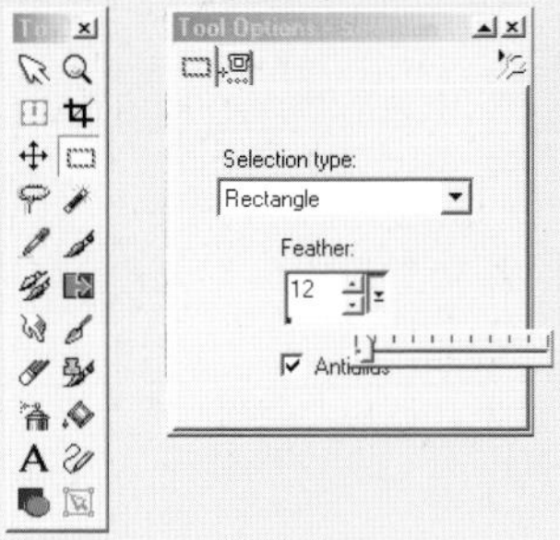

8

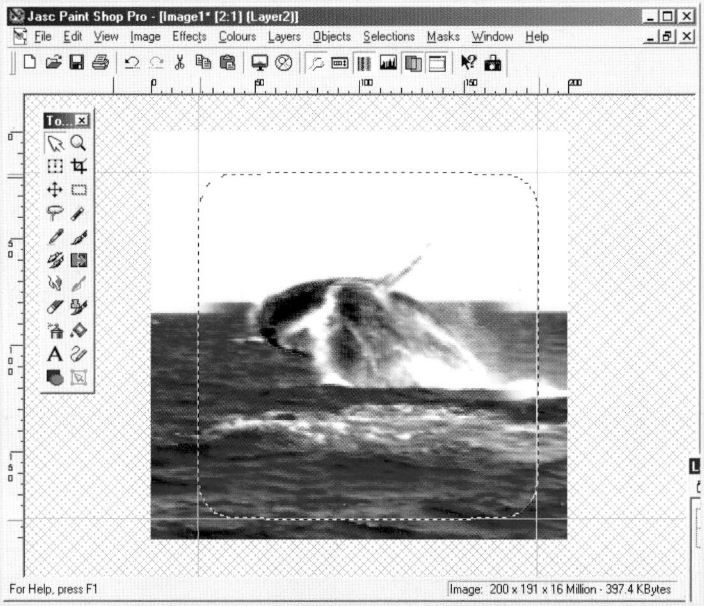

9

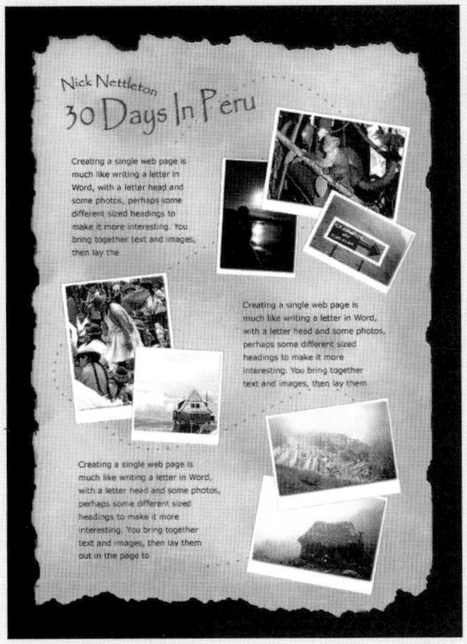

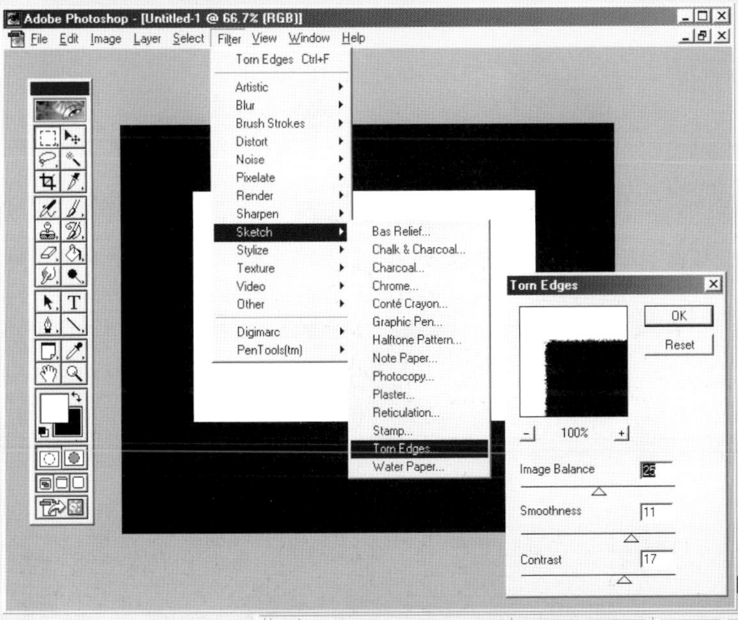

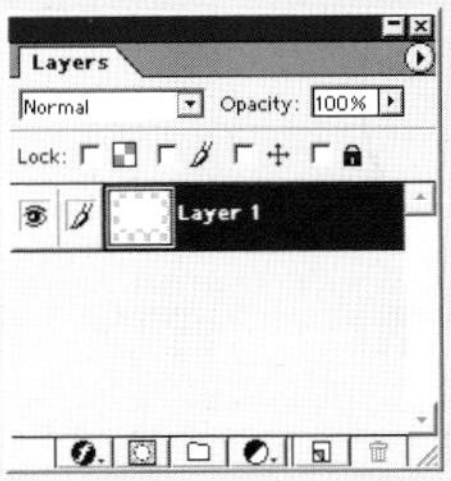

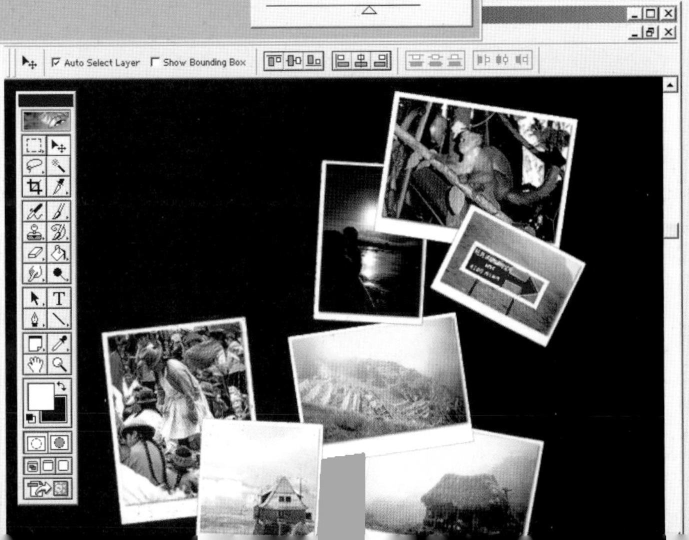

Quick scrapbook

❶ One final framing look for this project combines two effects in one. It's a scrapbook look, which is always perfect for spicing up vacation or party shots online. It's easy to do and looks impressive, and the variations are almost endless.

❷ First, collect the images you want, and prepare them in the normal way. You might want to make them quite dark and contrasty, with strong colour.

❸ Now create backing cards. In a new file, draw a white rectangle on a black background. (You may need to combine these into one bitmap graphic for the next bit to work.) Look for a filter or effect called *Torn Edges* or similar. If you can't find it, experiment with roughening filters. What you want is a subtle jagged edge on the white rectangle.

❹ Next, use your *Magic Wand*, with antialiasing (see page 130) turned on, to select the torn-edge rectangle. Copy it, paste it onto a new layer and delete the original layer, so you've got your backing card on a transparent background.

Now, for each photo, take a copy of this file, paste the photo into it and size everything up for a snug fit. Try not to get them all perfectly straight. Add a barely visible, tight drop shadow to lift the photos a bit.

❺ Finally, paste all your frame image combinations into one page in a jumbled fashion, and apply a soft drop shadow to the backing cards.

To finish the look, add in a tasteful textured background, with a heading to match.

PROJECT 15

CUTTTING IMAGES OUT

Getting creative with the borders of images in your Web design helps to add an element of surprise – or at least something less than predictable – to your site. It sets you apart from the crowd.

Another technique for breaking the boredom is to cut out the main subject of the image, and place it directly onto your background. You'll see this done a lot in magazines, where it helps to provide a contrast to the straight lines that dominate most print layouts.The process used to do this can be rather tricky until you get the hang of it. It takes patience and is not suitable for every photo. However, it does create a striking impression, and is well worth the effort for your homepage, or links that you want to really emphasise.

The first and most important thing is to work with a really big, hi-resolution image, so that you've got lots of margin for error. You should also try to use an image in which the edges between your subject and background are simple and clear: sharp, high-contrast, or with a distinct change in colour is good. Also, it's good to avoid subjects with lots of fiddly detail around the edge. If you start trying to cut out a picture of a skydiver with all their hair in the air, strands flying all over the place, then you're embarking on a very ambitious project indeed!

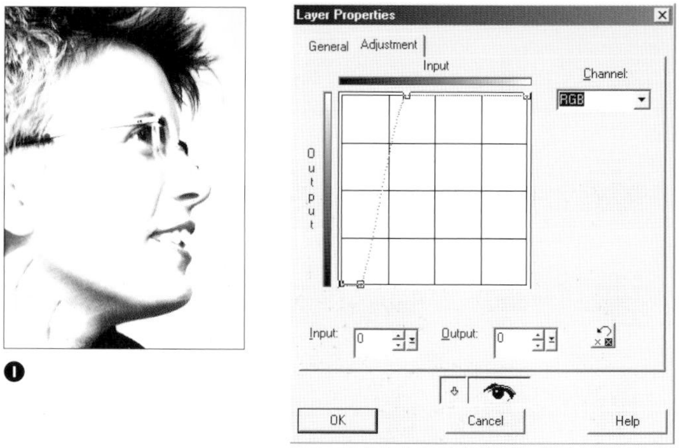

1

2

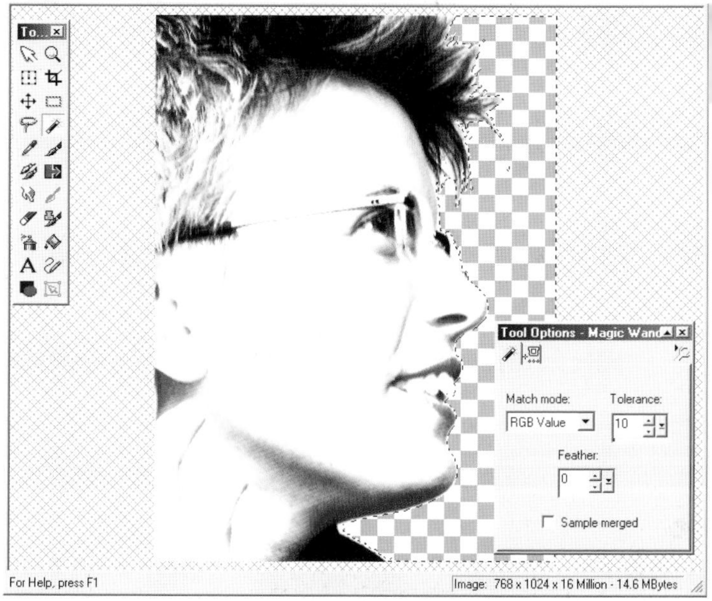

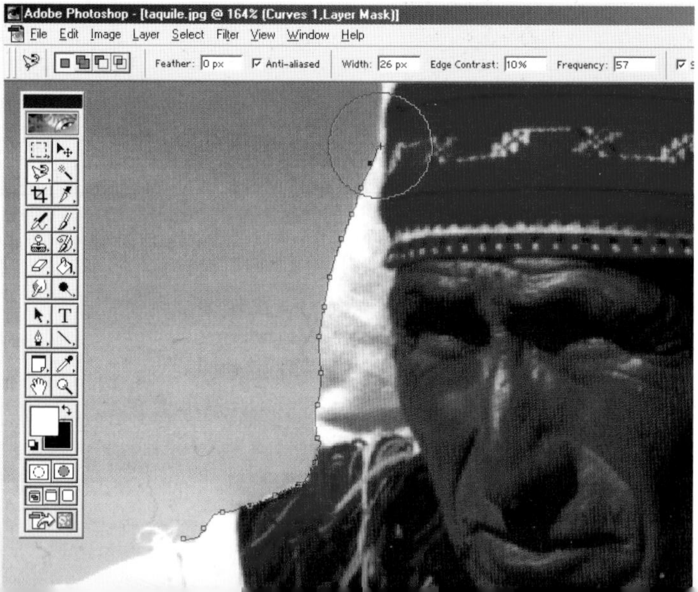

3

4

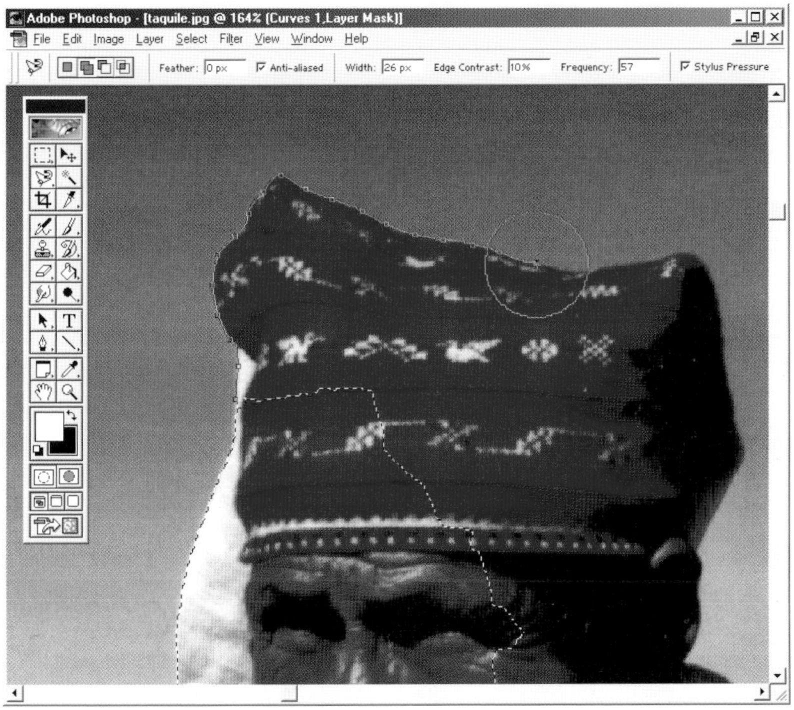

5

6

1 In an ideal world, the image you want to cut out will already have a broadly flat background with just a few tones in it. Or you may be able to make it more like this using your lighting tools.

2 In this case, just use your *Magic Wand* tool to instantly select areas of the same colour, and quickly tidy up the details using the following techniques. Use the *Tolerance* setting in your options to adjust how similar tones should be for the magic to work.

3 You can also do this manually. The tool for the job is the *Lasso*, or a *Magic Lasso* if you've got one, which tries to identify edges. Zoom in close to your image, and start drawing along the edge. This gets easier with practice, and you can always tidy things up later...

4 You don't need to do the whole thing in one go. Complete a small section of the image, then scroll across and start doing the next small bit, but this time holding the *Shift* key. This means that you are adding to what's already selected, rather than starting all over from scratch. You can also take away from selections, by holding the *Alt* or *Command* key and drawing around the area you don't want to be selected.

5 When you're happy with this, copy and paste the selection onto a new layer, put a background colour behind it, then zoom out from your cut out to see how it looks.

6 You might want to add a soft shadow behind the cut out, or even paint in your own realistic 3D shadow...

PROJECT 16

ICONS AND PHOTO GRAPHICS

Photos aren't just for use in Web photo galleries and scrapbooks, or to illustrate some text. You can also use them to liven up buttons and links. We talked a great deal about creating different types of graphics for these in the last chapter. However, all the graphics were abstract – they weren't actually pictures of anything. Given that almost nothing beats an image for focusing attention, a well-applied photo in your buttons can do a world of good. Cutouts, in particular, work well, along with extreme colour and lighting treatments to make your image more graphic in appearance, with greater impact.

Another way to add a pictorial element to your graphic is by using symbols, illustrations (or drawings) and icons, as the My Computer or Macintosh HD icon on your desktop does.

A good accompanying graphic on a button tells the whole story: your viewer doesn't even have to read the text, because they know what it's about already. If you're supremely confident, you might want to dispense with the text altogether, although this is a bold move indeed.

Getting images to work at small sizes can be challenging: there's no room for lots of detail, and your shapes and colour have got to be clear and obvious. You also need something succinct and to-the-point; complex messages aren't going to do the job. If the site is all about news, then get a picture of a newspaper, for example.

❶

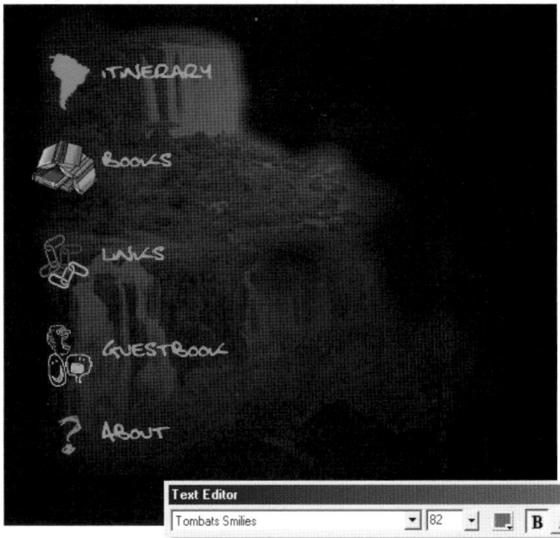

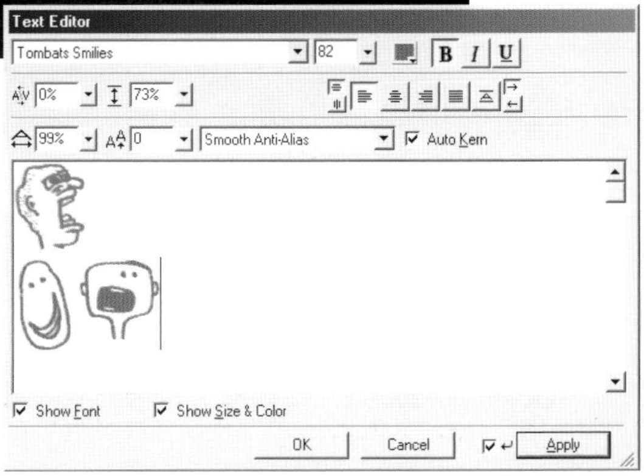

❷

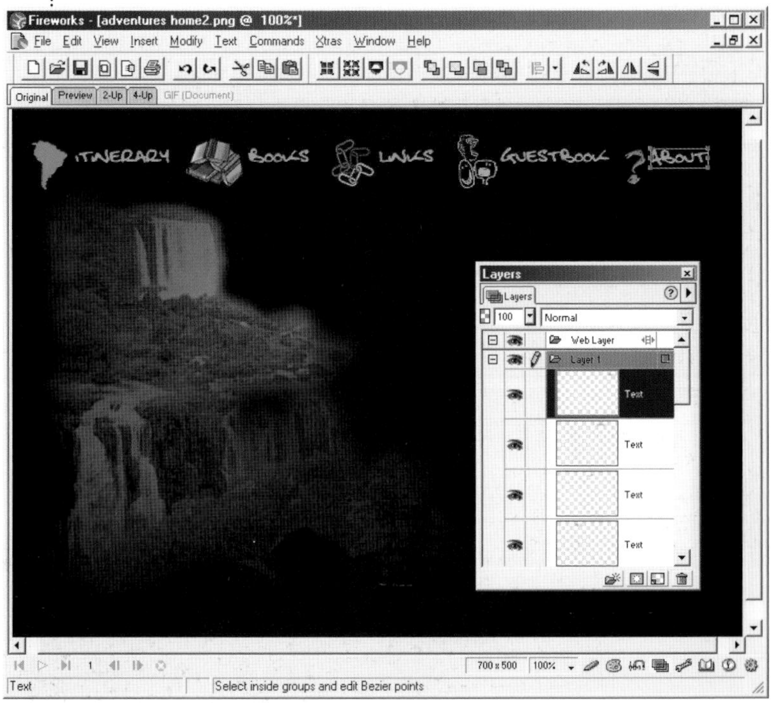

❸

4

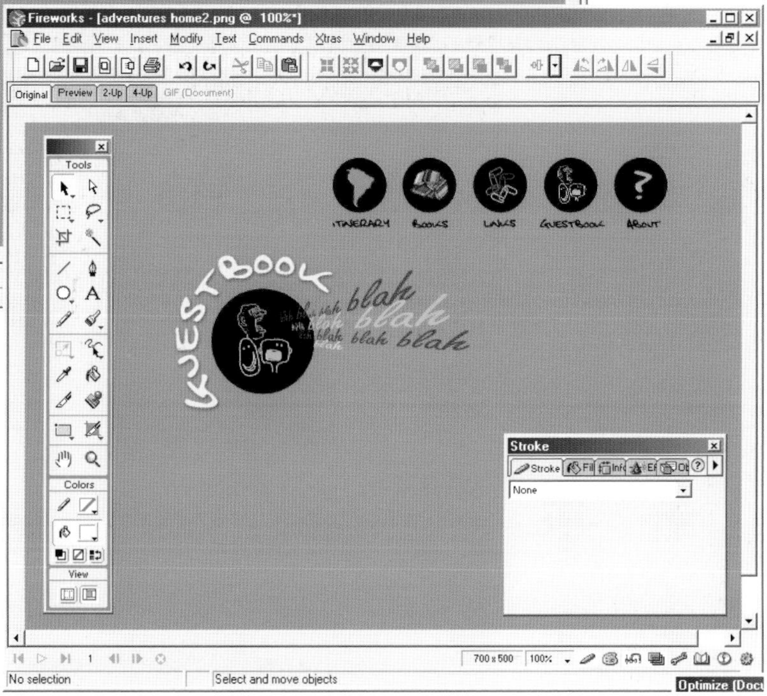

5

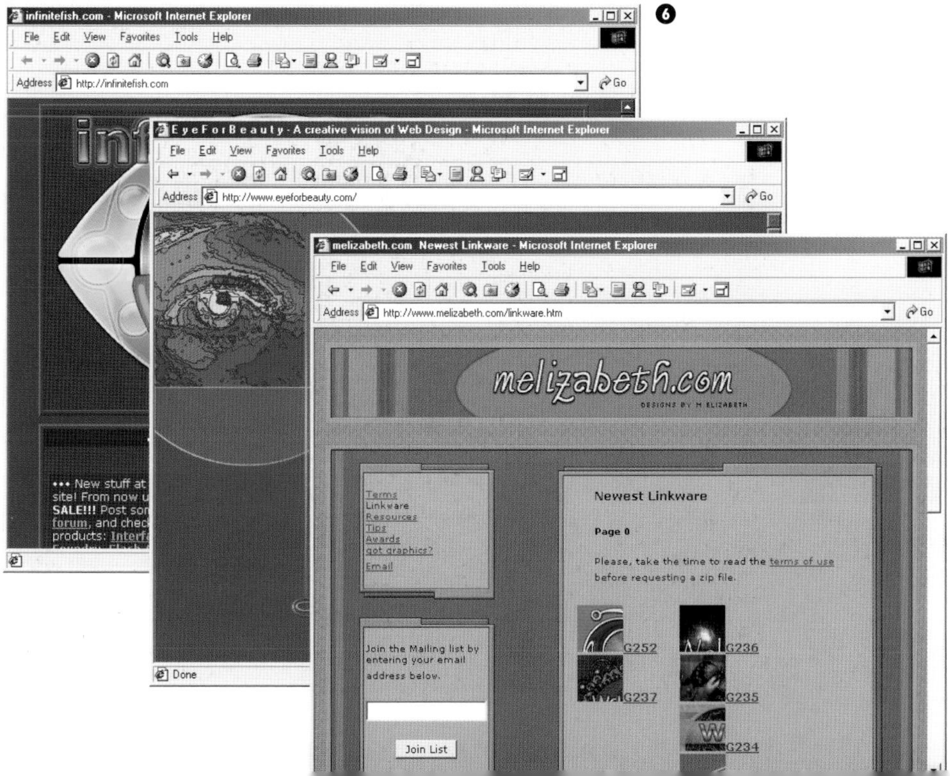

6

Graphical icons

❶ A few small pictures make this series of buttons a thousand times better. After all, wouldn't you prefer to always know where links go without having to read the words? The icons focus your attention and yet are subtle enough not to interfere with the main content of the page.

❷ You don't have to draw all these pictures by hand, though of course you can if you want to. The quickest way to get graphics is to use a Dingbat font. Wingdings 1 to 3, Webdings and Zapf Dingbats are good starting points, or you can get more experimental with Good Dog Bones and Tombat Smilies.

❸ You can use these in all kinds of ways. The obvious is to colour them in line with your website colour scheme and just sit them above, below or next to your link text.

❹ Or why not put them in a square or circle for an added sense of clickability?

❺ If you use a particular icon style for a link, then you might want to use it again in an adapted – and perhaps more elaborate – form in the heading of the page it's linking to. This provides a sense of continuity and reinforced identity for your viewers.

❻ There are also many sites on the Web where you can download popular icon graphics like these for free. Try ***http://infinitefish.com***, ***www.eyeforbeauty.com*** and ***www.melizabeth.com*** for starters. Always remember to check the copyright before using them, though.

Photo icons and thumbnails

❶ Photos, particularly of faces, have a special quality that instantly attracts people's attention. This is even more the case if they have a dramatic form or are easily recognisable. It's effective to use and exploit this in small details in your designs. The trouble is, getting your images to look right when they're very small is something of an art form. But there are three basic rules you can use: keep it simple; go for strong shapes and forms; and use high contrast, keeping it sharp.

❷ You should, of course, always try to make the image relate to what the link is about! Try browsing old photos to find details you can use. You need only a small image, so you can go for ultra-close-ups (as shown here) or use details from the background. You could use a front door or door knocker for a homepage link, for instance.

❸ You might want to just go square and simple with your photo icons, or use edge effects. This edge effect was done using the same techniques as are used for creating cutouts, but without following the edge of the object. It looks quick and scruffy, but it took a while to get the effect to look like that! You also need to make sure that the overall lighting and colouring in your icons matches up well. If you're having trouble doing this in a natural way, try applying a stronger effect across the board.

❶

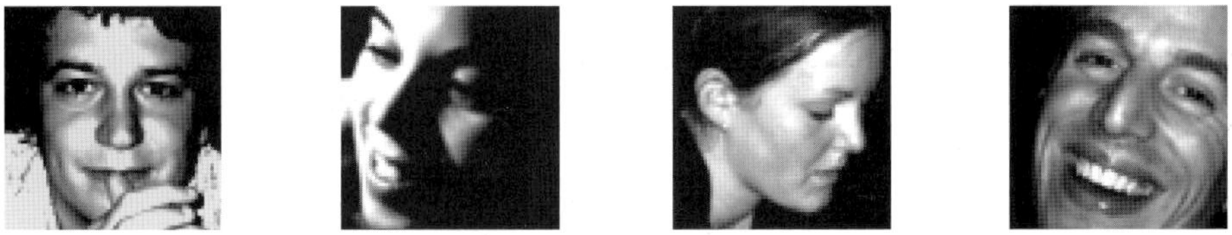

❷

❸

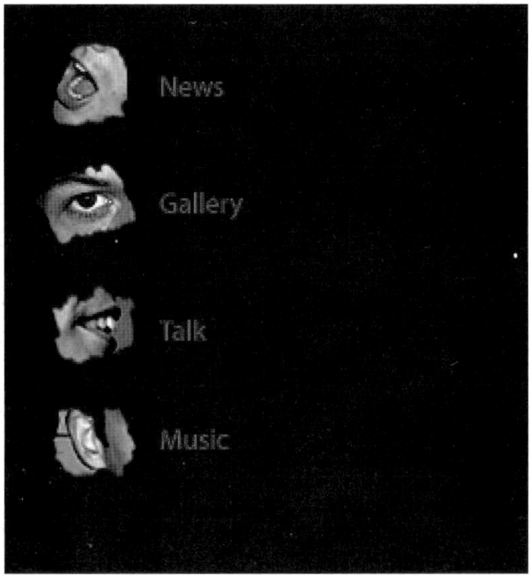

1

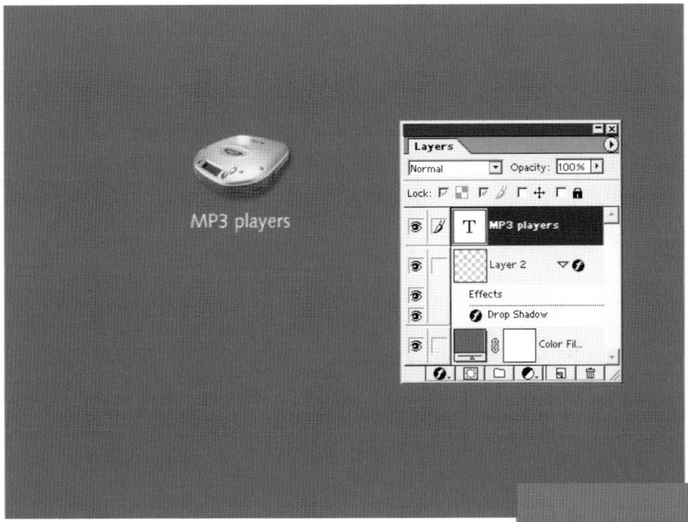

2

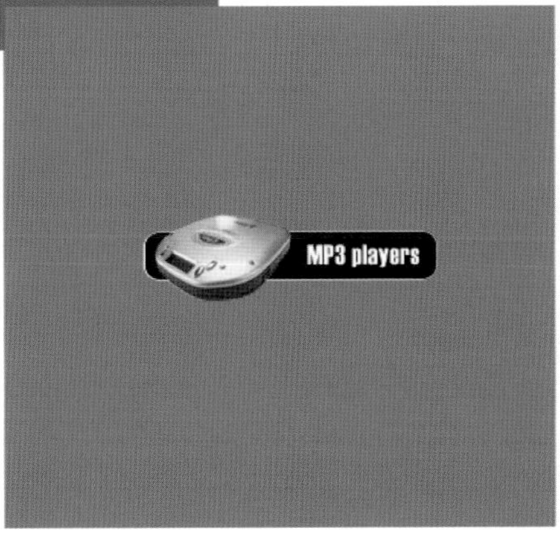

3

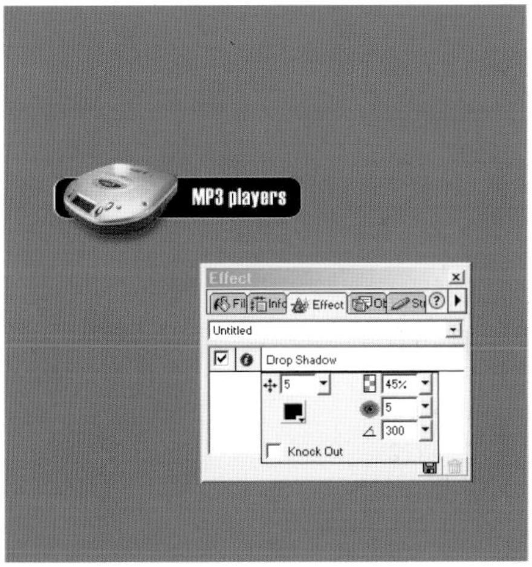

4

5

Using cutouts

1 Images that are cut out using the techniques from the previous project are particularly effective for links you want to draw attention to. This is also an excellent way to make use of the technique in your design, but without having to put all the effort in every time you want to make an update.

2 Try layering cutouts over the edge of your button, or just squeezing out of the edges of a circle. This effect, of cutting through graphics, adds to the sense that the image is floating over the page. This gives it depth, as well as breaking up the lines.

3 A little drop shadow helps to emphasise this effect, but keep it subtle or you'll ruin the classiness of your cutout.

4 You need to make sure that when you export your buttons and put them in your webpage, they all line up properly. Because the images are slightly different sizes – that's all part of the natural, irregular look – imagine a box around each graphic. Place a guide to mark its size and use this as a guideline when you're saving the individual files.

5 Because cutouts are so attention-grabbing, they're perfect for ads. You can give them the appearance of punching or cutting through the edge of the advertisement.

ABOUT TRANSPARENCY AND ALIASING

When you come to export your photo-based, and other, graphics into your webpage, and you've got them at an angle (as in the scrapbook design) or you're using cutouts, then you might want to use *Transparency* for the background colour. This is particularly useful if the background is a texture or gradient, because you can then be flexible about exactly where the graphic goes on your page, and change your mind at will.

If you're wondering why this is important, then imagine you've exported a graphic with a textured background, which doesn't match up seamlessly to the background at its final position in the webpage. You're going to get crude and unsightly edges showing, which will ruin the effect. *Transparency* is the solution, but this creates several problems of its own. The first is that you can use only the GIF format – JPEG doesn't support transparency. But that shouldn't matter too much, especially if you go for a low-colour posterized look in the photos.

A tougher problem to deal with is antialiasing, which means that sometimes you can't entirely take a transparent graphic intended for one background colour, and put it on an another. Aliasing is best described by imagining that when you draw a curve you can see it has jagged edges, because the very pixels which it is made up of are visible to the eye. Antialiasing is a process that dupes the eye into seeing a smooth curve by ever so slightly blurring the edges, so that the edge pixels have a colour that is mixed from the background and the foreground. The trouble is, you can't do this in a GIF where the background is transparent because, with the GIF format, a pixel is either completely transparent or not at all...

1

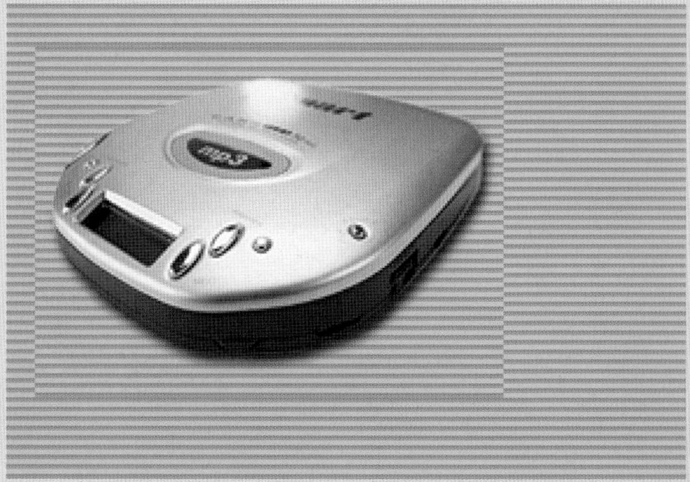

2

3

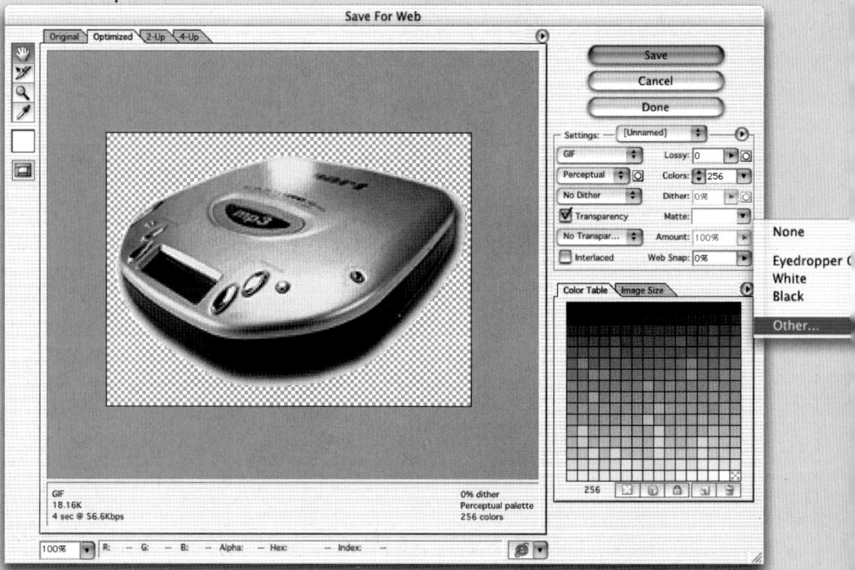

❹

❺

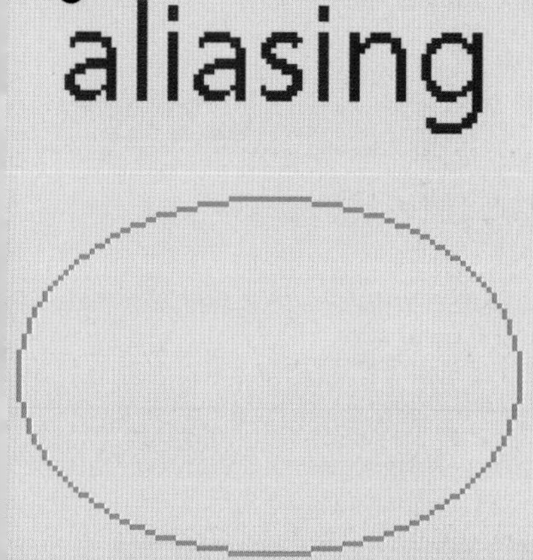

❻

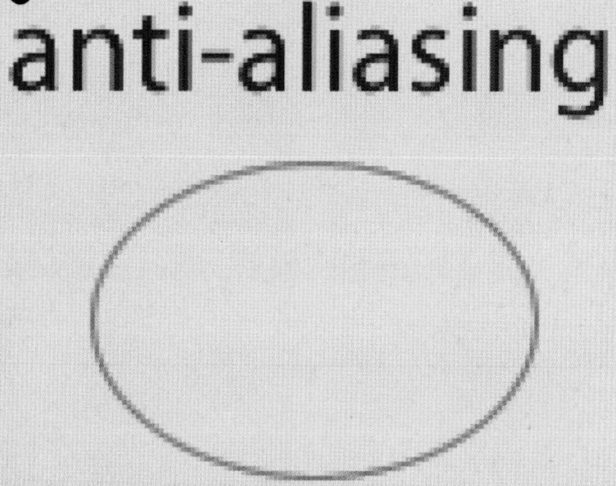

❼

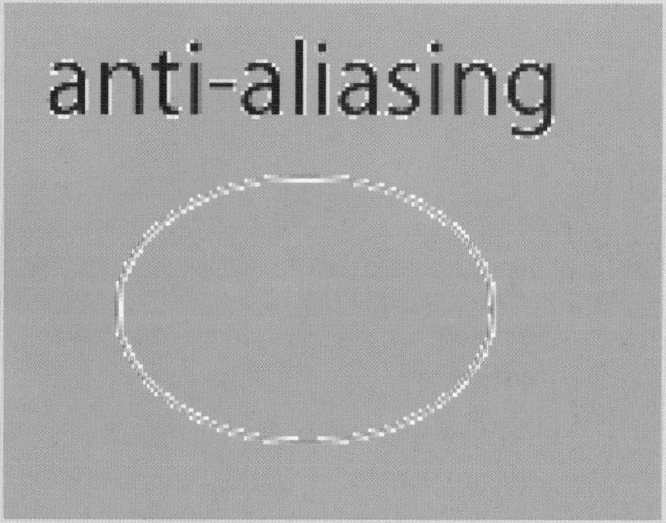

❶ It's good to use *Transparency* for the backgrounds of graphics, particularly if you're putting them on a textured or patterned background, or are not sure of the exact colour they will be on. It saves unsightly accidents!

❷ *Transparency* is easy to create. Delete the background layer in a bitmap application or, in Fireworks, change the *Canvas Color* setting to transparent. Then select the *Transparency* option when you export as a GIF.

❸ But if your graphic includes semitransparent pixels, in a drop-shadow for instance, you need to decide what to do, because in a GIF you can have only complete transparency. Usually, you'll have to use the *Matte* setting to choose an assumed background colour.

❹ And this means you've still got to be careful about what kind of background you're putting your image on, as you can see here. Unless, that is, it had no semitransparent pixels to start with. However, almost all images do, due to antialiasing.

❺❻ Aliasing – its antithesis – occurs when you see jagged edges on a line or text, because your eye can detect the pixels. Antialiasing smoothes the appearance by gently blurring the curve.

❼ The trouble is, if your background is transparent, this means the antialiased pixels have a part-transparent colour. However, the GIF format can't do partial transparency. Use the *Matte* colour to help it work out what to do, but this reduces the flexibility of using transparent GIFs, as you can see here.

PROJECT 17

ALIGNING AND SPACING IMAGES

Having created and prepared all your images, you need to get them into your webpage. This is just a matter of exporting and adding them in the same way as you add other types of graphics. However, sometimes it can be a little difficult to get the alignments and positioning just right. Often you want an image to align with a particular bit of text; other times, you want a series of images, perhaps of unusual shapes, to align with each other.

Much of design is about space and form. Getting things to line up properly, when they're meant to, is absolutely paramount, as is getting the spacing even between things. Often designers set a kind of semi-rule about the spacing between elements of the design. For example, you may choose to set related things to go 10 pixels apart and unrelated things 20 pixels apart. You don't have to stick to this rule at all times, but you may find that using this method improves your designs significantly.

Remember that by putting connecting elements of your design closer together, you're helping your viewers to make the connection quickly, without having to think or interpret it in any way. You're appealing to the already existing language of the human mind, and that is a very powerful thing to do. Also, by keeping your spacing regular and using common sizes, everything will look much tidier and better planned.

❶

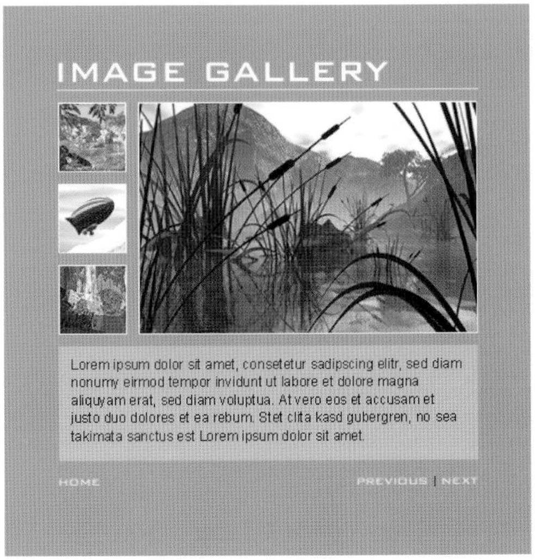

❷

❸

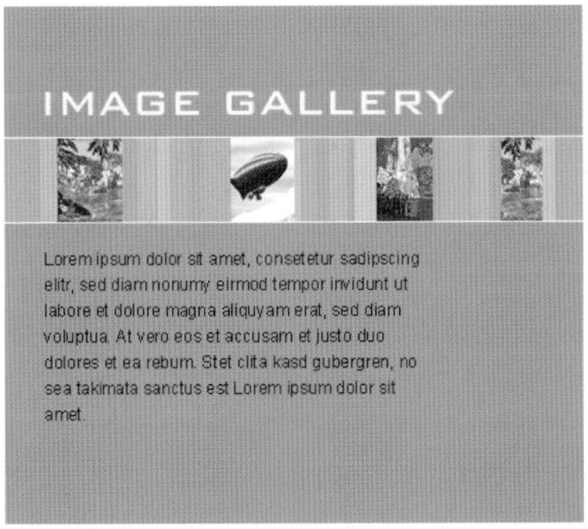

IMAGE GALLERY
Lorem ipsum dolor sit amet, consetetur sadipscing elitr, sed diam nonumy eirmod tempor invidunt ut labore et dolore magna aliquyam erat, sed diam voluptua. At vero eos et accusam et justo duo dolores et ea rebum. Stet clita kasd gubergren, no sea takimata sanctus est Lorem ipsum dolor sit amet.

4

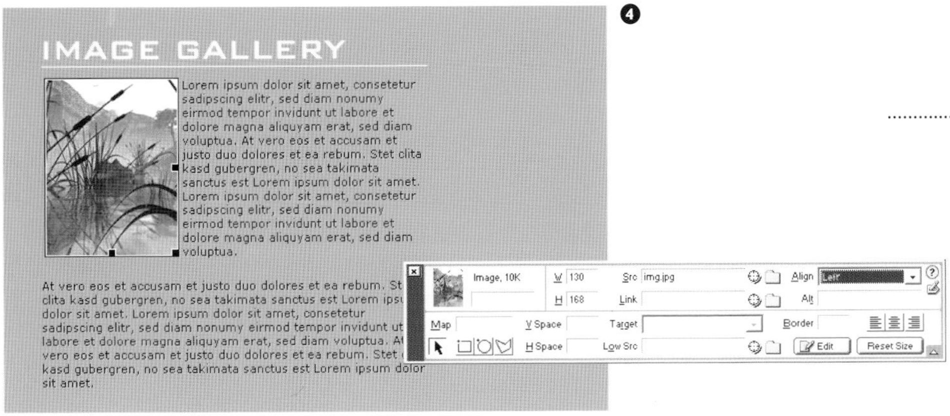

5

6

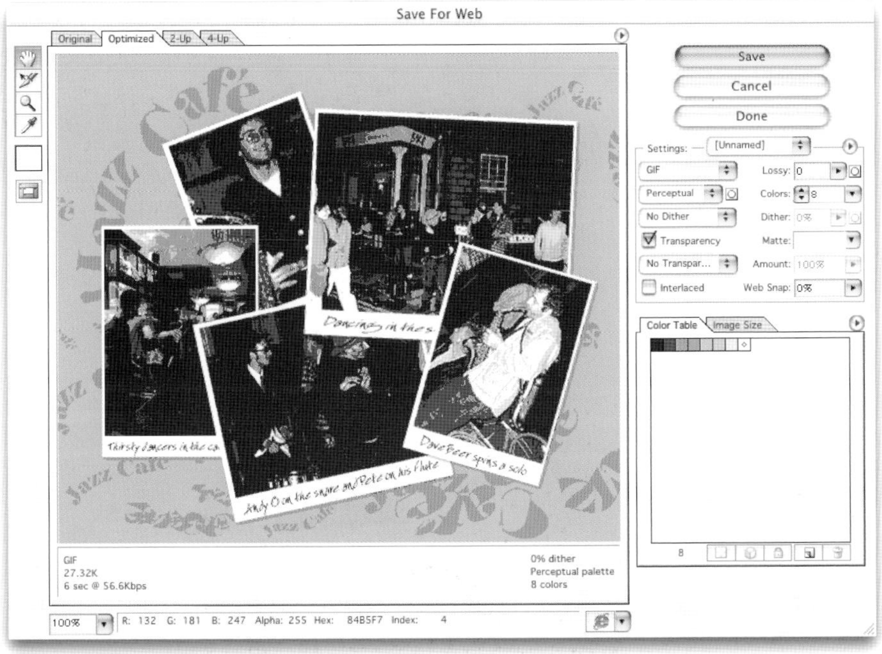

1 Try to use common sizes for your images. For example, you might want to go for thumbnails at 60 x 60 pixels, and big pictures at 300 x 200 pixels.

2 Regular spacing tends to look attractive with photos, and obviously works better with same-size pictures. It's also quick and easy to set up such spacing, using a single table with cell spacing set to 10, for instance. Here, the background becomes the border.

3 Here, in contrast, an irregular spacing has been created, using randomly sized (but finely tuned) table columns with different, but tonally similar, background colours.

4 Often you'll want to flow an image in with the text. You can use the image's *Align Left* and *Align Right* properties for a quick solution, but you might feel the spacing isn't great!

5 As an alternative, create a 1 x 1 table, both five pixels wider and five pixels taller than the image, and set the whole table to align left or right. Then set the inner cell's alignment properties to *Top* and *Left* or *Right* and pop your photo in it.

6 With a jumbled scrapbook look, the process can be difficult, although well worth the effort. If your photos are all tightly packed, you might be wise to just export it as one big image with some hefty compression. (Consider making GIF colour reduction an intended effect in itself.)

Alternatively, space things out a little, place guides around the images and use these to mark the edges when you crop out the individual graphics.

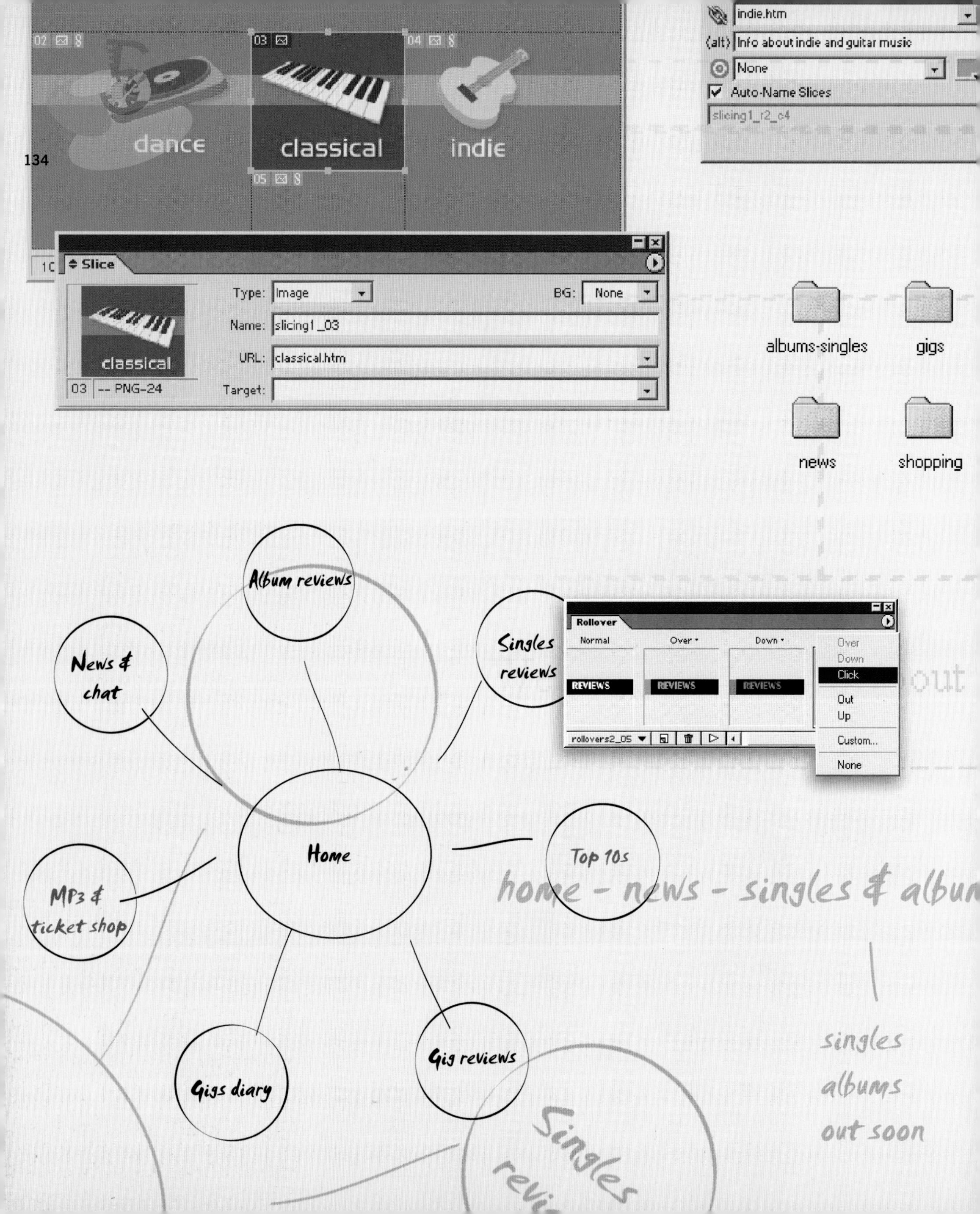
dance
classical
indie
indie.htm
(alt) Info about indie and guitar music
None
Auto-Name Slices
slicing1_r2_c4
Slice
Type: Image
BG: None
Name: slicing1_03
URL: classical.htm
Target:
03 -- PNG-24
albums-singles
gigs
news
shopping
Album reviews
News & chat
Singles reviews
Home
Top 10s
MP3 & ticket shop
Gigs diary
Gig reviews
Rollover
Normal
Over
Down
REVIEWS
Over
Down
Click
Out
Up
Custom...
None
rollovers2_05
home - news - singles & albun
singles
albums
out soon

CHAPTER 5

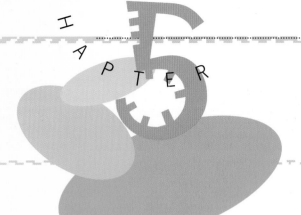

Navigation & Rollovers

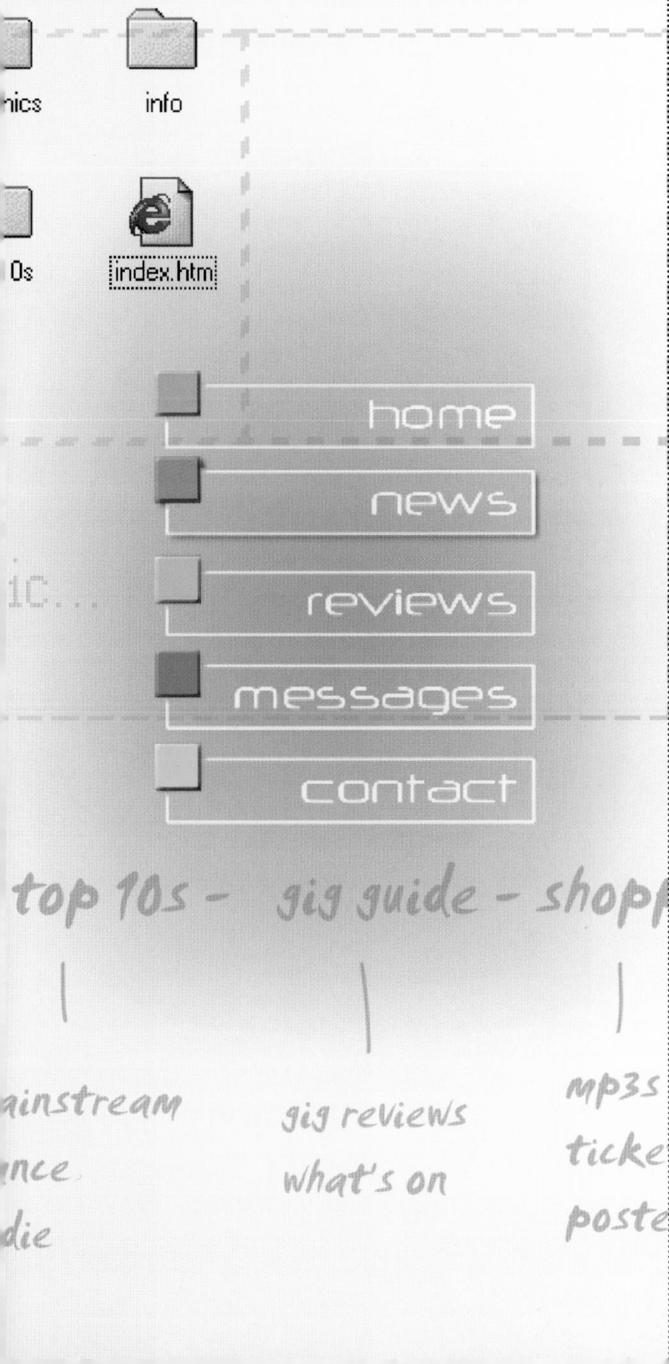

Whatever the claims for the digital world, computer screens can supply only a two-dimensional image, and the long-promised benefits of virtual reality have yet to find a mass market. But interactive technologies, whether based on TV or cell phones, will be a huge growth area over the next few years. Design forms that can work with the interactive dimension, such as Web design, offer unique, creative opportunities to get your message across. As a Web designer, you should be looking to make the most of this. But how...?

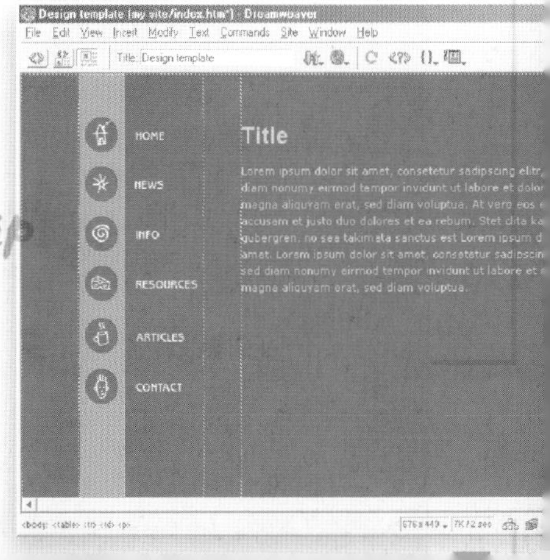

PROJECT 18

PLANNING YOUR NAVIGATION

Navigation is to Web design what the Sun is to our Solar System: it's a beacon for your users, and everything revolves around it. The whole principle of the Internet is built on the idea of getting from A to C by clicking on B, and creating a good website means getting this absolutely right.

There's a general rule that states you should have the same unerring navigation on every page of your site, and there is good sense in this. While you may know your website inside out, it's a mystery to others. Like exploring the streets of a town you've never visited before, it's hard to know which street goes where, and two wrong turns is all it takes to lose your way. Now imagine if there were no signposts. No doubt you've found yourself in websites like this before.

Presumably, you want people to visit your website, get as much out of it as possible and come back regularly. This means holding their hand as they find their way around. Your navigation is like a series of signposts to all the major attractions on your site. Choose them well, label them clearly and point your visitors in the right direction. If you don't take the time to do this thoroughly, much of the rest of the effort you put in will be a waste of your time.

❷

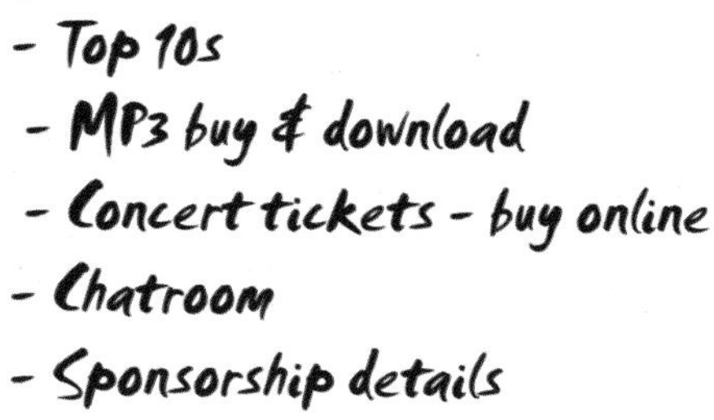

❶

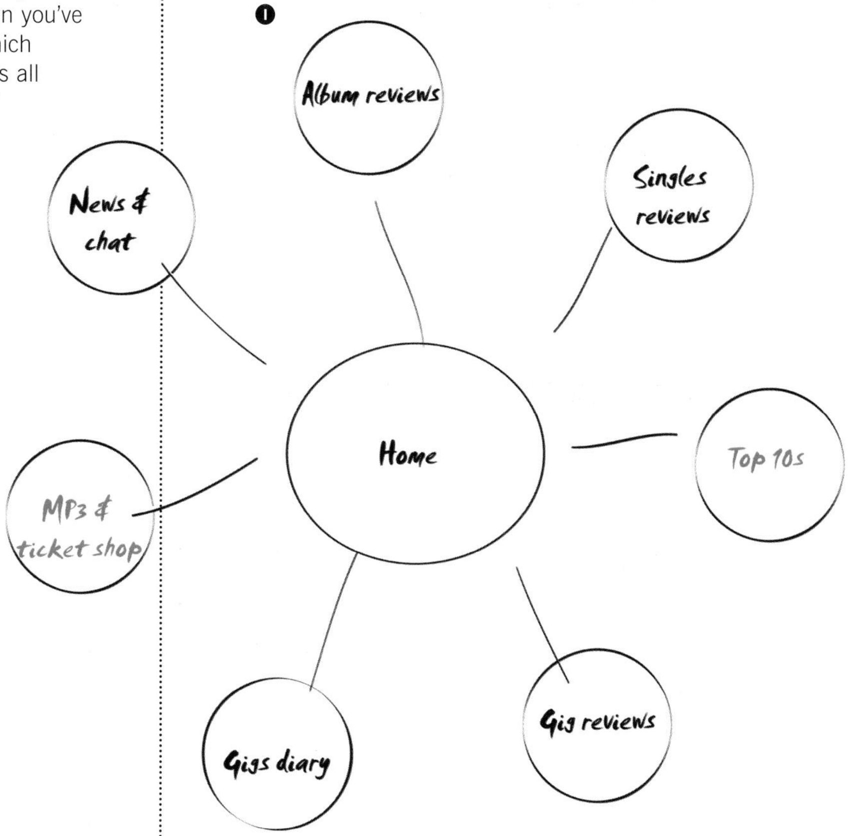

❸

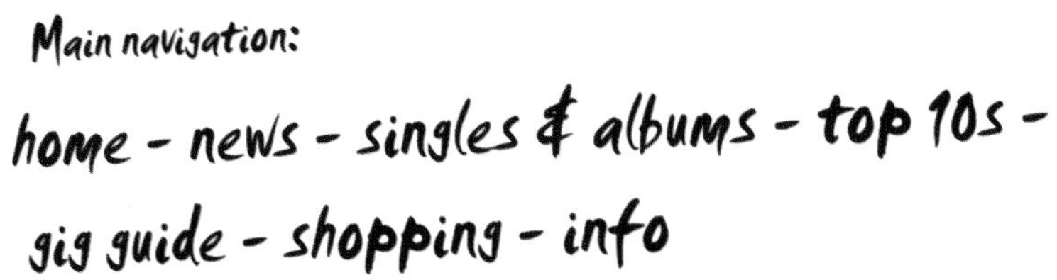

Main navigation:
home - news - singles & albums - top 10s -
gig guide - shopping - info

❹

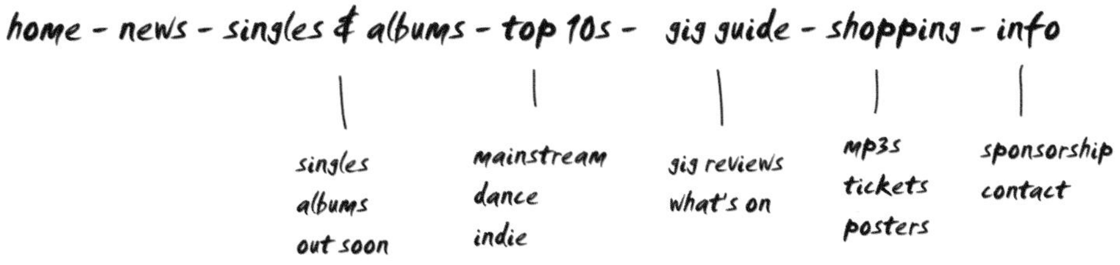

❺

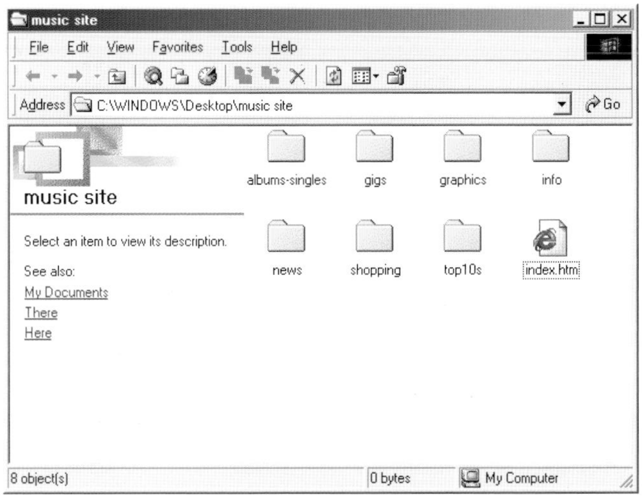

Organising your site

❶ Before you do anything else, you should make a written plan of your site and a list of the main links, like the one shown here. For example, imagine you're creating a site about music. You could organise it according to types of music (rock, soul, classical, country and western), according to the type of information (news, reviews, sound clips, message board), or many other ways.

❷ It's up to you, but if you have a specific objective for your site, make another list of what you think the most important features might be. You might have an MP3 shop for music clips and downloads (perhaps your own?), previews, contact information...

❸ From these, you can work out a list of things for your navigation. Don't make it too long or complicated: five to seven links is good, but ten should be the maximum. If you've got more than that, try reorganizing or dividing them into groups, which you can make a feature of on your site.

❹ As your website gets larger, you'll find that some sections have more pages than others, and you might want to sub-group these to make it easy for your visitors to navigate. You can also create mini navigations for individual sections.

❺ Name all your webpage files sensibly, so you know what's what. You might even want to put different sections in various subfolders within your site folder, and put graphics files in a dedicated images folder.

Navigation design

1 *There are many ways you can incorporate your navigation into the design of your page, but the most important thing is to make sure that it is clear, and a leading feature of your design. Nothing's more frustrating than a pretentious navigation scheme...*

2 *The most popular options are to place navigational tools across the top and down the left, integrating with your logo. The advantages are numerous but, most importantly, it means you can always have navigation in the same place, leaving plenty of room for you to get creative with the content.*

3 *If you're expecting to have a lot of links, a vertical navigation scheme is probably the best bet, because you're not going to run out of space – see* ***www.netmag.co.uk****, shown here. It's important to plan for growth when you're first designing a site; in a month or so, you might want to add some new features or sections.*

4 *You need to make sure that the names or labels you use for your buttons are obvious, so people know exactly what they'll get when they go there. Remember: it might take a minute or more for them to actually get to the page, which is always frustrating, so you don't want to disappoint them. But you also want to make sure that every time you update the site you don't have to change the navigation buttons, or keep making new ones, because that's a pain. Choose labels that are generic, and point them to a page with subheadings or further links to the updated content. Always, plan for growth.*

1

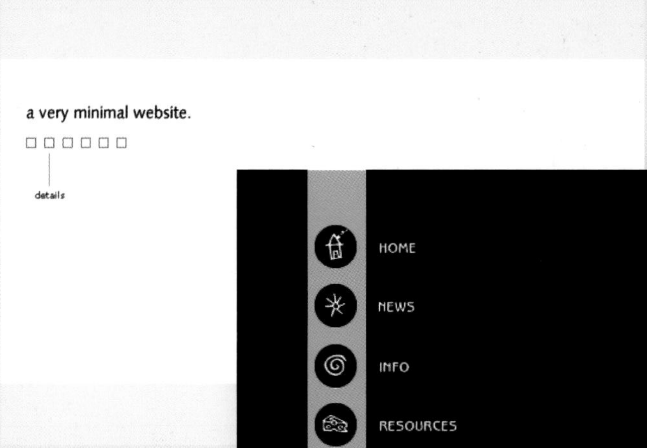

2

3

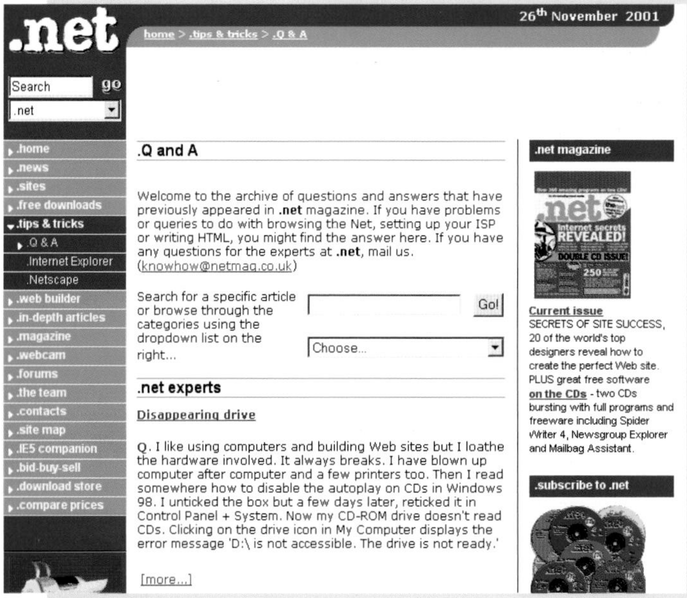

4

5

6

7

8

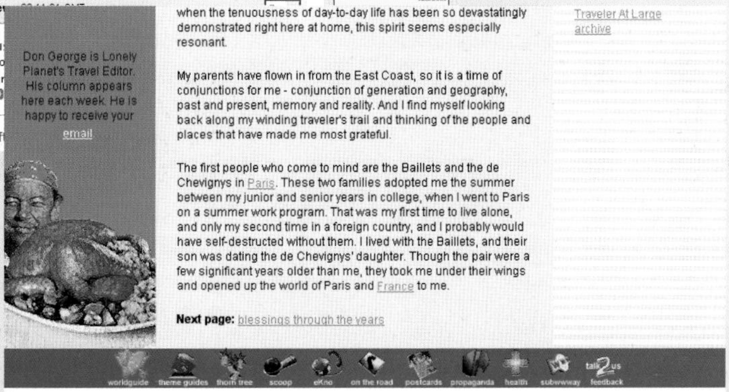

Multinavigation

5 *The term 'navigation' (or nav) in Web design is no accident: it's about helping people find their way around a strange place. If your website is interesting, your visitors will probably want to look at several different things. It's good when you're on a website to be able to jump from one page straight to something else that sparked interest, without having to hit the Back button. See if you can make this easy for your users, as* ***www.bbc.co.uk*** *has done.*

6 *There's no reason why you can't use a subnavigation for this purpose – especially if you've got a lot of links, or have gone for subsections in your site. One technique is to have subheadings under your main links. With a horizontal style, you can have another navigation bar under the first, which appears when the user moves into different sections. See how it has been done at* ***www.creativebase.com****.*

7 *Or you can combine both top and left-hand navigation to great effect.* ***www.computerarts.co.uk*** *uses main links at the top, and secondary links down the side. This works extremely well for large sites like this.*

8 *Many sites have the main navigation tools repeated at the bottom, often just as plain text links that can be loaded quickly. This is really useful on sites with longer pages. It's pleasant to find something to spark your interest as soon as you finish reading, without having to scroll back up. This is what* ***www.lonelyplanet.co.uk*** *has done in this example.*

PROJECT 19

CREATING SIMPLE NAVIGATION

It's important to concentrate on the navigation of your site, so that it is the best you can create, and it loads quickly. Spending time getting it right now will pay dividends later. It's far better to attract people to your site from the outset than try to win them back with a redesigned site later!

Preparing graphics

❶ Here's a navigation bar designed using techniques from previous chapters. Designing your bar to look like a single, integrated graphic helps to organise your webpage.

❷ This design uses a simple blue rectangle with evenly spaced black circles to hold the icons, which are from the free Dingbat font Good Dog Bones (visit *www.fonthead.com*).

❸ You can also design an appearance for the button when the user arrives on the page it links to. Here, it's all blue. This is achieved using a blue layer or object over the top with the *Blending Mode* set to *Color*.

❹ To export the graphics, you could create just one file, then change the text and icon for each button, or crop the buttons from your initial design. To do this, place guides evenly around the buttons, save a copy of the file for each, then open and crop that copy.

❺ Keep the crop fairly close, because if there's too much space in the graphic, your users will see the Internet Explorer or Netscape Hand cursor before their mouse is actually over the icon or text, which is confusing.

❻ For each button, optimize and save a normal version first, with the blue *Color* layer or object invisible. Then do an 'on' version with this layer showing. Name the files clearly – say, home.gif and home_on.gif.

❼ Finally, crop out and export a blank version of the button, to use as a background tile for the navigation.

❷
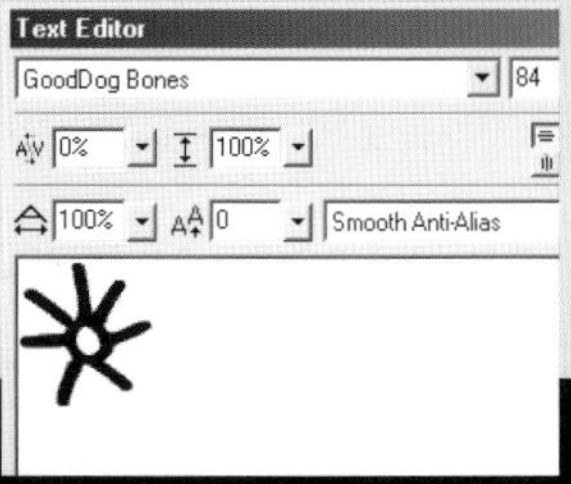

❶❸
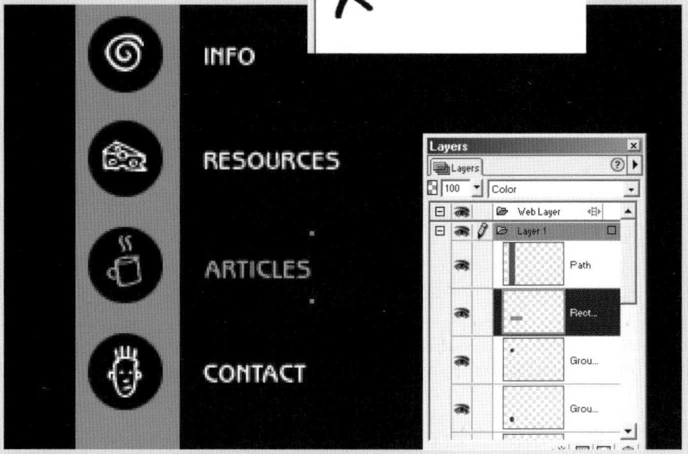

❹

❺
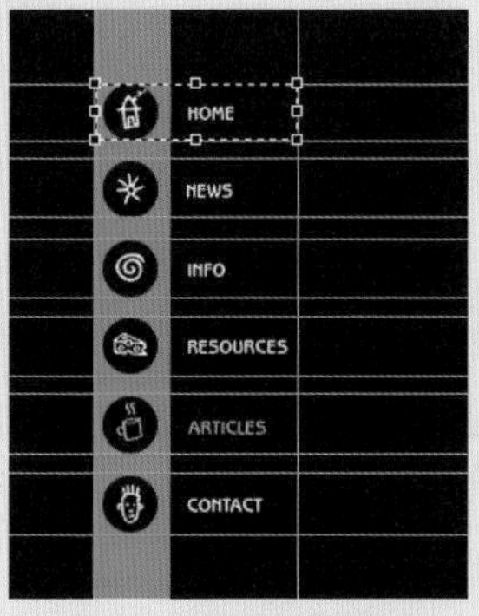

❻❼
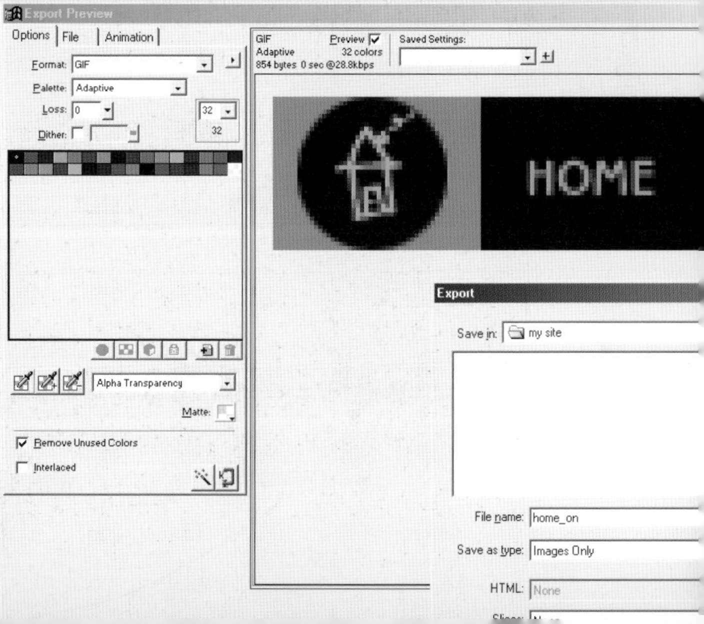

8 9 10 11 12

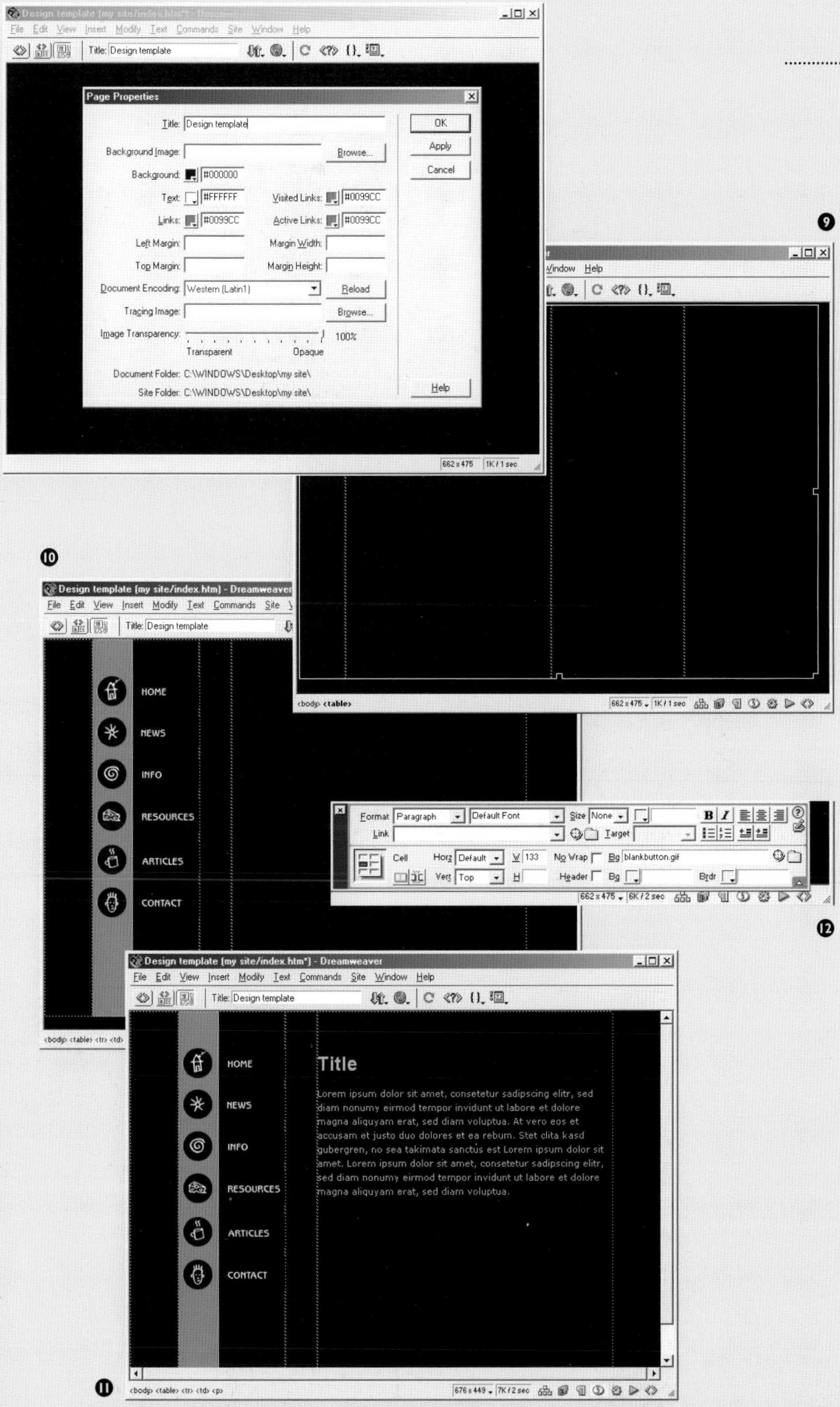

Making the nav bar

8 Navigation, along with a logo and masthead, is usually the first thing to do when you're creating a new webpage, because everything else hinges on it. So create a new webpage and set the background colour and other elements.

9 You're going to put the navigation all in one column, and rely on the graphics to create the appearance of two columns. But you still need to think about creating a space to put the rest of the page in, and you can do this using the same table. Try using a four-column, one-row table, set to 100 per cent height. The first column, made about 20 pixels wide, simply creates a spacious margin down the left.

10 The second column holds the navigation (and you'd probably put the logo in here too). So use the blank button as a tiling background graphic for this cell, and then add in navigation graphics using their *Vertical Spacing* setting to space them out as we did in the original design.

11 The third column is to create spacing – called a gutter – between the navigation and the main content. Use a clear 40 pixels here, to make it obvious. The final column is for the main content of the page. Set this to 400 pixels wide.

12 For different pages in the site, set one of the nav buttons to the 'on' look simply by selecting the graphic and browsing to the 'on' version of the image file.

PROJECT 20
IMAGE MAPS

As mentioned in the previous project, it can be effective design to have your navigation appear as a single visual graphic, rather than just a series of buttons. And it keeps things tidy.

You don't have to use the obvious button-and-label format for your navigation – particularly on the homepage, where you can splash out a little more and worry less about how much space is left over for the real content. In fact, some navigation ideas are just begging for a more pictorial presentation. A site about a journey you've made is one obvious example. Here you can allow a map of the journey to almost completely take over the homepage, and make different parts of it clickable, so that it becomes the navigation in itself.

This is taking navigation as a single graphic to the extreme, but cropping out using the technique you've learned really isn't the way forward. There is a much better option available in Web design, which allows you to export the graphic as one single file, add it to your webpage, and then, using your Web authoring software, you can mark out different areas on the image with various live links. This is different from the usual way of adding links to graphics, which allows you to have just one link for the whole image.

This technique is called an image map, and it's easy to do in most Web design software (although you'll find many free applications, like Netscape Composer, don't include the feature). If you're strapped for cash, pick up the free trial or demo version of a commercial application.

1

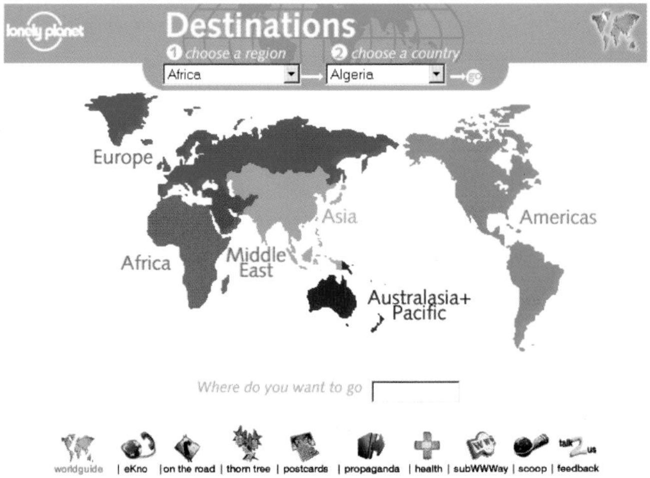

2

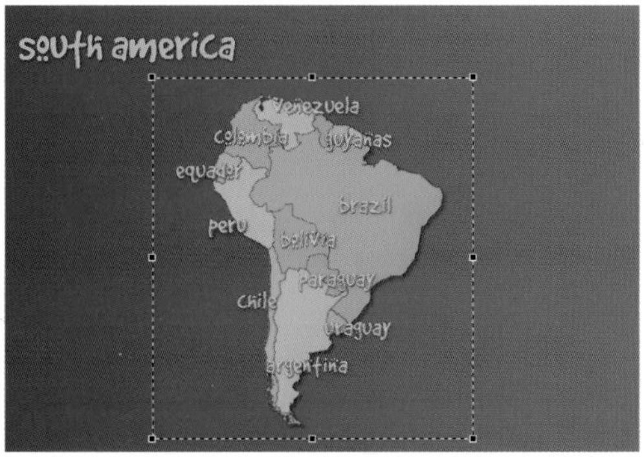

3

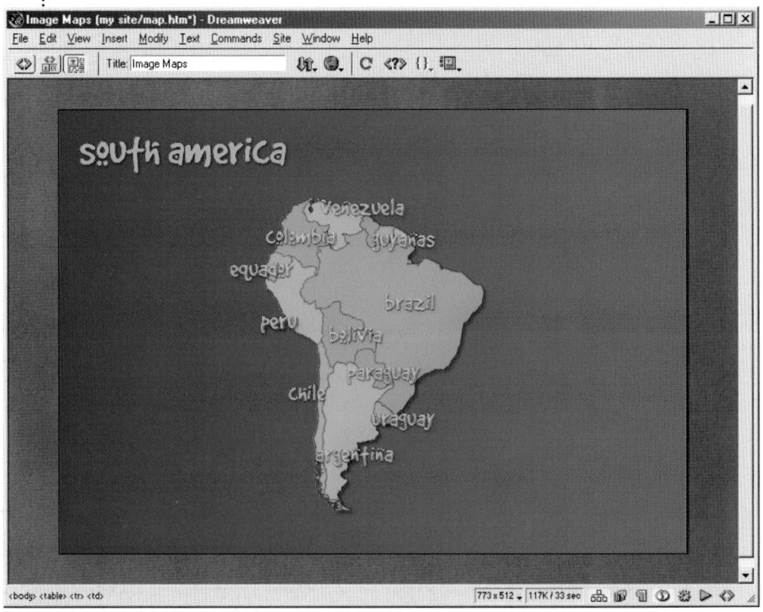

4

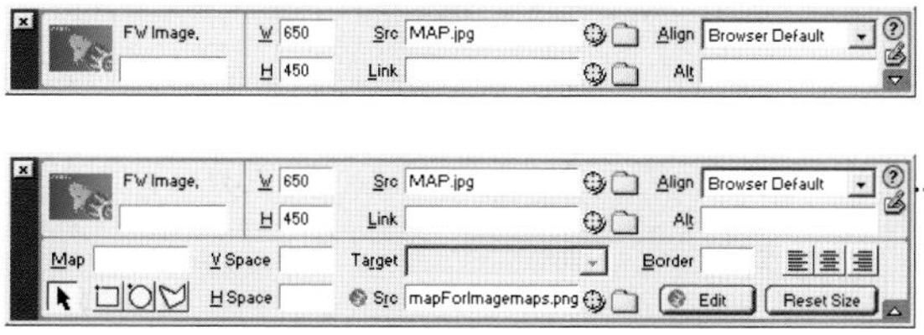

5

6

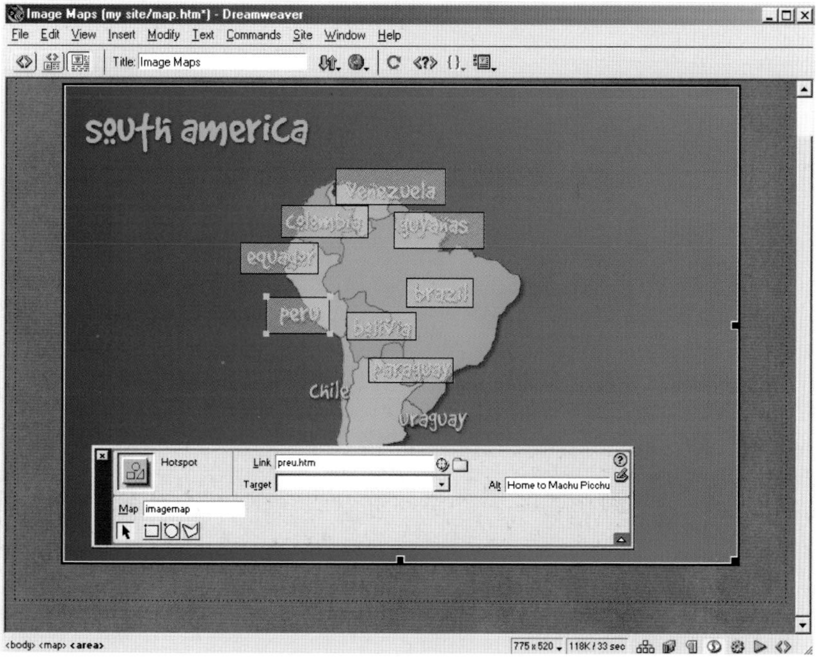

In Dreamweaver

❶ Travel sites are perfect for applying a more visual approach to your navigation, at least on the homepage. (You might need the space for something else on other pages.) But you can also apply this as a visual metaphor for a website on almost any topic. After all, finding your way around a website is rather like driving around a foreign country.

❷ You can use the techniques from the last few chapters to create this image, combining photos with graphics. Then crop and export them as a single, compressed GIF or JPEG.

❸ Bring the image into your homepage in the usual way, add the frills around the site, and centre as in chapter 2.

❹ Now apply the image map: exactly how this works depends on your software, but it is broadly similar across the board. In Dreamweaver, you select the image, then use the tools in the bottom section of your *Properties* palette. If you can't see this, click the little *Down* arrow at the bottom left.

❺ Then use one of the drawing tools to individually mark out the live, or 'hotspot', areas. You can have rectangles, circles or irregular polygon shapes. Use the *Pointer* tool (arrow) to tweak the points and select different hotspots.

❻ Finally, fill in the link and target for each hotspot. Use the *Alt* field to add text for a tool tip that shows if you hover your cursor over the hotspot for few moments.

Photoshop and Fireworks

❶ If you don't have image maps in your Web software, you can create them directly within some graphics software, including ImageReady (which comes bundled in with Photoshop) and Fireworks. In ImageReady, you have *Rectangle*, *Circle* and *Polygon Image Map* tools, and an *Image Map Select* tool, all hiding under the same button. Use these to draw, tweak and select hotspots on your graphic.

❷ Open the *Image Map* palette from your *Window* menu, and use this to set the link, target and *Alt text* for each hotspot.

❸ In ImageReady, you export your graphic using an *Optimize* palette, as in Fireworks, and choose *Save Optimized* from the *File* menu. When you do this, make sure *Save As Type* is set to *HTML and Images*. Image maps are a feature of HTML – not of graphics files.

❹ Finally, open the webpage – that is, the HTML file – created by ImageReady, and either adapt this according to what you want, or copy the graphic and hotspots into your existing homepage.

❺ In Fireworks, the process is almost exactly the same, but you use your normal *Select* tool to select and modify hotspots. You can see them in your *Layers* palette too. Use your normal *Object* palette to set their individual properties.

These appear blue, but you can easily hide them by hiding the *Web Layer*. Remember to set *Save As Type* to *HTML and Images* settings.

❶

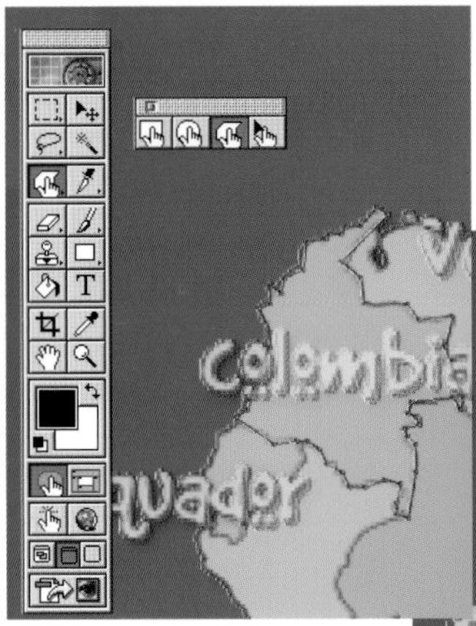

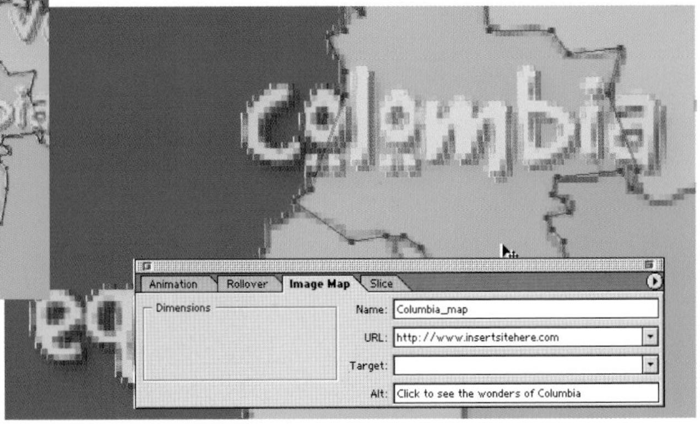

❷

❸

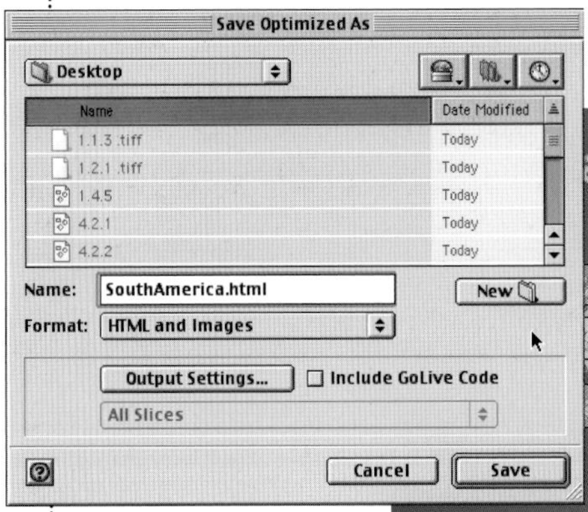

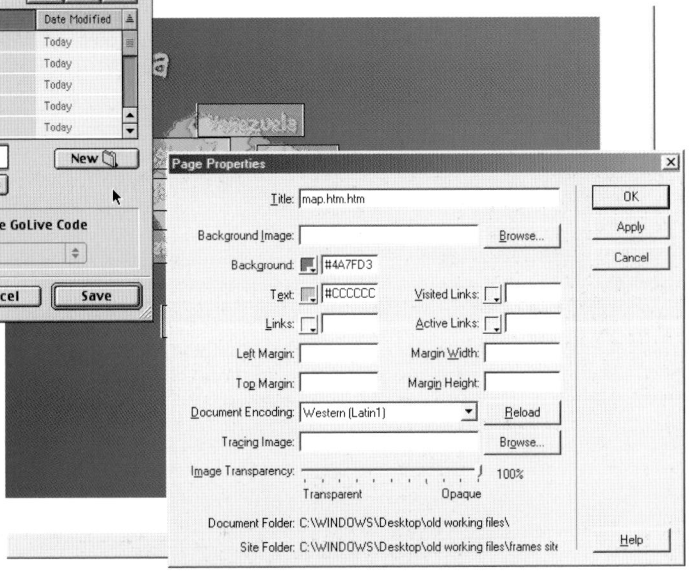

❹

❺

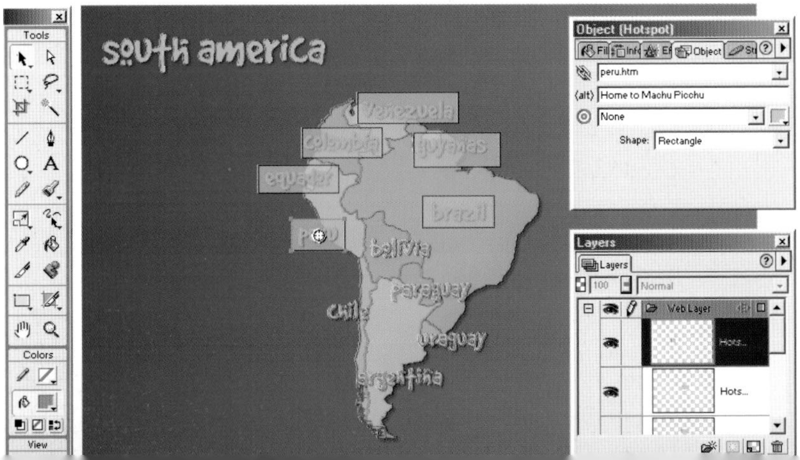

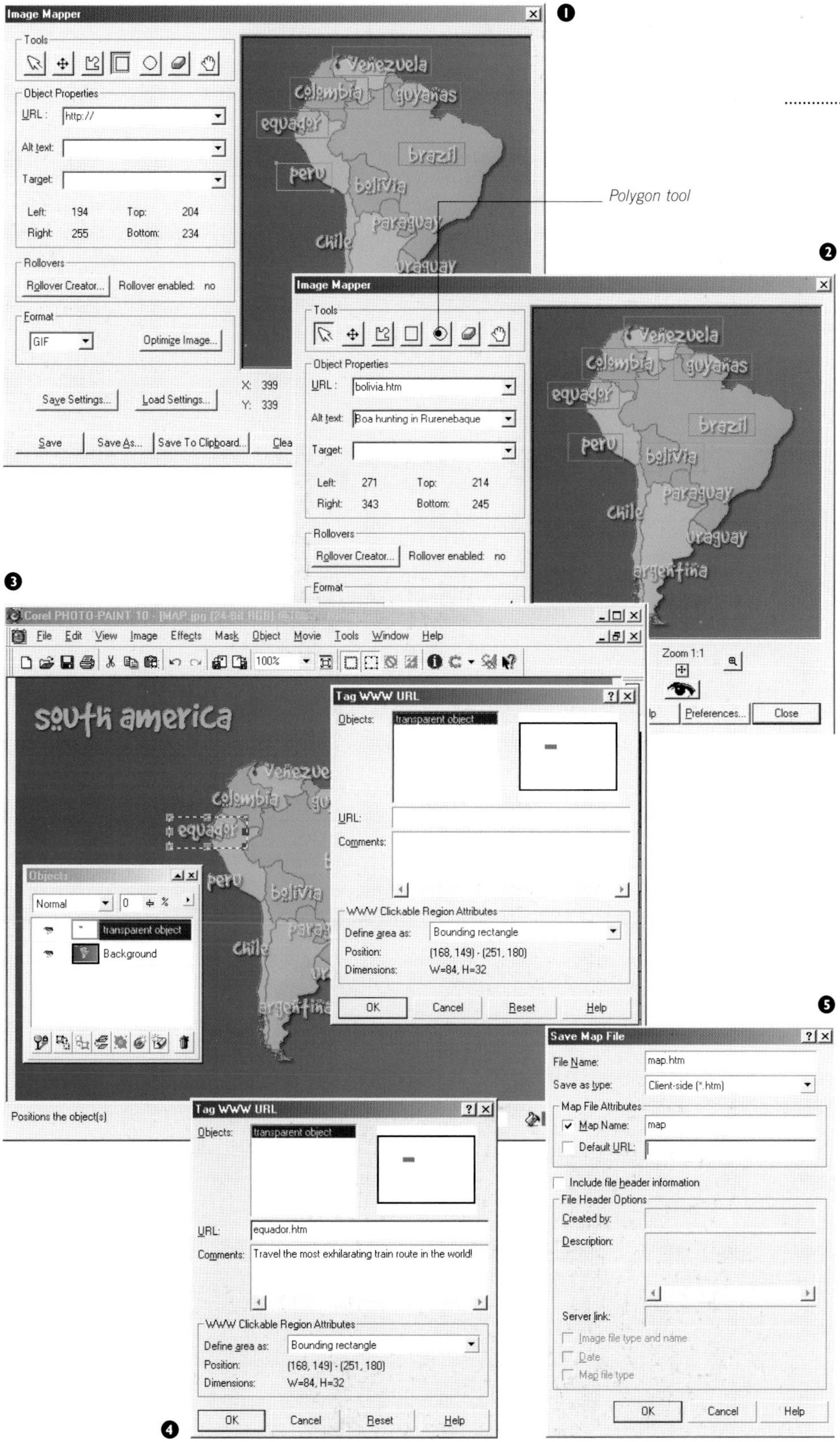

Paint Shop Pro and Photo-Paint

1 You can also create image maps in Paint Shop Pro, using the *File* > *Export* > ***Image Mapper*** command, which opens a dedicated dialog. The tools across the top achieve all the same things as those in the other packages do. If you get stuck with the *Polygon* tool, remember to doubleclick to end *Polygon* tool use.

2 Complete the link's *Alt text* and, if necessary, *Target* for each hotspot. Then use the *Optimize Image* button to compress the file. Finally, click the *Save As* button to export the HTML and image file for your image-mapped graphic.

3 Corel Photo-Paint supports creating image maps too, although this is done through a somewhat complex series of dialogs. Create areas you want for hotspots as individual objects. A transparent rectangle over your existing design for each hotspot does the trick, then choose *File* > *Publish to the Web* > ***HTML***.

4 Send links and comments (which become the tool tip) for the relevant objects, then battle your way through all the optimization dialogs until you finally reach the *Save Map File* dialog box...

5 Set *Save As Type* to *Client-side*, choose a *Map Name* (anything will do), leave *Default URL* alone and forget the rest. Finish up and you should find you have one HTML file and one GIF or JPEG file, which you can develop as normal.

PROJECT 21
SLICING GRAPHICS

Image maps are a very quick and easy way to create exciting visual navigations, and it can be tempting to go to town with the graphics. But don't forget to keep an eye on the file size. As a guideline, a 50K graphic takes 10–20 seconds to appear on a 56K modem.

Image maps aren't always the best approach though, especially if you've got spacious, blank areas in the graphic eating up valuable file size. Slicing is a technique for getting around this, and is also a quick way to prepare ordinary graphics. It certainly leads to more exciting interactive possibilities.

In earlier projects you created navigation ideas in one file, then cropped out the individual buttons and put them together again in the HTML. And this is basically what slicing is about: cutting up a graphic and reassembling it with HTML. But by using the automatic features in many graphics applications, you can easily do this for much more complicated graphics and not worry too much about whether everything's going to work out right. You can focus on being creative while the software takes care of the rest for you.

In principle, the techniques are very easy. You just use a *Slice* tool to draw rectangles marking out how the complete graphic should be divided up, then hit the *Export* or *Save For Web* command, and you should end up with a series of graphics files and an HTML file which, if you open it in Internet Explorer or Netscape, holds the whole thing together seamlessly, as if it's a single image, using a complex table structure.

❶

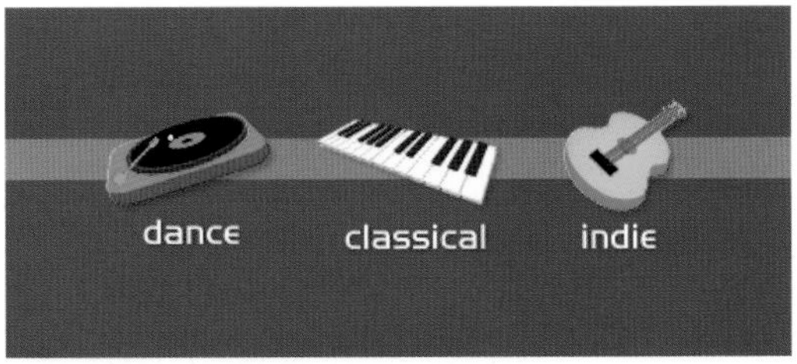

❷

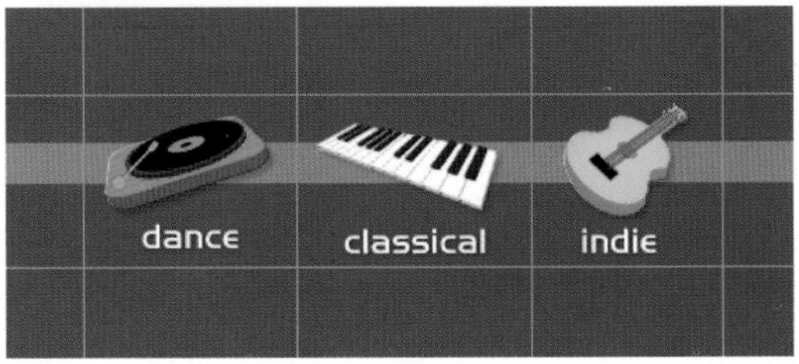

❸

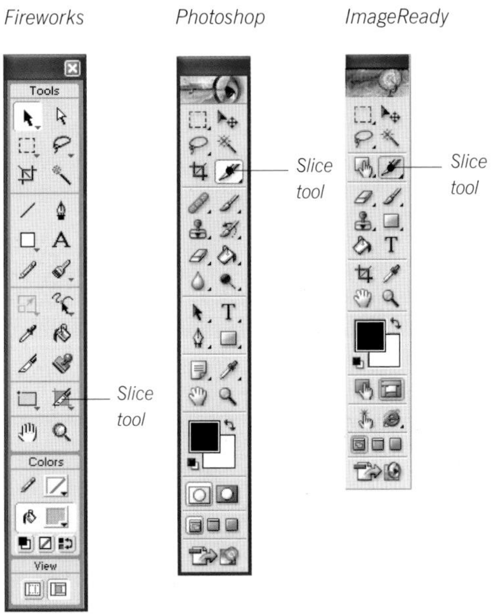

❹

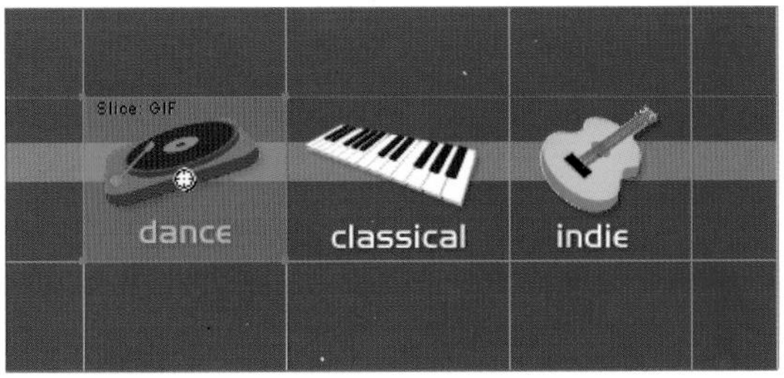

5

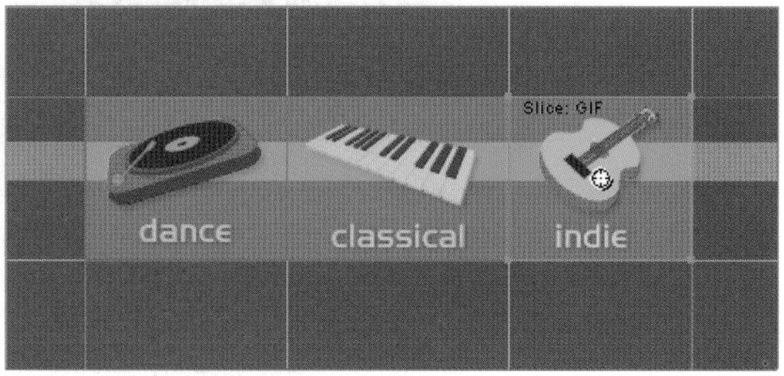

6

ImageReady

Fireworks

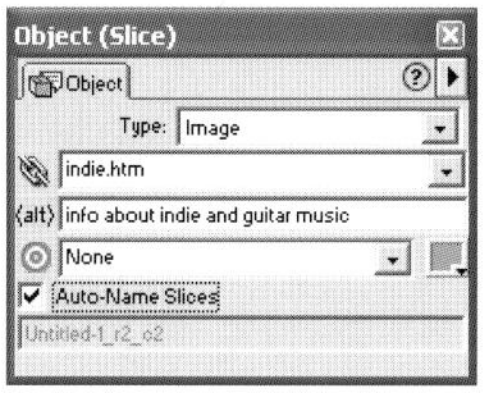

7

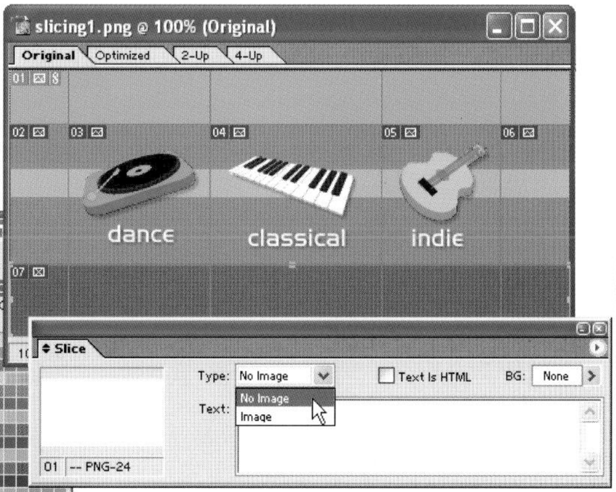

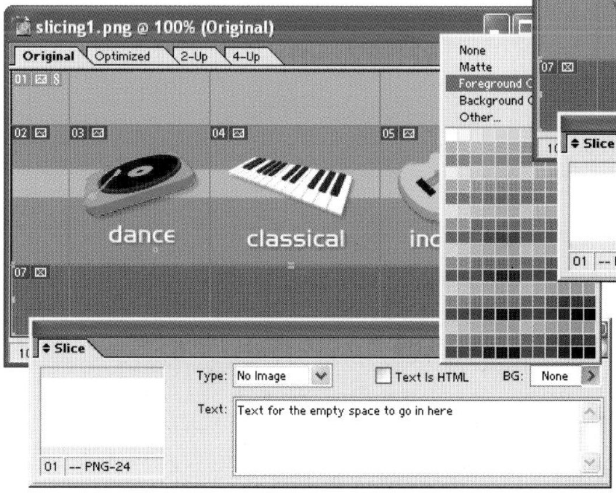

8

1 Let's begin with this simple navigation design. You could export this by individually cropping out the graphics, but once you've got the hang of slicing you'll find it much quicker to do it that way.

2 As before, start by dragging guides to mark button edges.

3 Photoshop, ImageReady and Fireworks all have a *Slice* tool in the toolbox, while Photoshop and ImageReady also have a *Slice Selector* for editing slices, hiding under their *Slice* tools. In Fireworks, you can just use the normal *Selection* tools.

4 **5** To create a slice, use this tool to draw a rectangle matching your guides, to mark out the area of the graphic. Do the same for each graphic you want to export, making sure your slices match up exactly.

6 In Fireworks, use your *Objects* palette to set a link for the individual slice. In Photoshop, use your *Slice Selector* and doubleclick the slice. In ImageReady just open the *Slice* palette. As is the case with image maps, the *Alt text* is a pop-up image.

7 One advantage to the slicing technique is that you can set individual slices to be 'blank' – just an empty cell with a flat background colour. This helps you save on file size, and you should use it in all empty areas of your design. (In Fireworks, this is called a *Text* slice.)

8 You can type text to appear in these cells, directly into the *Text* box. This appears as normal HTML text, and you can apply fonts, sizes and so on to it later. Don't forget to set the background colour for the cell while you're at it.

9 Before you finish off, prepare compression in the usual way. You can apply individual compression settings to each slice if you like, by just selecting the slice, then using your normal optimization tools.

10 Finally, use your normal *Save For Web*, *Save Optimized* or *Export* command to save the whole thing – graphics, HTML and all – into your Web folder. Don't forget to select the *HTML and Images* option.

11 Paint Shop Pro works slightly differently: as you do with image maps, you use a dedicated dialog, located under *File > Export > Image Slicer*. You can use the grid (#) tool to create a grid for the table, use the *Slice* (or *Knife*) tool to move the edges and split slices, and the *Rubber* to combine slices.

12 Use the *Pointer* tool to select your individual slices and set their links, pop-up text and so on. Use the *Optimize Cell* button to apply specific compression settings for your different slices. Finally, hit *Save* to export the whole thing.

13 If you open the webpage that goes with the graphic in your Web authoring application, you'll see how it works, although it might not look exactly right. Don't worry about this – it should be fine when you see it in the browser.

9

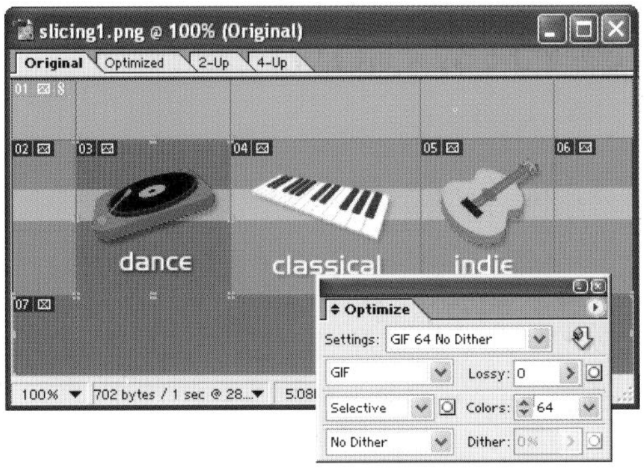

10

11

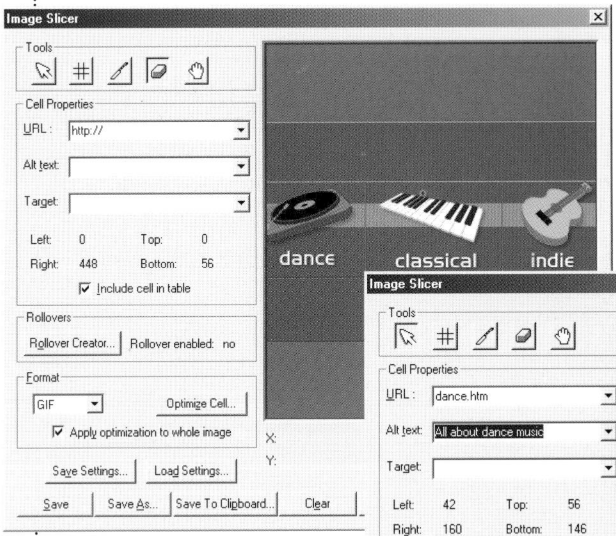

12

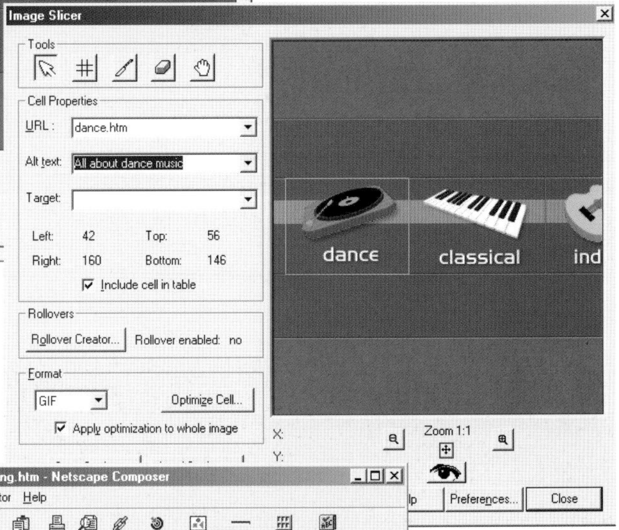

13

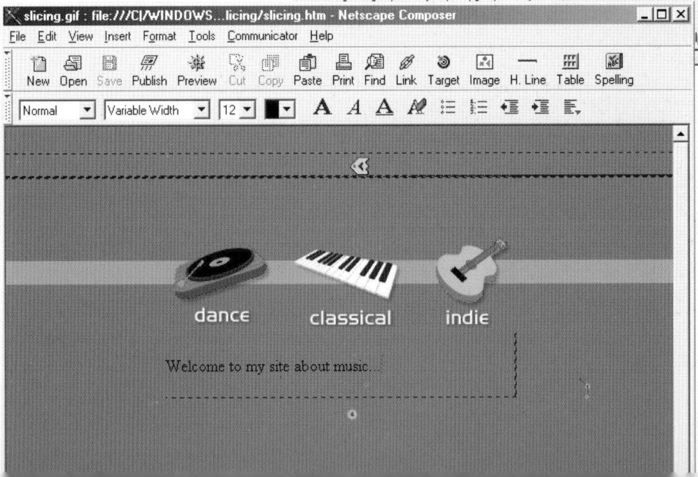

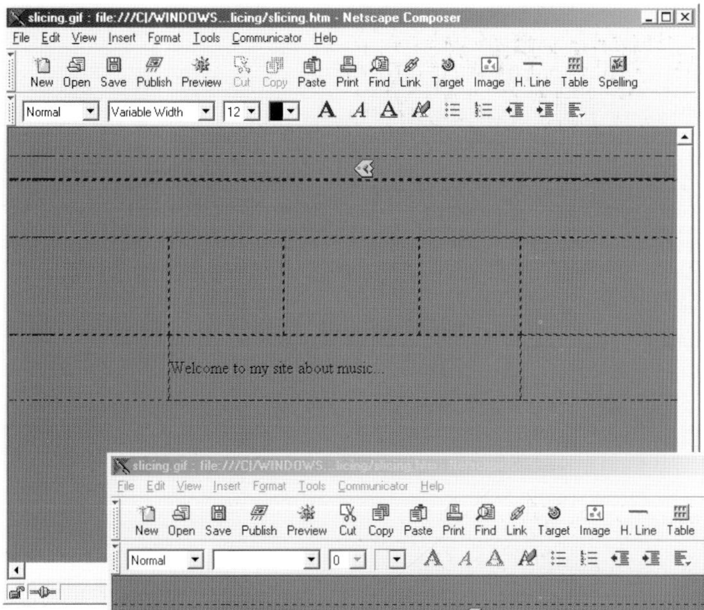

14

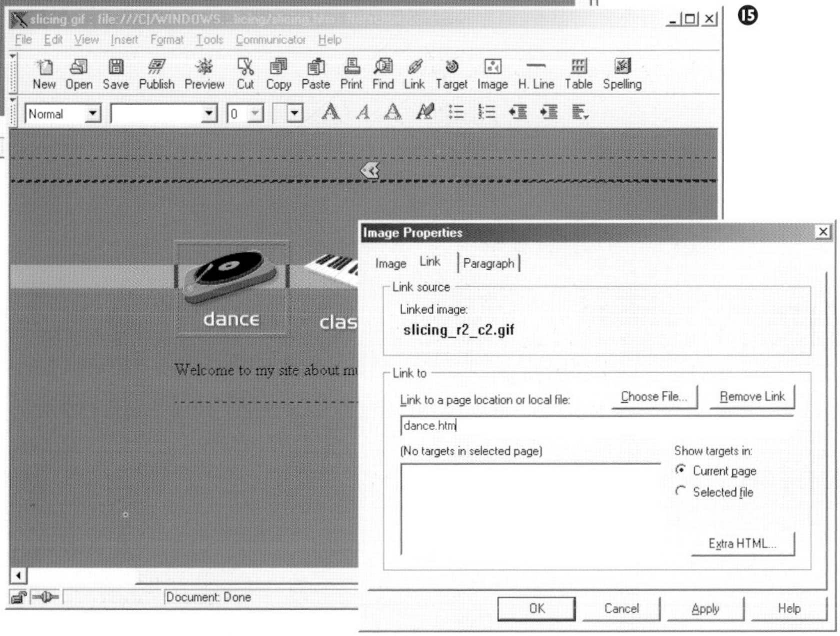

15

16

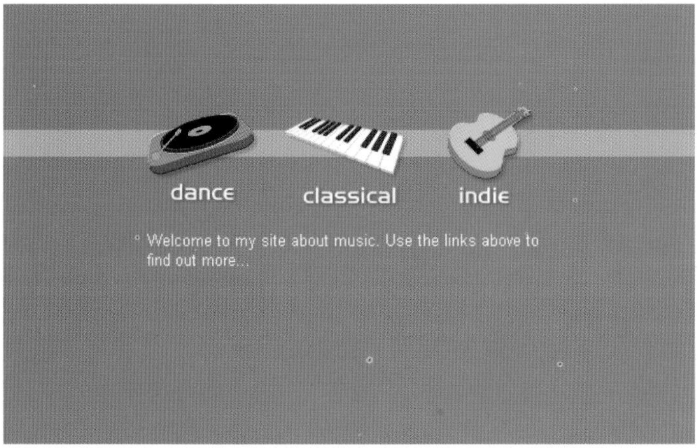

14 The software has created a table with a complex combination of rows and columns with merged cells, as you can see here. To add the graphic to an existing webpage template, all you need to do is copy the whole thing and paste it in. The table structure that holds it all together is finely balanced, so you need to avoid changing it, unless you take a great deal of care. If you do need to change something, it's best to go back to your graphics software and make the amendments there.

15 But you can still select each individual graphic in the table, and set particular properties, like the link and target or the background colour of the table and individual cells. In fact, it's often easier to set links here, where you can browse to the actual link, rather than in your graphics application where you have to work out for yourself what the link is.

16 If you have any empty cells, check that there really is no lurking graphic in them eating up valuable download time for your users. And of course change the font, size, colour and so on of any text you put in these cells. Be careful to ensure that the text won't overflow the length of the cell, because this will mess up your design.

PROJECT 22
ROLLOVERS

One feature of the Web that makes it unique from most other media is that it is interactive: it responds to what the user does, and what your viewer gets to see depends on what they do. You should aim to make the most of this because even the simplest touches can alter the entire user experience.

Perhaps the simplest and most common interactive feature on the Internet, apart from links themselves, is the rollover. A rollover occurs when you move your mouse over a button and it changes. Perhaps it glows, changes colour or appears to lift a notch out of the page. The important thing is that it changes form in some way.

For a normal navigation, a button is simply a single graphics file. In a rollover, when your cursor moves over the graphic, the browser instantaneously swaps it for a different graphic file, which is almost exactly the same – it is the difference that creates the effect. When you move your cursor away, the graphic swaps back.

In Project 19 you created 'on' versions of your buttons (see page 140) – you could also use these to create a rollover effect. Most Web design software and Web graphics applications include features for automatically adding rollovers to buttons, using a *Behaviors* or *Rollovers* palette or command. All you have to do is design and specify the 'mouse over' version of the graphic.

It's important to make sure the graphic file is only as big as the button: you don't want to swap a massive graphics file to create this effect for a small button, because it's got to be downloaded and stored in memory beforehand, to ensure the effect is instantaneous.

1

2
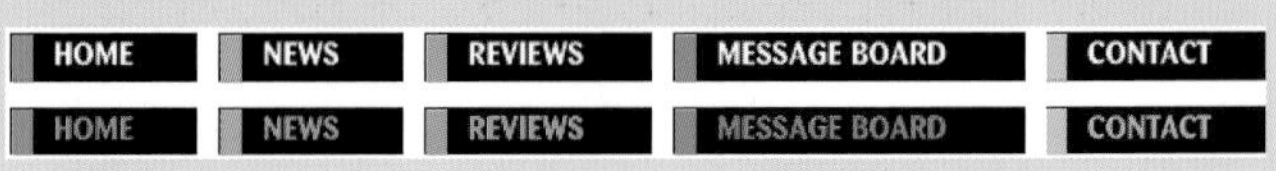

3
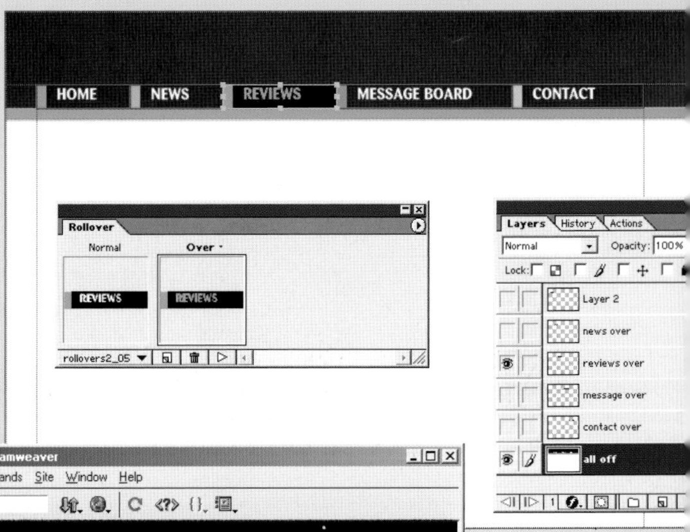

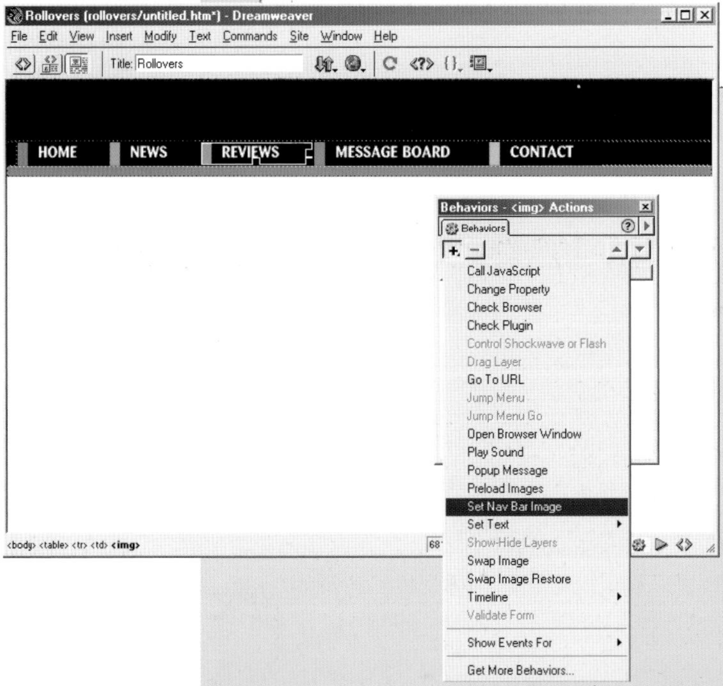

4

❺

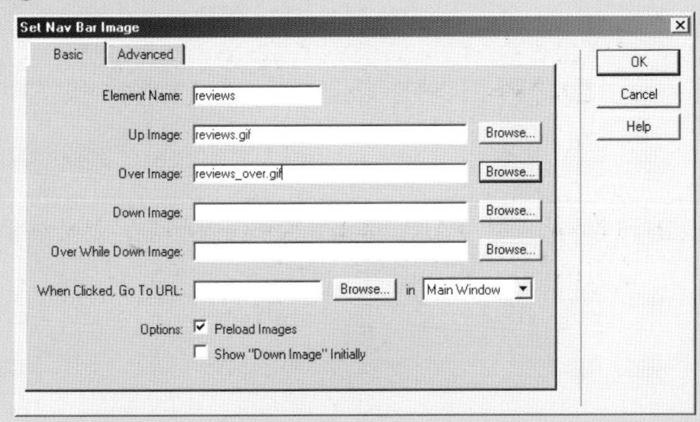

❻

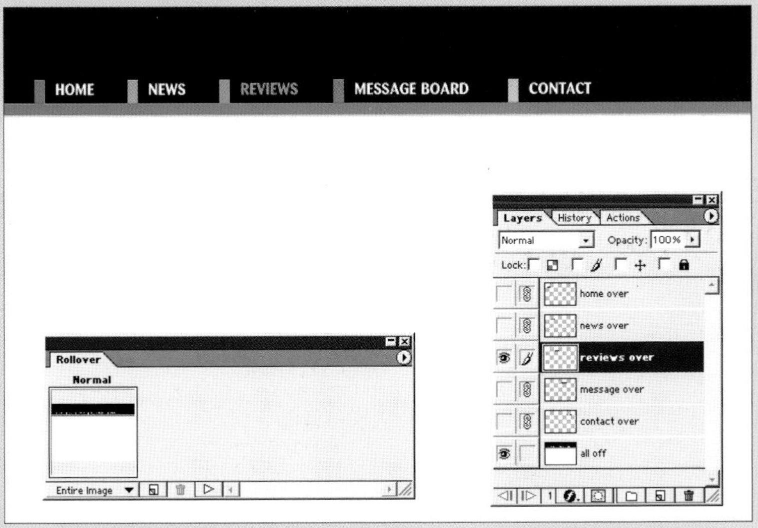

❶ Here's a simple design for rollovers. However, you can amend it to make it as complex as any of the graphics created in this book. Each section has a different colour, but the labels are white until you rollover them, at which point they change to the appropriate colour (see 'Reviews' button).

❷ All the rollover instructions are stored in the HTML, not the image. You can set this up either from your Web authoring application, or directly in your graphics software. If you decide on the former, start by exporting the buttons individually, with separate files for both the *Off* and *Over* states.

❸ If you choose the latter, in Photoshop it's very easy indeed. You just set up the different *Off*, *Over* and other states in seperate layers.

❹ Start up your Web app and select the first image. Open the *Behaviors* palette and click the menu marked '+'. Choose *Set Nav Bar Image*.

❺ You will get a dialog where you can browse and select a graphics file for the *Up* state, *Over* state, and also for the *Down* and *Over While Down* states, if you want. Leave the *Preload Images* option ticked – this makes sure there is no delay in the effect when it is seen over the Web. And that's all there is to it.

❻ The process is different in graphics software, and in some respects it is easier. If you are using Photoshop, create your buttons in the usual way, but put them all in one file with each *Over* state button on a new layer. Then open this file in ImageReady, and open your *Rollover* palette.

7 Hide the *Over* button layers, so only the normal button is visible, then draw guides and create slices for each of your buttons.

8 For each button, select its slice, click the *New State* icon at the bottom of your *Rollover* palette, and swap the visibility of the layers to show only the clicked version of that button. That's all there is to it!

9 You can click the little headings above the thumbnails in your palette to open a menu giving you a choice of different button states. You can also preview how they work by using the *Play* button at the bottom of the palette, and then interacting with the main image.

10 Finally, crop your design to the edges of your navigation, and export the whole thing just as you did with a normal sliced graphic. Then open the page in your Web authoring application and edit it from there.

In Fireworks, you can use the easy Button Editor, by selecting *Insert* > *New Button*. With this window all your tools work in the normal way, and you can design or paste in your graphics. Using the tabs at the top, you can create graphics for the different button states, and use the *Copy* button at the bottom right to use a previous state as a starting point for the next graphics.

7

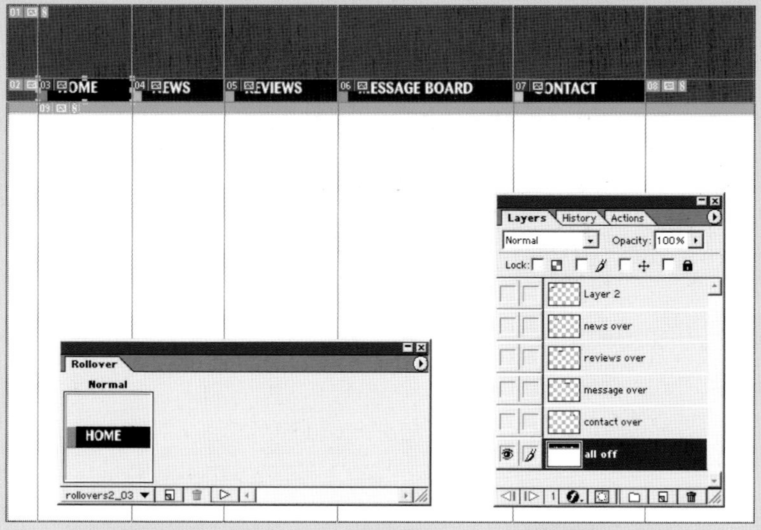

8

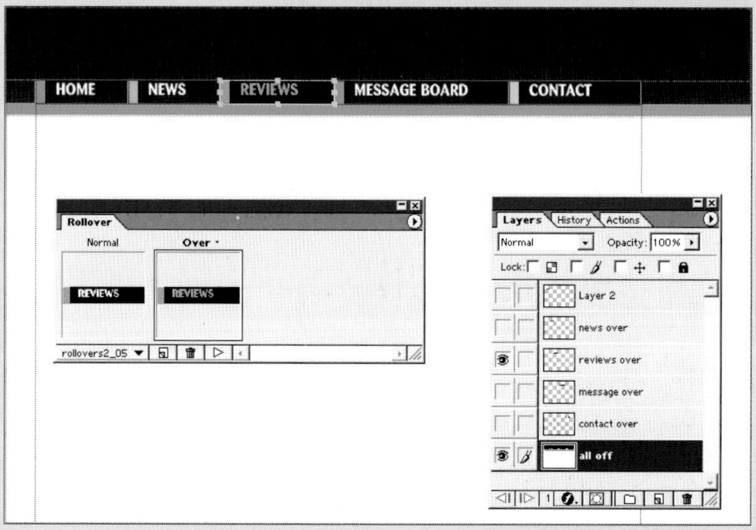

9

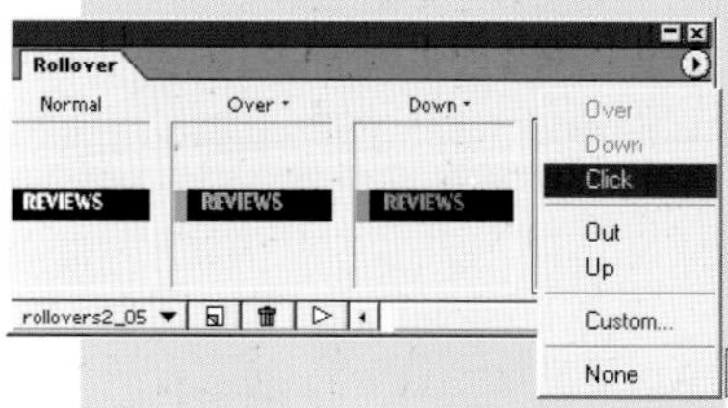

10

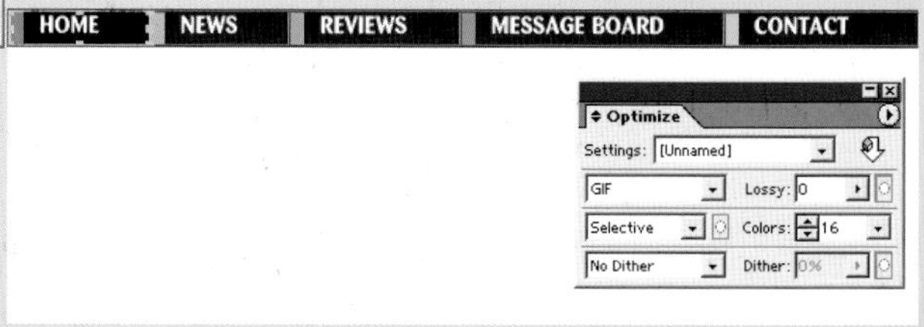

11

12

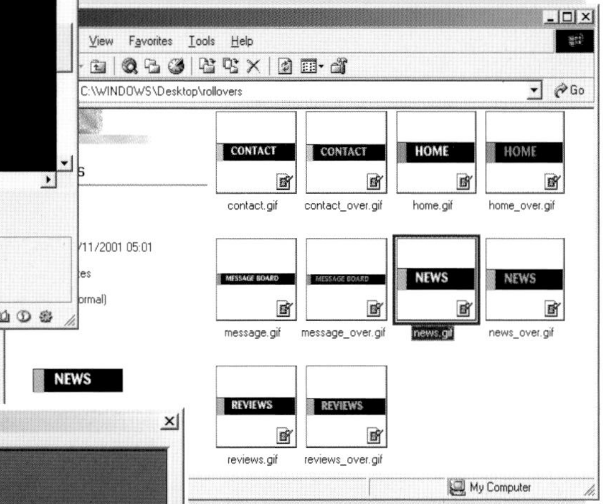

13

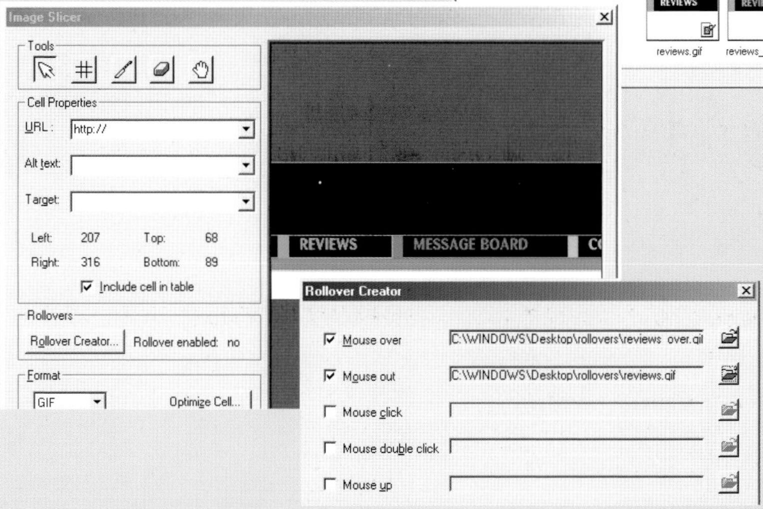

14

15

16

17

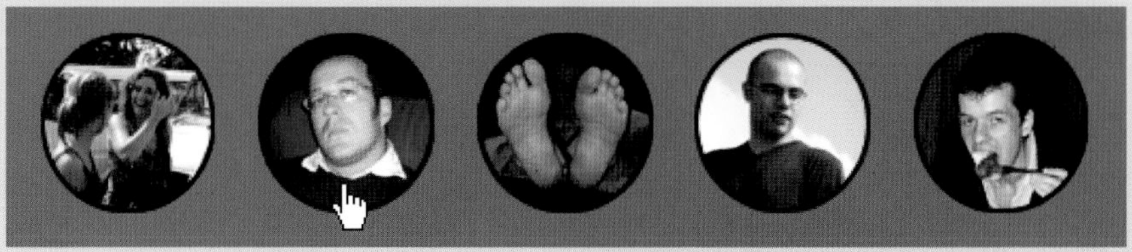

⓫ Setting up rollovers in Paint Shop Pro is extremely easy, but you'll have to create, optimize and save the *Over* and other button states first. Remember to put them all somewhere safe in your website folder, and make sure, of course, that they're exactly the right size.

⓬ Now open the *Image Slicer*, as before, and set up your slices, selecting each slice one by one, and then click the *Rollover* creator button.

⓭ This opens a simple dialog where you can select the button states you want to create, and browse to the appropriate graphics files. Then just save the whole lot. Next, you should open the webpage in your browser to check that it works.

Finally, click the *Save* button to export the table, complete with rollovers.

⓮ The key design aspect in rollovers is to think about how the interaction works – the effect is attention-grabbing, so you want to give thought to how and why it works. The design here is very simple, yet it's also very effective, and you can apply the colour change idea in different ways...

⓯ A popular effect is to make a button appear to lift out of the page. For this, you just nudge it a few pixels up and left, and apply a bit of shadow.

⓰ Another is to have an arrow that appears by the link as you roll over it. This uses the same rollover techniques, but different graphics.

⓱ With photos, you can have them in black-and-white or tinted, and then show a full-colour version for the rollover.

re:media
home
books
MUSIC
Lorem ipsum dolor sit amet, consetetur sadi
tempor invidunt ut labore et dolore magna a
At vero eos et accusam et justo duo dolores
gubergren, no sea takimata sanctus est Lore
dolor sit amet, consetetur sadipscing elitr, se
invidunt ut labore et dolore magna aliquyam
At vero eos et accusam et justo duo dolores
gubergren, no sea takimata sanctus est Lore
dolor sit amet, consetetur sadipscing elitr, se
invidunt ut labore et dolore magna aliquyam
KIT USED
Just a little bit of text...
KIT USED
Lorem ipsum dolor sit amet, consetetur sadipscing elitr, sed diam nonumy eirmod tempor invidunt ut labore et dolore magna aliquyam erat, sed diam voluptua. At vero eos et accusam et justo duo dolores et ea rebum. Stet clita kasd gubergren, no sea takimata sanctus est Lorem ipsum dolor sit amet.
Done
Untitled Document (frames site/blank.htm*) - Dreamweaver
File Edit View Insert Modify Text Commands Site Window Help
Title: re:media

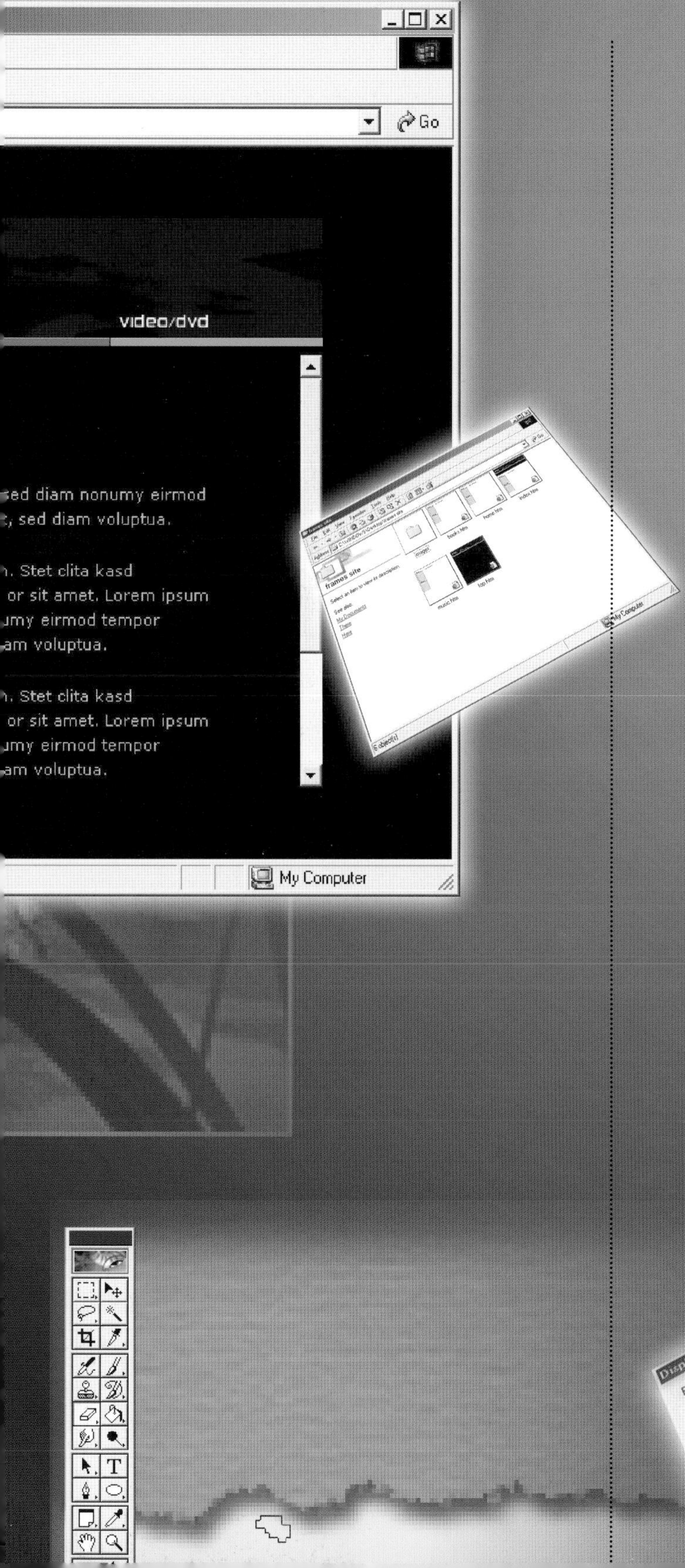

CHAPTER 6

Advanced Techniques

If you ever get frustrated while you're creating webpages, don't worry – all Web designers do at some point, and it is usually because they can't get the tools to do what they want them to do. However, with the right skills, you can do just about anything you want. In this chapter we cover some of the more advanced techniques that are useful for creating impressive websites.

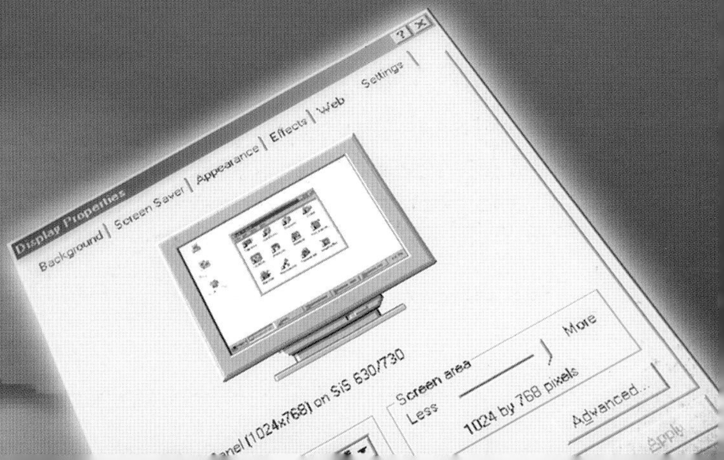

PROJECT 23
SPACE AND SHAPE

Much of design is about organising information visually, and finding innovative ways to get an idea across. This is particularly important in Web design, because it's not as easy to read text on a screen as it is in print. In addition, most Web users tend to scan pages for particular pieces of information or links quickly, and then move on. This means that you've really got to grab their attention, and deliver your message fast and effectively.

Good design has the advantage of instant communication: you don't have to read a picture, you just have to see it. And you can exploit this when you're creating a website by finding ways to present information visually – like the interactive map you created in the last chapter. This has far more impact than a simple list of places, but you'd be surprised how many sites don't bother putting any effort into this. Other ideas include weather charts, league tables, graphs, etc.

Often, though, the text is what it's all about, and here design plays its role in making that text accessible – that is, easy to scan and digest. There are myriad techniques you can use to achieve this, which we have already covered, such as splitting columns and creating subheadings, highlighting and emphasising key items, or illustrating your point. Over the next few pages, we'll look at some simple techniques to take this even further...

1

2

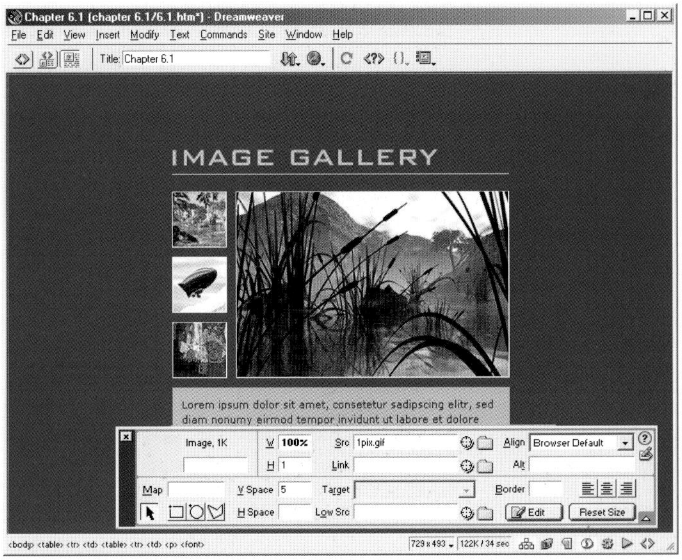

❸

❹

❺

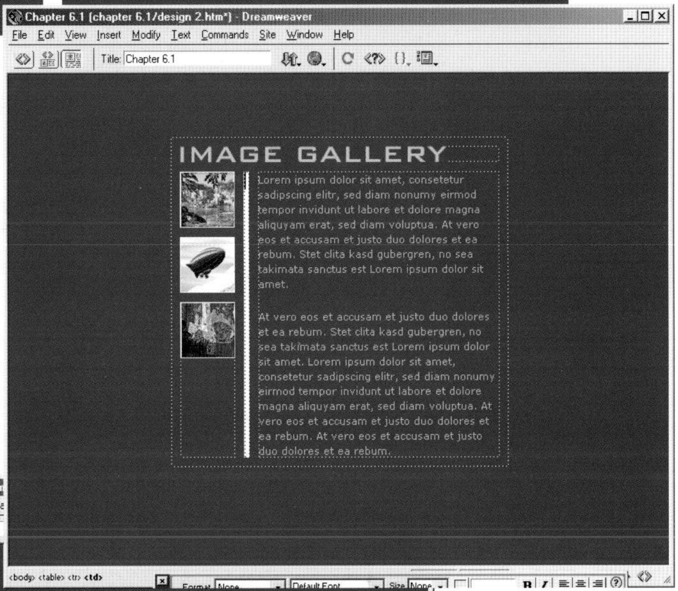

❻

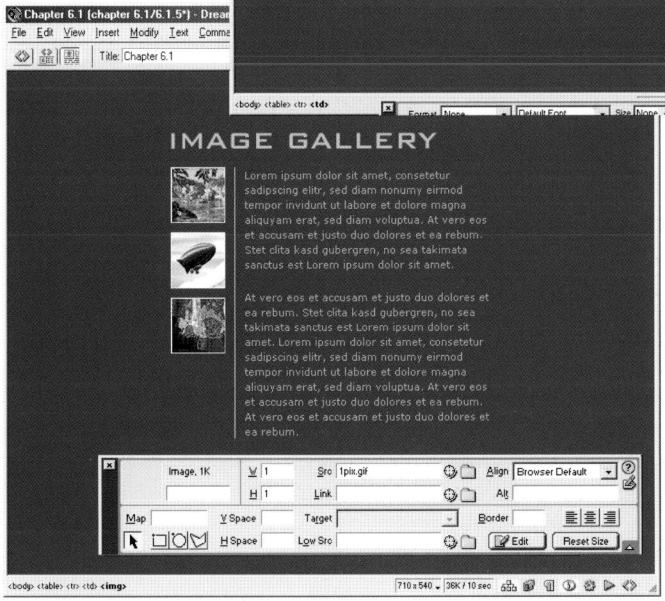

Lines

❶ The line must be the single most important tool in page design for swiftly and effectively separating one piece of information from another. Sadly, there is no *Line* tool in most Web authoring software. You can use the *Horizontal Rule*, but you can't reliably control its colour and size in all browsers.

❷ One effective option is to create a tiny black (or any colour) GIF graphic, just 1 x 1 pixels. Add this to your webpage, and then set its width to 100 per cent, so it stretches right across the table cell.

❸ You could do something similar for a vertical line, setting the alignment of the graphic to *Left*. But you'll find you have to give an exact height, such as 300, rather than a percentage-based height, for it to work.

❹ This isn't very flexible, especially as fonts appear at different sizes for different users, so you can never be sure how deep the text will run. And you might not be convinced about the accuracy of the spacing. But there is an option...

❺ Try adding a new column, setting its background colour to black and its width to 1. You will notice a problem when you do this. Netscape 4.x doesn't display empty table cells, so most software will automatically add in a space character, but this will make the cell too big. If it doesn't, you won't see your supposed line at all in Netscape 4.x.

❻ So create a transparent 1 x 1-pixel GIF, and put this in the cell at its usual size, in place of the space character.

Boxouts

Careful use of lines is effective for marking out different areas of a webpage. But another technique is using different background colours to create what designers call boxouts. These are ideal for little snippets of information or links. You will have seen similar things in magazines.

❶ To create the simplest kind of boxout, you can just add a two-row table, 160 pixels wide and with cell padding set to eight pixels. Put a heading in the top cell, content in the bottom cell, and set their background colours.

❷ To add a border, create a new 1 x 1 table with cell padding at one or two. Set its background colour to the border colour, then copy and paste the previous box inside this. (The built-in table border setting can be unreliable.)

❸ It would be attractive to do something a little more graphical, though. For this design, the main part of the box doesn't need to change – you just need a graphic for the top and the bottom.

❹ Create your graphic in the normal way, using the exact background colour of the webpage. Use guides to mark the top and bottom parts, then crop and export them.

❺ Next create a three-row table and set its background colour. Add the graphics in the top and bottom rows.

Add another table in the middle row, with cell padding set to eight, to create a margin, and paste in your content.

❶

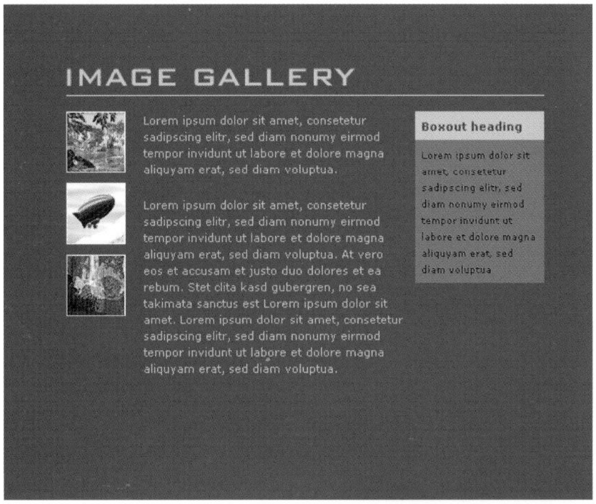
IMAGE GALLERY
Lorem ipsum dolor sit amet, consetetur sadipscing elitr, sed diam nonumy eirmod tempor invidunt ut labore et dolore magna aliquyam erat, sed diam voluptua.
Lorem ipsum dolor sit amet, consetetur sadipscing elitr, sed diam nonumy eirmod tempor invidunt ut labore et dolore magna aliquyam erat, sed diam voluptua. At vero eos et accusam et justo duo dolores et ea rebum. Stet clita kasd gubergren, no sea takimata sanctus est Lorem ipsum dolor sit amet. Lorem ipsum dolor sit amet, consetetur sadipscing elitr, sed diam nonumy eirmod tempor invidunt ut labore et dolore magna aliquyam erat, sed diam voluptua.
Boxout heading
Lorem ipsum dolor sit amet, consetetur sadipscing elitr, sed diam nonumy eirmod tempor invidunt ut labore et dolore magna aliquyam erat, sed diam voluptua

❷

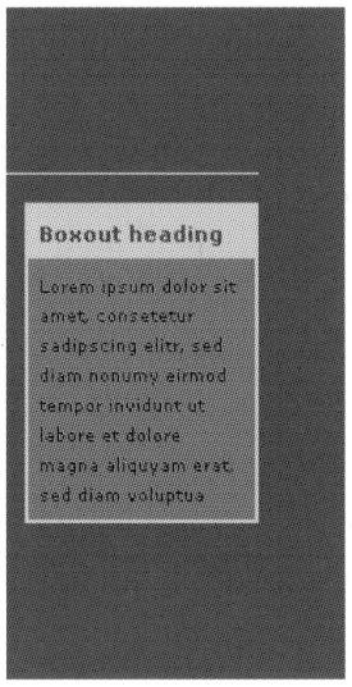
Boxout heading
Lorem ipsum dolor sit amet, consetetur sadipscing elitr, sed diam nonumy eirmod tempor invidunt ut labore et dolore magna aliquyam erat, sed diam voluptua

❸

IMAGE GALLERY
KIT USED
LINKS
Morning in Loch Fynn
Lorem ipsum dolor sit amet, consetetur sadipscing elitr, sed diam nonumy eirmod tempor invidunt ut labore et dolore magna aliquyam erat, sed diam voluptua. At vero eos et accusam et justo duo dolores et ea rebum. Stet clita kasd gubergren, no sea takimata sanctus est Lorem ipsum dolor sit amet.
HOME
PREVIOUS | NEXT

❹

KIT USED
LINKS

❺

KIT USED

❻

LERY
KIT USED
LINKS

❼

KIT USED

❽

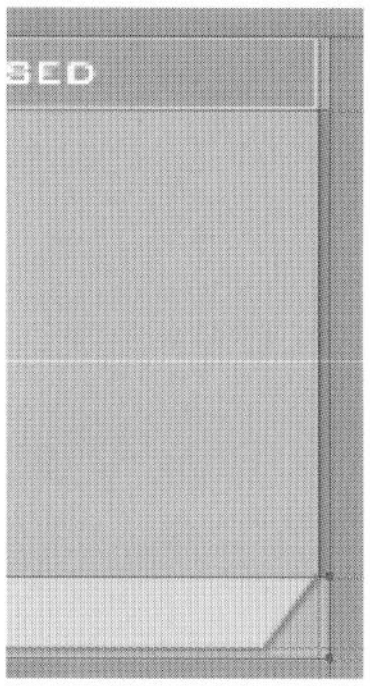

❾

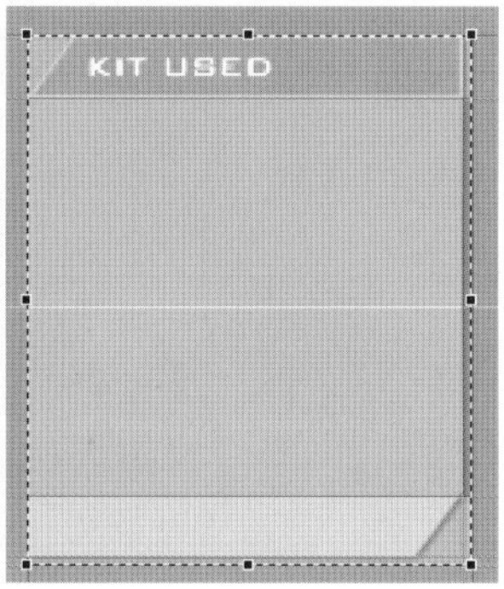
KIT USED

❿

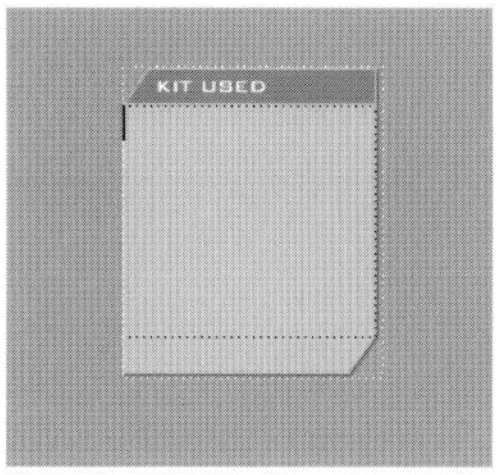
KIT USED

⓫

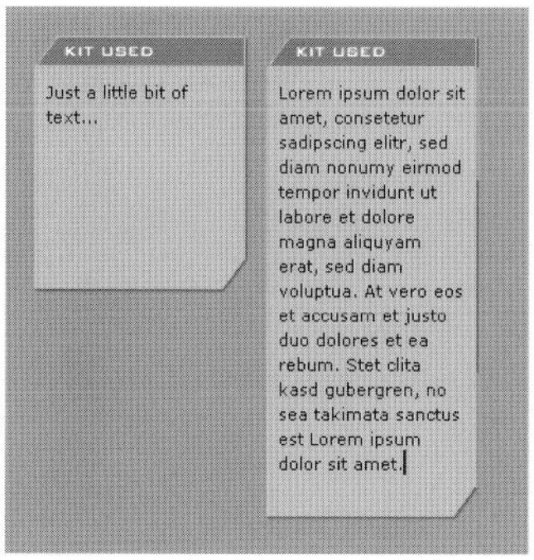
KIT USED
Just a little bit of text...
KIT USED
Lorem ipsum dolor sit amet, consetetur sadipscing elitr, sed diam nonumy eirmod tempor invidunt ut labore et dolore magna aliquyam erat, sed diam voluptua. At vero eos et accusam et justo duo dolores et ea rebum. Stet clita kasd gubergren, no sea takimata sanctus est Lorem ipsum dolor sit amet.

⓬

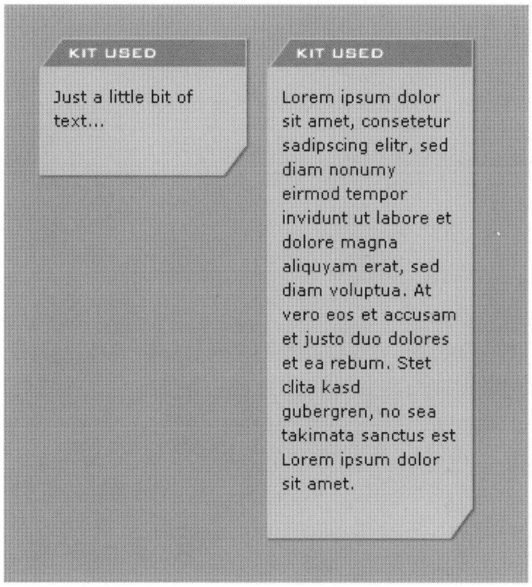
KIT USED
Just a little bit of text...
KIT USED
Lorem ipsum dolor sit amet, consetetur sadipscing elitr, sed diam nonumy eirmod tempor invidunt ut labore et dolore magna aliquyam erat, sed diam voluptua. At vero eos et accusam et justo duo dolores et ea rebum. Stet clita kasd gubergren, no sea takimata sanctus est Lorem ipsum dolor sit amet.

❻ You may or may not have noticed a cheat in this webpage, though. In the initial design there was a tiny drop shadow around the box, which was left out in the slicing, because it's a little more difficult to do. But design is as much about the fine details as the big ones – and this one makes a big difference.

❼ To add it in, use guides to mark the outer boundaries of the shadow in the design, then extend both the header and footer slices for the box to fit. You'll also have to deepen the footer slice.

❽ Then create a new slice for the side shadow, as shown, and a *No Image* or *Text* slice for the central text area.

❾ Crop the box to its boundaries, then export the whole thing – slices, graphics, HTML and everything – to your website folder.

❿ Open the webpage in your authoring application, and you should have a near-perfect template boxout, which you can just copy and paste with different heading graphics for different boxes. You'll need to add a 1 x 1 table with cell padding set to eight in the central text area, though, to create a margin…

⓫ If you have only a small amount of text, you'll find the box is too big, but if you have too much text, the right-hand shadow is too small. To solve this, replace the shadow graphic with a 1 x 1-pixel transparent GIF, then use the shadow graphics file as a background image for the cell…

⓬ Here is what the finished boxouts look like.

ABOUT PAGE SIZES

One of the major problems confronting Web designers is that everybody has different computers. Some people use PCs while others have Macs; some people use Internet Explorer while others have Netscape. Some set their fonts to display large; others prefer to set them small.

This, to be frank, is a complete pain, and as you become more ambitious in your ideas for websites, you will discover that a great idea that took a lot of effort just won't work on some people's computers. The way to prevent this from happening too much is to keep on checking your site, as you work, on as many different systems as possible.

There's one issue that you can avoid up front, however, simply by knowing about it, and that's screen size. While you may have a 17-inch monitor with the resolution set to 1024 x 768 pixels or higher, not everyone does. And this means they will have less space to view a page than you have. It's easy to forget this when you're designing but, if you do, you'll find that a lot of people in the world get to see only the left half of your website, unless they scroll sideways, which is highly frustrating.

Similarly, if you're creating the type of page that's intended to be viewed completely within a single screen – with no downward scrolling – then you'll have to go one step further and think about page height as well as page width. It can become a real challenge to fit everything in. So what sizes should you use to get the desired results?

1

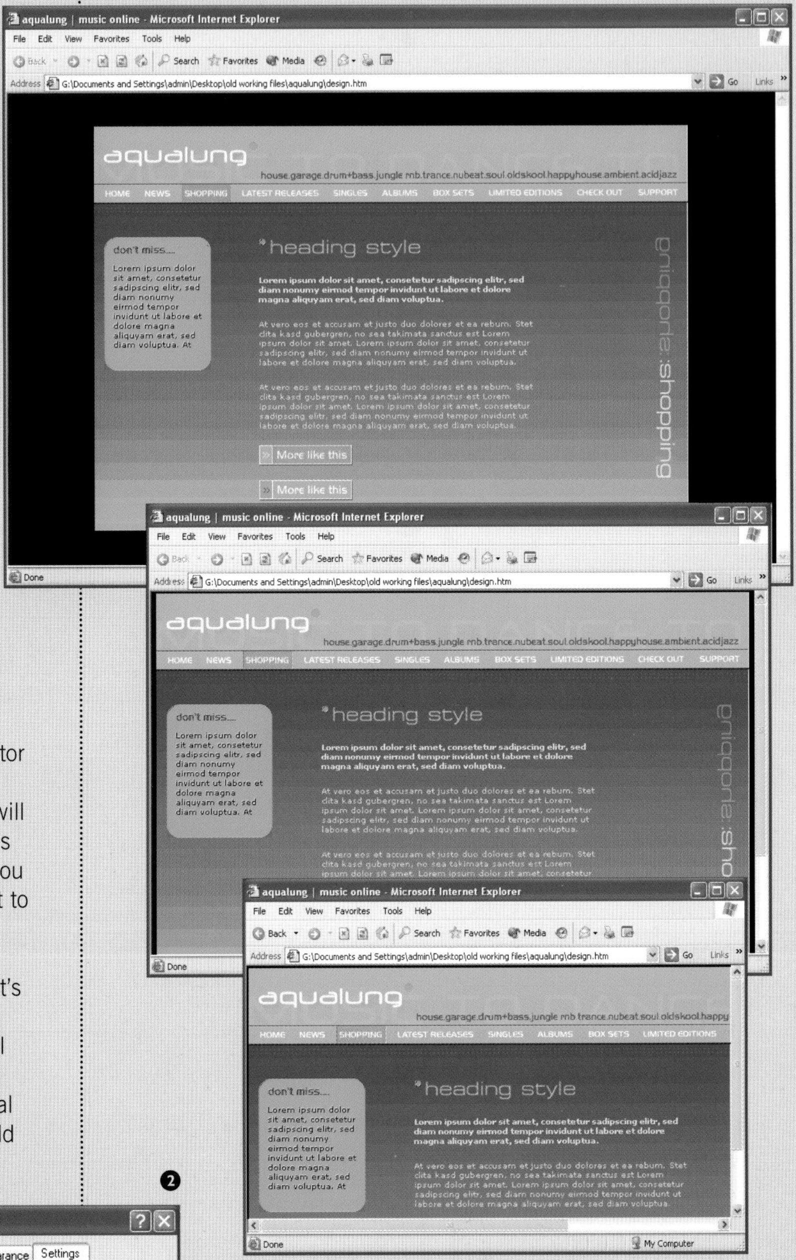

2

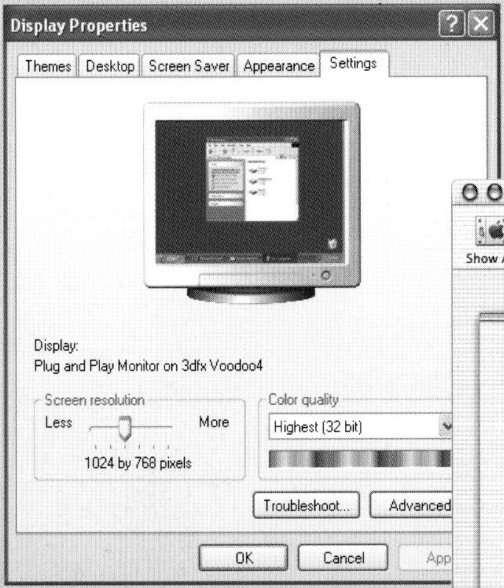

3

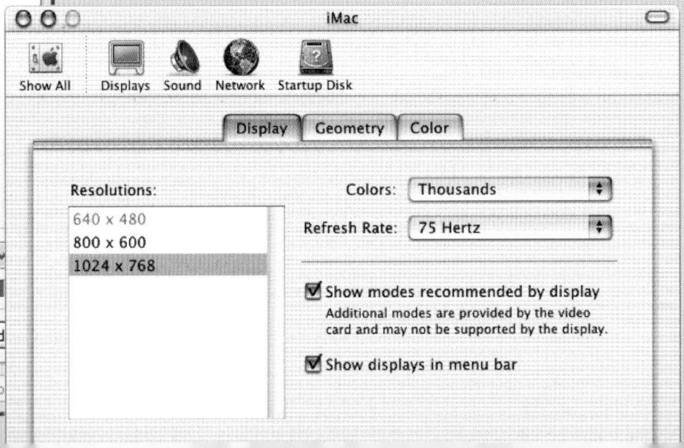

4

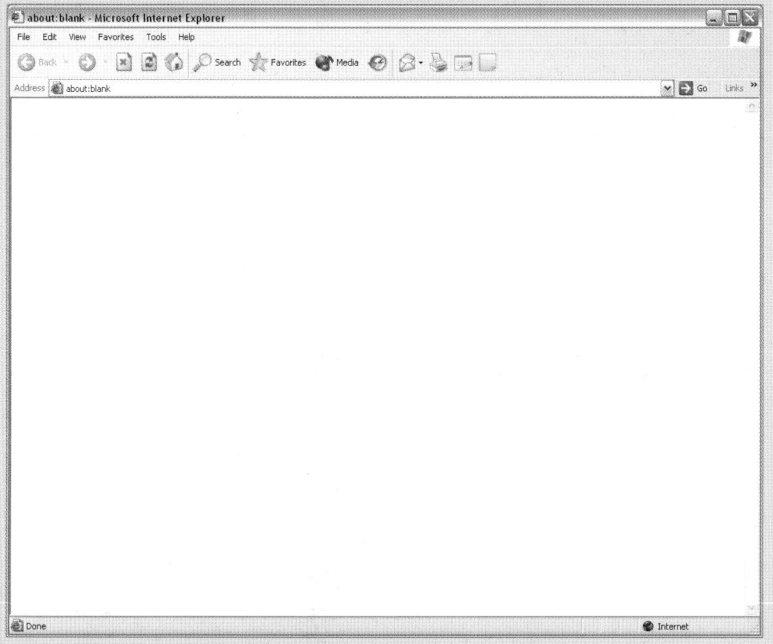

5

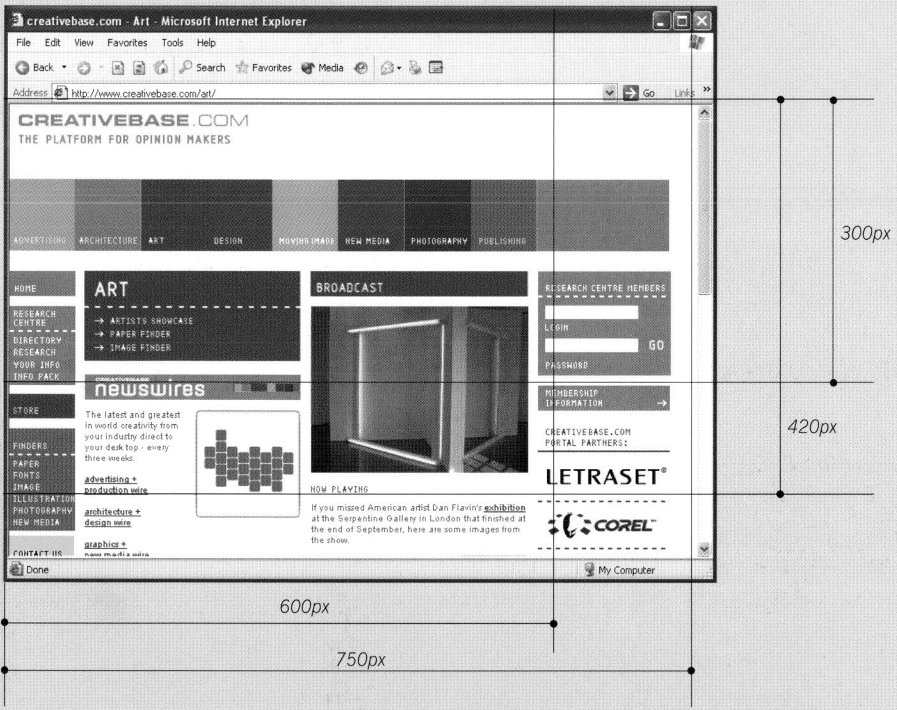

❶ While larger monitors are rapidly coming down in price, there are still a lot of people out there with 800 x 600 pixel displays. Some may even have 640 x 480, especially on a laptop. These are the same pixels that you use to measure the size of images and the tables on your webpage.

❷ You can see what your own resolution is, and change it to see how your webpage will look on other screens. In Windows, right-click on your desktop, choose Properties and go to the Settings tab.

❸ On a Mac, open the Displays dialog from your Apple menu, where you can also adjust your screen resolution as well as the colour settings.

❹ After you take into account scroll bars, menus, toolbars, taskbars, and all the other interface items that clutter up most users' screens, there's not a lot of space left: about 760 x 420 pixels in a maximised browser window on an 800 x 600 display, or 600 x 300 on a 640 x 480 display. Another factor is the individual computer as well.

❺ So what do you do? Most Web designers opt to squeeze all the important content into a 600-pixel wide page area, so that even if the user has a tiny screen, the site will still work for them. Then less important bits go in the 600 to 760 pixel area. Height-wise, 300 pixels is a very small area, so unless you're prepared to seriously compromise your design, you might have to give up on the idea of a nonscrolling design for the smallest screens. But 420 pixels, although small, is perfectly workable.

PROJECT 24
ELASTIC GRAPHICS

The easy way to deal with the screen-size problem is, before you do anything else, put a two-column, 760-pixel wide table in your webpage, and set the columns to 600 and 160 pixels respectively. Then put everything within these columns. You can align the table left or centre.

If you've got a lot of content, though, this can lead to very long pages; and for the many people with larger screens, it leaves a huge amount space around the page area. Many designers prefer instead to make use of the full window area, creating a page design that's capable of stretching and resizing itself in order to fit the space available. This may sound complicated, but it's not too difficult if you use percentages, rather than exact pixels, to specify the size of your tables.

Of course, you instantly start to lose control over spacing, but then you never get perfect control in Web design anyway, particularly with respect to the size fonts appear at. And for this reason, the techniques in this project are a boon, even if you prefer to go for a fixed-width page design.

The main problem involves graphics similar to the ones we used for the boxouts in the first project of this chapter. If you don't know how wide the boxout is going to be, what do you do about the heading and footer? You can't just ignore the problem. If your heading graphic stops short of the edge of the boxout, it's going to look terrible.

Also remember that, even if you're creating an elastic design, you've still got to make sure it all fits within a smaller screen. You'll need to keep checking your work with your browser at different sizes, to make sure all is well.

1

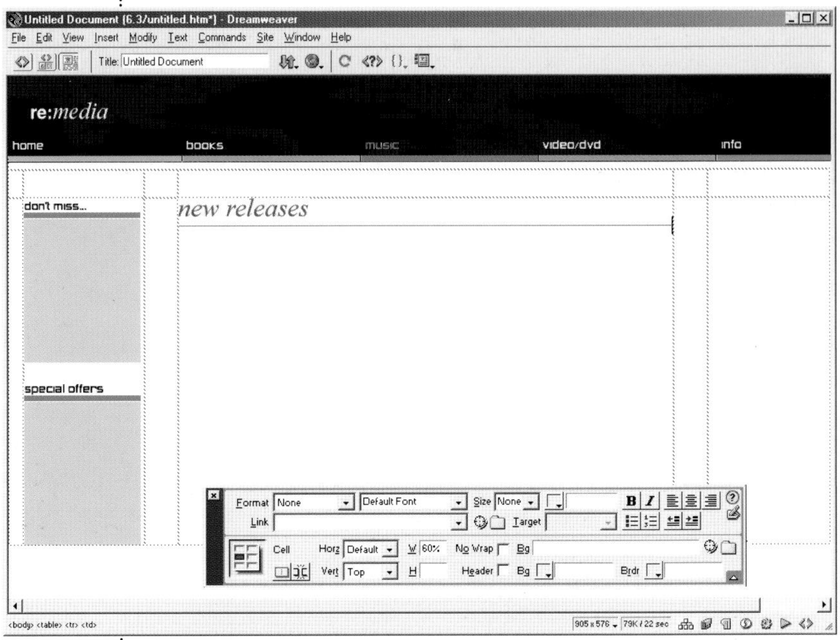

2

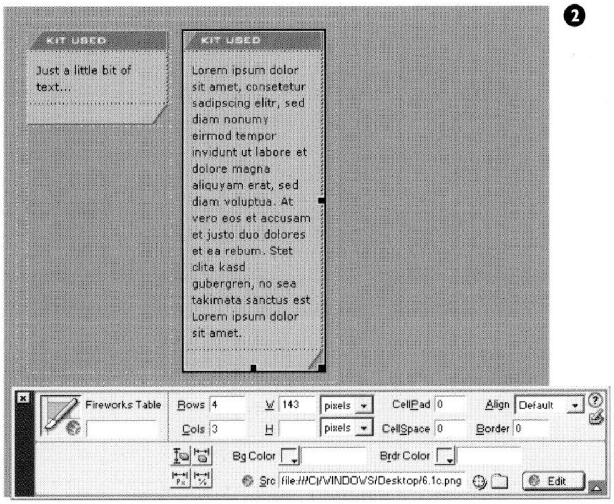

3

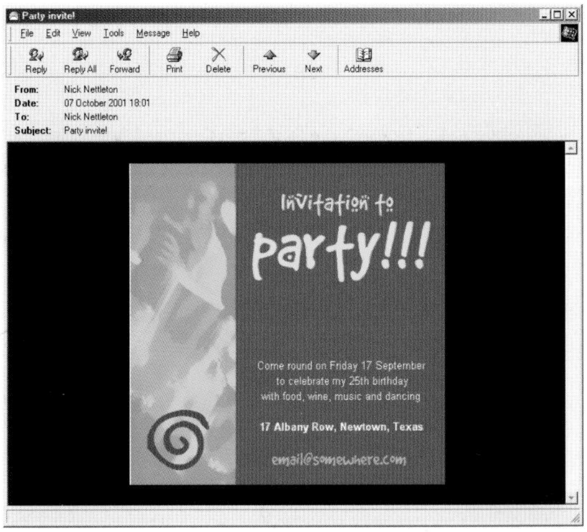

4

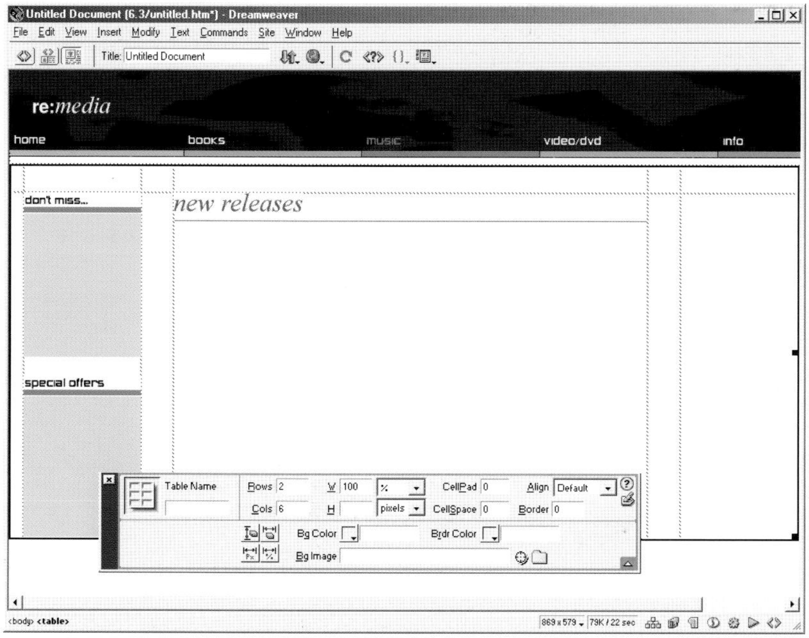

5

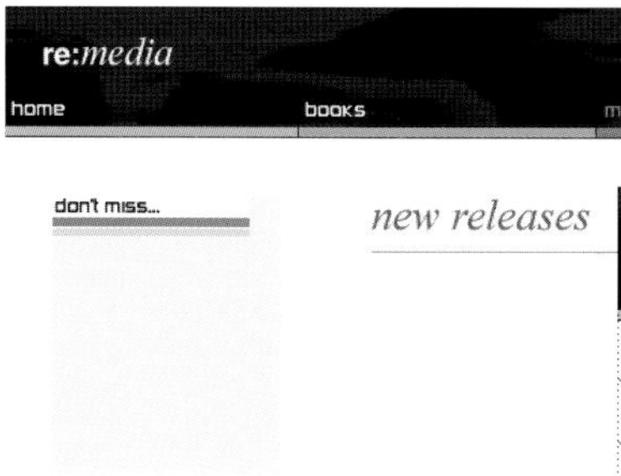

6

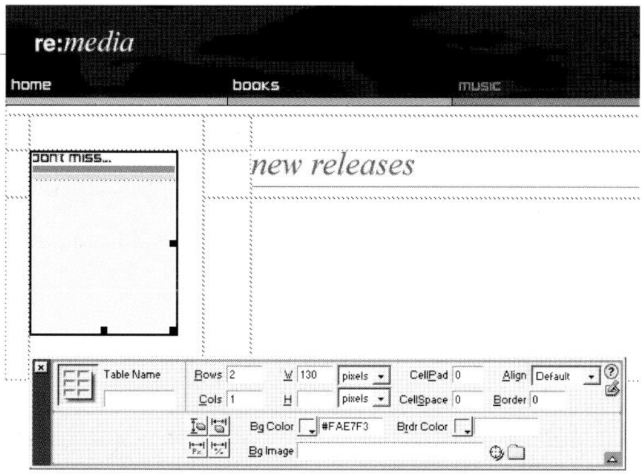

7

Table sizes

1 Stretchy webpages are based on setting the size of your tables and cells using percentages. Alternatively you can just leave it blank, in which case the browser will make a guess as to how to evenly fit the content in.

2 Often you'll want the main content area of your page to stretch to fit the content you put in, so you should leave the height settings blank.

3 Or, if you want to align something smaller vertically within the page, you can put it in a 1 x 1 table with height set to 100 per cent and *Align* set to middle.

4 It's a good idea to specify a table width in a percentage (type 100 per cent, for example), or exact pixels (450, say). Otherwise you might not get the results you're intending.

5 You can also set individual column widths in percentages. But the trouble comes if you want just the left-most column, say, to be exactly 130 pixels in a table that has its overall width set in percentages. You can type 130 in the box, but the browsers won't always respect your wishes!

6 The solution is to allow the columns to flow more naturally, and to put another table within the left-most column with its width set to exactly 130, and use this to hold the content.

7 Another problem with elastic webpages occurs if you use a decorative background in parts of the page that will stretch, like in the masthead shown here. This is because the graphic won't stretch along with them.

Creating a tile

8 The solution to this is to continue the background design through the clear-space areas, using a seamless background tile, like in the boxouts created before. The background design was very simple here, though, and you didn't have to do anything to make it seamless.

9 With designs like this, however, you'll have to put more effort into getting the tile to work properly...

10 Paint Shop Pro has a quick *Convert To Seamless* command in the *Selections* menu, but to be honest the results aren't always that great. You can also use the *Effects* > *Reflection Effects* > ***Pattern*** option, but please take care – you may end up with tacky results.

11 Adobe ImageReady has an excellent *Tile Maker* tool, under *Filters* > ***Other***. The *Kaleidoscope* option is perhaps best avoided, but the *Blend Edges* technique is effective for many types of images, using a feathering effect to achieve a seamless result.

Photo-Paint has a similar tool, under *Effects* > *Distort* > ***Tile***. However, as in Paint Shop Pro, the 'seamless' look can sometimes be disappointing, especially around the corners.

12 So you might be better off doing it by hand – especially for graphics where a washy, feathered effect is the last thing you want. Using *Filters* > *Other* > ***Offset*** (in Photoshop or ImageReady), ***Effects*** **>** or by hand if you have no similar option, shift your image across and wrap the edges around, so that you can see the seams...

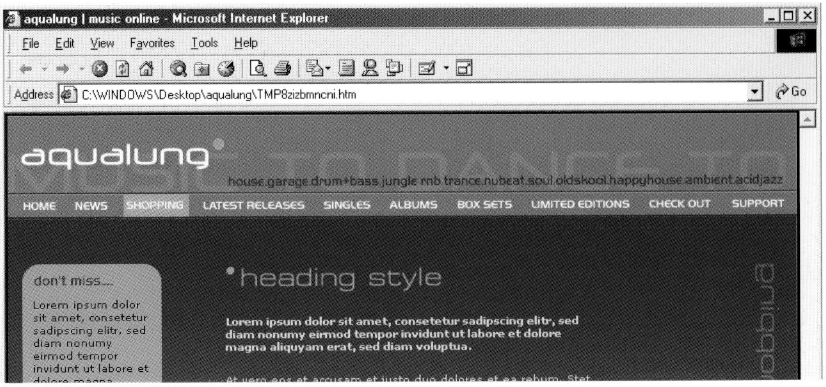

8

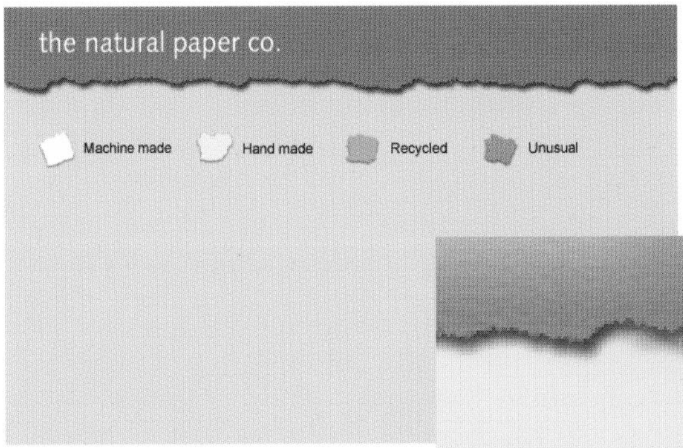

9

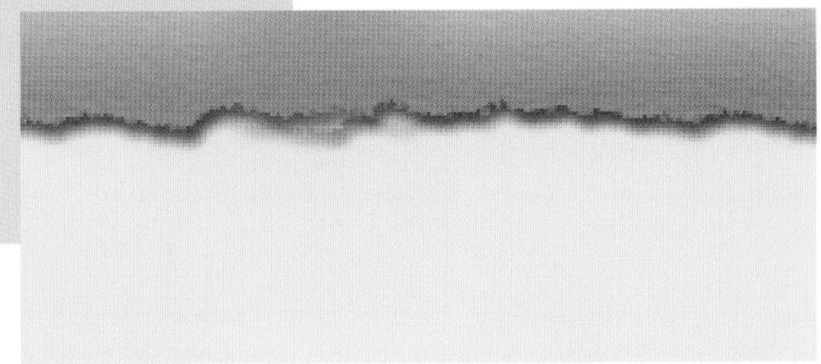

10

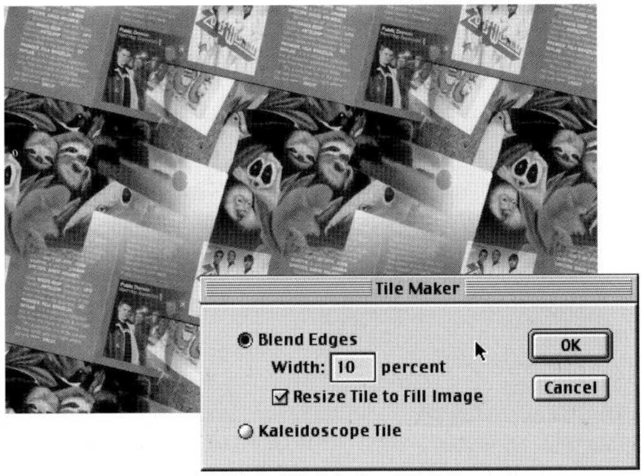

11

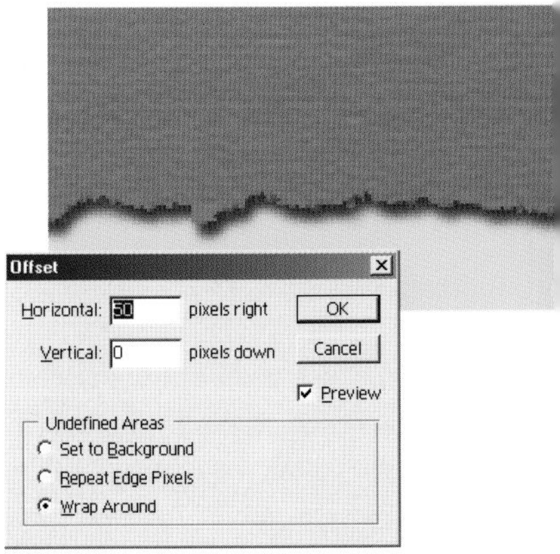

12

13

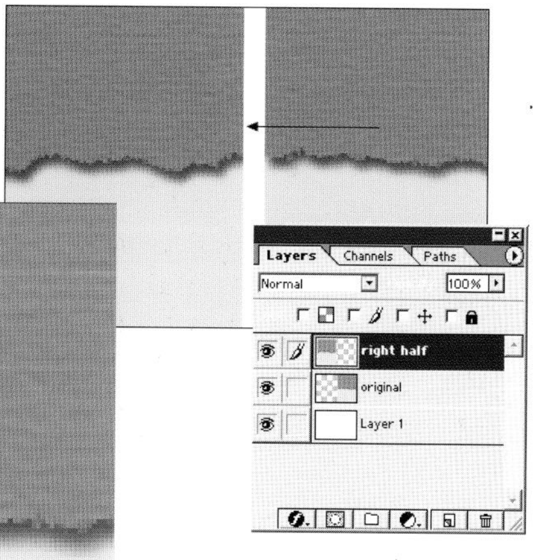

14

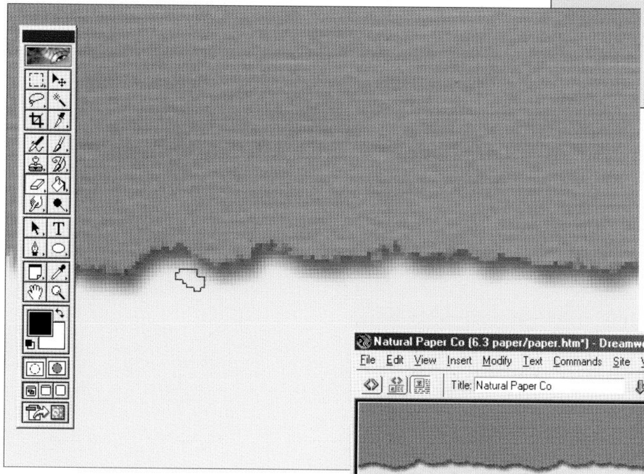

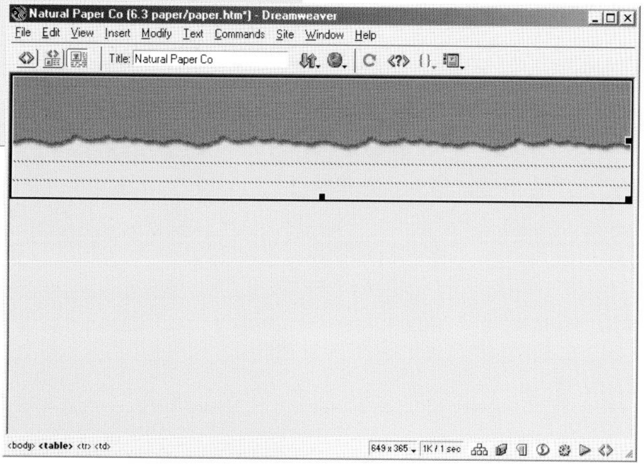

15

16

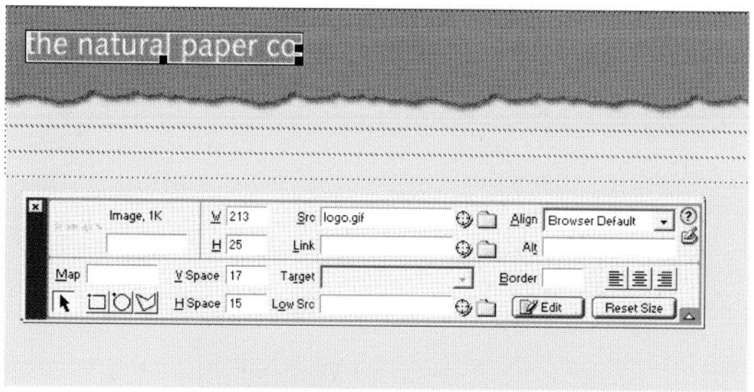

17

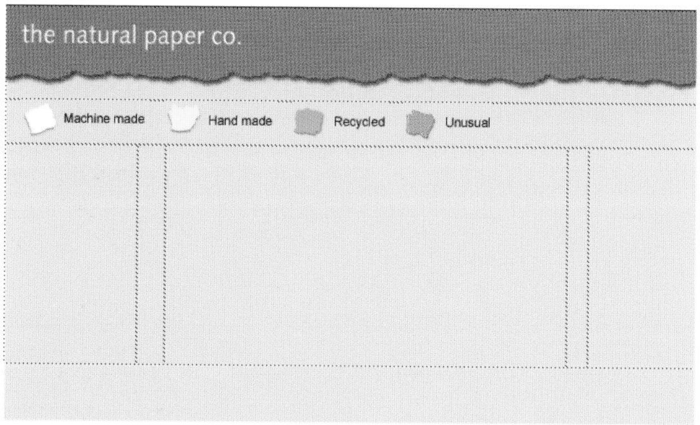

13 You can do this by selecting the right half of your image and copying it onto a new layer. Then shift the original to the right, move the copy to the left and line them up…

14 Now, using your normal graphics tools, work on the seam areas to blend them. In particular, you may find your *Clone* tools useful.

Export your graphics in the normal way. In particular, it's a good idea to use a transparent background for graphics intended for a textured background so you can avoid problems with seams.

15 Once this is done, start on the webpage proper. You'll probably want all margins set to 0 for this as well as a three-row table – one for the header, one for the navigation and the third for main content. Add your tile as the background image for the header cell, and use this cell's height setting so you can see the whole tile.

16 Set this cell's vertical alignment to *Top*, and add the logo in here. To get the positioning of the logo right, use its horizontal and vertical spacing settings.

Add your buttons in the second row, using their spacing settings to get the positioning right, and use the row's height setting to create space above and below the navigation.

17 Finally, in the bottom row add a new table with, say, five columns, and use these to hold your content in the usual way…

PROJECT 25
FRAMES

One technique that has been extremely popular in Web design is using frames, although some designers avoid them. Frames are very hard to use well. You've probably seen websites that have a scroll bar floating in the webpage, rather than at the side, and you can use it to scroll a particular bit of the page, while the rest stays right where it is. This is done using frames.

The browser window is divided up into subwindows (called frames), in the same way as your e-mail program has subwindows – one for your folders, one for a list of messages and perhaps one for previewing messages. You can control the width of these borders, and even make them invisible, which is what most designers do. You can also choose to hide the scroll bars on certain windows. This is why a page using frames doesn't appear to be made of different windows.

Each frame contains a separate HTML page, and behaves in just the same way as a normal browser window – it is just smaller. You also need a webpage that will tell the browser about the different frames – how many there are, what size they are and what other properties they have, as well as the address of the webpage that each one should open. The address of this file is also what you should link people to, for the complete webpage experience.

1

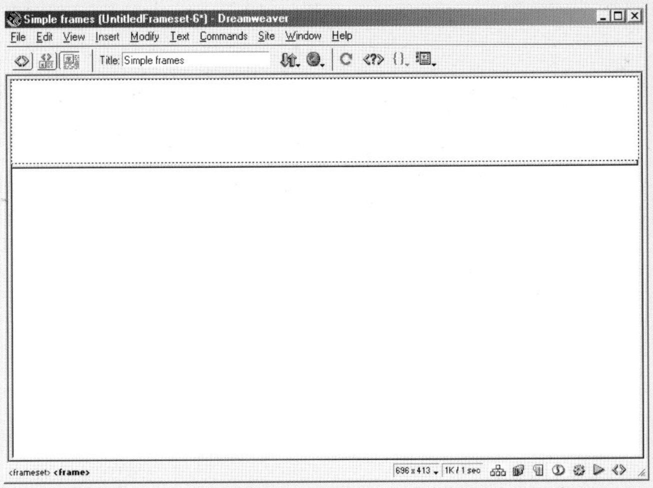

2

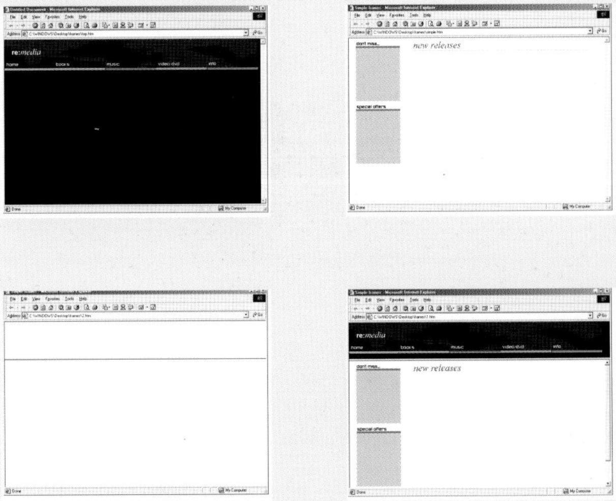

3

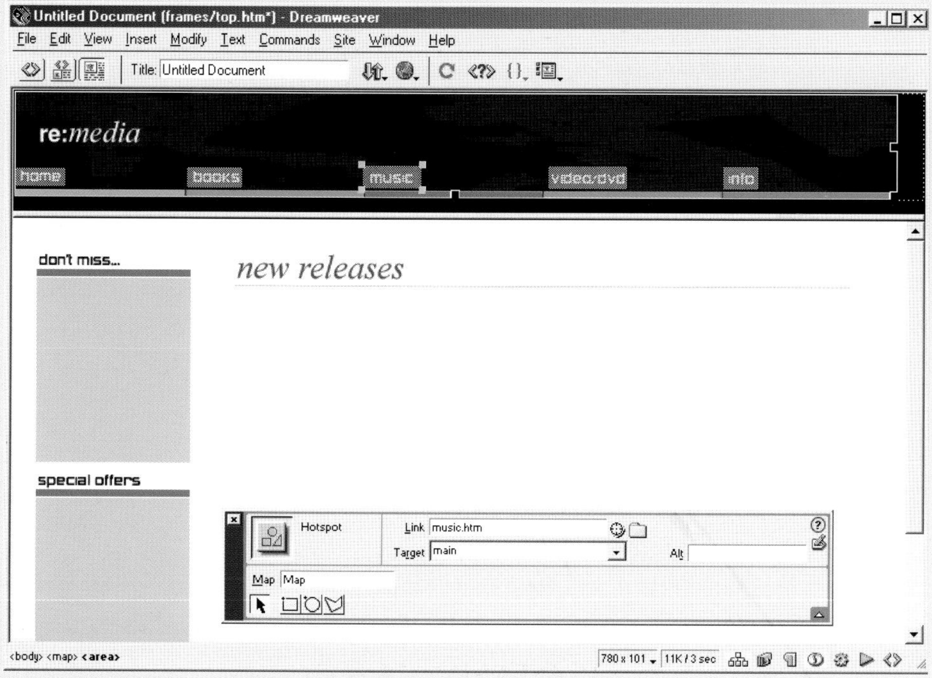

4

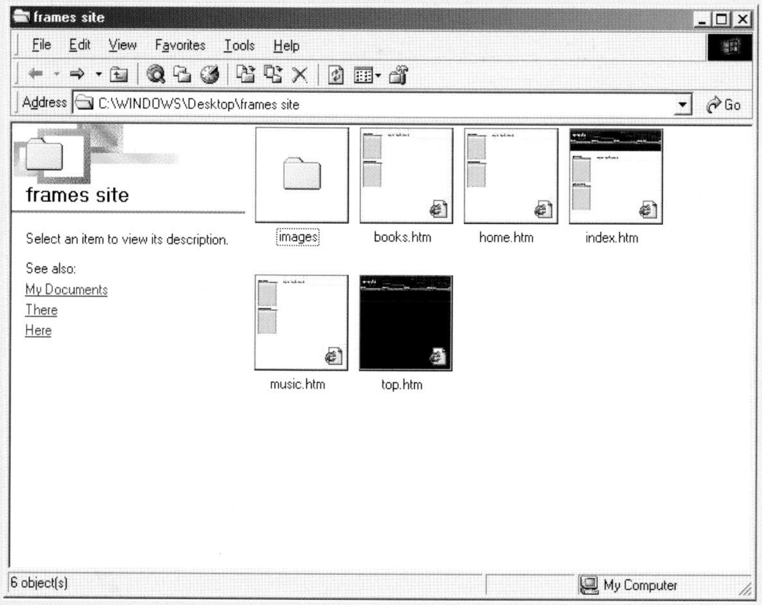

1 Setting up frames is a fiddly process at first, but it can make changing something across your whole site much easier later. The classic example is a two-frame layout, with one for the navigation across the top and the other for the main content.

2 You create one webpage for the overall frameset, as it is called, and then one page for each frame. In this case there is a page containing the logo, masthead and navigation and another page for the content.

3 For a whole site, you still need to create different content pages for the various sections. But the idea is that you set the links in the navigation to change only the page in the bottom frame, leaving everything else just where it is. Do this by giving the bottom frame a name – 'main', for example – and then setting the *Target* of the link to 'main'. This is the same *Target* that, if you set it to '_blank', opens the page in a new window. This means you can use the same frameset and the same navigation page throughout your site. So if you want to change the frames later, or update your navigation, you only have to edit one file.

4 Normally, you should give your frameset the file name of the homepage – index.htm or index.html – because this is the file you want to open automatically when people come to your site.

The use of frames is one of those techniques that works differently in different software. You need to use your Web authoring application for this – graphics software won't do the job. But most of these include a palette or toolbox for working with frames, as well as a *Frame Properties* inspector or dialog.

❺❻ You should find that your software has a selection of common prefab framesets you can use by clicking a button or dragging into your page, such as the simple two-down or two-across set-up. Take your pick...

❼ You should also be able to click-and-drag frame borders to position them exactly where you want them, or manually set their individual sizes. It's a good idea to fix a navigation frame to the exact size of the nav bar.

❽ You can give your frames sizes in exact pixels or percentages, just like a table. You can also give them relative sizes, which are each represented by an *. So if you've got one at frame at 1* and another at 2*, then the first frame will take up one-third of the space, and the second frame two-thirds of the space (so it's twice the width or height). For the style we're using, just set the nav frame to 90 pixels, and the other frame to 1*, so it simply fills the rest of your main browser window.

❾❿ If you wanted to have your whole page scrolling, but floating in the middle of the window, you could create a frameset like this. The heights and widths of all the frames are set to 1*, except the middle one, which is set at 600 x 420 pixels (in order to fit most screen sizes).

5

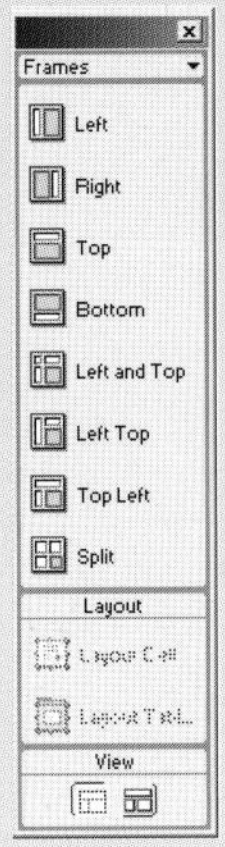

6

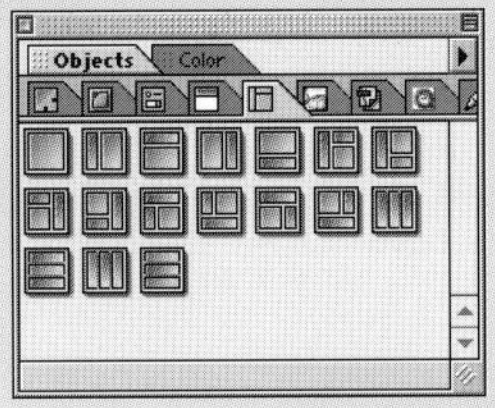

7

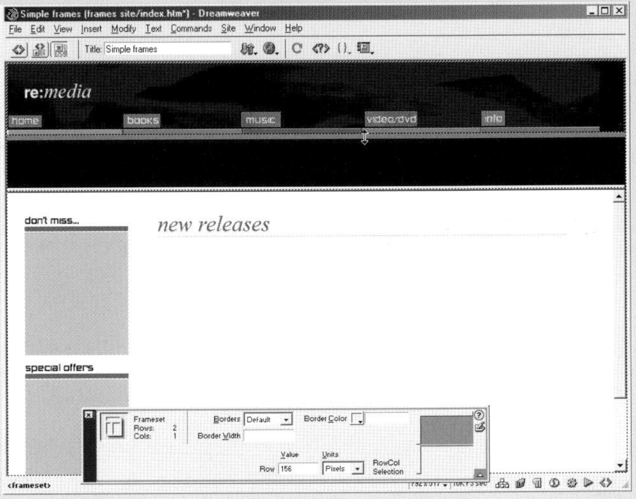

8

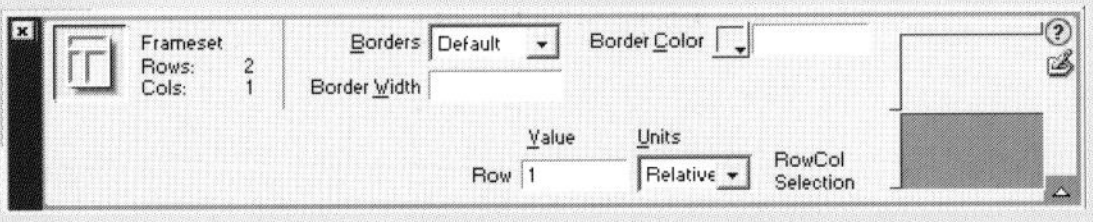

9

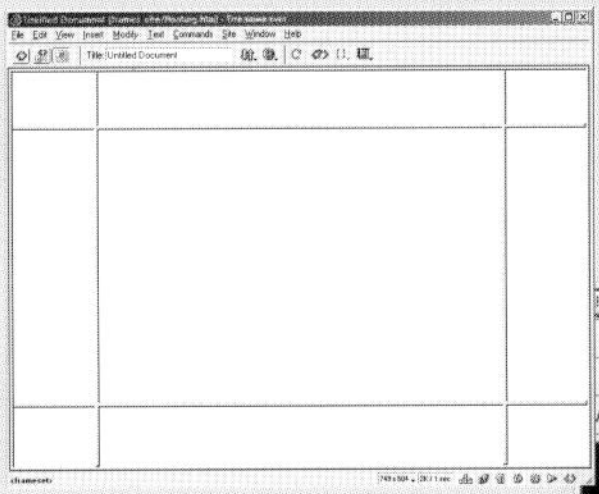

10

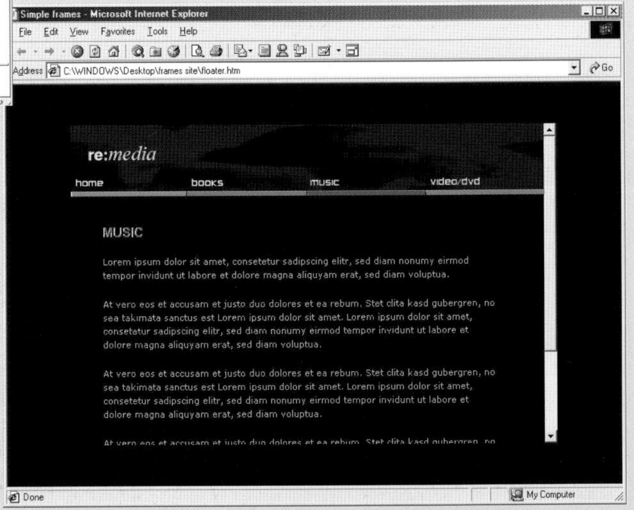

11
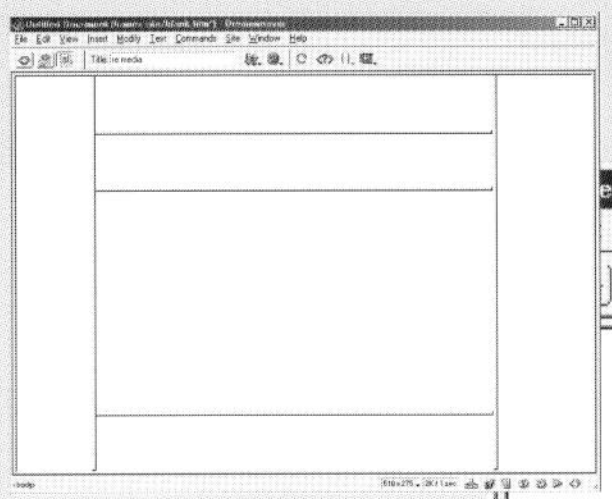

12
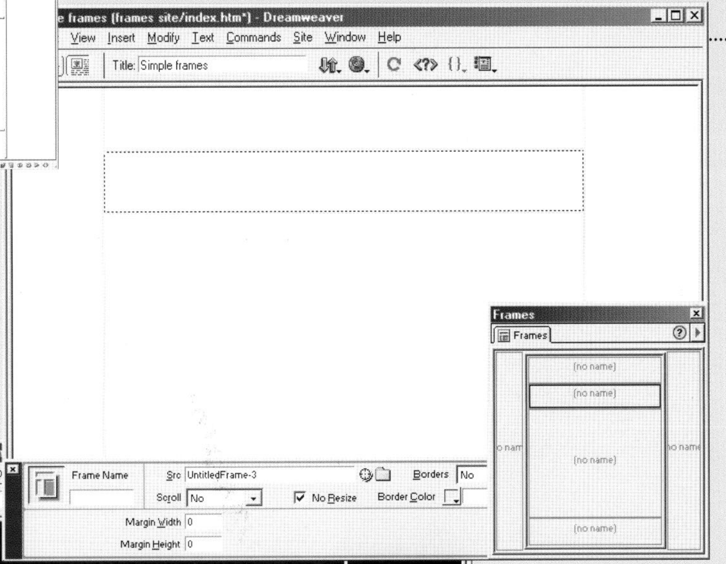

13
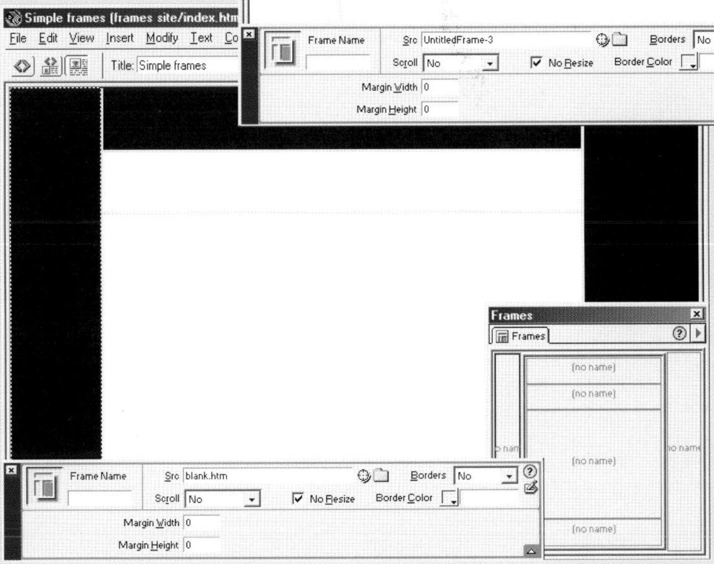

14
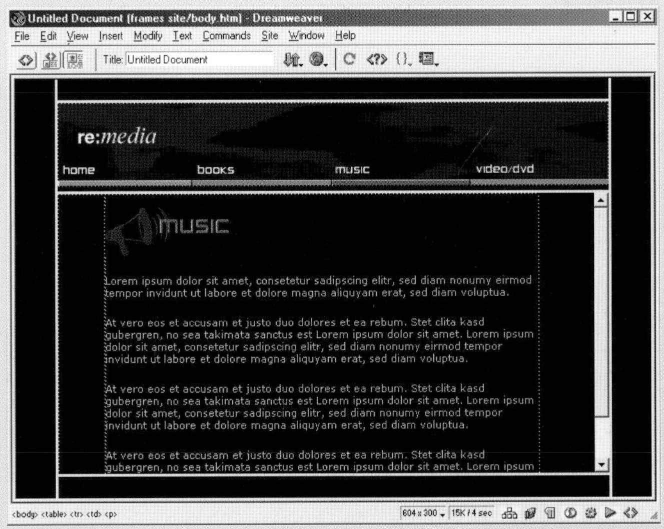

15
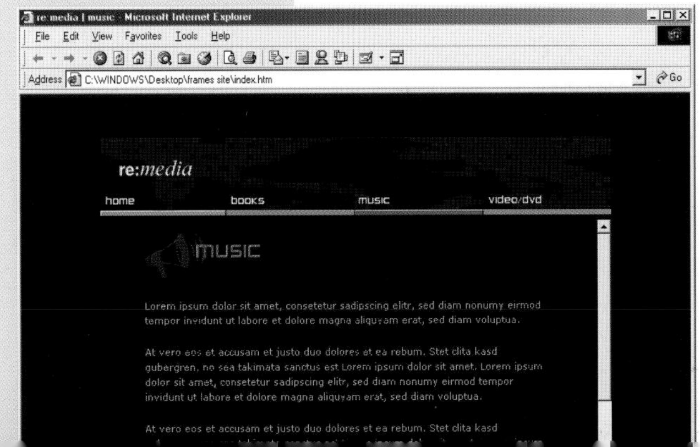

11 Finally, settle on this frameset layout, with two rows in the middle: one for the nav, one for the main content.

12 Before you move on with the design, select the overall frameset and then the individual frames, and set all their properties. Next, hide all borders, and set *Margin Heights* and *Margin Widths* to 0 (these are inner margins for each frame). Finally, choose the *No Resize* option so users can't make a mess of your design and choose which frames do and don't have scroll bars.

13 You should be able to edit each frame's page individually. The easy part is the frames you want to be empty – they're just there to create space. All you need do is set a background colour for one and give it a title, then save it as 'blank.htm', and use the same file to go in other blank frames. When you select a frame, you should see an SRC property (link) and an icon where you can browse to choose the HTML file you want.

14 In the navigation window, create the logo, masthead and nav just as you would normally. But don't worry about the main content section, because that goes in the final window.

15 Finally, open the frameset page in your Web browser and check it all works properly.

Jasc Animation Shop - [fish anim.gif [1:3] - Frames]
File Edit View Animation Effects Window Help
Zoom: 1:3
F:1 D:7
F:2 D:7
F:5 D:7
Go To Frame...
Animation Properties...
Shift+Alt+Enter
View Animation
Edit the properties of the current animation
Forever
Layers
History
Actions
Normal
Opacity: 100%
Lock:
Layer 1 copy
Layer 1
Background

CHAPTER 7

Animation

Animation for the Web is all about putting design in motion. Like rollovers, even the slightest touch of animation on a webpage can transform its appeal for your users. Serious animation is an artform in itself, but simple animation works well on the Web, and you can easily create your own to work well with your overall design.

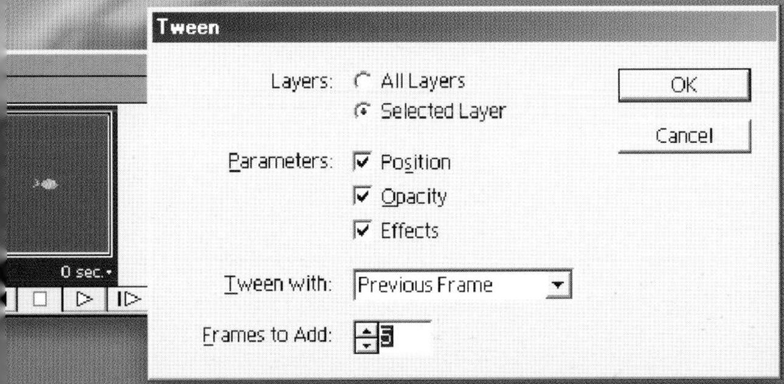

PROJECT 26

HOW ANIMATION WORKS

Animation is such a diverse and exciting topic that it really demands a book of its own. We can cover only the barest introduction here: for more, see the *Web Animation* book in this series.

There is more than one way to create animation for the Web. The simplest, which we'll look at here, is GIF animation. This is the same file format and uses many of the same techniques that you have used to create the graphics throughout this book.

Other techniques include using Macromedia's Flash, which has become incredibly popular over the last couple of years, and DHTML (Dynamic HTML) animation. Although powerful, this is tricky to get working right and is therefore best used in moderation.

Almost all animation, including GIF animation, works like a film: a series of static images are displayed one after the other in a rapid sequence, and this gives the illusion of motion. With GIF animation, all these images are included in a single GIF, but as you can imagine, file size increases in direct proportion to the number of frames you use.

Fortunately, the frame rate doesn't need to be that fast to create a realistic animation – 9 or 12 per second is ample for the Web. And you can use techniques for looping and slowing down animations to get more impact per kilobyte of download.

1

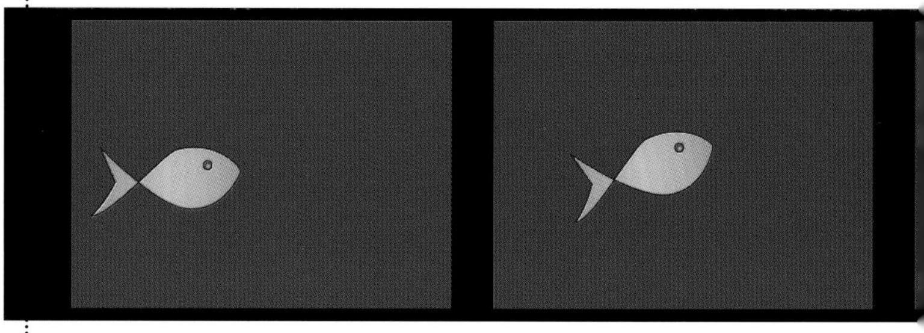

2

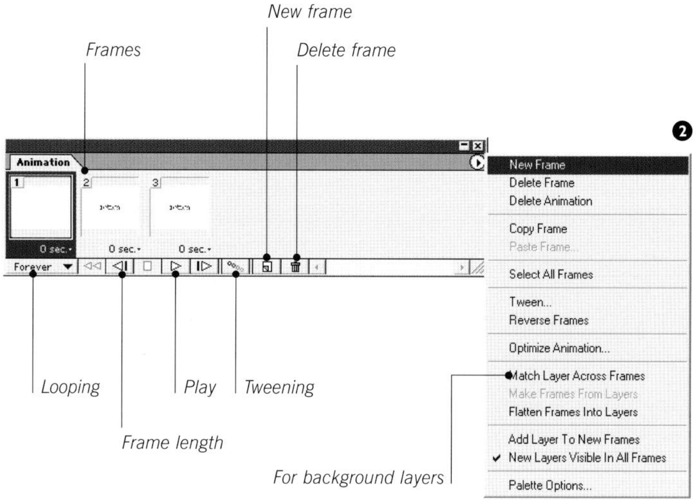

3

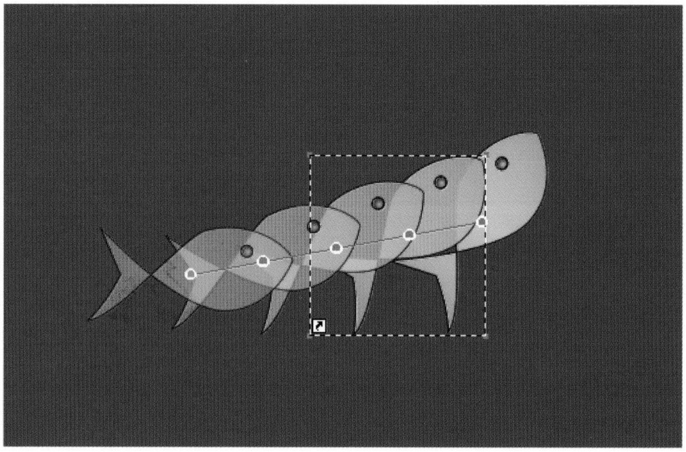

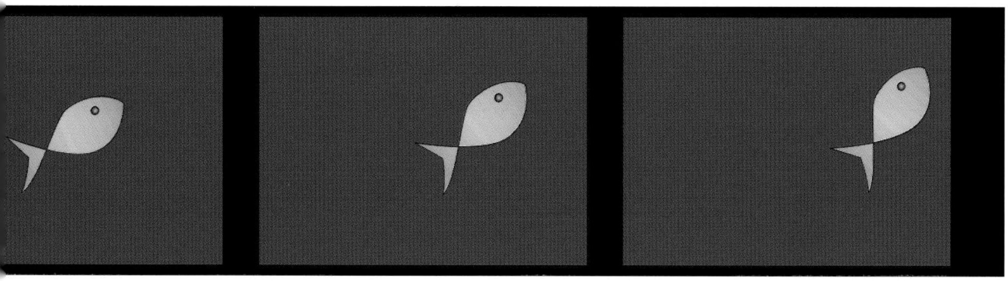

❶ Animation using the GIF format is quite simply a series of images, or frames, squeezed into a single GIF file, together with information about how long each frame lasts, whether the end loops back to the beginning, and so on. Sometimes these frames are called layers – not to be confused with the layers used in most graphics applications.

❹

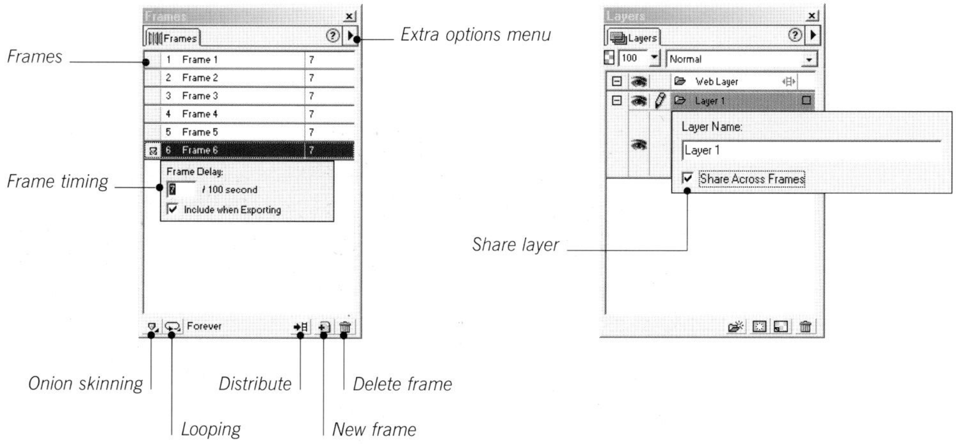

❷ You need dedicated tools in your graphics application to create animation. Photoshop owners should use ImageReady's *Animation* palette, which includes just about everything you need. The content of a layer is the same on all frames, although you can change its position, visibility, transparency, blending and effects. For other animation, put your different images on separate layers, and change which is visible for each frame.

❸ The *Tweening* feature allows you to create just the beginning and end points of a stretch of animation, and the software works out all the in-between points. This is very useful, but you do have to give it as much help as possible. Of course, it can't write a script for you, but it can make an object appear to move or change colour.

❹ Fireworks, which has superb animation facilities, uses a *Frames* palette that is much like ImageReady's *Animation* palette, and has most of the same controls. Onion skinning allows you to see and work on several frames at once. In Fireworks you don't have to create your animation on different layers first – you can have completely different layers on different frames if you like. For *Tweening*, you have to turn a graphic into a symbol, using *Insert* > ***Convert to Symbol***, and then tween it using your *Modify* > ***Symbol***... menu. You can share a layer across frames by doubleclicking it on your layers palette.

5 Paint Shop Pro users should use Animation Shop. Its main work area is effectively your *Animation* palette, with all your control in the interface around it. Animation Shop has no object tweening, but it does have a range of quick and easy image and text effects, as well as transitions, which you can apply from the *Effects* menu. To set frame properties, such as timing, right-click and select that option.

6 Like Fireworks, Corel Photo-Paint's animation tools are built directly into the package, although they work somewhat differently: you don't have an animation palette as such, but a 'Movie docker' – really a toolbar for stepping through frames, adding new ones and previewing your animation. Basically, on each frame you should create the design you want, then combine it with the background, using *Object > Combine* before you move on.

7 Usually when you're creating an animation, you'll want to have much the same image on different frames, adding incremental changes between them. This means it's a good idea to use layers that are the same on all frames. Use a *Share Layer* or *Match Layer Across Frames* feature, so that when you want to change something you have to change it only once rather than going into every frame in your animation, which would be terribly boring. This would be ideal if you wanted a background for the goldfish animation, for instance...

5

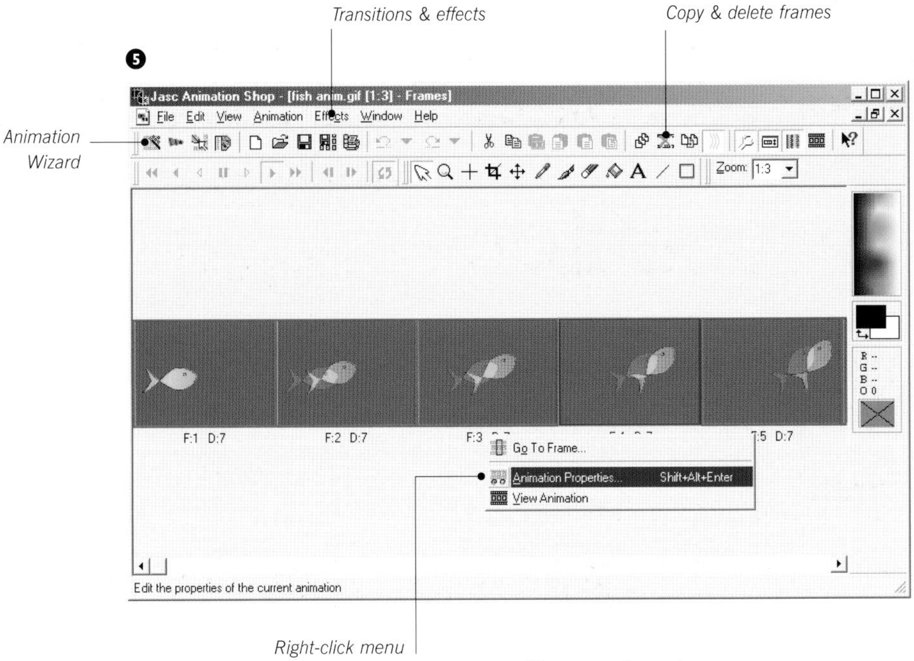

6

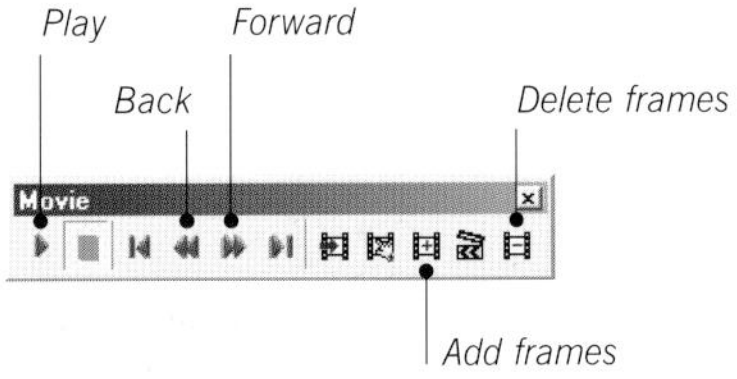

7

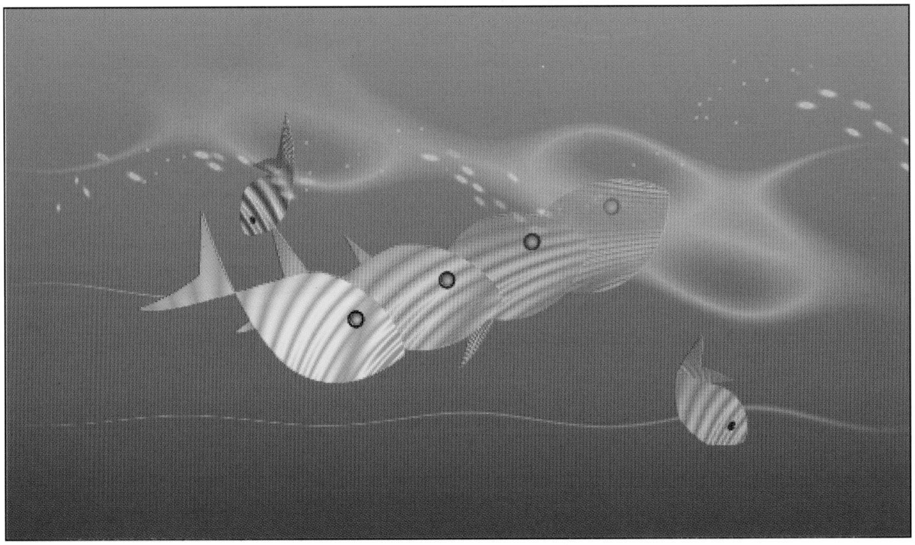

8

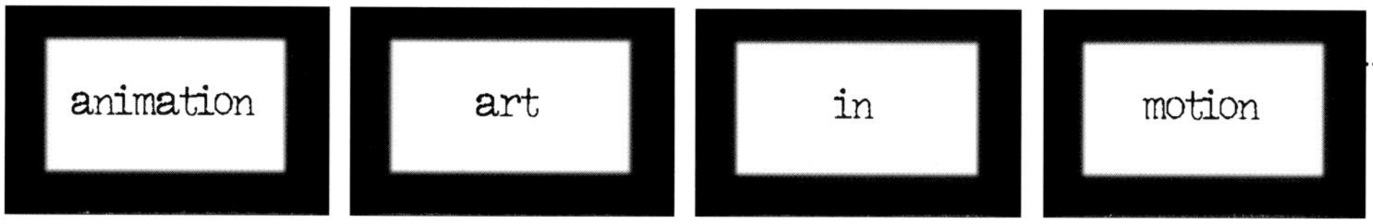

9

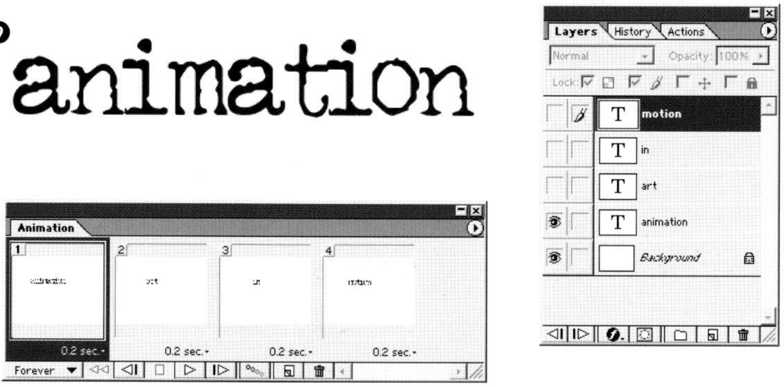

10

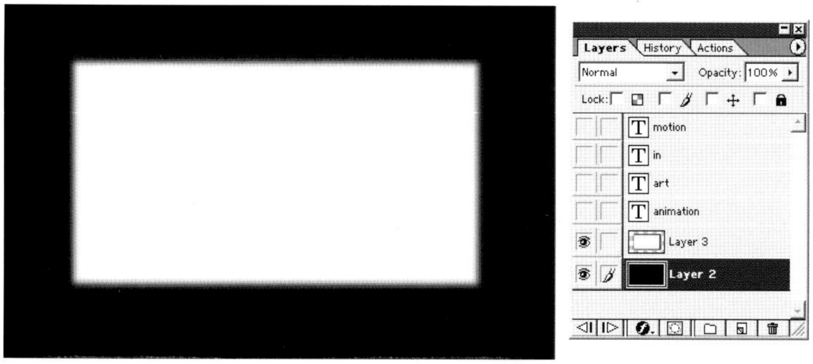

11

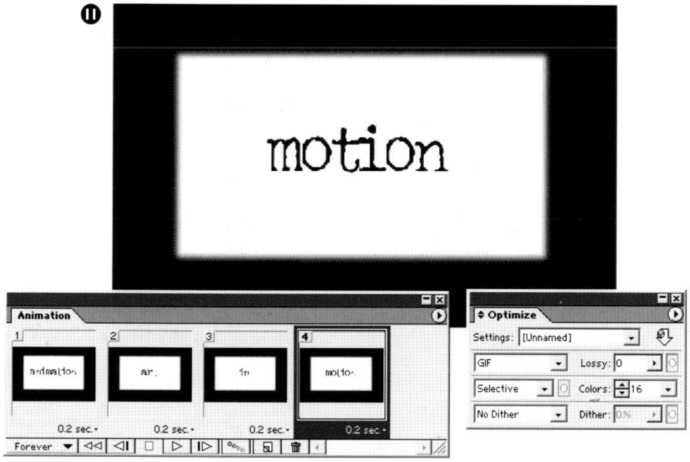

12

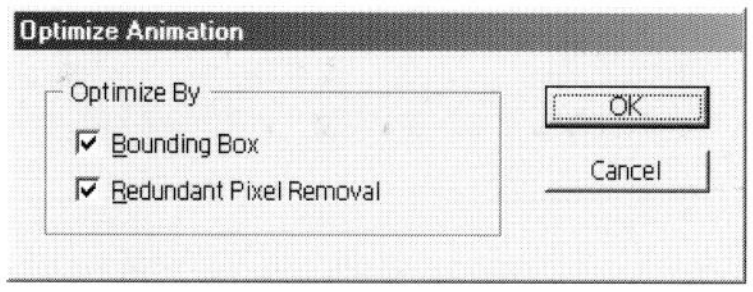

8 The simplest kind of animation involves an image that changes for each frame, with no pretence to the illusion of movement. This works well with text, allowing you to make good use of a small space. Remember, while you might have frames running at 100 milliseconds each for some types of animation, you can make a single frame last as long as you wish, for example, one-quarter second per word.

9 To create this effect, simply type the first word centred on the first frame. Then duplicate this frame a few times, and change the text that appears for each subsequent frame (with new *Layers* or *Objects* depending on your software). Set the timings as you go.

10 The background is simply a white rectangle, blurred, on its own layer. Here it has been set to be visible on all frames of the animation. The font used is called GF Halda – you can pick it up free at ***www.flashkit.com***.

11 The final process is to crop, prepare and export the animation. Remember, it has to be a GIF file, and you export this in the normal way. The file is going to be much larger, though, because you've effectively got a file for each frame of your animation, all bundled into one.

12 Some applications, including ImageReady and Fireworks, include tools for compensating by only storing the background image once, since this doesn't change. In Fireworks, use the *Share Layer* option. In ImageReady, choose *Optimize Animation* from the *Animation* palette menu, and check both boxes in there.

PROJECT 27
TWEENING

Tweening is a process that enables you to create designs for particular points in an animation, called keyframes. This is immensely useful as your animation becomes more complex, or seeks the illusion of gradual change, because to do it by hand is difficult and laborious.

The intelligence your software can apply to this process escalates in almost direct proportion to how much you pay for it. If you want help to make a stick man walk, you'll have to spend several thousands – perhaps not the right investment at this stage. But with a little cunning and creative thought, you can produce realistic effects with the simpler tweening tools for position, colour, transparency and so on that you'll find in ImageReady and Fireworks.

Now you're going to animate the fish graphic, which was shown in the previous chapter, to create a file that you can put across the top of a webpage as a pleasant surprise for visitors. It's got a simple form, which makes the whole process much easier: you can get away without moving limbs and so on. And by scaling, rotating and distorting the shape of the fish as it moves, you can give it a 3D illusion of swimming nearer and further away. You can also emphasise this by changing the speed of the animation at different points. Things seem to move more slowly when they're further away, and the darting movements of fish can easily be mimicked using these techniques.

1

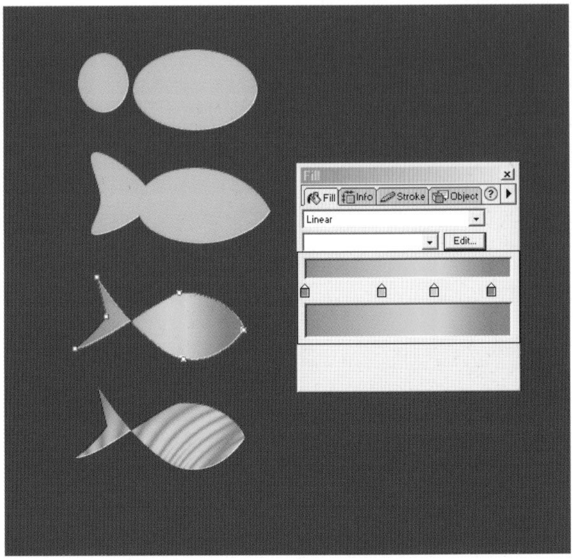

2

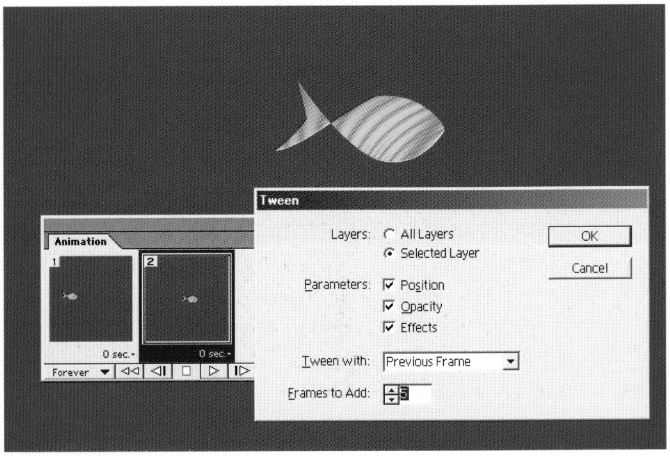

3

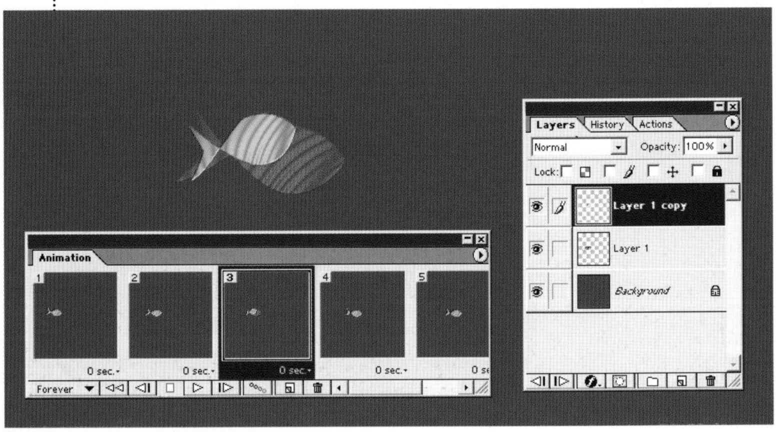

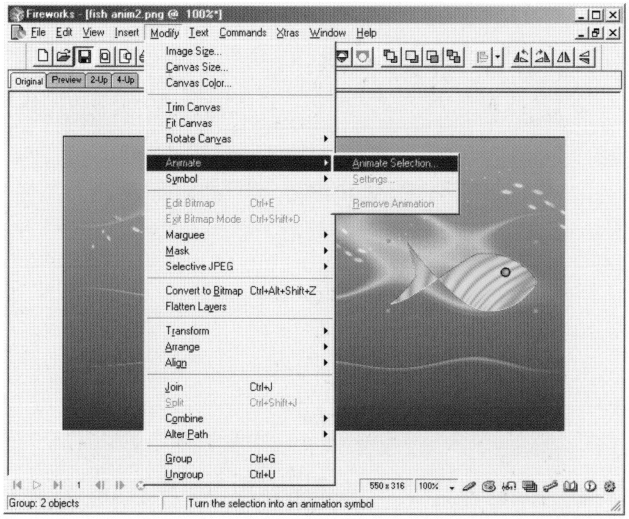

4

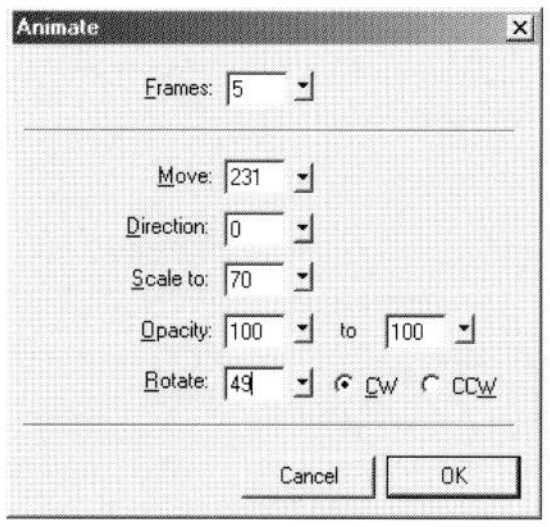

5

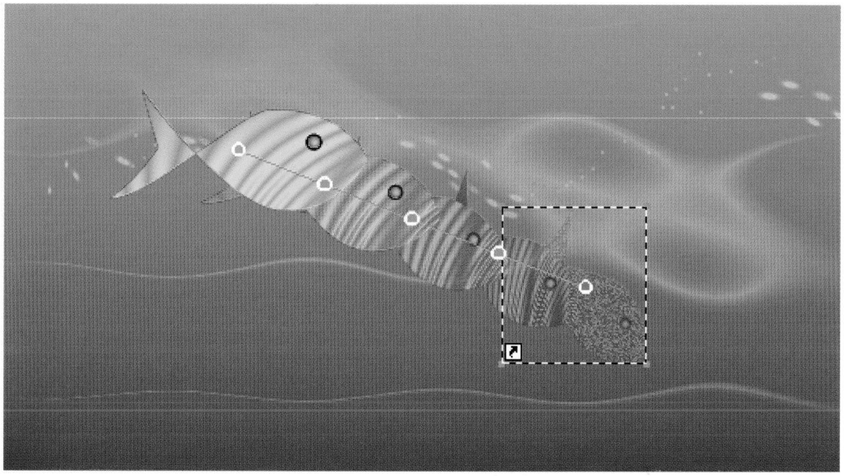

6

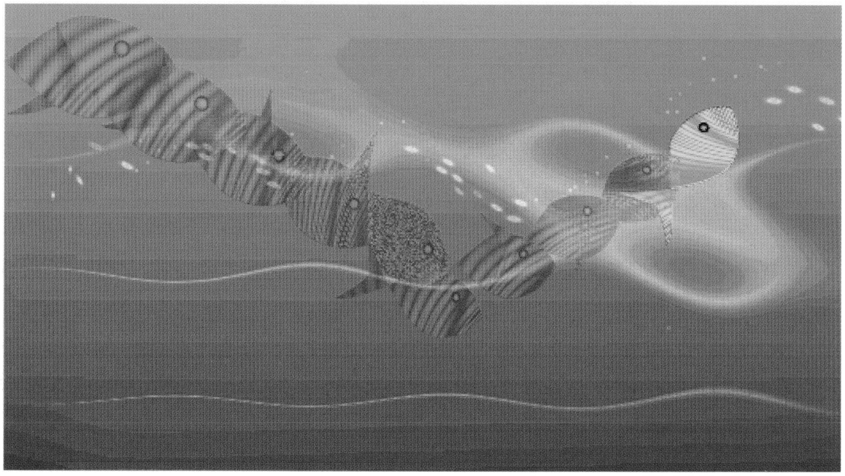

7

1 Create the fish by just drawing a couple of circles, distorting them and using a few gradient fills to give it exotic stripes. The background is also a collection of distorted ellipses with gradient fills, where one of the gradient colours is the same as the background.

2 The next stage is to get the fish moving. In ImageReady, simply create a new frame, change the position of the fish, then click the *Tween* button and set your options in here. The software does all the rest, but you might need to set your background layer to *Match Across all Frames*.

3 You can't tween scaling and rotating in ImageReady, but you can use this animation as a starting point to make distortions manually to each frame. Duplicate the layer, change and distort the new version, and make the previous layer invisible. Don't delete it, or you'll lose it entirely.

4 5 Fireworks' tweening is much more powerful. The easiest way to use it is to group your fish as one object (*Control* or *Apple* + *G*), then select *Modify* > *Animate* > ***Animate Selection***. This provides a dialog in which you can choose all your settings.

6 Hit *OK* and turn *Onion Skinning* on, so you can see the animation work. You can now transform, move and adapt your fish as a single object.

7 To continue in either application, add a new frame at the end and repeat the process for your new stretch of animation, ensuring that the beginning matches the way in which the last stretch ended.

PROJECT 28
ANIMATED ROLLOVERS

For our final project in the book, we're going to create a sophisticated and eye-opening animated rollover effect. This is difficult, so it might take a few tries to get it right, but don't give up. The idea is that when you roll over a link, a little icon image of a closed eye opens. When you roll out, the eye closes. First, we create the animation of a closing eye; then set it in reverse and save it. Next, we create a simple rollover using static images of the closed and open eye for the mouseout and mouseover states – this is done in the normal way. Finally, we export the animated files at exactly the right dimensions, and replace the static GIF files with these animated versions...

❶ First, draw the eyeball. Here we begin with a simple oval, using a soft grey-blue to white gradient to give it a rounded, 3D look, and an almost transparent layer of red with a veiny texture over the top for some extra detail. The iris and pupil use the same gradient-plus-texture technique, which we finish off with highlights – some sharp, some soft and blurry.

❶

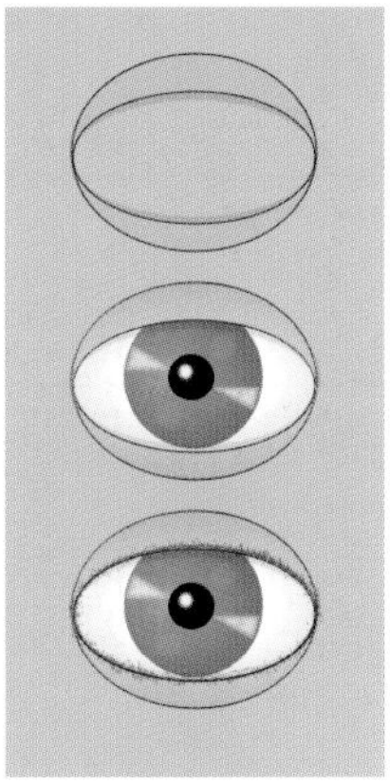

❷

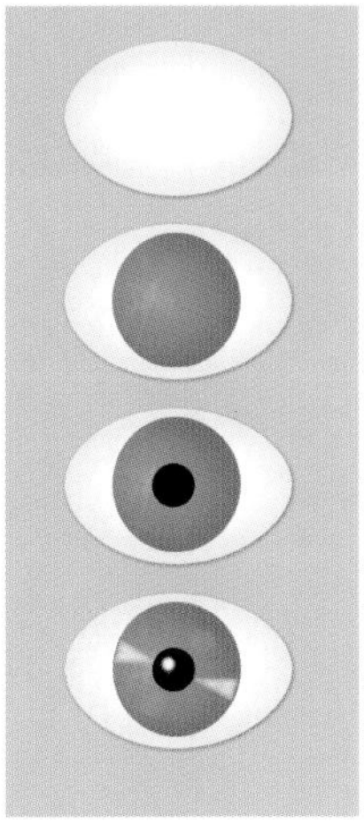

❸

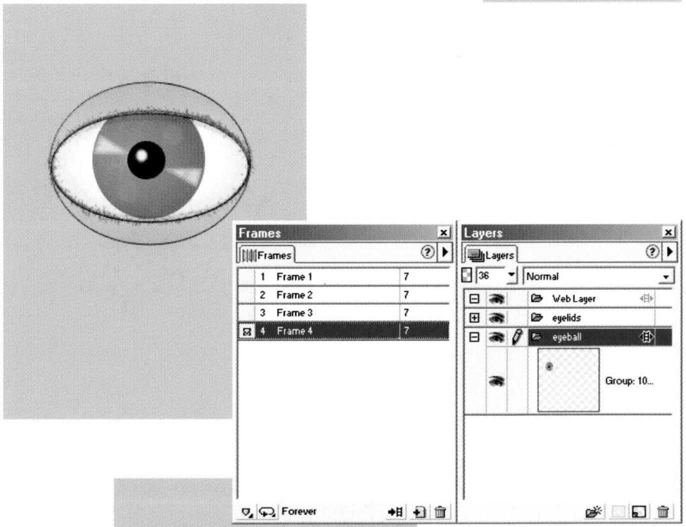

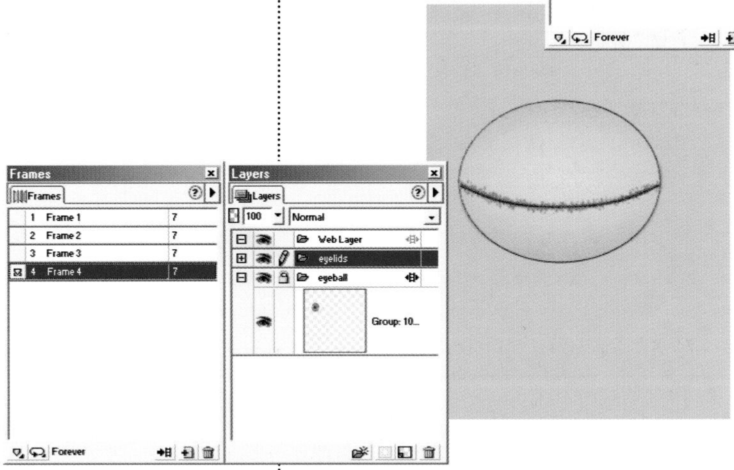

❹

❺

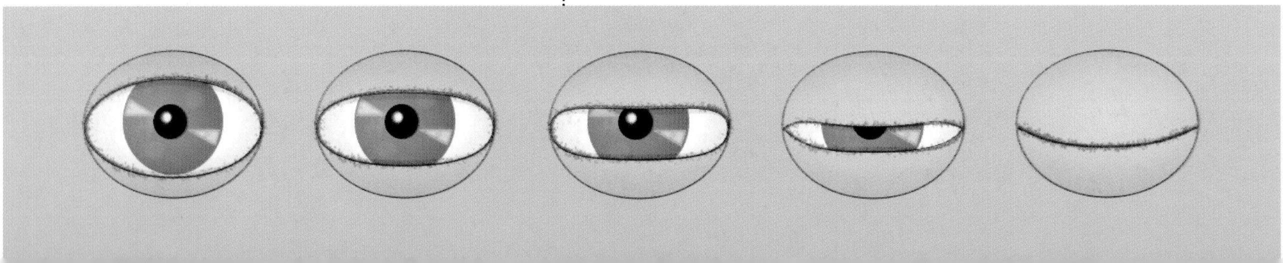

6

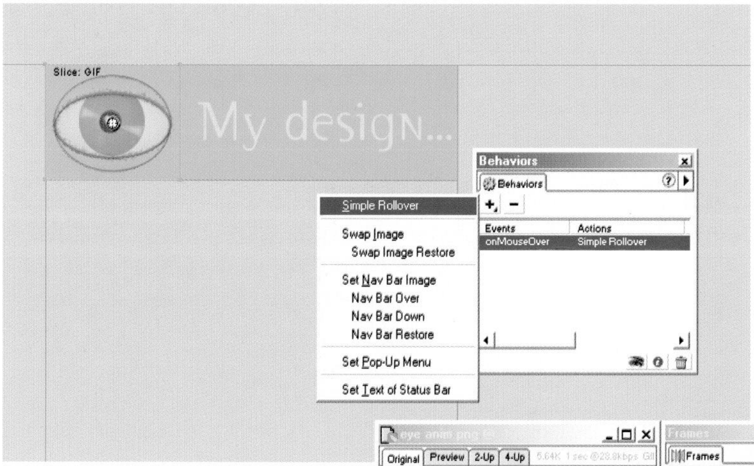

7

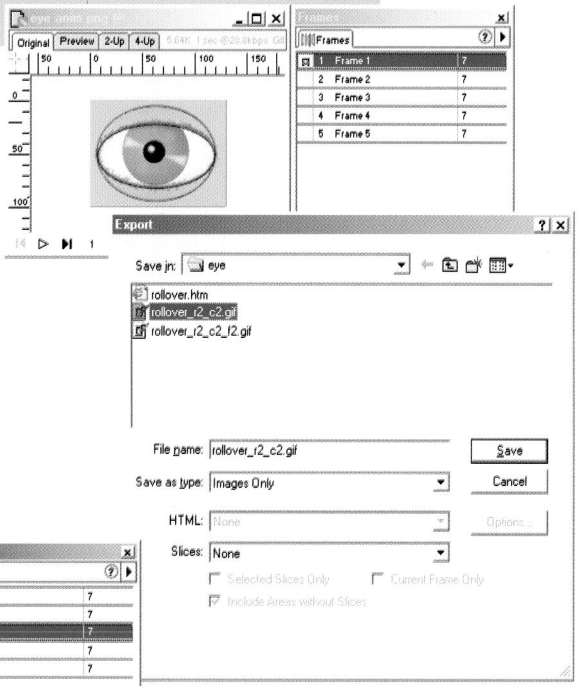

8

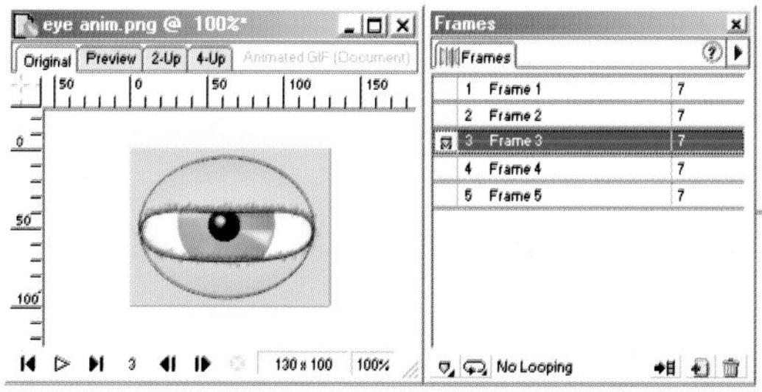

9

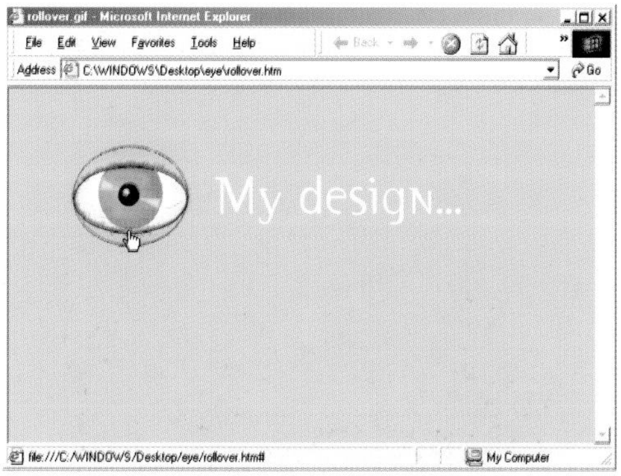

❷ Next, draw and colour some eyelids, and add a soft shadow just below and above the bottom lids. Put the eyeball underneath, and complete your eye with some lashes.

❸ Save a copy of this for later, then duplicate this first frame three or four times. If possible, set the layers for the ball of the eye to share across frames.

❹ On the last frame, bring the two eyelids, shadows and eyelashes together to a closed position, being careful to remember how you do it.

❺ Now repeat this exactly for the layers in between, but so the eye is a little more closed with each layer as you go.

❻ Save this file, then create a new file with just the 'open' and 'closed' frames, using these to set up a rollover in the normal way. Export the rollover, and check all is working correctly…

❼ Now replace the static images with animations. Take a copy of the rollover images, in case things go wrong, and doublecheck the exact dimensions. Open your animation, make sure it is exactly the same size, and set it to not loop. Now optimize and export it, saving over the mouseout static GIF file.

❽ Next take a copy of the original animation file, and shift all the frames around so the eye appears to open rather than close…

❾ Finally, export this animation over the mouseover GIF file, then open the webpage in your browser and check that it all works.

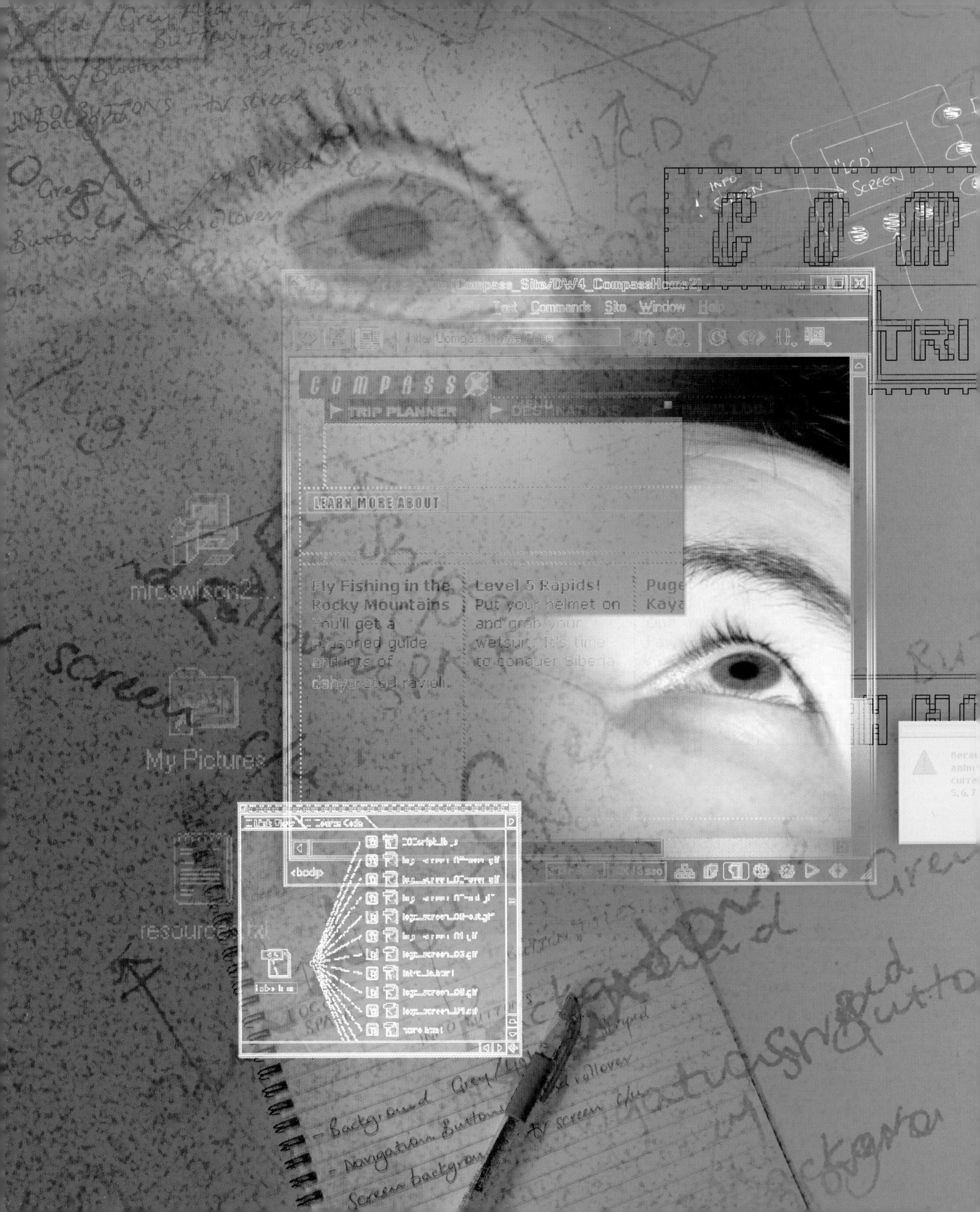

Commands Site Window Help
COMPASS
TRIP PLANNER
LEARN MORE ABOUT
Fly Fishing in the Rocky Mountains
You'll get a seasoned guide and lots of dehydrated ravioli.
Level 5 Rapids!
Put your helmet on and grab your wetsuit. It's time to conquer Siberia
My Pictures
resources.txt
<body>

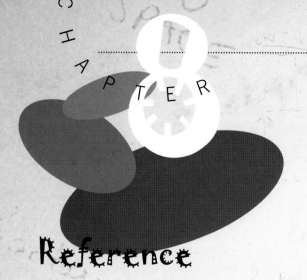

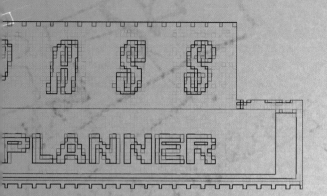

CHAPTER 8

Reference

Glossary

aliasing The term describing the jagged appearance of bitmapped images or fonts, either when the resolution is insufficient or when they have been enlarged.

anchor A hyperlink that takes you to another part of the same Web page, rather than to a sub-page or another site elsewhere on the Web.

animated GIF A GIF file containing more than one image. Many programs, including Web browsers, will display each of the images in turn, thus producing an animation.

animation The process of creating a moving image by rapidly moving from one still image to the next. Animations are now commonly created by means of specialist software that renders sequences in a variety of formats, typically QuickTime, AVI and animated GIF.

antialias/antialiasing A technique of optically eliminating the jagged effect of bitmapped images or text reproduced on low-resolution devices such as monitors. This is achieved by adding pixels of an in-between tone – the edges of the object's colour are blended with its background by averaging out the density of the range of pixels involved.

attribute The specification applied to a character, box or other item. Character attributes include font, size, style, colour, shade, scaling, kerning, etc.

authoring tool/application/program Software that enables you to create interactive presentations, such as those used in multimedia titles and on certain websites. Authoring programs provide text, drawing, painting, animation and audio features and combine these with a scripting language that determines how each element of a page behaves.

bevel A chamfered edge applied to type, buttons or selections to emphasise a 3D-effect.

Bézier curve A curve whose shape is defined by a pair of 'direction lines' at each end. Drawing programs usually allow you to draw Bézier curves by dragging out the direction lines with a pen tool.

bitmap An array of values specifying the colour of every pixel in a digital image.

bitmapped font A bitmapped font is one in which the characters are made up of dots, or pixels, as distinct from an outline font which is drawn from vectors. Bitmapped fonts generally accompany PostScript Type 1 fonts and are used to render the fonts' shapes on screen.

bitmapped graphic An image made up of dots, or pixels, and usually generated by 'paint' or 'image-editing' applications, as distinct from the 'vector' images of 'object-oriented' drawing applications.

body One of the main structures of an HTML document, falling between the header and the footer.

brightness The strength of luminescence from light to dark.

browser/web browser Program that enables the viewing or 'browsing' of World Wide Web pages across the Internet. The most common browsers are Netscape's Navigator and Microsoft's Internet Explorer. Version numbers are important, as these indicate the level of HTML that the browser supports. Another browser, 'Opera', is competitive because of its compact size, efficient performance and security. It is rapidly gaining popularity.

cell A space containing information in the rows or columns of a table. **cell padding** The space between cells in a table. **cell spacing** The number of pixels between cells in a table.

clip art/clip media Collections of (usually) royalty-free photographs, illustrations, design devices and other pre-created items, such as films, sounds and 3D wireframes.

colour depth This is the number of bits required to define the colour of each pixel. Only one bit is required to display a black-and-white image, while an 8-bit image can display either 256 greys or 256 colours, and a 24-bit image 16.7 million colours (eight bits each for red, green and blue, equating to 256 x 256 x 256).

colour picker The term describing a colour model when displayed on a computer monitor. Colour pickers may be specific to an application such as Adobe Photoshop, a third-party colour model such as PANTONE, or to the operating system running on your computer.

complementary colours On a colour wheel, two colours directly opposite each other that, combined, form white or black depending on the colour model (subtractive or additive).

compression The technique of rearranging data so that it either occupies less space on disk or transfers faster between devices or on communication lines. Different kinds of compression techniques are employed for different kinds of data. Applications, for example, must not lose any data when compressed, while photographic images and films can tolerate a certain amount of data loss. Compression methods that do not lose data are referred to as 'lossless', while 'lossy' is used to describe methods in which some data is lost. Films and animations employ techniques called 'codecs' (compression/decompression).

contrast The degree of difference between adjacent tones in an image (or on a computer monitor) from the lightest to the darkest. 'High contrast' describes an image with light highlights and dark shadows, but with few shades in between, while a 'low contrast' image is one with even tones and few dark areas or highlights.

copyright The right of a person who creates an original work to protect that work by controlling how and where it may be reproduced.

copyright-free A misnomer used to describe ready-made resources such as clip art. In fact, resources described as such are rarely, if ever, 'copyright free'. Generally it is only the licence to use the material which is granted by purchase.

density The darkness of tone or colour in any image. In a transparency this refers to the amount of light that can pass through it, thus determining the darkness of shadows and the saturation of colour. A printed highlight cannot be any lighter in colour than the colour of the paper it is printed on, while the shadows cannot be any darker than the quality and volume of ink that the printing process will allow.

digitize To convert anything, for example text, images or sound, into binary form so that it can be digitally processed, manipulated, stored and reconstructed. In other words, transforming analog to digital.

dingbat The modern name for fonts of decorative symbols, traditionally called printer's 'ornaments', or 'arabesques'.

dither(ing) The term describing a technique of 'interpolation' that calculates the average value of adjacent pixels. This technique is used either to add extra pixels to an image – to smooth an edge, for example, as in 'antialiasing' – or to reduce the number of colours or greys in an image by replacing them with average values. These conform to a predetermined palette of colours, such as when an image containing millions of colours is converted ('resampled') to a fixed palette ('index') of 256 colours – in Web use, for example. A colour monitor operating in 8-bit colour mode (256 colours) will automatically create a dithered pattern of pixels. Dithering is also used by some printing devices to simulate colours or tones.

domain name system/service (**DNS**) The description of a website's 'address' – the means by which you find or identify a particular website, much like a brand name or trademark. A website address is actually a number that conforms to the numerical Internet protocol (IP) addresses that computers use for information exchange, but names are far easier for us to remember. Domain names are administered by the InterNIC organisation and include at least two parts: the 'subdomain', typically a company or organisation; and the 'high-level domain', which is the part after the first dot, such as in '.com' for commercial sites, '.org' for non-profit sites, '.gov' for governmental sites, '.edu' for educational sites, and so on.

dots per inch (**dpi**) A unit of measurement used to represent the resolution of devices such as printers and imagesetters and also, erroneously, monitors and images, whose resolution should more properly be expressed in pixels per inch (ppi). The closer the dots or pixels (the more there are to each inch), the better the quality. Typical resolutions are 72 ppi for a monitor, 600 dpi for a laser printer and 2450 dpi (or more) for an imagesetter.

download To transfer data from a remote computer, such as an Internet server, to your own. The opposite of upload.

drop shadow A shadow projected onto the background behind an image or character, designed to 'lift' the image or character off the surface.

dynamic HTML/DHTML (Dynamic HyperText Markup Language) A development of HTML that enables users to add enhanced features such as basic animations and highlighted buttons to webpages without having to rely on browser plug-ins.

export A feature provided by many applications to allow you to save a file in a format so that it can be used by another application or on a different operating system. For example, an illustration created in a drawing application may be exported as an EPS file so that it can be used in a page-layout application.

eyedropper tool In some applications, a tool for gauging the colour of adjacent pixels.

face Traditionally the printing surface of any metal type character, but nowadays used as a series or family name for fonts with similar characteristics, such as 'modern face'.

file extension The term describing the abbreviated suffix at the end of a filename that describes either its type (such as .EPS or .JPG) or origin (the application that created it, such as QXP for QuarkXPress files).

file format The way a program arranges data so that it can be stored or displayed on a computer. Common file formats are TIFF and JPEG for bitmapped image files, EPS for object-oriented image files and ASCII for text files.

File Transfer Protocol (FTP) A standard system for transmitting files between computers across the Internet or a network. Although Web browsers incorporate FTP capabilities, dedicated FTP applications provide greater flexibility. Typically, when creating a webpage, an FTP application will be used to upload this to the Web.

frame A way of breaking up a scrollable browser window on a webpage into several independent windows. Frames enable one to fix arbitrary sections of the available browser window space – e.g., a logo, a menu button bar or an animation can be placed in one part of the browser window while another part is left available for information from a different webpage.

frame (**2**) A single still picture from a film or animation sequence. Also a single complete image from a TV picture.

font Set of characters sharing the same typeface and size.

font file The file of a bitmapped or screen font, usually residing in a suitcase file on Mac OS computers.

form A special type of webpage which provides users with the means to input information directly into the website. Form pages are often used to collect information about viewers, or as a way of collecting password and username data before allowing access to secure areas.

gamma A measure of the contrast in a digital image, photographic film or paper, or processing technique. Gamma curves can be used within the software that may come with a scanner so that you can preset the amount of light and dark, and contrast on input.

GIF (Graphics Interchange Format) One of the main bitmapped image formats used on the Internet. It was devised by CompuServe, an Internet Service Provider that is now part of AOL. GIF is a 256-colour format with two specifications, GIF87a and, more recently, GIF89a, the latter providing additional features such as the use of transparent backgrounds. The GIF format uses a 'lossless' compression technique, or 'algorithm', and thus does not squeeze files as much as the JPEG format, which is 'lossy'. For use in Web browsers, JPEG is the format of choice for tone images, such as photographs, while GIF is more suitable for line images and other graphics.

graduation/gradation/gradient The smooth transition from one colour/tone to another. The relationship of reproduced lightness values to original lightness values in an imaging process, usually expressed as a tone curve.

home page The main, introductory page on a website, usually with a title and tools to navigate through the rest of the site. Also known as index page or doorway.

host A networked computer that provides services to anyone who can access it, such as for e-mail, file transfer and access to the Web. When you connect to the Internet and select a website, information will be transferred to you from the host's computer. Users' computers that request services from a host are often referred to as 'clients'.

HSL (Hue, Saturation, Lightness) A colour model based upon the light transmitted either in an image or in your monitor – hue being the spectral colour (the actual pigment colour), saturation being the intensity of the colour pigment (without black or white added), and brightness representing the strength of luminance from light to dark (the amount of black or white present). Variously called HLS (hue, lightness, saturation), HSV (hue, saturation, value) and HSB (hue, saturation, brightness).

hue A colour as found in its pure state in the spectrum.

HTML (HyperText Markup Language) The code that websites are built from. HTML is not a programming language as such, but a set of 'tags' that specify type styles and sizes, the location of graphics, and other information required to construct a webpage. To provide for increasingly complex presentations such as animation, sound and video, the basic form of HTML is seeded with miniature computer programs, or applets.

HTML table A grid on a webpage consisting of rows and columns of cells allowing precise positioning of text, pictures, film clips or any other element. A table can be nested within another table. Tables offer a way of giving the appearance of multi-column layouts. They can be visible, with cells framed by borders, or invisible and used only to demarcate areas containing the elements on the page. A table is specified in terms of either a pixel count, which fixes its size irrespective of the browser or screen resolution used to view it, or as a percentage of the available screen space, allowing resizing to fit the browser window.

Hypertext Transfer Protocol (http) A text-based set of rules by which files on the World Wide Web are transferred, defining the commands that Web browsers use to communicate with Web servers. The vast majority of World Wide Web addresses, or 'URLs', are prefixed with 'http://'.

icon A graphical representation of an object (such as a disk, file, folder or tool) or of a concept or message used to make identification and selection easier.

image map An image that features a set of embedded links to other documents or websites. These are activated when the mouse is clicked on the appropriate area. Often the 'front page' of a website contains such a map.

image slicing The practice of dividing up a digital image into rectangular areas or slices, which can then be optimized or animated independently for efficient Web presentation. Programs that enable you to slice images automatically generate an HTML code that puts the slices back together on a webpage.

index page The first page of any website that is selected automatically by the browser if it is named 'default.htm,' 'default.html', 'index.htm' or 'index.html'.

interactive Any activity that involves an immediate and reciprocal action between a person and a machine (for example, driving a car), but more commonly describing dialog between a computer and its user.

interface This is a term most used to describe the screen design that links the user with the computer program or website. The quality of the user interface often determines how well users will be able to navigate their way around the pages within the site.

interlacing A technique of displaying an image on a webpage in which the image reveals increasing detail as it downloads. Interlacing is usually offered as an option in image-editing applications when saving images in GIF, PNG and progressive JPEG formats.

Internet The worldwide network of computers linked by telephone (or other connections), providing individual and corporate users with access to information, companies, newsgroups, discussion areas and much more.

ISP (Internet Service Provider) Any organisation that provides access to the Internet. At its most basic this may be a telephone number for connection, but most ISPs also provide e-mail addresses and webspace for new sites.

JavaScript A 'scripting' language that provides a simplified method of applying dynamic effects to webpages.

JPEG, JPG The Joint Photographics Experts Group. An ISO (International Standards Organization) group that defines compression standards for bitmapped colour images. The abbreviated form, pronounced 'jay-peg', gives its name to a 'lossy' (meaning some data may be lost) compressed file format in which the degree of compression from high compression/low quality to low compression/high quality can be defined by the user.

kerning The adjustment of spacing between two characters (normally alphanumeric) to improve the overall look of the text.

keyline A line drawing indicating the size and position of an illustration in a layout.

layout A drawing that shows the general appearance of a design, indicating, for example, the position of text and illustrations. The term is also used when preparing a design for reproduction, and to describe the way a page is constructed in desktop publishing programs.

link A pointer, such as a highlighted piece of text in an HTML document or multimedia presentation, or an area on an image map, which takes the user to another location, page, or screen just by clicking on it.

lossless/lossy Refers to data-losing qualities of different compression methods: lossless means that no image information is lost; lossy means that some (or much) of the image data is lost in the compression process.

midtones/middletones The range of tonal values in an image anywhere between the darkest and lightest, usually referring to those approximately halfway.

multimedia Any combination of various digital media, such as sound, video, animation, graphics and text, incorporated into a software product or presentation.

paragraph In an HTML document, a markup tag <P> used to define a new paragraph in text.

palette This term refers to a subset of colours that are needed to display a particular image. For instance, a GIF image will have a palette containing a maximum of 256 individual and distinct colours.

pixel (Picture Element) The smallest component of any digitally generated image, including text, such as a single dot of light on a computer screen. In its simplest form, one pixel corresponds to a single bit: 0 = off, or white, and 1 = on, or black. In colour or grayscale images or monitors, one pixel may correspond to up to several bits. An 8-bit pixel, for example, can be displayed in any of 256 colours (the total number of different configurations that can be achieved by eight 0s and 1s).

plug-in Subsidiary software for a browser or other package that enables it to perform additional functions, e.g., play sound, films or video.

raster(**ization**) Deriving from the Latin word 'rastrum', meaning 'rake', the method of displaying (and creating) images employed by video screens, and thus computer monitors, in which the screen image is made up of a pattern of several hundred parallel lines created by an electron beam 'raking' the screen from top to bottom at a speed of about one-sixtieth of a second. An image is created by varying the intensity of the beam at successive points along the raster. The speed at which a complete screen image, or frame, is created is called the 'frame' or 'refresh' rate.

rasterize(d) To rasterize is to electronically convert a vector graphics image into a bitmapped image. This may introduce aliasing, but is often necessary when preparing images for the Web; without a plug-in, browsers can only display GIF, JPEG and PNG image files.

resolution The degree of quality, definition or clarity with which an image is reproduced or displayed, for example in a photograph, or via a scanner, monitor screen, printer or other output device.

resolution (2): monitor resolution, screen resolution The number of pixels across by pixels down. The three most common resolutions are 640 x 480, 800 x 600 and 1024 x 768. The current standard Web page size is 800 x 600.

RGB (Red, Green, Blue) The primary colours of the 'additive' colour model, used in video technology, computer monitors, and for graphics such as for the Web and multimedia that will not ultimately be printed by the four-colour (CMYK) process. CMYK stands for 'Cyan, Magenta, Yellow, BlacK'.

rollover The rapid substitution of one or more images when the mouse pointer is rolled over the original image. Used extensively for navigation buttons on webpages and multimedia presentations.

rollover button A graphic button type that changes in appearance when the mouse pointer moves over it.

saturation A variation in colour of the same total brightness from none (grey) through pastel shades (low saturation) to pure (fully saturated) colour with no grey.

scan(**ning**) An electronic process that converts a hard copy of an image into digital form by sequential exposure to a moving light beam such as a laser. The scanned image can then be manipulated by a computer or output to separated film.

shareware Software available through user groups, magazine cover disks, etc. Although shareware is not 'copy protected', it *is* protected by copyright and a fee is normally payable for using it, unlike 'freeware'.

spacer A blank, transparent GIF, one pixel wide, used to space elements on a webpage.

tag The formal name for a markup language formatting command. A tag is switched on by placing a command inside angle brackets – i.e., < and > – and switched off again by repeating the same command but inserting a forward slash before the command. For example, <bold> makes text that follows appear in bold, while </bold> switches bold text off again.

text path An invisible line, either straight, curved or irregular, along which text can be forced to flow.

thumbnail A small representation of an image used mainly for identification purposes in an image directory listing or, within Photoshop, for illustrating channels and layers. Thumbnails are also produced to accompany PictureCDs, PhotoCDs and most APS and 35-mm films submitted for processing.

TIFF, TIF (Tagged Image File Format) A standard and popular graphics file format originally developed by Aldus (now merged with Adobe) and Microsoft, used for scanned, high-resolution, bitmapped images and for colour separations. The TIFF format can be used for black-and-white, grayscale and colour images, which have been generated on different computer platforms.

tile, tiling Repeating a graphic item and placing the repetitions side-by-side in all directions so that they form a pattern.

transparency Allows a GIF image to be blended into the background by ridding it of unwanted background colour.

tween(ing) A contraction of 'in-between'. An animator's term for the process of creating transitional frames to fill in-between key frames in an animation.

typeface The term (based on 'face' – the printing surface of a metal type character) describing a type design of any size, including weight variations on that design such as light and bold, but excluding all other related designs such as italic and condensed. As distinct from 'type family', which includes all related designs, and 'font', which is one design of a single size, weight and style. Thus 'Baskerville' is a type family, while 'Baskerville Bold' is a typeface and '9 pt Baskerville Bold Italic' is a font.

Uniform Resource Locator (URL) The unique address of every webpage on the WWW. Every resource on the Internet has a unique URL which begins with letters that identify the resource type, such as 'http' or 'ftp' (determining the communication protocol to be used), followed by a colon and two forward slashes.

vector A mathematical description of a line that is defined in terms of physical dimensions and direction. Vectors are used in drawing packages (and Photoshop 6 upwards) to define shapes (vector graphics) that are position- and size-independent.

vector graphics Images made up of mathematically defined shapes, such as circles and rectangles, or complex paths built out of mathematically defined curves. Vector graphics images can be displayed at any size or resolution without loss of quality, and are easy to edit because the shapes retain their identity, but they lack the tonal subtlety of bitmapped images. Because vector graphics files are typically small, they are well suited to Web animation.

webpage A published HTML document on the World Wide Web, which forms part of a website.

Web server A computer ('host') that is dedicated to Web services.

website The address, location (on a server) and collection of documents and resources for any particular interlinked set of webpages.

World Wide Web (WWW) The term used to describe the entire collection of Web servers all over the world that are connected to the Internet. The term also describes the particular type of Internet access architecture that uses a combination of HTML and various graphic formats, such as GIF and JPEG, to publish formatted text that can be read by Web browsers. Colloquially termed simply 'the Web' or, rarely, by the shorthand 'W3'.

World Wide Web Consortium (W3C) The global organisation that is largely responsible for maintaining and managing standards across the Web. It is chaired by the UK's Tim Berners Lee, progenitor of the Web.

Index

Useful Websites

Download resources
www.fontparadise.com
www.acidfonts.com
www.flashkit.com
www.fontaddict.com
www.fontalicious.com
www.fonts.com
http://htmlgear.lycos.com
www.brainjar.com
www.eyeforbeauty.com
http://infinitefish.com
www.sweetaspirations.com
www.melizabeth.com
www.thepluginsite.com
www.iconfactory.com
www.freephotoshop.com

Tutorials, articles, news, pictures...
www.webmonkey.com
www.alistapart.comwww.wired.com
www.computerarts.co.uk
www.createonline.co.uk
www.creativepro.com
www.maccentral.com
www.creativebase.com
www.webreference.com
www.planetphotoshop.com
www.zooworld.net
www.internet.com
www.wired.com
www.webmasterbase.com
www.tutorialfind.com

Fun
www.the5k.org
www.surfstation.lu
www.pixelsurgeon.com
www.shockwave.com
www.linkdup.com
www.australianinfront.com.au

Software
www.adobe.com
www.macromedia.com
www.jasc.com
www.microsoft.com
www.apple.com
www.ulead.com
www.corel.com
www.netscape.com

Acknowledgements

This book would not be possible without the help of a great many people, but special thanks are due to Bob Carney, for Mac expertise and doing some of the screen shots; Ed Ricketts for his fine command of the English language; and Harv for his inimitable sense of humour.

But most of all to Penny for your unstoppable support and many excuses to get away from my computer. This book is dedicated to you.

Thanks also to everyone in the photos: Aaron, Annelise, Bobbio, David, Sarah, Esther, Ali, Garrick, Harv, Matthias, Andy Mac, Rach, Dave's band, the people of Los Uros, the Baku jazz players, Vix, Jo King, Gary, Gary, La, Pat Piano, Caroline, the whale of Valdez (thanks Jo), Rosie Ray, Brynn, the boatman and Emily.